D1507667

Advances

in COMPUTERS
VOLUME 58

Advances in
COMPUTERS

Highly Dependable Software

EDITED BY

MARVIN V. ZELKOWITZ

Department of Computer Science
and Institute for Advanced Computer Studies
University of Maryland
College Park, Maryland

VOLUME 58

ACADEMIC PRESS

An imprint of Elsevier Science

Amsterdam Boston Heidelberg London New York Oxford
Paris San Diego San Francisco Singapore Sydney Tokyo

Academic Press
An imprint of Elsevier Science
525 B Street, Suite 1900, San Diego, California 92101-4495, USA
http://www.academicpress.com

First edition 2003

Library of Congress Cataloging in Publication Data
A catalog record from the Library of Congress has been applied for.

British Library Cataloguing in Publication Data
A catalogue record from the British Library has been applied for.

ISBN: 0-12-012158-1
ISSN (Series): 0065-2458

⊗ The paper used in this publication meets the requirements of ANSI/NISO Z39.48-1992 (Permanence of Paper).

Printed in Great Britain by MPG Books Ltd, Bodmin, Cornwall

Contents

Software Development Productivity

Katrina D. Maxwell

Transformation-Oriented Programming: A Development Methodology for High Assurance Software

Victor L. Winter, Steve Roach and Greg Wickstrom

Bounded Model Checking

Armin Biere, Alessandro Cimatti, Edmund M. Clarke, Ofer Strichman and Yunshan Zhu

Advances in GUI Testing

Atif M. Memon

Software Inspections

Marc Roper, Alastair Dunsmore and Murray Wood

Software Fault Tolerance Forestalls Crashes: To Err Is Human; To Forgive Is Fault Tolerant

Lawrence Bernstein

Advances in the Provision of System and Software Security— Thirty Years of Progress

Rayford B. Vaughn

Contributors

Prof. Armin Biere received a diploma in computer science and the title Dr.rer.nat. from the University of Karlsruhe, Germany, in 1993 and 1997, respectively. In 1997/1998 he worked as a PostDoc at CMU and then joined the EDA startup Verysys. Since 2000 he is an assistant professor for computer science at ETH Zurich, Switzerland.

Prof. Larry Bernstein is currently the Industry Research Professor of Software Engineering at Stevens Institute of Technology in Hoboken, New Jersey. He is on the board of Center for National Software Studies and he is director of the New Jersey Center for Software Engineering. He had a 35-year distinguished career at Bell Laboratories managing large software projects. He is a Fellow of both the Institute of Electrical and Electronics Engineers and the Association for Computing Machinery.

Dr. Alessandro Cimatti is a Research Scientist at Institute for Scientific and Technological Research (IRST) in Trento, Italy, where he is the head of the Formal Methods group. He has participated in and lead several industrial technology transfer projects aiming at the application of formal methods to the development of industrial critical systems. His main research interests include symbolic model checking, the NuSMV OpenSource project, and the application of model checking to automated task planning, safety analysis, and to the verification of multi-agent systems and model-based diagnosis systems.

Prof. Edmund M. Clarke received a B.A. degree in mathematics from the University of Virginia, Charlottesville, VA, in 1967, an M.A. degree in mathematics from Duke University, Durham NC, in 1968, and a Ph.D. degree in Computer Science from Cornell University, Ithaca NY, in 1976. Before joining CMU he was at Duke University and Harvard University. In 1995 he became the first recipient of the FORE Systems Professorship, an endowed chair in the School of Computer Science. Dr. Clarke has served on the editorial boards of Distributed Computing and Logic and Computation and is currently on the editorial board of IEEE Transactions in Software Engineering. He is editor-in-chief of Formal Methods in Systems Design. He is on the steering committees of two international conferences, Logic in Computer Science and Computer-Aided Verification. He was a cowinner along with Randy Bryant, Allen Emerson, and Kenneth McMillan of the ACM Kanellakis Award in 1999 for the development of Symbolic Model Checking. For this work he also received a Technical Excellence Award from the Semiconductor Research Corporation in 1995 and an Allen Newell Award for Excellence in Research from the Carnegie Mellon Computer Science Department in 1999. Dr. Clarke is a Fellow of the Association for Computing Machinery, a member of the IEEE Computer Society, Sigma Xi, and Phi Beta Kappa.

Dr. Alastair Dunsmore received the B.Sc. and Ph.D. degrees in computer science from the University of Strathclyde, Glasgow, Scotland. He is currently employed in industry as a Java Developer. His research interests include software inspection, Java, UML, and Object-Oriented systems.

Dr. Katrina D. Maxwell, a leading international expert in the area of software development productivity, is currently a Partner at Datamax. She specializes in data analysis, productivity benchmarking and software metrics research. Dr. Maxwell is the author of "Applied Statistics for Software Managers" published by Prentice-Hall. Her research has appeared in IEEE Transactions on Software Engineering, IEEE Software and Management Science.

Prof. Atif M. Memon is an assistant professor in the Department of Computer Science, University of Maryland. He received his BS, MS, and Ph.D. in Computer Science in 1991, 1995, and 2001, respectively. He was awarded a Gold Medal in BS. He was awarded a Fellowship from the Andrew Mellon Foundation for his Ph.D. research. He is the inventor of the GUITAR system (guitar.cs.umd.edu) for GUI testing. His research interests include program testing, software engineering, artificial intelligence, plan generation, and code improving compilation techniques. He is a member of the ACM and the IEEE Computer Society.

Prof. Steve Roach received his Ph.D. from the University of Wyoming in 1997. Prior to that he developed process control, data acquisition, and process modeling software for insitu chemical and environmental engineering firms. He has contributed to NASA's Amphion deductive synthesis system and developed application software for the Cassini mission to Saturn. He is currently an Assistant Professor of Computer Science at the University of Texas at El Paso where he is a member of the Software Engineering Research Group.

Prof. Marc Roper obtained his BSc (Hons) degree in Computer Science from the University of Reading in 1982. After a brief period working as a programmer for Mars Group Services he moved to Sunderland Polytechnic as a research assistant in 1983 and was appointed lecturer in 1986. He was awarded his PhD in Computer Science from the CNAA in 1988. In 1989 he joined the Computer Science Department at the University of Strathclyde in Glasgow Scotland as a lecturer and was appointed senior lecturer in 1996. His research interests are in the development and rigorous evaluation of technologies to support the construction, comprehension and validation of reliable large-scale software systems.

Dr. Ofer Strichman received his B.Sc. and M.Sc. from the Technion, Israel, in Operations Research and Systems Analysis. He received his Ph.D from the Weizmann Institute, where he worked, under Amir Pnueli, on translation validation for compilers, Bounded Model Checking, and other topics in formal verification. His research interests include formal equivalence checking, decision procedures in first order logic, SAT procedures, and selected areas in operations research. He is currently a post-doc at Carnegie Mellon University.

Prof. Rayford Vaughn is currently a professor of computer science at Mississippi State University where he teaches and conducts research in the areas of Software Engineering and Information Security. Prior to joining the University, he completed a twenty-six year career in the Army where he commanded the Army's largest software development organization and created the Pentagon Single Agency Manager organization to centrally manage all Pentagon IT support. While on active duty with the Army, he served a three-year assignment with the National Security Agency's National Computer Security Center where he authored national level computer security guidance and conducted computer security research. After retiring as a Colonel in June 1995, he accepted a position as a Vice President of Integration Services, EDS Government Systems where he was responsible for a wide variety of technical service contracts and customer satisfaction. Dr. Vaughn has over 40 publications to his credit and is an active contributor to software engineering and information security conferences and journals. He holds a PhD in Computer Science from Kansas State University.

Greg Wickstrom is a Principle Member of Technical Staff at Sandia National Laboratories. He joined the labs in 1983 with an associate's degree in Electronic Engineering Technology from Valparaiso Technical Institute. He continued his education to receive a BSEET and then received a MSCS degree in 1995. Greg spent his first few years at Sandia developing instrumentation for a laser physics lab. He then developed a cryptographic authenticator for a military communications application. For the latest half of Greg's career he has been working a various aspects of security systems for the nation's weapons systems. His most recent assignment has been to improve the development infrastructure of these systems with respect to assurance, cost, and schedule. Most recently, Greg is determining where and how formal methods can be incorporated into this new development infrastructure.

Prof. Victor Winter received his Ph.D. from the University of New Mexico in 1994. His specific research interests include high-assurance software development, program transformation, semantic models, language design, theory of computation, automated reasoning, reactive systems, and virtual reality environments. From 1995 to 2001, Dr. Winter worked at Sandia National Laboratories as a member and later on the principal investigator of the High Integrity Software program. He is currently an Assistant Professor of Computer Science at the University of Nebraskaat Omaha. More information about his research can be found at http://www.ist.unomaha.edu/faculty/winter/index.htm.

Prof. Murray Wood received the BSc (Hons) and the PhD degrees in Computer Science from the University of Strathclyde in 1983 and 1988, respectively. He was appointed lecturer in Computer Science at the University of Strathclyde in 1987 and senior lecturer in 2000. His main interests are in software architecture and design, software inspection and empirical evaluation.

Dr. Yunshan Zhu did his undergraduate study at the University of Science and Technology of China. Yunshan received his Ph.D. in computer science from University of North Carolina at Chapel Hill in May 1998. He was a visiting scientist/postdoc at Carnegie Mellon University from 1997 to 1998. Yunshan is currently a member of the advanced technology group in Synopsys.

Preface

This volume of **Advances in Computers** is the 58th in this series. This series, which has been continuously published since 1960, presents in each volume six or seven chapters describing new developments in software, hardware, or uses of computers. As machines continually get smaller, faster, and less expensive, they are becoming increasingly important in many facets of our everyday lives—which leads us to the theme of this volume "highly dependable software." As computers take over the controls of many devices our very lives may be at stake. It may be an inconvenience if your VCR or digital watch fails, but the consequences can be much more severe if the computer controlling the steering or brakes of your automobile fails. You want software (and hardware) to do what it was intended to do. You want it to be dependable, highly dependable in fact.

Dependability comes in various forms. You certainly want software to be reliable and not fail. But you also want it to be useful—you want to understand the controls and user interface. You want it to be secure from outside tampering and immune from hackers. You want it to be maintainable to allow for requested changes. You want it to be efficient. You want it to be available whenever it is needed. Because of these many demands dependability becomes a hard characteristic to define and even harder to achieve in practice. In this volume we present seven chapters that address various aspects of how to make software more dependable.

In order to increase dependability of a system, we have to be able to measure it in order to know when it is increasing or decreasing. Chapter 1, "Software Development Productivity" by Katrina D. Maxwell, is all about measuring software development. In this chapter the emphasis is on productivity measures, but the basic concept of collecting data to measure relevant attributes is critical for any development environment, and all too often, is ignored in most development environments. There is a continuing need to make software engineering more of an engineering discipline by including the measurement and data collection aspects of the other engineering sciences.

Chapter 2, "Transformation-Oriented Programming: A Development Methodology for High Assurance Software" by Victor L. Winter, Steve Roach and Greg Wickstrom discusses one particular development method called Transformation-Oriented

Programming (TOP) as a mechanism for using formal methods to help convert a formal specification of a program into software. The authors built the High Assurance Transformation System (HATS) as an implementation of the TOP method and show how HATS can be used to develop a portion of a secure operating system.

Model checking is another formal model for verifying the correctness of a software specification for software that enters one of many states. Many model checkers use the binary decision diagrams (BDD) as the method for checking the specification. The problem, however, is that the number of possible states to check overwhelms the capacity of most computers. Various methods have been introduced to limit the size of this state space explosion. In Chapter 3, Armin Biere, Alessandro Cimatti, Edmund M. Clarke, Ofer Strichman and Yunshan Zhu present "Bounded Model Checking," where the authors present their Bounded Model Checking (BMC) process for limiting this state explosion.

Today, most interaction with computers is via an interface consisting of a mouse for input, and windows with pull down menus, scroll bars, radio buttons, and other forms of interaction with the user. Testing a graphical user interface (GUI) is similar to the model-checking problem of Chapter 3 in that the interface can enter one of many states. Testing the interface, however, requires more of an interactive testing process than in traditional model checking. In Chapter 4, "Advances in GUI Testing," Atif M. Memon discusses how graphical user interfaces can be effectively tested.

In today's fast-paced computer world, 1976 is ancient history. However, in 1976 Michael Fagan of IBM developed a process called software inspections for discovering flaws in software development. Although inspections have repeatedly been shown to be effective, they are still not universally used. Why? Current research is still looking at ways to make inspections more effective, and more importantly, more relevant to companies so that they will be used. In Chapter 5, "Software Inspections" by Marc Roper, Alastair Dunsmore, and Murray Wood, the authors explore the history of inspections and discuss some of the recent research in this area.

"Software Fault Tolerance Forestalls Crashes: To Err Is Human; To Forgive Is Fault Tolerant" by Lawrence Bernstein in Chapter 6 addresses a different issue. Whereas the first 5 chapters focus on removing errors prior to release of the software, this chapter looks at the problem of users obtaining software with errors. How can systems continue to operate in the face of errors and how can users measure the impact that errors have on their use of the software? Can the software be tolerant of its own failures? How can systems be designed with appropriate redundancy much like redundancy in hardware? And finally, how can software be designed that minimizes the appearance of such problems? These are all issues discussed in this chapter.

The last chapter by Rayford B. Vaughn is entitled "Advances in the Provisions of System and Software Security—Thirty Years of Progress." Security is certainly an aspect of making a dependable system. In this chapter, Dr. Vaughn discusses the evolution of the various security policies that ensure appropriate secure behavior. Most computer professionals have heard of security terms such as the "Bell and LaPadula security model" and the "Orange book." This chapter discusses the evolution of these and other security policies over the past thirty years.

I hope that you find these articles of interest. If you have any suggestions of topics for future chapters, or if you wish to be considered as an author for a chapter, I can be reached at mvz@cs.umd.edu.

Marvin Zelkowitz
College Park, MD, USA

Software Development Productivity

KATRINA D. MAXWELL

Datamax
7 bis bld. Foch
77300 Fontainebleau
France
kmaxwell@datamax-france.com

Abstract

This chapter explains what software development productivity is and why it is important. It discusses the various ways of measuring software size and project effort using examples from past research. An overview of productivity factors considered in prior research is also presented. A methodology for determining influential productivity factors in software project data is briefly described. This is followed by a case study that shows what one bank learned from the productivity analysis of their software project data. Finally, the author shares her practical real-life experiences of benchmarking software development productivity.

1. Introduction

Software is everywhere. In the modern world, software is a fundamental element of the infrastructure of industry, commerce and government. Companies whose primary business is to sell books, insurance or savings accounts, or to manufacture cars, telephones or cameras have increasingly found that they are also in the business of software development. Although software development lies on the critical path of their activities—to many, software development remains mysterious and uncontrollable. Companies that are used to applying quantitative techniques to other parts of their business still hesitate to apply similar techniques to software development, in spite of over 30 years of research in this subject.

Engineering techniques that use metrics, measurements and models to make quantitative assessments of the productivity and cost of software development were first introduced in the late 1960s. Why aren't they being used more? One explanation is that senior managers may be more concerned about the strategic and operational impact of the software than they are in its production. Even if the software is a success from the development standpoint (i.e., on time and within budget), they will still consider the project a failure if the implementation of the software does not have the desired effect (e.g., were the company's business processes improved?). Another explanation is that today's software managers never received any education in this subject. Until recently, these techniques were not taught in most undergraduate degree programs related to computer science [39]. As software-producing companies rarely provide such training themselves, a software manager with no time to read academic journals might not even be aware that such practices exist.

In this chapter, I will focus on developing your awareness of software development productivity. Let's start by answering a key question—Why is measuring software development productivity important? There are several reasons you might like to measure software productivity. First of all, if you can determine what factors have an impact on productivity, this will give you some clues as to how to improve your software development process. Perhaps you would like to know if your productivity is improving. If you don't know your initial productivity level, you won't be able to tell if you are getting any better. Development cost depends on productivity. If you know what software development productivity to expect for certain types of applications, then you can better estimate the cost of development—next time. Time-to-market is also related to productivity. Finally, you can compare your productivity rates externally. Are you doing better than your competitors? If you want to benchmark your productivity rates with other companies, then you have to use the same variable definitions as they do. As we will see, definitions can vary enormously.

2. What is Software Development Productivity?

Productivity is typically defined as output divided by the effort required to produce that output. For example, the productivity of a car manufacturing line can be described as the number of cars produced per 24 hours. The output is the quantity of cars produced. It is much more difficult to measure software development productivity. Just what is the output we should measure? If a software developer works for one day, just what has he or she achieved at the end of it? A better understanding of the customer's requirements, a better design, some coding or testing? Or perhaps the day was spent documenting how the application works, learning a new tool, or training a new colleague. If a team of software developers work together for months (or years) to develop an application, how do we quantify what they have produced? Although not perfect, we traditionally use the size of the software as the output measure for software development productivity.

2.1 Software Size Measurement

How do you measure software size? Is it the number of bytes the software takes up on the disk? The lines of code? The number of screens? The number of data elements? A measure which takes into account what the software actually does? Just what does software size mean? Researchers have been pondering this question for years. The inability of the software engineering community to reach consensus on the definition of software size is believed by some to be the single most significant factor holding back the increasing use of complex metrics for estimation, control and comparison [43]. Many software size metrics now exist, the most common of these are lines-of-code and function points.

2.1.1 Lines-of-code

Lines-of-code means you count the lines of code in the application. Exact definitions can vary. Let's take a trip back in time to see how this definition has evolved.

In 1976, J.D. Aron published "Estimating resources for large programming systems" [3]. This paper is based on IBM's Federal Systems Division's experiences developing large software projects (from 1959). The output measure used is the number of deliverable instructions. These include source statements and data descriptions written by the programmer in a macro-assembly language. He also notes that the method is not precise, and that the estimator should never allow himself to treat answers as anything other than an approximate representation of system size.

In Walston and Felix's classic 1977 study at IBM [51], their measure of output is the number of lines of delivered source code. Source lines are defined as 80-character source records provided as input to a language processor. They include job control languages, data definitions, link edit language, and comment lines. They do not include reused code.

The lines-of-code definition used in Conte et al.'s 1986 book [17] is any line of program text that is not a comment or blank line, regardless of the number of statements or fragments of statements on the line. This includes all lines containing program headers, declarations, and executable or non-executable statements. They note that in 1986 this was the predominant definition used by researchers. They also note that they do not advocate developing computer programs without comments, which are a valuable aid during program development and maintenance.

So on one hand we have the problem that if we include comments in the definition of lines-of-code we encourage programmers to add unnecessary comments to their programming in order to create the illusion of high productivity by increasing their output. On the other hand, if we don't include comments, we discourage programmers from spending their time making their program understandable to others, because doing so takes time that could be spent coding. This is one of the reasons that we do not measure the productivity of individuals, but of entire software development projects.

Conte et al.'s book also discusses the question of whether or not reused code should be included in the lines-of-code measure and if so, what adjustment should be made, by referring to research available at the time. The major question being does the size of the software simply equal the amount of new code plus the reused code? Should the number of lines of reused code be adjusted down because simply copying code is easy and requires little effort, or should it be left as is because it is sometimes necessary to adapt code to fit the existing system and this takes extra time? The researchers agreed that, at most, it could be equally difficult to adapt used code or to rewrite it completely; however, they disagreed about the amount of adjustment needed for easier cases.[1] Conte concluded that there was no consensus about how to compute this "equivalent size."

---

[1] If the reused code does not include comments, I would say that it could be even more difficult to adapt it than to rewrite it completely.

Ten years on, in a 1996 study of the European Space Agency (ESA) software project database [33], source lines of code (SLOC) is defined as the amount of non-blank, non-commented delivered lines of code. Adaptation adjustment factors are used to adjust the size of reused code when available, otherwise only the size of new code is included.

The growing need to be as precise as possible, especially about reuse issues, has led to longer and more complicated lines-of-code definitions. In 2001, Boehm et al. [12] used a Software Engineering Institute (SEI) definition checklist for logical source statements to define the COCOMO II line of code measure, which differs somewhat from the SEI default definition. This checklist takes more than 4 pages of the book. Briefly, SLOC is the amount of non-blank, non-commented logical source statements. They include code produced by programming, conversion with auto-mated translators, code copied or reused without change, and modified code. They exclude code generated with source code generators, or removed code. The origin of the code counted can be new code, previous versions or releases, reuse libraries, or other software components or libraries. They don't include code taken from another product, commercial-off-the-shelf software (COTS), government furnished software (GFS), vendor-supplied language support libraries, operating systems or utilities (un-modified), local or modified language support libraries or operating systems in their definition.

There has been much discussion concerning the validity of using lines-of-code in the measurement of productivity. According to Jones [23] there are three serious problems associated with lines-of-code:

1. The number of lines-of-code is dependent on the language used. Higher level languages, such as Ada and C, appear less productive then low-level languages such as Assembler, because fewer lines are required to generate the same functionality.
2. There is no international standard for a line of code that encompasses all procedural languages.
3. Software can be produced by program generators, graphic icons, etc. which makes the effort of producing lines of code irrelevant.

Other disadvantages with the lines-of-code measure include the fact that coding is only a minor part of the effort required to produce software. In addition, the actual lines of code that will be required cannot be estimated very accurately before starting the project. Estimating software size early is important in order to estimate the cost of software development [35,43]—one of the main reasons you may be interested in knowing your software development productivity. This is because the forecasted effort can be roughly estimated as the reciprocal of past productivity (also known as the project delivery rate) multiplied by the estimated size.

Although the lines-of-code metric is the subject of much debate, the fact remains that it is considered by many organizations as a more practical productivity metric than the currently available alternatives [11], particularly in the domain of space, military and industrial applications. In a recent study of the European Space Agency software project database, lines-of-code was the only size measure available [13].

2.1.2 Function Points

In 1979, Albrecht [2] developed a new measure of software size—function points. While lines-of-code size software from the developer's point of view, function points are based on the functionality of the software as seen by the user [38]. Albrecht calculated the total number of function points by weighting the sums of five different factors: inputs, outputs, inquiries, logical files and interfaces.

- Inputs: e.g., transactions to create, modify or delete records in logical files.
- Outputs: e.g., reports.
- Inquiries: e.g., on-line inquires supported by the application.
- Logical files: logical files updated by the application.
- Interfaces: logical files accessed by the application but not updated by it.

One advantage of function points is that they can be estimated during the requirements phase. This also means that the downstream costs of changing requirements can be quantified. In addition, using metrics such as the cost per function point in contracts helps everyone involved (clients, accountants, project managers, contract officers and attorneys) understand software economics better [24].

One of the main disadvantages of the initial function point method is that it was created and used primarily in business systems environments. For other types of software that have high algorithmic complexity but low numbers of inputs and outputs, such as technical or scientific applications, the Albrecht function point method gives misleading counts [23]. It is for this reason that some later function point methods, for example, Feature Points [23] and Experience [32], also include measures of the number of algorithms in the application. In addition to different counting rules, some of the function point counting methods, for example, IFPUG [38], adjust the size for a number of external complexity factors, and some, for example, Experience, do not.

Since Albrecht's initial work, close to 40 different methods of measuring functionality have been developed—IFPUG, Mark II, 3D, Asset-R, Feature Points, Experience and Cosmic, just to name a few [1,32,38,41,43,47]. While each performs well in the particular environment for which it is intended, the proliferation of different function point counting methods means that few companies count software size in the same way. As software development productivity is a function of software size, this makes comparisons of software productivity across organizations and countries very difficult.

In 1993, work began to develop a technology independent international standard for functional size measurement under the guidance of the International Organization for Standardization committee for software engineering standards (ISO/IEC JTC1/SC7 Working Group 12) [43]. The first part of the standard "Definition of the Concepts of Function Size Measurement" was published in June 1998. This part identifies the common fundamental characteristics of functional size measurement methods. It also defines a set of generic mandatory requirements for a method to be called a Functional Size Measurement (FSM) method. The role of the standard is to promote the consistent interpretation of FSM principles.

As of June 2002, agreement had not been reached regarding the four other parts of the standard:

- Part II: Compliance Assessment of Software Size Measurement Methods
  Will establish a framework to assess the extent of compliance of a particular FSM method with Part I.

- Part III: Verification of an FSM Method
  Will provide the process and the criteria against which specific claims (for example, accuracy, reliability, . . .) of an FSM method can be verified.

- Part IV: FSM Reference Model
  Will provide reference points against which users of the verification process can assess the effectiveness of an FSM for different software types in various software environments.

- Part V: Determination of Functional Domains for use with FSM
  Will establish a standard for mapping functional user requirements to one or more functional domains. Exactly what type of software belongs in a functional domain, for example, MIS, real time or scientific software, will be clearly defined.

That nearly 10 years on, agreement has not been reached on an international standard for functional size measurement is not surprising. Each different function point method is supported by consultants, tools, companies and conferences with a vested interest to not change their unique product or service. It is in their interest to make sure that the method on which they have based their business will comply with future standards. And there is no better way to do this then to participate in making those standards, hence the difficulty in reaching consensus. Nonetheless, the eventual publication of an international standard for functional size measurement will not drastically reduce the number of different functional sizing methods. The main difference is that there will be a compliance assessment and verification of the strengths and weaknesses of each method's performance sizing different types of software. This way, companies can select the method most suitable for their purposes.[2] Thus, it is highly improbable that there will ever be one single functional sizing method used worldwide.

2.2   Effort Measurement

How should you measure effort? Should you measure it in hours or months? Should you include management time, support staff time, or just developers time? Should you include unpaid overtime? Should you include the effort the customer spent working on the project? How many phases should you include in the definition of effort—from requirements specification through installation, or feasibility study through testing? Let's take a look at how some large multi-company databases have defined effort.

In the ESA database [33], effort is measured in person-months and is defined as beginning at specification delivery and ending at customer acceptance. It covers all directly charged labor on the project. As the data comes from companies in several different countries, each having a different definition of a month of work, each company also provides data about the number of hours in their person-month. The effort data is then adjusted to person-months of 144 hours based on this information so that the effort data is comparable.

In COCOMO II [12] effort is expressed in person-months. This is the amount of time one person spends actually working on the software development project for one month. Each person-month is equivalent to 152 hours of working time. It excludes holidays, vacations, and sick leave. It covers all directly charged project effort. For example, it includes project managers and program librarians, but excludes computer center operators, secretaries, higher management, and other jobs considered as overheads. For the waterfall process model, the effort is defined as beginning at software requirements review and ending at software acceptance review. For a second type of process model, project effort is defined as starting with life cycle objectives and ending with initial operational capability. For both process models, software development activities such as documentation, planning and control, and configuration management are included, while database administration is not.

---

[2]I hope that this international standard will be made freely available so that the many small to medium size software producers will read it. If it is too difficult or costly to find out what the standards are they will never be used.

In the Experience database [32], effort is measured in hours. It covers all directly charged labor on the project, defined as the work carried out by the software supplier from the beginning of the requirement specification phase to customer delivery.

In the International Software Benchmarking Standards Group (ISBSG) database [20], effort is measured in hours. It includes all personnel effort needed to complete a software development project including over-time, whether paid or unpaid. It includes the effort of the client representatives as well as the effort of the IT personnel. It excludes public holidays, annual leave, sick leave and non-project related training. Project effort is collected from feasibility study through implementation/installation/user training.

Effort is notoriously difficult to measure accurately, even within a company. In addition to making sure that everyone collects effort using the same definition, other sources of error include late time sheets, missing cost codes, or misallocation of time for various reasons. In a recent article [45], Martin Shepperd and Michelle Cartwright recount the experience of assisting one organization with its effort estimating practices. When they cross-validated the total effort of one project using three different sources in the company, they found that total effort differed in excess of 30%.

With effort measurement as with size measurement, it is important that you decide what you are going to do and then do it consistently.

3. What Factors Can Have an Impact on Productivity?

Productivity rates are highly variable across the software development industry [4]. Business sector, requirements volatility, application language, hardware platform, tool use, quality requirements and hundreds of other parameters can affect productivity. An overview of some of the productivity factors considered by past researchers can be found in Table I. Walston and Felix [51] found 29 factors that were significantly correlated with productivity at IBM. Bailey and Basili [5] identified 21 productivity parameters in an analysis of data from the NASA/Goddard Space Flight Center. At ITT, Vosburgh et al. [49] found 14 significant productivity factors, with modern programming practice usage and development computer size playing important roles. Boehm's first COCOMO model [10] was based on 15 software factors. However, such major factors as application type and programming language were omitted in these models.

Several studies look at the relationship between productivity rates and the type of software being developed [18,29,42]. Real-time software was found to have the lowest productivity in a study by Stephenson [46]. Vosburgh et al. [49] identified 3 different programming environments with business applications having the highest

TABLE I

OVERVIEW OF SOME PRODUCTIVITY FACTORS CONSIDERED IN RESEARCH FROM 1976–1996

Some major productivity factors	ESA data	A[a]	B	C	D	E	F	G	H	I	J	K	L	M	N	O	P	Q	R
Country	X											X							
Company	X																		
Category/type	X											X	X		X		X		
Industrial/business environment	X														X				
Language	X	X	X			X							X	X					
Team size	X	X					X			X	X					X			
Duration	X	X					X			X	X					X	X		
Project size	X		X			X			X		X		X				X	X	
Required software reliability	X							X	X										
Execution time constraint	X							X	X						X			X	X
Main storage constraint	X							X	X						X			X	X
Virtual machine volatility	X							X											
Programming language experience	X			X				X	X					X				X	X
Modern programming practices	X		X	X	X			X	X	X			X	X	X	X		X	X
Tool use	X			X	X			X	X	X			X	X	X	X		X	
Product complexity				X				X	X					X	X	X		X	X
Analyst capability					X			X						X	X	X			
Applications experience				X	X			X	X					X	X	X			X
Programmer capability				X	X			X	X					X					
Virtual machine experience				X		X		X	X					X					X
Amount of documentation							X			X									X
Overall personnel experience									X	X			X					X	X
Customer interface complexity				X					X					X	X			X	X
Design volatility				X					X	X				X		X		X	X
Hardware concurrent development									X					X		X		X	X
Quality assurance					X					X					X				
Development environment (on-line)		X				X								X	X				X

[a]Table II describes the research referred to by each letter.

Reproduced from Maxwell, K., Van Wassenhove, L. and Dutta, S., Software development productivity of European space, military and industrial applications. *IEEE Transactions on Software Engineering.* © 1996 IEEE. Used with permission.

average productivity followed by normal-time and real-time applications. Maxwell and Forselius [32] found that the type of business for which the software was developed explained most of the productivity variation in the Experience database. Higher productivity was found in the manufacturing, wholesale and retail, and public administration sectors, and lower productivity was found in the banking and insurance sectors.

Aron [3] found that the productivity variation of a number of IBM projects involving systems programs and business applications was due to differences in system difficulty and project duration. He also adjusted his cost estimate for the use of higher-level languages. Kitchenham [26] found that productivity varied with programming language level and working environment. Productivity has also been found to vary with tool use [32,33], user interface type [32], requirements volatility [32], programmer experience [10,23,29,48,49,51], hardware constraints [10,49], team size [14,17, 22,33], duration [3,9,33], project size [2,8,17,22,25,32,33,42,49] and modern programming practices [6,10,15,23,33,49], among other factors. It should be noted that many of these findings differ and are limited to programming environments similar to those studied.

Several studies have also found differences in the factors that explain productivity in a single company, and the factors that explain the productivity of multi-company databases [13,21,35]. In one study productivity factors common to both the ESA database and one company's database were analyzed [35]. In the ESA database, productivity depended on the application category, language, required software reliability, main storage constraint, and the use of modern programming practices or software tools. Productivity in the company was a function of only two factors: the application language and the start year. An overview of the major databases that include productivity factors can be found in Table II.

As is evident in Table II, some of the databases studied measured software size in lines-of-code and some used function points. Does measuring size, and hence productivity, differently have an impact on the variables that are found to be important? Apparently not. In a little known comparative study of the ESA database and the Laturi database (now called Experience), the authors found that although the two databases studied used different measures of size, effort and productivity, and contained very different types of projects, the similarity of the results was quite striking [34]. In both databases, company differences explained the greatest amount of productivity. In both databases, a 2-class model based on application category and language was found to explain the greatest amount of productivity variation. And in both databases, software development productivity had been significantly increasing over time.

One of the difficulties in maintaining a software metrics database is that the factors that are important can change over time. In Tables III and IV, you can see the evo-

TABLE II
SOME REFERENCES FOR DATABASES WHICH INCLUDE PRODUCTIVITY FACTORS 1976–2002

Reference	No. projects	Environment	Scope	Size measure	Database code in Table I
Maxwell 2002 [37]	63	Bank	One company	F.P.	
Lokan et al. 2001 [30]	208/60	Mixture/not identified	Multi-company/one company	F.P.	
Lokan 2001 [31]	465	Mixture	Multi-company	F.P.	
Boehm et al. 2000 [12]	161	Mixture	Multi-company	L.O.C. (sometimes converted from F.P.)	
Jeffery et al. 2000 [21]	145/19	Mixture/business	Multi-company/one company	F.P.	
Maxwell and Forselius 2000 [32]	206	Business software	Multi-company	F.P.	
Briand et al. 2000 [13]	160/29	Space-military-industrial/military	Multi-company/one company	L.O.C.	
Maxwell et al. 1999 [35]	108/29	Space-military-industrial/military	Multi-company/one company	L.O.C.	
Walkerden and Jeffrey 1999 [50]	19	Not identified	One company	F.P.	
Maxwell et al. 1996 [33]	99	Space/military/industrial	Multi-company	L.O.C.	ESA data
Kraut and Streeter 1995 [28]	65	Telecommunications	One company	L.O.C.	
Nevalainen and Mäki 1994 [40]	120	Commercial	Multi-company	F.P.	O
Putnam and Myers 1992 [42]	1486	Mixture (primarily Business systems)	Multi-company	L.O.C.	P
Kitchenham 1992 [26]	108	Not identified (probably Commercial)	One company	F.P.	M
Jones 1991 [23]	4000	Mixture (primarily Systems and MIS)	Multi-company	F.P. (converted from L.O.C.)	L

(continued on next page)

TABLE II — *Continued*

Reference	No. projects	Environment	Scope	Size measure	Database code in Table I
Banker et al. 1991 [6]	65	Bank maintenance projects	One company	F.P. and L.O.C.	D
Cusumano and Kemerer 1990 [18]	40	Mixture	Multi-company	L.O.C.	K
Card et al. 1987 [16]	22	Space (NASA/Goddard)	One company	L.O.C.	I
Conte et al. 1986 [17]	187	Mixture	Multi-company	L.O.C.	J
Vosburgh et al. 1984 [49]	44	Mixture (from ITT)	Multi-company	L.O.C.	Q
Behrens 1983 [8]	24	Data processing	One company	F.P.	E
Bailey and Basili 1981 [5]	18	Space (NASA/Goddard)	One company	L.O.C.	C
Boehm 1981 [10]	63	Mixture	Multi-company	L.O.C.	G
Brooks 1981 [15]	51	Mixture (from Walston–Felix)	One company	L.O.C.	H
Lawrence 1981 [29]	278	Commercial	Multi-company	L.O.C.	N
Belady and Lehman 1979 [9]	37	Not identified	One company	L.O.C.	F
Albrecht 1979 [2]	22	IBM data processing	One company	F.P.	B
Schneider 1978 [44]	400	Mixture (mainly military)	Multi-company	L.O.C.	
Walston and Felix 1977 [51]	60	Mixture (from IBM)	One company	L.O.C.	R
Aaron 1976 [3]	9	IBM large systems	One company	L.O.C.	A

TABLE III
EVOLUTION OF SOFT PRODUCTIVITY FACTORS IN COCOMO DATABASE

Soft productivity factors	COCOMO 1981 (15 factors)	COCOMO II (22 factors)
Programmer capability	X	X
Analyst capability	X	X
Product complexity	X	X
Time constraint	X	X
Required software reliability	X	X
Multi-site development		X
Documentation match to life cycle needs		X
Personnel continuity		X
Applications experience	X	X
Use of software tools	X	X
Platform volatility		X
Storage constraint	X	X
Process maturity		X
Language and tools experience		X
Required development schedule	X	X
Database size	X	X
Platform experience		X
Architecture and risk resolution		X
Precedentedness		X
Developed for reuse		X
Team cohesion		X
Development flexibility		X
Modern programming practices	X	
Programming language experience	X	
Computer turnaround time	X	
Virtual machine experience	X	
Virtual machine volatility	X	

lution of the productivity factors collected, or no longer collected, in the COCOMO and Experience databases. In addition, even if the same productivity factor is collected, its definition can change over time. What was considered an average level of tool use in 1986, might be considered a low level of tool use by 1996. "Modern programming practices" is another variable which is hard to define consistently over time. What was modern in the past is no longer modern today, and what is modern today did not exist in the past. So just what does "modern" mean? Modern compared to now, or modern compared to what was available at the time? (This variable has been dropped from COCOMO II [12].) As practices change, new variables need to be collected, definitions need to evolve, and past data needs to be adjusted in order for data to remain comparable.

TABLE IV
EVOLUTION OF SOFT PRODUCTIVITY FACTORS IN EXPERIENCE DATABASE

Soft productivity factors	Experience v1.4 (15 factors)	Experience v2.0 (21 factors)
Customer involvement	X	X
Performance and availability of the development environment	X	X
IT staff availability	X	X
Number of different stakeholders		X
Pressure on schedule		X
Impact of standards	X	X
Impact of methods	X	X
Impact of tools	X	X
Level of change management (*Requirements volatility in v1.4*)	X	X
Process maturity		X
Functionality requirements		X
Reliability requirements		X
Usability requirements		X
Efficiency requirements	X	X
Maintainability requirements		X
Portability requirements		X
Staff analysis skills	X	X
Staff application knowledge	X	X
Staff tool skills	X	X
Project manager's experience		X
Team skills	X	X
Software's logical complexity	X	
Installation requirements	X	
Quality requirements	X	

4. How to Identify Influential Factors[3]

So finally, you have decided what data to collect and what definitions you are going to use. You've made sure that everyone is measuring in the same way and you are the proud owner of a software metrics database. Great, but do you know how to make the most of this valuable asset? As we have seen in the previous section categorical variables such as language, development platform, application type, and tool use can be important factors in explaining the productivity of your company's software projects. However, analyzing a database containing many non-numerical variables is not a straightforward task.

---

[3]This section was adapted from Chapter 1 in K.D. Maxwell, "*Applied Statistics for Software Managers*" published by Prentice-Hall PTR in June 2002. It is provided here with permission of Prentice-Hall PTR.

Data Analysis Methodology	
Step 1:	Validate your data
Step 2:	Select the variables and model
Step 3:	Perform preliminary analyses (using graphs, tables, correlation and stepwise regression analyses)
Step 4:	Build the multi-variable model (using analysis of variance)
Step 5:	Check the model

FIG. 1. Data analysis steps.

Statistics, like software development, is as much an art as it is a science. Choosing the appropriate statistical methods, selecting the variables to use, creating new variables, removing outliers, picking the best model, detecting confounded variables, choosing baseline categorical variables, and handling influential observations all require that you make many decisions during the data analysis process. Decisions for which there are often no clear rules. What should you do? Read my book "Applied Statistics for Software Managers" [37]. Using real software project data, this book leads you through all the steps necessary to extract the most value from your data. First, I describe in detail my methodology for analyzing software project data. You do not need to understand statistics to follow the methodology. I simply explain what to do, why I do it, how to do it, and what to watch out for at each step.

Common problems that occur when analyzing real data are thoroughly covered in four case studies of gradually increasing complexity. Each case study is based around a business issue of interest to software managers. You will learn how to determine which variables explain differences in software development productivity. You will look at factors that influence time to market. You will learn how to develop and measure the accuracy of cost estimation models. You will study the cost drivers of software maintenance, with an emphasis on presenting results. Finally, you will learn what you need to know about descriptive statistics, statistical tests, correlation analysis, regression analysis, and analysis of variance.

In this section, I briefly describe my data analysis methodology (Fig. 1) and the reasons why I undertake each step.

4.1　Data Validation

The most important step is data validation. I spend much more time validating data than I do analyzing it. Often, data is not neatly presented to you in one table, but is in several files that need to be merged and which may include information you do not need or understand. The data may also exist on different pieces of paper.

What do I mean by data validation? In general terms, I mean finding out if you have the right data for your purpose. It is not enough to write a questionnaire and get people to fill it out; you need to have a vision. Like getting the requirement specifications right before starting to develop the software. Specifically, you need to determine if the values for each variable make sense.

If you haven't collected the data yourself, start off by asking these questions:

- What is this data?
- When was the data collected?
- Why was the data collected?
- Who collected it?
- How did that person ensure that everyone understood the definitions?
- What is the definition of each variable?
- What are the units of measurement of each variable?
- What are the definitions of the values of each variable?

Other typical questions I ask when validating software project databases include [36]: What does a zero mean? Does it mean none, is it a missing value, or is it a number which has been rounded to zero? And if a value is missing, does that indicate no value or don't know? The response "other" is also problematic, especially when collecting data for benchmarking. "Other" can represent a variety of different things (e.g., tools, languages, methods) for different organizations.

Why Do It?

You can waste months trying to make sense out of data that was collected without a clear purpose, and without statistical analysis requirements in mind. It is much better to get a precise idea of exactly what data you have and how much you trust it before you start analyzing. Regardless of whether the data concerns chocolate bar sales, financial indicators, or software projects, the old maxim "garbage in equals garbage out" applies. If you find out that something is wrong with the raw data after you have analyzed it, your conclusions are meaningless. In the best case, you may just have to correct something and analyze it all again. However, if the problem lies with the definition of a variable, it may be impossible to go back and collect the data needed. If you are collecting the data yourself, make sure you ask the right questions the first time. You may not have a second chance.

4.2   Variable and Model Selection

Once we understand what data we actually have, we need to determine what we can learn from it. What possible relationships could we study? What possible relationships should we study? What relationship will we study first? Your answers to the last two questions will depend on the overall goals of the analysis.

Why Do It?

The data may have been collected for a clearly stated purpose. Even so, there might be other interesting relationships to study that occur to you while you are analyzing the data, and which you might be tempted to investigate. However, it is important to decide in advance what you are going to do first and then to complete that task in a meticulous, organized manner. Otherwise, you will find yourself going in lots of different directions, generating lots of computer output, and becoming confused about what you have tried and what you have not tried; in short, you will drown yourself in the data. It is also at this stage that you may decide to create new variables or to reduce the number of variables in your analysis. Variables of questionable validity, variables not meaningfully related to what you want to study, and categorical variable values that do not have a sufficient number of observations should be dropped from the analysis.

4.3   Preliminary Analyses

Before running "blind" statistical tests, I check that the assumptions underlying them are true. In addition, I like to get some first impressions of the data. My objective is not a complete understanding of all possible relationships among all the variables. For example, in Step 2, variable and model selection, I could decide that my first goal is to determine which of the variables collected have an influence on productivity. To achieve that goal, I undertake the following preliminary analysis steps before building the multi-variable model (Step 4).

4.3.1   Graphs

Histograms

To start, I look at a graph of each numerical variable individually to see how many small values, large values, and medium values there are, that is, the distribution of each variable. These are also called histograms.

Why Do It?

I want to see if the variables are normally distributed. Many statistical techniques assume that the underlying data is normally distributed, so you should check if it is. A normal distribution is also known as a bell-shaped curve. In a bell-shaped curve,

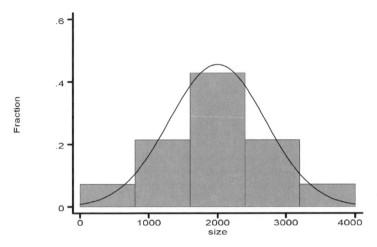

FIG. 2. Example of a normal distribution—hypothetical data.

most values fall in the middle, with few very high and very low values. The histogram of an approximately normally distributed variable will look like Fig. 2. This shows the distribution of the sizes of a hypothetical group of software development projects. From this histogram, we can see that most projects in the group are around 2000 function points, and only a small number are less than 800 or more than 3200 function points. (n.b. the y-axis label "Fraction" refers to the percentage of projects that fall into one of the intervals. For example, 0.4 = 40% of projects.)

If the histograms show that some variables are not normally distributed (which is often the case with the size, effort, duration and productivity found in **real** software project databases), it is common to transform these variables by taking their natural log. Fig. 3 shows the size distribution of one bank's software project database. In this real-world example, *size* is not normally distributed. Almost 80% of projects are less than 800 function points. However, ln(*size*) looks more normally distributed (Fig. 4). Thus the bank should use ln(*size*) in their models, not *size*.

4.3.2 Two-Dimensional Graphs

I also make graphs of the dependent variable against each independent numerical variable. The dependent variable is the variable you want to model—for example, productivity. The independent variables are the variables you think could explain the differences in the productivity of your projects—for example, size.

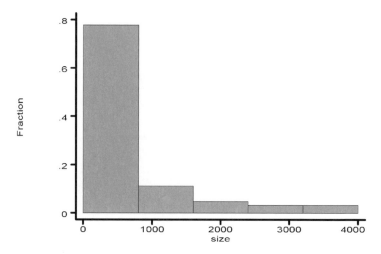

FIG. 3. Histogram showing distribution of software size (*size*)—real data.

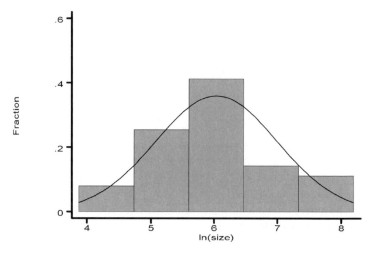

FIG. 4. Histogram showing distribution of ln(*size*)—real data.

Why Do It?

A picture is worth a thousand words. I highly recommend visualizing any relationship that might exist between the dependent and independent variables before running "blind" statistical tests. It is important to see if the relationship is linear as our

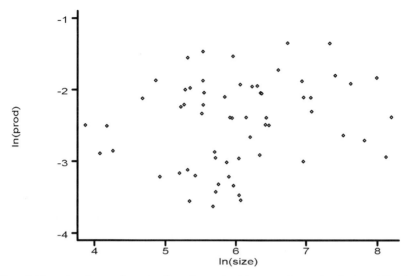

FIG. 5. Example of a two-dimensional graph—productivity vs. software size (both variables have undergone a log transformation).

statistical tests are based on linear relationships and will "ignore" non-linear relationships. A relationship is linear if you can fit one straight line through the data points, and this represents them well. Fig. 5 shows an example of a two-dimensional graph using two variables from one bank's software project database. Here productivity is a function of size. Both variables have undergone a natural log transformation.

4.3.3 Tables

I print out the average value of the dependent variable and the number of observations it is based on for each value of each categorical variable. In Example 1, we can see the mean (or average) value of productivity (*prod*) for each value of the categorical variable user interface.

```
----------------+------------------------
User Interface | N (prod)   mean (prod)
----------------+------------------------
          GUI |    4         0.2016
       TextUI |   58         0.0943
----------------+------------------------
```

EXAMPLE 1. Mean productivity by user interface type.

The 4 graphical user interface (GUI) applications seem a lot more productive than the 58 text user interface (TextUI) applications.

Why Do It?

We make tables to see if there is a big difference in the productivity needed by category and to start formulating possible reasons for this.

4.3.4   Correlation Analysis

Another assumption of the statistical procedure I use to build a multi-variable model is that independent variables are independent; that is, they are not related to each other. There is a very quick way to check if the numerical variables are independent: correlation analysis. I use Spearman's rank correlation coefficient because it tests the relationships of orders rather than actual values. This is important as some of our variables may be measured using subjective scales (e.g., *t01–t15* in Table V). Another important feature of Spearman's rank correlation coefficient is that it is less sensitive to extreme values than the standard Pearson correlation coefficient.

4.3.5   Stepwise Regression Analysis

Performing multiple regression analyses allows us to determine the relative importance of each independent, numerical variable's relationship to the dependent variable.

Why Do It?

Because stepwise regression analysis is automatic and very simple to run, I always like to see how good a model can be built by just using the non-categorical data. In addition to learning if the non-categorical variables collected are very important indicators of productivity, this also gives me a quick idea of what performance the categorical data is going to have to beat.

4.4   Building the Multi-Variable Model

I call the technique I've developed to build the multi-variable model "stepwise ANOVA" (analysis of variance). It is very similar to forward stepwise regression except I use an analysis of variance procedure to build models with categorical variables. This procedure allows us to determine the influence of numerical and categorical variables on the dependent variable. The model starts "empty" and then the variables most related to productivity are added one by one in order of importance until no other variable can be added to improve the model. The procedure is very labor-intensive because I make the decisions at each step myself; it is not automatically done by the computer. Although I am sure this could be automated, there are some advantages to doing it yourself. As you carry out the steps, you will develop a better understanding of the data. In addition, in the real world, a database often contains many missing values and it is not always clear which variable should be added at each step. Sometimes you need to follow more than one path to find the best model.

4.5   Checking the Model

Before we can accept the final model found in the previous step, we must check that the assumptions underlying the statistical tests used have not been violated. In particular, this means checking that:

- Independent numerical variables are approximately normally distributed.
- Independent variables are not strongly related to each other.
- The errors in our model should be random and normally distributed.

In addition, we also need to check that no single project or small number of projects has an overly strong influence on the results.

4.5.1   Numerical Variable Checks

When I have my final model, I need to check that all the independent numerical variables present in the final model are not strongly linearly related to each other. In other words, I need to check for multicollinearity problems. Why would this cause a problem? If two or more explanatory variables are very highly correlated, it is sometimes not possible for the statistical analysis software to separate their independent effects and you will end up with some strange results. Exactly when this will happen is not predictable. So, it is up to you to check the correlations between all numerical variables. To avoid multicollinearity problems, I do not allow any two variables with an absolute value of Spearman's rho greater than or equal to 0.75 in the final model together.

You should also be aware that there is always the possibility that a variable outside the analysis is really influencing the results. Always ask yourself if your results make sense and if there could be any other explanation for them. Unfortunately, we are less likely to ask questions and more likely to believe a result when it proves our point.

4.5.2   *Categorical Variable Checks*

Strongly related categorical variables can cause problems similar to those caused by numerical variables. Unfortunately, strong relationships involving categorical variables are much more difficult to detect. How do we check that categorical variables are not related to each other or to the numerical variables in the model?

To determine if there is a relationship between a categorical variable and a numerical variable, I use an analysis of variance procedure. It is more difficult to determine if there is an important relationship between two categorical variables. To check this, I first calculate the chi-squared statistic to test for independence. From this I learn if there is a significant relationship between two categorical variables, but not the extent of the relationship. If there is a significant relationship, I need to look closely at the two variables and judge for myself if they are so strongly related that there could be a problem.

If I find any problems in the final model, I return to the step where I added the correlated/confounded variable to the variables already present in the model, take the second best choice, and rebuild the model from there. I do not carry out any further checks. The model is not valid, so there is no point. We have to start again.

4.5.3   *Testing the Residuals*

In a well-fitted model, there should be no pattern to the errors (residuals) plotted against the fitted values (Fig. 6). The term "fitted value" refers to the productivity

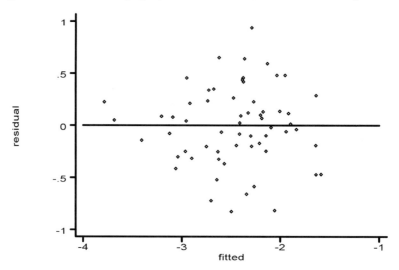

FIGURE 6. Example of plotting residuals.

predicted by our model; the term "residual" is used to express the difference between the actual productivity and the predicted productivity for each project. Your statistical analysis tool should calculate the predicted values and residuals automatically for you. The errors of our model should be random. For example, we should not be consistently overestimating small productivities and underestimating large productivities. It is always a good idea to plot this relationship and take a look. If you see a pattern, it means that there is a problem with your model. If there is a problem with the final model, then try the second best model. If there is a problem with the second best model, then try the third best model, and so on.

You should also make a histogram of the residuals to check that they are approximately normally distributed.

4.5.4 Detecting Influential Observations

How much is our final model affected by any one project or subset of our data? If we dropped one project from our database, would our model be completely different? I certainly hope not. But we can do better than hope; we can check the model's sensitivity to individual observations. Projects with large predicted errors (residuals) and/or projects very different from other project's values for at least one of the independent variables in the model can exert undue influence on the model (leverage). I check this with a statistic called Cook's distance.

5. Case Study[4]

In this case study, I will show you what can be learned from the productivity analysis of one bank's software metrics database. The initial database contained 29 variables for 63 completed software development applications. As the project data had already been entered into a software management data collection tool, which included definitions of all the variables, I did not have to spend too much time trying to understand the data and correcting mistakes. The bank collected this data to help manage project portfolios. The project's manager provided data at the end of each project. One person entered all project data into the database and validated it. In addition to the data file, I received a copy of the Experience software tool (http://www.sttf.fi), a database parameter file, and a productivity factor definition file. The database parameter file defined each categorical variable value's code. For example, app $= 406$ corresponded to a transaction processing application. Nonetheless, an initial face-to-face meeting with the data provider was necessary to fully understand everything I was given. I then consolidated all the information I needed to understand the data into a variable definition table (Table V).

[4]This section was adapted from Chapter 2 in K.D. Maxwell, "*Applied Statistics for Software Managers*" published by Prentice-Hall PTR in June 2002. It is provided here with permission of Prentice-Hall PTR.

TABLE V
VARIABLE DEFINITIONS

Variable	Full name	Definition
id	identification number	Each completed project has a unique identification number. (Originally, each project was given a name instead of a number, but I replaced these names for data confidentiality reasons.)
size	application size	Function points measured using the Experience method.
effort	effort	Work carried out by the software supplier from specification until delivery, measured in hours.
duration	duration	Duration of project from specification until delivery, measured in months.
start	exact start date	Day/month/year application specification started.
app	application type	401 = Customer service (CustServ) 402 = Management information system (MIS) 406 = Transaction processing (TransPro) 407 = Production control, logistics, order processing (ProdCont) 408 = Information/on-line service (InfServ)
har	hardware platform	1001 = Networked (Network) 1002 = Mainframe (Mainfrm) 1003 = Personal computer (PC) 1004 = Mini computer (Mini) 1005 = Multi-platform (Multi)
dba	DBMS architecture	1602 = Relational (Relatnl) 1604 = Other (Other) 1605 = Sequential (Sequentl)
ifc	user interface	2001 = Graphical user interface (GUI) 2002 = Text user interface (TextUI)
source	where developed	7001 = In-house (Inhouse) 7004 = Outsourced (Outsrced)
lan1 *lan2* *lan3* *lan4*	language used	Up to four languages were used per application. They could be used in any order; thus, *lan1* is not necessarily the most important language. Too many codes to list here; however, codes of special interest include: 2617 = COBOL 2660 = Telon

(*continued on next page*)

TABLE V — *Continued*

Variable	Full name	Definition
t01	customer participation	How actively customer took part in development work: 1 = Very low; none 2 = Low; passive; client defined or approved < 30% of all functions 3 = Nominal; client defined and approved 30–70% of all functions 4 = High; active; client defined and approved all of most important functions, and over 70% of others 5 = Very high; client participated very actively, thus most functions were slightly volatile and changes had to be made
t02	development environment adequacy	Performance level of tool resources and equipment during project: 1 = Very low; continuous shortcomings in devices, building of test environments and testing required special arrangements 2 = Low; shared equipment/machine resources; delays in some work stages (e.g., compiling and testing) 3 = Nominal; enough during development work; a workstation for everybody 4 = High; enough to deal with capacity peaks (efficiency, storage, response time) 5 = Very high; dedicated, over-dimensioned development environments, in practice only for this project
t03	staff availability	Availability of software personnel during project: 1 = Very low; big problems with key personnel availability; lots of simultaneous customer and maintenance responsibilities; special know-how required 2 = Low; personnel involved in some other simultaneous projects and/or maintenance responsibilities 3 = Nominal; key members involved in only one other project 4 = High; project members involved almost full-time 5 = Very high; qualified personnel available when needed; full-time participation
t04	standards use	Level and use of standards: 1 = Very low; standards developed during project 2 = Low; some standards, but not familiar ones; more must be developed for some tasks 3 = Nominal; generally known standards applied in environment before; some tailoring needed 4 = High; detailed standards applied in same environment for some time 5 = Very high; stable and detailed standards; already familiar to team; use controlled

(*continued on next page*)

TABLE V — *Continued*

Variable	Full name	Definition
t05	methods use	Level and use of methods: 1 = Very low; no modern design methods; mostly meetings; used by individuals 2 = Low; use beginning; traditional concepts employed (structural analysis and design, top–down design, etc.) 3 = Nominal; generally known methods used 4 = High; methods integrated in detail and most activities covered; support existed; used by everyone 5 = Very high; methods used during entire life cycle; methods tailored for specific needs of project; methods supported for individual projects
t06	tools use	Level and use of tools: 1 = Very low; minimal tools: editors, compilers, and testing tools 2 = Low; basic tools: interpreters, editors, compilers, debuggers, databases, and libraries 3 = Nominal; development environment, database management system (DBMS), and support for most phases 4 = High; modern tools like CASE, project planners, application generators, and standardized interfaces between phases 5 = Very high; integrated CASE environment over entire life cycle; all tools support each other
t07	software's logical complexity	Computing, I/O needs, and user interface requirements: 1 = Very low; only routines; no need for user interface; simple databases 2 = Low; functionally clear; no algorithmic tasks; database solution clear 3 = Nominal; functionally typical; normal, standard database; no algorithms 4 = High; processing more demanding; database large and complex; new requirements for user interfaces 5 = Very high; functionally and technically difficult solution; user interface very complex; distributed databases
t08	requirements volatility	Volatility of customer/user requirements during project: 1 = Very low; no new features; standard components; conversions only 2 = Low; some changes to specifications; some new or adapted functions; some minor changes in data contents 3 = Nominal; more changes to specifications, but project members could handle them; impact minor ($< 15\%$ new or modified functions) 4 = High; some major changes affecting total architecture and requiring rework; 15–30% of functions new or modified 5 = Very high; new requirements added continuously; lots of rework; more than 30% new or modified functions compared to original requirements

(*continued on next page*)

TABLE V — *Continued*

Variable	Full name	Definition
t09	quality requirements	Quality goals of software: 1 = Very low; no quality requirements; "quick-and-dirty" allowed 2 = Low; basic requirements satisfied (documentation, implementation testing, system testing, and module testing); no statistical controls or reviews 3 = Nominal; proper documentation of critical features; design- and implementation-tested; modules/job flows tested; walk-throughs; maintenance work planned 4 = High; formal reviews and inspections between all phases; attention to documentation, usability, and maintenance 5 = Very high; quantified quality requirements; 100% satisfaction of technical and functional goals; maintenance work minimal
t10	efficiency requirements	Efficiency goals of software: 1 = Very low; no efficiency requirements needing attention or planning 2 = Low; efficiency goals easy to reach; requirements below average 3 = Nominal; capacity level of software stable and predictable; response time, transaction load, and turnaround time typical 4 = High; specific peaks in capacity, response time, transaction processing, and turnaround time reached by specific design and implementation techniques 5 = Very high; efficiency essential; strict efficiency goals needing continuous attention and specific skills
t11	installation requirements	Training needs for users and variants of platform: 1 = Very low; no training needs; < 10 users 2 = Low; some training; about 10 users; creation of basic data only minor 3 = Nominal; typical training; 10–50 users; some conversions of old data 4 = High; large-scale training for several organizations; < 1000 users; extra software for conversions; possible parallel runs; several platforms 5 = Very high; > 1000 users; long expected lifetime; several user organizations; several different platforms
t12	staff analysis skills	Analysis skills of project staff at kick-off: 1 = Very low; no experience in requirements analysis or similar projects 2 = Low; < 30% of project staff with analysis and design experience in similar projects 3 = Nominal; 30–70% of project staff with analysis experience; one experienced member 4 = High; most members of staff with experience in specifications and analysis; analysis professional in charge

(*continued on next page*)

TABLE V — *Continued*

Variable	Full name	Definition
		5 = Very high; project staff composed of first-class professionals; members have strong vision and experience with requirements analysis
t13	staff application knowledge	Knowledge of application domain in project team (supplier and customer): 1 = Very low; team application experience < 6 months on average 2 = Low; application experience low; some members have experience; 6–12 months on average 3 = Nominal; application experience good; 1–3 years on average 4 = High; application experience good both at supplier and customer sites; 3–6 years on average; business dynamics known 5 = Very high; both supplier and customer know application area well, including the business; > 6 years' average experience
t14	staff tool skills	Experience level of project team (supplier and customer) with development and documentation tools at project kick-off: 1 = Very low; team has no experience in necessary tools; team's average experience < 6 months 2 = Low; tools experience less than average; some members have experience with some tools; 6–12 months on average 3 = Nominal; tools experience good in about half the team; some members know development and documentation tools well; 1–3 years on average 4 = High; most team members know tools well; some members can help others; 3–6 years on average 5 = Very high; team knows all tools well; support available for specific needs of project; > 6 years' average experience
t15	staff team skills	Ability of project team to work effectively according to best project practices: 1 = Very low; scattered team; minimal project and management skills 2 = Low; some members with previous experience on similar projects; not united as a group 3 = Nominal; most members with experience on similar projects; commitment on project goals good; no motivation to utilize real team spirit 4 = High; group very active and knows how to exploit team effectiveness 5 = Very high; very anticipatory team; team can solve in an innovative way most personal and team problems; superior spirit

The size of projects in this database range from 48 function points to 3634 function points; the average project size is 671 function points. Effort ranges from 583 to 63,694 hours, with an average of 8110 hours. Project duration ranges from 4 months to 54 months; the average project duration is 17 months.

Whatever we are going to find out from our data analysis, it is important to remember that it is only true for similar projects, that is, projects with sizes, efforts, and durations within the domain of this database. My conclusions will not apply to projects in this bank that are smaller than 48 function points, or that used less than 583 hours of effort, or that were less than four months in duration. They will also not apply to projects bigger than 3634 function points, or projects that used more than 63,694 hours of effort, or projects longer than 54 months in duration.

5.1   Data Validation

While validating the data I noticed that some variables had missing values. The DBMS architecture (*dba*) was missing for two projects. In addition, two projects did not have valid language data. On closer inspection of the data, I found out that Project 12, which does not have a value for *lan1*, does have one for *lan2*. Project 24 has no language at all. I contacted the data provider for more information. First of all, I learned that the two projects with a missing *dba* value were "client application" development projects and did not have a database. Thus, they did not have any DBMS architecture. So in this case, missing data means "none." I was told that the project with no language at all actually used a development tool called *Clipper*. It had not been entered in the database because it was not one of the choices in the list. I created a new code, *2670*, for *Clipper*. Finally, I learned that for the project with a *lan2* and no *lan1*, there was only one language used, the language listed in *lan2*. Until this conversation, I had assumed that *lan1* was the most important language, *lan2* the second most important language, etc.; however, I learned that this was not the case. The languages were input in any order, not in order of importance. There was no information about the percentage use of each language. This was bad news for me; from previous research, I knew that language was important and it would have been interesting to look at the effect of language on productivity in the bank. I was planning to use *lan1* as the principal language to do this.

I also noticed one outlier because of its very high productivity, approximately 0.53 function points/hour. It was over twice as productive as the next highest rated project in the database. When I contacted the data provider to find out more, I learned that this project was an **exceptional** project. It was the only Macintosh project the bank ever had. More importantly, it was outsourced at a fixed price. So it was the only project in the database where the actual effort was not really known. The effort input in the database was derived from the outsourcing price. As this price was fixed, and it was impossible to know if the developing company made or lost a lot of money on it, the derived effort value was not comparable with the other projects' efforts. As this project was neither a typical project for this bank, nor was its productivity reliable, I dropped it from the analysis.

5.2 Variable and Model Selection

Because I couldn't make use of the language variable in the traditional way, I needed to find a way to transform the language information I did have into something useful. First, I decided to try grouping projects that used the same combinations of languages together. I found 32 different language combinations for 63 projects. This meant that, on average, there were two projects per language combination— not enough to make any meaningful conclusions. In addition, most language combinations containing enough observations to analyze used COBOL, so perhaps they weren't really that different. I then decided it might be interesting to see if productivity was different for projects that used one language, two languages, three languages, or four languages, so I created the variable *nlan*—number of languages used. I thought that perhaps it might be less productive to use many languages in a project. In addition, as some research has suggested that using Telon can improve productivity, I decided to create a new categorical variable, *telonuse*, which was 1 if Telon was one of the languages used and 0 if it was not.

I also created the following new variables:

- *syear*—As it could be interesting to see if productivity had increased or decreased over time, I decided to create one new variable by extracting the year from the exact start date of the project. I used this variable for making graphs and tables.

- *time*—This is the variable I used in the regression and ANOVA models to represent time. I calculated it from the start year:

$$time = syear - 1985 + 1,$$

thus *time* is 1 in 1985, 2 in 1986, etc. (n.b. 1985 was the minimum value of *syear*). Why do I do this? Why not just put *syear* in the models? First of all, it is common practice in time series analysis to do this. It is not the actual year that matters, just the fact that a year is one year more than the previous year (or one year less than the following year). In addition, should I have to transform *syear* by taking its natural log, ln, I will find that the natural logs of large numbers like 1985, 1986, etc. are not very different ($\ln(1985) = 7.5934$; $\ln(1990) = 7.5959$, $\ln(1993) = 7.5973$). It will look like time does not vary very much. This will have a bizarre influence on the results. The logs of smaller numbers are more differentiated. In addition, if time has an exponential effect on productivity and I try to calculate e^{syear}, I will get a number so big that it will overload the computer.

- *prod*—If I want to study productivity, I must have a variable that measures productivity.

$$prod = size/effort.$$

Model Selection

My goal in this study is to determine which variables explain the productivity differences among software development projects in this bank. Once I understood the variable definitions and decided which variables to use, this is the model I selected.

$$prod = f(size, \ effort, \ duration, \ app, \ har, \ ifc, \ source, \ t01–t15, \ nlan,$$
$$telonuse, \ time).$$

What is the relationship between productivity and the size of the application, the amount of effort spent, the duration of the project, the type of application, the type of hardware, the user interface, whether or not the development was outsourced, the 15 different productivity factors, the number of languages used, Telon use and time?

5.3   Analysis Results

I've highlighted some of the most interesting productivity analysis findings in this section. From the histogram step in the preliminary analysis, I learned that the productivity factors, *t01–t15*, were approximately normally distributed in the sample. I've printed out two histograms so you can see how I interpret them (Figs. 7 and 8).

The definitions of these factors were chosen especially so that most projects from a diverse group of companies and industries would be average and the distributions would be normal. This is the case in the larger multi-company database from which this subset was taken. However, in this bank, I noted some differences.

- Most applications had high customer participation (*t01*) (see Fig. 7).
- No application had big problems with key personnel availability (*t03*) (see Fig. 8).
- No project needed standards development (*t04*).
- No application used an integrated CASE environment (*t06*).
- The logical complexity of the software was on the high side (*t07*).

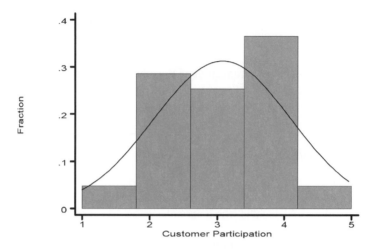

FIGURE 7. Distribution of *t01* (customer participation).

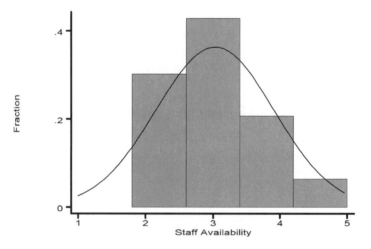

FIGURE 8. Distribution of *t03* (staff availability).

- Requirements volatility was quite high. Half the applications had high or very high requirements volatility. No application had very low requirements volatility (*t08*).
- No application had zero quality requirements—"quick-and-dirty" would never be allowed in a bank. About 75% of the applications had high to very high quality requirements (*t09*).

TABLE VI

SUMMARY OF CORRELATION COEFFICIENTS

Variables	Num obs	Correlation
t06 and *time*	62	0.54
t07 and *effort*	62	0.59
t07 and *size*	62	0.57
t11 and *nlan*	62	0.58
t12 and *t15*	62	0.53
t09 and *t10*	62	0.60
size and *duration*	62	0.54
effort and *size*	62	0.75
effort and *duration*	62	0.75

- Some level of attention and planning was needed for the efficiency requirements of all applications. Efficiency requirements were also on the high side (*t10*).

- All applications required some kind of user training (*t11*).

- For most projects, the analysis skills of the project staff at the time of kick-off were high. Most people had experience with specification and analysis, and the project manager was a professional analyst (*t12*).

- Tools experience was on the high side (*t14*).

During the correlation analysis step of the preliminary analysis, I searched the correlation output for any significant correlation coefficients greater than |0.5|. The summary is presented in Table VI. Note that these results are based on 62 projects, not 63, because one outlier was detected and removed during the data validation step. From this summary we learn that tools use (*t06*) increased over time. Projects with higher logical complexity (*t07*) often required more effort and were bigger in size. The more development languages used in a project (*nlan*), the higher its installation requirements (*t11*). Staff analysis skills (*t12*) and staff team skills (*t15*) are positively correlated; project staff with good analysis skills generally have good team skills, too. Quality (*t09*) and efficiency requirements (*t10*) are also positively correlated; projects with high quality requirements often have high efficiency requirements too. Size, effort, and duration are all positively correlated with each other; bigger projects usually take longer and require more effort. The correlations between effort and size, and effort and duration are so strong that these pairs of variables should not be in the final model together (risk of multicollinearity).

I also thought it would be interesting to see how time was related to the different factors. Table VII summarizes all significant correlations involving time. I discussed

TABLE VII
VARIABLES CORRELATED WITH *time*

Variable	Num obs	Correlation
t05	62	0.30
t06	62	0.54
t08	62	−0.43
t14	62	0.28
t15	62	0.27
duration	62	−0.35
nlan	62	0.32

the correlation analysis results with the data provider to see if they made sense in the context of his company. He agreed with the results and was able to provide some explanations.

The increased level and use of methods (*t05*) over time indicate some process improvement in the company. The level and use of tools (*t06*) also increased over time. Requirements volatility (*t08*) decreased over time as well. This could be because the company learned better requirements management. Staff tool skills (*t14*) and team skills (*t15*) increased over time. This is because staff turnover was low, another factor that increased organizational learning. Project duration decreased over time. This could be the result of process improvement in the company. The number of languages (*nlan*) increased over time. This was due to the development of more three-tier architecture projects at the end of the time period.

I ended up with the following final productivity model that passed all the model checks. Note that productivity, duration and size required log transformations (*lprod*, *ldur* and *lsize*).

Final Model

```
. fit lprod ldur lsize t09 t14 t10
   Source |       SS      df      MS              Number of obs = 62
---------+------------------------------          F(5, 56)      = 17.80
   Model | 13.6939918   5 2.73879836              Prob > F      = 0.0000
Residual | 8.61777376  56 .153888817              R-squared     = 0.6138
---------+------------------------------          Adj R-squared = 0.5793
   Total | 22.3117655  61 .365766648              Root MSE      = .39229
---------------------------------------------------------------------------
```

```
lprod |    Coef.    Std. Err.     t     P>|t|  [95% Conf. Interval]
---------+------------------------------------------------------------
  ldur |  -.7223637   .1020141  -7.081  0.000  -.9267224    -.518005
 lsize |   .4475299   .0633893   7.060  0.000   .3205459     .574514
   t09 |  -.190931    .0855067  -2.233  0.030  -.3622215  -.0196405
   t14 |   .144847    .0518125   2.796  0.007   .0410541    .2486399
   t10 |  -.1437862   .0711115  -2.022  0.048  -.2862396  -.0013328
 _cons |  -2.406596   .478281   -5.032  0.000  -3.364708  -1.448484
---------+------------------------------------------------------------
```

The equation as read from the final model's output is:

$$\ln(prod) = -2.406596 - 0.7223637 \times \ln(duration) + 0.4475299 \times \ln(size)$$
$$- 0.190931 \times t09 + 0.144847 \times t14 - 0.1437862 \times t10.$$

How did I read the equation off the output? The equation is a linear equation of the form $y = a_0 + a_1x_1 + a_2x_2 + a_3x_3 + a_4x_4 + a_5x_5$. y is $\ln(prod)$, x_1 is $\ln(duration)$, and x_2 is $\ln(size)$, and so on. a_1–a_5 are the coefficients (*Coef.*) from the output. The constant (_cons), a_0, is -2.406596, the coefficient of $\ln(duration)$, a_1, is -0.7223637, the coefficient of $\ln(size)$, a_2, is 0.4475299, and so on.

In a presentation or report, I give the results in the form of an equation for *prod*, not $\ln(prod)$. I find it is easier for people to understand. Keep in mind that most people don't want to know how you analyzed the data or the equation; they just want to know the management implications. I almost never include an equation in an oral presentation. By all means, prepare some slides about the methodology and the equation, but do not show them unless specifically asked to go into the details in public.

To transform $\ln(prod)$ into *prod*, I take the inverse natural log (or e) of each side of the equation. To do this accurately, I use all seven significant digits of the coefficients from the output. However, when I present the equation, I round the transformed coefficients to four digits.

This results in the following equation for productivity (*prod*):

$$prod = 0.0901 \times duration^{-0.7224} \times size^{0.4475} \times e^{-0.1909 \times t09}$$
$$\times e^{0.1448 \times t14} \times e^{-0.1438 \times t10}.$$

5.4 Interpreting the Equation

How can I interpret this equation? Let's look at the influence of the productivity factors on the value of productivity (*prod*). First, I calculate the value of each produc-

TABLE VIII
PRODUCTIVITY FACTOR MULTIPLIERS

Defn.	Value	t09 multiplier	t14 multiplier	t10 multiplier
very low	1	*0.826190	1.155863	*0.866073
low	2	0.682589	1.336019	0.750082
average	3	0.563948	1.544254	0.649626
high	4	0.465928	1.784946	0.562623
very high	5	0.384945	2.063152	0.487273

TABLE IX
NORMALIZED PRODUCTIVITY FACTOR MULTIPLIERS

Defn.	Value	t09 multiplier	t14 multiplier	t10 multiplier
very low	1	*1.465	0.748	*1.333
low	2	1.210	0.865	1.155
average	3	1	1	1
high	4	0.826	1.156	0.866
very high	5	0.683	1.336	0.750

tivity factor multiplier (Table VIII); that is, what is e to the power $-0.190931 \times t09$ when $t09$ is 1, when it is 2, etc.?

It is easier to think of an effect on productivity as being more or less than average. To do this, I calculate the normalized productivity factor multipliers by dividing each variable's multiplier by its average value (Table IX).

From Table IX, I can easily see that if all other variables remain constant, the effect on productivity (*prod*) of low quality requirements (*t09*) as opposed to average quality requirements is to increase productivity by 21%. On the other hand, if quality requirements are very high, I can expect productivity to be about 32% lower (1–0.683) than for an identical project with average quality requirements. Staff tool skills (*t14*) and efficiency requirements (*t10*) can be interpreted in the same manner. The quality requirements (*t09*) multiplier has the largest spread, from 0.683 to 1.465, thus quality requirement differences have a stronger impact on productivity than staff tool skills (*t14*) or efficiency requirements (*t10*). You can also deduce this from the equations because *t09*'s coefficient has the largest absolute value.

You should also keep in mind that no project in the database actually had very low quality requirements or efficiency requirements (denoted by * in Tables VIII and IX). So although the model says that very low quality requirements would increase productivity by 46.5% compared with average quality requirements, we cannot be completely sure about this. However, within the bank, this should not pose a problem because the bank is unlikely to ever undertake a project with either very low quality requirements or very low efficiency requirements.

What about the effects of duration and size on productivity? What can I learn from the equations? The coefficient of duration is approximately -0.72. This means that for every 1% increase in duration, productivity is expected to decrease by 0.72%, all other variables remaining constant. For example, if duration is increased by 5%, productivity should decrease by 3.6%. The coefficient of size is approximately 0.45. Assuming that all other variables remain constant, this means that for every 1% increase in size, productivity should increase by 0.45%.

5.5   Management Implications

The data provider was surprised to learn that bigger projects had higher productivities. As past research had indicated that there were large diseconomies of scale, the trend in the bank was to break large software development projects into smaller projects. However, these smaller projects' proportionally larger overhead probably made them less productive. Project duration had an impact on productivity in this bank. Can the bank do anything to reduce the duration of their projects?

Of the three significant productivity factors, quality requirements, efficiency requirements, and staff tool skills, only the level of staff tool skills is controllable. The quality and efficiency requirements of the projects are fixed. Tool skills are very important in the banking sector. It is important for a project team to be fully trained in all development and documentation tools. The bank could improve this by carefully selecting a small portfolio of development and documentation tools to use in their projects, sticking to their choice for a number of years, fully training their staff to use these tools, and reducing staff turnover. The implications of changing tools should be considered very carefully. Even if a better tool becomes available, the cost of retraining everyone may not make the change worthwhile.

It is also worth noting that many of the variables considered did not have a significant impact on productivity. None of the categorical variables, application type, hardware platform, user interface, number of languages used, Telon use, or whether or not the project was outsourced, explained any additional variation in productivity once size, duration, quality and efficiency requirements, and staff tool skills were taken into consideration. In addition, only 3 of the 15 productivity factors explained any variation in productivity. Does that mean that collecting the other 12 was a waste of time? Only 58% of the variation in productivity was explained by the variables collected. This means that 42% of the variation is still unexplained. Are there other variables that should have been collected? Before deciding what to collect or not collect in the future, we should first determine if any of the collected variables influenced project duration and cost. You must also keep in mind that a variable that is not important today might be important in the future, so you may want to collect it anyway.

6. Benchmarking Software Development Productivity[5]

Many companies want to improve the delivery of software solutions to their customers through better quality, reduced development time and lower costs. One key step in the continuous process of optimizing software development is to benchmark software development productivity (Fig. 9).

Benchmarking → Detailed analysis → Action plan → Implementation → Benchmarking

FIGURE 9. The place of benchmarking in the continuous process of improvement.

Benchmarking provides a diagnosis of actual performance and potential for improvement. Benchmarking also helps to identify levers for improvement and to prioritize actions. Benchmarking leads to more effective project and resource management (e.g., defining people skills and training needs, setting objectives and reviewing performance, choosing techniques and budgeting), increased staff motivation, and software process improvement.

However, this is easier said than done. The fact is, whether you are benchmarking an organization or simply a project, it all boils down to one thing—data.

Do you have the necessary data in your company? Is your data valid and comparable? Where can you access data from other organizations? To help you answer these questions and avoid some common serious mistakes in the benchmarking process, I've summarized my practical real-life experiences with software project data collection and benchmarking efforts in this section.

6.1 Planning for Data Collection

First of all, you can't benchmark data if you haven't collected it. In addition, you need to decide exactly what you are going to do with the data **before** you start col-

---

[5]This section was adapted from K.D. Maxwell, Collecting data for comparability: benchmarking software development productivity. *IEEE Software.* © 2001 IEEE. It is provided here with permission of the IEEE.

lecting it. If you work for a large company, consider asking the market or operations research department to help design your benchmarking questionnaire. Software managers know about software; data analysts know about questionnaire development. Collecting the right data for your purposes might require a multifunctional team effort.

When I receive a new software project database, I usually need to spend much more time understanding and validating the data than I do actually analyzing it. You can greatly reduce the risk of collecting the wrong data and the effort spent validating it if you spend more time up-front defining what variables to collect and how to measure them [27]. Think about how you collect data in your company. How careful are you? Do you ensure that everyone understands the definitions? How do you ensure uniformity over the years? Has your definition of effort evolved over time? Have you always counted support staff effort and tracked management time? If the person initially in charge of collecting the data has left the company, is the current person collecting the data in exactly the same way, using the same definitions? Even assuming that you have a high-quality data collection process for estimating cost and comparing project productivity within your company, if you want to benchmark against other companies the critical question is: Is your data comparable?

6.2   Benchmarking and Data Comparability

Given the various definitions of effort and size that exist, if they do not pay attention to data comparability, two companies measuring the same project can end up with very different sizes and efforts. As productivity is calculated by dividing these two error-prone terms, benchmarking productivity is potentially extremely inaccurate. For example, let's assume that Companies A and B have developed the exact same insurance software application and used exactly the same effort. However, Company A uses the IFPUG 4.0 method [19] which doesn't count algorithms, and Company B uses the Experience 2.0 function point method [41] which does count them. This results in a 20% greater function-point count for Company B. In addition, Company B does not count the effort of installation at the customer site, whereas Company A does, and this results in a 20% lower effort for Company B. So, for Company A, 100 function points divided by 400 hours equals 0.25 function points per hour. For Company B, 120 function points divided by 320 hours equals 0.375 function points per hour. Because Company B divides a 20% larger size by a 20% smaller effort, it calculates its productivity as 50% higher than Company A.

Obviously, you need to beware of comparability errors. If you think that comparability errors exist, rather than calculate a single productivity value, calculate a probable range of productivity values assuming an error in both terms.

If you want a dependable benchmark of software development productivity, make every effort possible to measure in exactly the same way. One way to compare your data to similar benchmarking data is to collect effort in hours by phase and staff type, and to keep the detailed breakdown of the function-point count so that you can create the different effort and function-point metrics. Another way is to decide in advance which benchmarking database you want to use and to collect your data using its definitions. If benchmarking is something you plan to do on a regular basis, you should collect your data with a tool used by other companies that also want to benchmark. In addition, verify that the benchmarking database you use contains projects that the data collector has carefully validated.

6.3   Benchmarking and Project Comparability

Even if you are measuring productivity in exactly the same way, you must also benchmark against similar projects. It is not enough to measure a project's size and effort and compare it with a large database's average productivity. As we have seen, productivity rates are highly variable across the software development industry. Hundreds of factors can affect productivity, and it is the identification and interaction of these factors that make comparing productivity rates very difficult. This is why software development databases should be statistically analyzed to determine the factors that contribute most to the specific database's productivity variation. Once you've identified the variables—or combinations of variables—that explain most of the database's productivity variation, you can limit your comparisons to projects similar to your own.

For example, if you developed a project using Cobol on a mainframe, and language and platform are important factors in explaining productivity differences in the database, then you should only benchmark your productivity against other projects using Cobol on a mainframe platform. On the contrary, if your project uses case tools and using the tools does not explain the differences in productivity of the database projects, there is no point in limiting your comparisons to other projects that also use case tools. So, either verify that the benchmarking service statistically analyzes the data and informs you of the key factors, or that it provides you with the raw data so that you can do so yourself. Also, pay attention to how many projects the benchmark is based on for each subset of data. You might consider a benchmark more reliable if it is based on 20 projects rather than four. Benchmarking against up-to-date data is also important.

6.4   Benchmarking Data Availability

Although many companies would like to benchmark projects, few contribute data to multicompany databases. Data is needed on a regular basis to keep these ser-

TABLE X
SOURCES OF SOFTWARE PROJECT BENCHMARKING DATA

Name of service provider	Website
Experience benchmarking	http://www.datamax-france.com/benchmk.htm
INSEAD/European Space Agency	http://www.insead.fr/~rise
International Software Benchmarking Standards Group	http://www.isbsg.org.au
NASA Software Engineering Laboratory database [7]	http://www.dacs.dtic.mil/databases/sled/sel.shtml
Software Productivity Research	http://www.spr.com

vices up-to-date. Although large companies with well-established metrics programs, high project turnover, and data analysis competency might be content to benchmark projects internally, smaller companies do not have this option. These companies must look to benchmarking services for access to numerous recent, comparable projects. (See Table X.) In addition, most cost estimation tool vendors have databases that you can use for benchmarking.

7. Conclusions

The productivity of different car manufacturing lines can be easily compared. There is not much ambiguity about the definition of a car. The same cannot be said about software development. As we have seen, the output of a software development project is neither easily defined, nor easily measured. The explanation behind much of the software development productivity variation among companies may simply lie in the unlimited number of definitions of software size and project effort. It is for this reason that the collection of comparable software project data is crucial.

Once you have a software project database, your company possesses a valuable asset. You can determine the factors that influence the productivity of software development projects in your company. You may find that some of these important factors are given and unchangeable; for example, certain applications of a particular type may always be more difficult and associated with lower productivity rates. However, some variables, such as choice of tool, may be within your control. In addition, if your company has a well-established metrics program and a high project turnover, you have a definite advantage. You can benchmark your projects internally and avoid many of the measurement comparability problems associated with multi-company databases.

In addition to productivity analyses, you can determine the variables that have an impact on software development duration (i.e., time-to-market). You can also use your data to calibrate cost estimation tools. And while you're at it, why not see how accurate of a cost estimation model you can build with your own data? Extract the most value you can from your data collection efforts. Use this knowledge to guide, and defend, your future actions. Recommendations backed up by hard data carry more weight with upper levels of management.

In your quest for productivity improvements, don't neglect quality. If the cars have to be recalled, if the software is full of bugs... don't expect to be congratulated on your high productivity. It does not matter how fast you are if no-one wants to buy your product, or use your services again. Nor does it matter how productive you are during software development if time-consuming problems are just postponed to the software maintenance phase. While important, software development productivity is only one part of the total picture.

REFERENCES

[1] Abran A., et al., in: S. Oligny (Ed.), *COSMIC-FFP Measurement Manual, version 2.0*, Software Engineering Management Research Laboratory, Université du Québéc à Montreal, Canada, 1999, http://www.lrgl.uqam.ca/cosmic-ffp.

[2] Albrecht A.J., "Measuring application development productivity", in: *Proceedings of the Joint SHARE/GUIDE/IBM Application Development Symposium, Monterey*, 1979, pp. 83–92.

[3] Aron J.D., "Estimating resources for large programming systems", in: J.M. Buxton, P. Naur, B. Randell (Eds.), *Software Engineering: Concepts and Techniques*, Litton Education Publishing, New York, 1976, pp. 206–217.

[4] Arthur L.J., *Measuring Programmer Productivity and Software Quality*, John Wiley & Sons, New York, 1985.

[5] Bailey J.W., Basili V.R., "A meta-model for software development resource expenditures", in: *Proceedings of the 5th International Conference on Software Engineering, San Diego*, 1981, pp. 50–60.

[6] Banker R.D., Datar S.M., Kemerer C.F., "A model to evaluate variables impacting the productivity of software maintenance projects", *Management Science* 37 (1) (1991) 1–18.

[7] Basili V., Zelkowitz M., McGarry F., Page J., Waligora S., Pajerski R., "SEL's software process-improvement program", *IEEE Software* 12 (6) (1995) 83–87.

[8] Behrens C.A., "Measuring the productivity of computer systems development activities with function points", *IEEE Transactions on Software Engineering* SE-9 (6) (1983) 648–652.

[9] Belady L.A., Lehman M.M., "The characteristics of large systems", in: P. Weger (Ed.), *Research Directions in Software Technology*, MIT Press, Cambridge, 1979, pp. 106–142.

[10] Boehm B.W., *Software Engineering Economics*, Prentice-Hall, Englewood Cliffs, NJ, 1981.

[11] Boehm B.W., "Improving software productivity", *IEEE Computer* 20 (1987) 43–57.

[12] Boehm B.W., Abts C., Brown A.W., Chulani S., Clark B.K., Horowitz E., Madachy R., Reifer D., Steece B., *Software Cost Estimation with COCOMO II*, Prentice-Hall, Upper Saddle River, 2000.

[13] Briand L., El Emam K., Maxwell K., Surmann D., Wieczorek I., "An assessment and comparison of common software cost estimation modeling techniques", in: *Proceedings of the 21st International Conference on Software Engineering, Los Angeles*, 1999, pp. 313–322.

[14] Brooks F.P., in: *The Mythical Man-Month: Essays on Software Engineering*, Addison-Wesley, Reading, MA, 1975.

[15] Brooks W.D., "Software technology payoff: some statistical evidence", *The Journal of Systems and Software* **2** (1981) 3–9.

[16] Card D.N., McGarry F.E., Page G.T., "Evaluating software engineering technologies", *IEEE Transactions on Software Engineering* **SE-13** (7) (1987) 845–851.

[17] Conte S.D., Dunsmore H.E., Shen V.Y., *Software Engineering Metrics and Models*, Benjamin/Cummings Publishing Company, Menlo Park, 1986.

[18] Cusumano M.A., Kemerer C.F., "A quantitative analysis of U.S. and Japanese practice and performance in software development", *Management Science* **36** (11) (1990) 1384–1406.

[19] *Function Point Counting Practices Manual, Release 4.0*, International Function Point Users Group, Westerville, OH, 1994.

[20] P. Hill (Ed.), *The Benchmark Release 6*, International Software Benchmarking Standards Group, Warrandyte, Victoria, Australia, 2000, pp. 77–78.

[21] Jeffery R., Ruhe M., Wieczorek I., "A comparative study of two software development cost modeling techniques using multi-organizational and company-specific data", *Information and Software Technology* **42** (14) (2000) 1009–1016.

[22] Jeffrey D.R., "Time-sensitive cost models in the commercial MIS environment", *IEEE Transactions on Software Engineering* **SE-13** (7) (1987) 852–859.

[23] Jones C., *Applied Software Measurement: Assuring Productivity and Quality*, McGraw-Hill, New York, 1991.

[24] Jones C., "Software change management", *Computer* (1996) 80–82.

[25] Jones T.C., "The limits of programming productivity", in: *Proceedings of the Joint SHARE/GUIDE/IBM Application Development Symposium, Monterey*, 1979, pp. 77–82.

[26] Kitchenham B.A., "Empirical studies of assumptions that underlie software cost-estimation models", *Information and Software Technology* **34** (4) (1992) 211–218.

[27] Kitchenham B.A., Hughes R.T., Linkman S.J., "Modeling software measurement data", *IEEE Transactions on Software Engineering* **27** (9) (2001) 788–804.

[28] Kraut R.E., Streeter L.A., "Coordination in software development", *Communications of the ACM* **38** (3) (1995) 69–81.

[29] Lawrence M.J., "Programming methodology, organizational environment, and programming productivity", *The Journal of Systems and Software* **2** (1981) 257–269.

[30] Lokan C., Wright T., Hill P.R., Stringer M., "Organizational benchmarking using the ISBSG data repository", *IEEE Software* **18** (5) (2001) 26–32.

[31] Lokan C.J., "Impact of subjective factors on software productivity", in: *Proceedings of the 7th Australian Conference on Software Metrics, Melbourne*, 2001.

[32] Maxwell K., Forselius P., "Benchmarking software development productivity", *IEEE Software* **17** (1) (2000) 80–88.

[33] Maxwell K., Van Wassenhove L., Dutta S., "Software development productivity of European space, military and industrial applications", *IEEE Transactions on Software Engineering* **22** (10) (1996) 706–718.

[34] Maxwell K., Van Wassenhove L., Dutta S., "Benchmarking: the data contribution dilemma", in: *Proceedings of the 1997 European Software Control and Metrics Conference*, The ESCOM Conference, Reading, MA, 1997, pp. 82–92.

[35] Maxwell K., Van Wassenhove L., Dutta S., "Performance evaluation of general and company specific models in software development effort estimation", *Management Science* **45** (6) (1999) 787–803.

[36] Maxwell K.D., "Collecting data for comparability: benchmarking software development productivity", *IEEE Software* **18** (5) (2001) 22–25.

[37] Maxwell K.D., *Applied Statistics for Software Managers*, Prentice-Hall, Upper Saddle River, 2002.

[38] Maya M., Abran A., Oligny S., St-Pierre D., Desharnais J.M., "Measuring the functional size of real-time software", in: R. Kusters, et al. (Eds.), *Project Control for 2000 and beyond*, Shaker Publishing Company, Maastricht, 1998, pp. 191–199.

[39] McConnell S., "Closing the gap", *IEEE Software* **19** (1) (2002) 3–5.

[40] Nevalainen R., Maki H., *Laturi-System Productivity Model Version 1.4, Technical Report 30.3*, Information Technology Development Center, Helsinki, 1994.

[41] Nevalainen R., Maki H., *Laturi-System Product Manual Version 2.0*, Information Technology Development Center, Helsinki, Finland, 1996.

[42] Putnam L.H., Myers W., *Measures for Excellence: Reliable Software on Time within Budget*, Prentice-Hall, Englewood Cliffs, NJ, 1992.

[43] Rehesaar H., "Software size: the past and the future", in: R. Kusters, et al. (Eds.), *Project Control for 2000 and beyond*, Shaker Publishing Company, Maastricht, 1998, pp. 200–208.

[44] Schneider V., "Prediction of software effort and project duration—four new formulas", *SIGPLAN Notices* **13** (6) (1978) 49–59.

[45] Shepperd M., Cartwright M., "Predicting with sparse data", in: *Proc. 7th International Software Metrics Symposium*, IEEE Computer Society, Los Alamitos, 2001, pp. 28–39.

[46] Stephenson W.E., "An analysis of the resources used in the safeguard system software development", in: *Proceedings of the 2nd International Conference on Software Engineering*, 1976, pp. 312–321.

[47] Symons C.R., "Function point analysis: difficulties and improvements", *IEEE Transactions on Software Engineering* **14** (1) (1988) 2–11.

[48] Thadhani A.J., "Factors affecting programmer productivity during application development", *IBM Systems Journal* **23** (1) (1984) 19–35.

[49] Vosburgh J., Curtis B., Wolverton R., Albert B., Malec H., Hoben S., Liu Y., "Productivity factors and programming environments", in: *Proceedings of the 7th International Conference on Software Engineering*, 1984, pp. 143–152.

[50] Walkerden F., Jeffrey R., "An empirical study of analogy-based software effort estimation", *Empirical Software Engineering* **4** (1999) 135–158.

[51] Walston C.E., Felix C.P., "A method of programming measurement and estimation", *IBM Systems Journal* **16** (1) (1977) 54–73.

Transformation-Oriented Programming: A Development Methodology for High Assurance Software[1]

VICTOR L. WINTER

Computer Science Department
University of Nebraska at Omaha
6001 Dodge Street, PKI 175A
Omaha, NE 68182
USA
vwinter@ist.unomaha.edu

STEVE ROACH

University of Texas at El Paso
El Paso, TX 79968
USA
sroach@cs.utep.edu

GREG WICKSTROM

Sandia National Laboratories
USA
glwicks@sandia.gov

Abstract

A software development paradigm known as Transformation-Oriented Programming (TOP) is introduced. In TOP, software development consists of constructing a sequence of transformations capable of systematically constructing a soft-

[1]This work was supported by the United States Department of Energy under Contract DE-AC04-94AL85000. Sandia is a multiprogram laboratory operated by Sandia Corporation, a Lockheed Martin Company, for the United States Department of Energy. Victor Winter was also partially supported by NSF grant number CCR-0209187.

ware implementation from a given formal specification. As such TOP falls under the category of formal methods.

The general theory and techniques upon which TOP is built is presented. The High Assurance Transformation System (HATS) is described. The use of the HATS tool to implement a portion of the functionality of a classloader needed by the Sandia Secure Processor (SSP) is described.

1. Background

Computer-enhanced problem solving has evolved dramatically over the past 50 years. When viewed in isolation, a computer is a device, that when presented a problem expressed in a binary language, will compute an answer also expressed in a binary language. While increases in processor speed and memory have been nothing short of astounding, the fundamental model of a computer as a function mapping binary inputs (i.e., programs and input data) to binary outputs has essentially remained unchanged. However, what have changed dramatically over the past 50 years are the techniques and approaches that can be employed to produce these binary inputs—in particular, binary programs.

Initially, the construction of binary programs was undertaken entirely by humans. Conceptually simple computations had to be described in terms of long sequences of 0's and 1's. Such program development was highly error prone. Even the slightest slip of the finger on the keyboard (or punchcard) would cause the program to fail. Furthermore, discovering the root cause of failure in programs written in machine code could require extremely complex analysis. Because of the cryptic notation and nature of feedback provided, the class of problems that could be effectively solved in this paradigm (i.e., the programs constructed) was (of necessity) quite modest when compared to modern standards. To assist in the development of software, tools were developed. Many of these tools partition software development into segregated activities where the responsibility of accomplishing a particular task fell predominantly upon either the developer (e.g., design) or the tool (e.g., compilation). Thus a crisp boundary existed between human tasks and computer tasks.

However, a dramatic blurring of this boundary is occurring. A plethora of tools and notations have been developed to assist the developer in virtually every aspect of software development including problem conceptualization, requirements elicitation, specification, design, code generation, and verification and validation. As a result, human activities and tool activities are becoming intertwined within software development paradigms. This chapter is devoted to *transformation-oriented programming* (TOP), an intertwined software construction paradigm for which formal verification can be used to provide assurance of correct software behavior.

1.1   Chapter Overview

This chapter has two parts. The first half is a general introduction to various paradigms of programming with particular attention given to TOP. The second half is a more detailed description of a specific tool called HATS and an application demonstrating its use. In the following section, we discuss high consequence systems and motivate the need for improvement in software development practices, in particular with respect to providing evidence in correct behavior. Section 3 describes current approaches to software development and puts transformation-oriented programming in the context of current work.

Section 4, *Transformation-Oriented Programming*, introduces transformations and rewriting as a mechanism for describing the conversion of data from one form to another. Section 5 extends the idea of transformation-oriented programming to include the creation of programs. The fundamental idea is that given a formal specification, a correct program can be created using a transformation tool. Section 6 describes a particular transformation tool called *HATS*, the High-Assurance Transformation Program.

In Section 7 we describe a specific application of transformation-oriented programming, the Sandia Secure Processor (SSP). This processor is intended to be an embedded processor interpreting a subset of the Java bytecode language for high-assurance applications. Transformations that implement the classloader for this processor are presented. Section 8 outlines work that must be done in order to validate the code generated by the transformations.

2.   High-Consequence Systems

Applications in which there is a high cost associated with failure are called *high-consequence systems*. In addition, if the cost of failure is measured in terms of human life we call the system a *safety-critical system*. In order for a high-consequence system to be certified for use, it typically must be demonstrated that the likelihood of a failure occurring during any given operational hour is on the order of 1-in-10^9. Such a system can be expected to fail only once every 114,155 years.

High-assurance software is software for which there is convincing evidence that the software possesses certain explicitly stated attributes (e.g., reliability). The attribute that one is generally most interested in here is *correctness*, which is the notion that the behavior of the software is in compliance with its intent (not just its specification). Because of the dominance of correctness as an attribute, the phrases *high assurance* and *high assurance of correctness* are often used synonymously. A *high-assurance system* is a system for which convincing evidence has been provided showing that its behavior will not result in a failure.

In spite of the dangers, software is being used at an accelerating rate to control systems that have the potential to affect the safety and well being of large numbers of people. For example, software plays a critical role in numerous systems such as antilock brakes, flight control systems, weapons systems, nuclear power plants, electrical power grids, and a wide variety of medical systems such as those for embedded cardiac support. As a result, the dependence of modern society on safety-critical software has become deeply rooted.

As society's appetite for *high-consequence* software increases, the importance of developing *high-assurance* software systems becomes essential. A key component of any construction technique claiming to produce high-assurance software is the ability to provide sufficiently convincing evidence, prior to fielding the system, that the software will function in its intended manner. In other words, when developing a high-consequence software system, it is not sufficient to merely build a dependable system. One must also be able to convince the stakeholders (e.g., society) that this system will function correctly if and when it is put into operation.

In this chapter, we assume that high-assurance software will be developed in two phases: a *formalization phase* and an *implementation phase*. Fig. 1 gives an overview of these two phases. The goal of the formalization phase is to understand an informally stated problem and express it in a formal framework. The artifact produced by the formalization phase is a formal specification. The implementation phase uses this formal specification as the basis for constructing an *implementation*. Here we define an implementation as representation of software that is either in an executable form or in a form that can be automatically translated (e.g., via a compiler) into an executable form. In the implementation phase, we assume that the formal specification is correct. This implies that the implementation phase will be considered successful if the software system developed satisfies the formal specification.

Though they are extremely important, the tools and techniques that can be brought to bear in the formalization phase of software development are beyond the scope of this chapter. Instead, our focus is on the implementation phase as it relates to high-assurance system development. When given a formal specification, our goal is to construct an implementation in which convincing evidence can be provided that the implementation satisfies the formal specification.

2.1   Building Software is Deceptively Hard

Software is malleable. This is both its strength and weakness and has often resulted in unrealistic expectations regarding (1) what software can and cannot do, (2) how easily something can be done in software, and (3) the level of effort required to effectively modify a software system. Unlike other engineered products

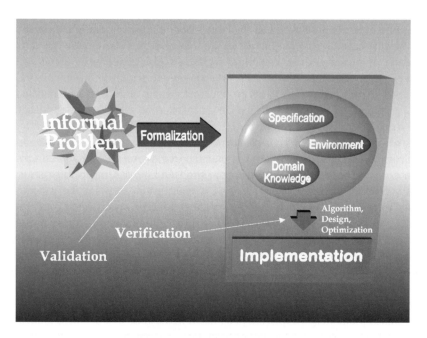

FIG. 1. High-assurance software development phases.

(e.g., a bridge or an airplane), modification of software does not require the replacement of tangible parts [18]. The malleable nature of software has frequently
resulted in system redesigns where many mechanical controls are re-implemented
in software. With mechanical controls, safety interlocks are common. If a mechanism fails, the interlock ensures the system remains in a safe state. With software systems, these controls may fail, and the software-based interlocks may also
fail, sometimes for the same reasons. An example of this is the Ariane 5 rocket
failure [8]. Another failure of this type occurred in the mid 1980s, the computer-
controlled Therac-25 radiation therapy machine delivered overdoses resulting in serious injury or death to at least six people. The Therac-25 reused software from
the Therac-20, but the Therac-20 had independent hardware protective circuits that
prevented an overdose. The Therac-25 depended solely on software [29]. In a well
designed system such as commercial aircraft, a single point of failure does not result in a system failure. However, in software, a failure can frequently be traced to
a single point. When considered in the context of a physical system, this can contribute to system failure. In this chapter, we restrict our attention simply to software
failures.

Software systems can easily become overly complex. "Computers often allow more interactive, tightly coupled, and error-prone designs to be built, and thus may encourage the introduction of unnecessary and dangerous complexity" [29]. A significant source of complexity arises from coupling of processes, which Chiles [10] and Dorner [13] independently suggest is difficult or impossible for humans to fully grasp. Analysis of major accidents such as nuclear power plant accidents and airline crashes invariably shows that these accidents are not caused by single component failures, but by highly complex, cascading sequences of events.

Software is buggy. The increased complexity in both product and process give rise to many new hazards. Oftentimes testing is used in hopes that hazards and errors will be discovered. Unfortunately, as the complexity of systems increase, a point of diminishing returns is reached. "Microsoft released Windows XP on Oct. 25, 2001. That same day, in what may be a record, the company posted 18 megabytes of patches on its Web site: bug fixes, compatibility updates, and enhancements" [32]. Microsoft is not alone. In [45] it was reported to the National Institute of Standards and Technology that 30–90% of labor expended to produce a working program is testing. Furthermore, the findings of the report indicated that even when using software engineering best practices, when counting all errors found during design, implementation, unit testing, integration testing, and maintenance of a software system, 5% of the errors are only discovered *after* the product is released. In 1999, the estimated cost due to software error in the aerospace industry alone was $6 billion dollars.

2.2   Software Development Risks

In a well-planned software project, the tools used, the techniques applied, and the resources allocated to various development activities should be appropriate for the actual risks faced in the project. In order to accomplish this, one must have a clear understanding of the nature and scope of the risks encountered in software development as well as what tools and techniques can be best applied to mitigate these risks. Overly optimistic misconceptions of software is a recipe for disaster, especially for high-consequence systems.

Abstractly speaking, risk is a combination of the likelihood of an undesirable event and the severity of its consequences. What constitutes risk with respect to a particular software product depends largely on the nature of the product as well as a given perspective (e.g., economic, environmental, etc.). For example, when developing commercial software in a highly competitive marketplace, *time to market* may be the most important factor in the risk equation from the standpoint of sales and profitability. In contrast, when developing software for niche markets, *development cost* may be the dominating factor. And when developing software for high-consequence systems, the primary factor is the ability to achieve high-assurance; that is, to convincingly demonstrate that the system will function as intended. A high-consequence software system for which such high-assurance cannot be provided is useless at best (because it will not be fielded) and extremely dangerous at worst (it is fielded and a failure is encountered).

So how does one address the risks associated with high-consequence software development? To date, some of the most promising tools and techniques for constructing high-assurance software are rooted in a form of mathematics that is known as *formal methods* [7,24,46]. The basic idea when using a formal method is to construct a particular artifact (e.g., a specification, or an implementation) in such a way that mathematical reasoning (i.e., calculation) can be used to answer certain questions— the most ambitious of which would be, "Is this program correct?".

3. Approaches to Developing High-Assurance Systems

There are many approaches to the development of software systems, and there are a large number of tools and notations available to assist software developers. Finding the right approach and using the right tools to develop a particular software system is key to achieving our software development goal. This section takes a brief look at some of these approaches. We use the term *paradigm* to mean a general approach to problem solving facilitated by a particular notation. In contrast, a *method* is defined here as a notation accompanied by a process. A process suggests a sequence of steps that a developer takes in order to produce some artifact such as a design or a test case. The notations and processes used influence how developers think about problems and software solutions. Frequently, different paradigms and methods can be combined, each being used to solve different parts of a larger problem.

Regardless of the paradigms or methods used to develop a software system, in order to successfully construct a software system, the following three steps must be accomplished: (1) the requirements of the system must be established; (2) the software must be designed; and (3) the design must be translated into machine executable code. This translation is typically accomplished in part by humans writing high-level language code, and in part by computers executing compilers, translators, interpreters, and assemblers. It is not necessary that the three steps be completed in a particular order, nor is it necessary for each step to have an artifact associated with it. A programmer who does not write a design on paper still has a design, even if its only manifestation is in the programmer's head. These steps may also be accomplished in strict sequence with no overlap as they are, for example, in the waterfall development process. Or they may be completed incrementally as they are in the spiral and evolutionary development processes. For high-assurance systems, there is the additional task of providing evidence that the software is correct.

3.1 Imperative Programming

It is widely accepted that the first imperative language was Fortran, and many other imperative languages followed, including Algol and Cobol [47]. In imperative programming, program variables hold the program state, and the primary unit of computation responsible for incremental change is the assignment statement. Control is dictated by various constructs such as the sequential composition operator as well as conditional statements, looping statements, jumps, and procedure calls. This provides a way in which solutions can be incrementally constructed. Block structuring provides a way of grouping code fragments such as statement sequences, and even other blocks into a unit or module. Such groupings can facilitate the understanding of the structures within a program at higher levels of abstraction than is possible when simply viewing a program as a composition of primitive statements. The introduction of block structuring has had a major impact on the ability of programmers to construct larger more complex software systems because it enables them to envision a software system in terms of an architecture consisting of blocks rather than statements. The primary tool support to programmers using the common imperative languages is editors, compilers, and debuggers.[2] The errors detected in this framework include syntax and type errors.

3.2 Object-Oriented Programming

As the problems to which software systems are being applied become more complex, software developers realize that more effort must be expended establishing the requirements and designing a solution. There is also the need to demonstrate that the software is adequate either through testing or through some other means. The management of complexity has become the primary consideration.

One approach to managing this complexity is to decompose software and encapsulate functionality into discrete units. Objected-oriented programming is the current dominant paradigm. It is an extension of imperative programming that encourages system decomposition in terms of *objects* and *classes*. The class is essentially an extension of the block structure in which a rich mechanism is provided for defining the internal state of an object as well as controlling the visibility of methods, variables, and types. Inheritance is a mechanism provided for defining new classes

---

[2]There are tools available that generate imperative language code such as code generators and report writers. These are considered in later sections.

based on other classes. Inheritance facilitates the creation of class hierarchies in which classes leverage off of the similarities between each other, thereby maximizing code reuse and understanding. Most object-oriented languages can trace their roots to Smalltalk. Object-oriented programming tends to require a greater emphasis on design and factoring than imperative programming does. While it is possible to implement an object-oriented design in an imperative language, some languages such as Eiffel, Java, and C++ more easily support inheritance, polymorphism, and encapsulation. Modern object-oriented software development environments facilitate the creation and modification of design documents such as diagrams in the Unified Modeling Language (UML). Some of these environments assist the user in the creation of high-level language code from design specifications.

3.3   Functional Programming

A alternative approach to problem decomposition is given in the functional programming paradigm. Here, programs are decomposed into functions, each of which may be arbitrarily complex. Once a function is written, it may be used without concern for the internal details. Functional programming paradigms typically provide a mathematically clean semantic framework (e.g., call-by-value parameter passing, type completeness, referential transparency) that encourages equational reasoning. Computation is accomplished by function evaluation. A purely functional language does not require variables or assignment statements. Iteration is accomplished through the use of recursion. The origins of functional programming are rooted in the Lambda Calculus. Lisp was the first functional language, and Common Lisp continues to be widely used in the field of artificial intelligence. Most modern functional languages provide a rich set of abstraction mechanisms. For example, ML offers *structures*, which are akin to classes as well as *functors*, which can be thought of as generalizations of structures.

3.4   Aspect-Oriented Programming

Not every problem can be cleanly decomposed into cohesive pieces. The motivation behind aspect-oriented programming [14,28] (AOP) is *separation of crosscutting concerns*. Concerns can range from high level, such as security, to low level, such as caching and buffering. An aspect is the embodiment of a concern. Other examples of aspects are: correctness/understandability, spatial efficiency, temporal efficiency, and error recovery. In standard object-oriented programming, it is difficult to separate these concerns into classes or objects. The source code that embodies an aspect is spread throughout many objects. AOP advocates the construction of systems by first specifying the various concerns and their relationships, then relying on the environment to automatically weave the code supporting the aspect with other code, forming a complex system that satisfies all aspects simultaneously. AOP extends object-oriented and imperative programming using all techniques available to achieve their goal of separation of concerns.

3.5   Declarative Programming

Declarative programming (or logic programming) provides an altogether different paradigm for solving problems [51]. In a declarative environment, properties of a system are stated in terms of logical formulas. These formulas are typically presented in predicate logic. Prolog, the most widely used declarative language, uses Horn-clauses, a subset of predicate logic. Programs do not state how a solution is to be computed. Instead, a problem (i.e., computation) is stated in terms of a query. When presented with a query, a declarative programming system uses a complex search algorithm (transparent to the user) based on resolution and backtracking in order to find an answer to the query. Declarative environments provide a powerful (and complex) computational framework; however, the implementations of these environments tend to be complex, and the search required by the implementation tends to require semantic information (e.g., the cut) to direct search by pruning the search tree. Declarative programmers still must develop designs and algorithms, but their designs and solutions are much different than imperative and object-oriented solutions are.

3.6   Formal "Methods"

As demonstrated by logic programming, formal notations may be used to describe not only the programs, but also the designs and requirements of the software system. We believe that in situations where the cost of failure is the overriding concern, as it is in high-consequence and safety-critical applications, formal approaches to software development are not just viable, but necessary. We use the term *formal method* to mean a language with formal syntax and semantics and a set of rules for inferring useful information from sentences written in the language [23]. Typically, we start with a set of requirements and then prove properties about the specification, derive an implementation, or prove that a given implementation satisfies the requirements.

The use of formal methods is not the norm in industry, even for high-consequence software. As Parnas explains,

> "When new methods do not catch on, there are two obvious possible explanations. Either the methods are not yet good enough, or practitioners are too conservative, unwilling to learn, and resistant to change. In most cases, there is truth

in both explanations. The best known formal methods clearly work, but it is equally clear that they require a lot of tedious writing of expressions that are difficult to read" [42].

It is true that the use of formal methods is expensive, in part because it requires time-consuming formulation of problems in a mathematically rigorous and precise manner. However, after the initial cost of formulation, the use of formal methods may actually drive down the cost of systems. As further evidence of their usefulness, note that in every case where formal methods were used under a NASA Formal Methods program [9], previously unknown errors were discovered. Examples of costly errors in mission software include the Mars Rover priority inversion and deadlock in the Deep Space 1 Remote Executive [21,22,27,44]. In spite of extensive testing and reviews using the best available methods, these errors persisted. These errors were discovered (or at least detected) using formal methods. In other words, even the best software practices deliver software with errors that can be detected using formal methods.

Formal methods work well for simple, textbook examples used in the classroom. Until recently, they have not competed well against traditional approaches for a class or size of programs of practical use, e.g., the kinds of programs that developers have succeeded at writing over the past fifty years. Current programs tend to be decomposable, with each unit significantly decoupled from other units, and they can be tested (though not completely or perfectly). However, we believe that software systems in the near future will be larger, more complex, not easily decomposed, and the components of this software will be tightly coupled with complex interactions. They will have many tedious details and require vast inputs and high speed. Some will control safety-critical systems. The system developer of the mid 21st century will require software tools to support program development, and the program support will be in the form of formal methods.

It is clear that formal methods hold great promise in the cost-effective construction of reliable software. It is equally clear that in order for formal methods to gain acceptance in the software development community, tools must continue to be developed to assist practitioners. This remainder of this section discusses some of the formal approaches that have been used successfully in industry.

3.7 Formal Specifications

A formal specification is the statement of a collection of properties that a system should satisfy, given in a formal language at some level of abstraction. The key difference between a specification and a program is that a specification must offer some abstraction of the problem. The examples of formal specifications have shifted over the past half-century. In the late 1950s, Fortran was considered a specification language. It dictated at some level of abstraction what a program was to do. The drive throughout computing history is to increase the power of translators that create executable code from specifications.

Current specification languages are much more sophisticated than Fortran. There are many such languages available, including report generator languages (fourth generation languages), model languages based on set theory and predicate logic such as Z and VDM, and algebraic specification languages such as CLEAR. Introductions to formal specifications are available [16,26,41].

A major benefit of formal specification is that many errors are caught simply by the act of specifying a system formally. For example, Mukherjee and Wichmann [40] describe the certification of a computerized voting system for the Church of England where the act of specifying the algorithm in VDM exposed several ambiguities in the English language description of the algorithm.

3.8   Theorem Proving

An automated theorem prover is a software system that takes a set of formulas as input and applies inference rules to derive new formulas that are logical consequences of the original formulas. Typical inference rules include modes ponens, resolution, and induction. Theorem provers are usually associated with a given logic, such as propositional, first-order, higher-order, or Horn-clause logic. They may be fully automated, or they may rely on interaction with humans to guide the search for a proof.

In theorem proving, we care about the form of the arguments. For example, given the statement "All men are mortal," and the statement "Socrates is a man," we can derive the statement "Socrates is mortal." As another example, given the two statements "All dogs are loyal" and "Uri is a dog," we can derive "Uri is loyal." Note that these two arguments have the same form. A theorem prover treats them in the same way.

In general, we start with a formula that is a formal specification S of program behavior and a set of formulas that describe the context C, including assumptions about the program and its environment. Then we try to demonstrate that for some formal model of the implementation I, $C \rightarrow (I \rightarrow S)$. If we succeed in proving this, then we can say that I is correct with respect to S and C.

As with testing, failed proofs can serve diagnostic purposes. "Why can't I prove it" is sometimes answered, "because I need more information" or perhaps "because it is wrong." Either of these answers can lead us to discover errors before the error manifests itself at runtime.

A recent example of the use of theorem provers in software development is the use of the PVS [48] theorem proving system in the verification of the AAMP5 processor [50]. A portion of the instruction set and register-level transfers were described formally, and PVS was used to demonstrate that the microcode correctly implemented the specified behavior of the instruction set. During this exercise, errors were discovered both during the specification of the system and during the proof process.

The Nqthm theorem prover [39] was used to verify the implementation of an assembly-level programming language called Piton, which supports constructs such as recursive subroutine call and return, stack-based parameter passing, and arrays. Piton is implemented via a mathematical function called a downloader that accepts a Piton program as input and produces a binary image as its output. This binary image can be run on the FM9001 processor. The downloader function can be decomposed into a compiler, assembler, and linker. The theorem that is proven is essentially the following: Let S_n denote the state (e.g., the answer) that is produced from running a well-formed Piton program p_0 for n steps. Let S'_n denote the state produced by downloading p_0 and running the resulting binary image on the FM9001 for k steps. Then S'_n is equivalent to S_n. Here, link tables are used to properly interpret S'_n enabling the extraction of the answer.

3.9   Model Checking

Model checking [25,38] is a technique used to test properties of programs by verifying the property using an exhaustive finite-state search of a model of a program. Because the state space of complex programs is too large for exhaustive search, a common approach is to abstract the program to a model and test properties of the model. If it is possible for the model to enter a state where a specified property does not hold, the model checker detects the error and provides a transition sequence leading to that state. Model checking is most often used to discover errors in concurrent systems such as deadlock and data race. Testing and debugging concurrent systems are notoriously difficult, and some recent NASA projects have suffered from defects in concurrent systems [21,22,27,44].

A standard technique used to discover errors in software systems via model checking follows the sequence given below.

- The developer determines desirable properties for a program (such as the avoidance of deadlock) and specifies these in the formal language required by the model checker.

- The developer manually abstracts the program source code to a model, attempting to be faithful to the relevant characteristics of the program.

- This model is encoded in the language of a model checker.

- The model checker is run. The model checker tests the properties in each state.
- If an error is discovered, a trace explaining an execution path reaching the error is reported by the model checker. The developer then attempts to map the error back to the program and verify that a corresponding error is present in the actual program. Either the model is corrected or the program is corrected, and the process is repeated.

Model checking is based on temporal logic. Temporal logic is a logic of state sequences. Thus, in temporal logic, formulas are not statically true: the truth-value may change depending on the state. Model checkers have been used to identify errors in software and protocols for concurrent, distributed, and reactive systems. Some of the most popular model checking systems available today include SPIN, SMV, and UPPAL. An introduction to model checking and these systems can be found in Berard et al. [4].

3.10 Synthesis

The goal of program synthesis is to automate the process of transforming a formal specification to code that is executable on a computer. Program synthesis is a mechanism for elevating the task of programming from code generation to specification generation [15]. An incomplete taxonomy of synthesis mechanisms includes the following:

- **Inductive synthesis**: In inductive synthesis, a program is obtained from a generalization of partial specifications. Given a set of both positive and negative examples, a program is generated that covers at least all the examples. Inductive synthesis usually requires a great deal of interaction with the programmer [17].
- **Deductive synthesis**: Deductive synthesis systems constructively prove a conjecture based on the specification. The three steps in the synthesis are to construct a formula, prove it, then extract instances of values bound to existential variables as the program. The resulting program is a logical consequence of the specification and the background theory. Three fundamental methods of deductive synthesis are:
  - **Transformational synthesis**. Transformation rules are applied to program specifications iteratively until an executable program is generated. This work is an outgrowth of optimization techniques. REFINE is one example of a transformational synthesis system [43].
  - **Schema guided synthesis**. Programs are designed by successive instantiation of templates. KIDS [49] and SPECWARE [37] are examples of this type of system.

- **Proofs as programs**. Proofs are the traditional approach to deductive synthesis [19,20,33,34]. A program is extracted from the proof. These systems take a specification of the form $\forall x \exists y : P(x) \rightarrow R(x, y)$ and prove a theorem of the form $\forall x : P(x) \rightarrow R(x, f(x))$. Here, P is some set of preconditions on the input variables x; y is a set of outputs; R is a set of post conditions constraining the outputs in terms of the inputs. The theorem prover constructs the term $f(x)$, that computes the outputs. Amphion [31] is an example of this type of program.

4. Transformation-Oriented Programming

Transformation-oriented Programming (TOP) is a software development paradigm that encourages viewing and manipulating a program in "terms of the whole" rather than in "terms of its parts." As such, this approach is well suited for an implementation phase that begins with a formal specification. This is one of the attributes that makes TOP a candidate for high-assurance software development.

The concept of understanding change (e.g., development) with respect to the whole is becoming widely used for commercial software development. For example, eXtreme Programming [3] advocates that software changes be undertaken in such a manner that a functioning product is produced each day. A similar approach is adopted by Microsoft. "A common practice at Microsoft and some other shrink-wrap software companies is the 'daily build and smoke test' process [36]. Every file is compiled, linked, and combined into an executable program every day, and the program is then put through a 'smoke test,' a relatively simple check to see whether the product 'smokes' when it runs... By the time it was released, Microsoft Windows NT 3.0 consisted of 5.6 million lines of code spread across 40,000 source files. A complete build took as many as 19 hours on several machines, but the NT development team still managed to build every day [58]. Far from being a nuisance, the NT team attributed much of its success on that huge project to their daily builds."

In TOP, the basic unit effecting change is the *transformational step*. A *term* is the data changed by a transformational step. In this context, it is helpful to think of a term as a structured representation of data such as a parse tree corresponding to a program string. The purpose of the term structure is to provide information (e.g., type information or contextual information) about data. This information typically provides the basis for defining change. How terms can be constructed, what information their structure can contain, and support for detecting inappropriate contexts for terms are areas currently being researched [11,12,53].

A *transformation rule* is a function from terms to terms. The syntax and semantics of transformation rules are discussed in more detail in Section 5.4. In the current section we develop some basic terminology. The *application* of a transformation rule T to a term P is generally written $T(P)$ and results in one of two possible outcomes: (1) the application produces a transformational step, in which case $P \neq T(P)$, or (2) the application fails to produce a transformational step,[3] in which case $P = T(P)$.

Let P_1 denote a term and T denote a transformation rule. If P_1 is constructed from other terms, it will be possible to apply T to more than one point in P_1. We choose any subterm x in P_1 and apply T. This results in a transformational step that produces a transformed term P_2. It is again possible to apply T to each point in P_2. In general for a given a set of transformation rules $\mathcal{R}$, and an input term P_1, a graph can be constructed reflecting all possible transformational steps. This graph describes a rewrite relation. In the graph, nodes denote unique terms, and directed edges denote transformational steps. A directed edge exists between P_i and P_j if and only if there exists a transformation rule, in $\mathcal{R}$, that when applied to a particular subterm in P_i yields P_j and $P_i \neq P_j$. It is worth noting that paths in this graph may be infinite and either non-cyclic or cyclic. In Fig. 2, the initial term is labeled P_1. The graph shows that if the transformation rule $R_1 \in \mathcal{R}$ is applied to P_1, the result is P_2. We label the node $P_2^{R_1}$ to indicate that P_2 was derived from P_1 by application of rule R_1. If instead transformation rule $R_2 \in \mathcal{R}$ is applied to P_1, the result is $P_2^{R_2}$. Note that in Fig. 2, $P_3^{R_2 R_1}$ could also be labeled $P_3^{R_1 R_2}$.

We define a *transformation sequence* as a path in a rewrite relation, i.e., the sequential composition of one or more transformational steps. In this path, nodes other than the initial and final nodes are referred to as *intermediate forms*. In practice, a transformation sequence is realized through the controlled application of a sequence of transformation rules to some initial term.

In TOP, software development consists of manipulating terms via transformation sequences. We want to develop a set of transformation rules $\mathcal{R}$, and define a *strategy* for the application of rules in $\mathcal{R}$ such that the endpoint of the transformation sequence defined by the strategy is our desired term. Strategies define how often, when, and where transformation rules are to be applied. Metaphorically, they play the role of a navigator within the rewrite relation. A strategy makes precise what it means to apply a transformation rule to a term in the case where the rule is applicable in various places.

---

[3] The ρ-calculus [11] is based on a different application semantics. Specifically, if an application of a transformation to a term is inappropriate then the empty term (actually an empty set) is returned.

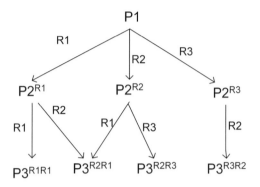

FIG. 2. A rewrite relation.

Below is an operational example of a strategy that exhaustively applies a transformation T to a term P_1. Mathematically speaking, we say this strategy computes a fixed-point of T.

```
Repeat
     Let P₁ denote the current form of the term.
     Scan P₁ from top to bottom and apply T to every
         point in P₁.
     Let P₂ denote the result of step 2.
Until P₁ = P₂
```

The next sections give two concrete examples of transformation-oriented approaches to problem solving. In the examples, the intent is not to focus on notation and technical detail, but rather on the spirit of transformation-oriented problem solving.

4.1   Example

Consider the problem of translating an internally stored tree structure into a string that can be written to a file. When a tree is represented as a string, parentheses provide a way of encoding the tree's structure. For example, a parenthesized expression having the form

$$(root\ subtree_1\ subtree_2 \ldots subtree_n)$$

can be used to denote a tree having n children whose root node has the label *root* and whose immediate children are described by the expressions *subtree₁ subtree₂ ...* *subtreeₙ*, respectively. Consider a tree consisting of five nodes, *A, B, C, D,* and *E.*

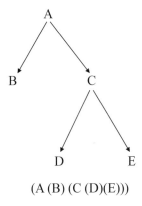

(A (B) (C (D)(E)))

FIG. 3. Tree and term structure.

Node A is the root, B and C are the immediate children of A, and D and E are immediate children of C. The structure of the tree as well as its term representation are shown in Fig. 3.

For larger trees it is difficult to write the corresponding parenthesized expression if one proceeds in a strictly left-to-right fashion. (Consider a tree with 30 nodes, for example.) This difficulty arises because the relationship between a partial solution and the whole solution is not immediately obvious at any given time. (See Table I.) In contrast, if we approach the construction of the expression from the perspective of the whole, the complexity of the problem vanishes. We proceed in a top–down manner producing a sequence of increasingly refined expressions. We initially denote the expression for the entire tree by the variable X_1. We then examine the root and children of X_1 and use the information obtained from this analysis to construct our first intermediate form. Suppose that the root node of X_1 has the label A and that A has two children. The expression $(A\ X_{1.1}\ X_{1.2})$ describes this refinement. Here

TABLE I

COMPARISON OF APPROACHES

Left-to-right approach	Refinement-based approach
$(A$	X_1
$(A(B)$	$(A\ X_{1.1}\ X_{1.2})$
$(A(B)(C$	$(A\ (B)\ X_{1.2})$
$(A(B)(C(D)$	$(A\ (B)\ (C\ X_{1.2.1}\ X_{1.2.2}))$
$(A(B)(C(D)(E)$	$(A\ (B)\ (C\ (D)\ X_{1.2.2}))$
$(A(B)(C(D)(E)))$	$(A\ (B)\ (C\ (D)\ (E)))$

$X_{1.1}$ and $X_{1.2}$ are variables denoting the expressions corresponding to the children of A. Parentheses are always introduced in a balanced fashion. Furthermore, the relationship between $(A\ X_{1.1}\ X_{1.2})$ and the initial tree is straightforward. We can now refine any of the variables in our expression in the manner that we used to refine X_1, producing an even more complex expression that still has balanced parenthesis. This refinement process continues until our expression is free from any variables, at which point we have our result. Table I compares the left-to-right approach and the refinement-based approach for our example.

4.2   Example

In this example, we consider compiling simple programs consisting of a single assignment statement into a sequence of RISC assembly instructions. This machine has a large number of registers, and the instruction set includes instructions for loading from memory to registers, storing from registers to memory, and adding the values in registers. The instruction set is described below.

LD R1 Addr	Load register R1 with the value in memory address Addr
ST Addr R1	Store the value in register R1 into memory address Addr
ADD R1 R2 R3	Store the sum of the values in registers R2 and R3 into register R1

The following partial grammar describes a small language where a *program* can be a high-level program or a low-level program. A high-level program consists of a single assignment of an expression to an address. A low-level program is a sequence of assembly instructions. Initially, expressions in high-level programs are either the address of a value or a term consisting of the sum of two other expressions. However, *intermediate forms* of expressions are also possible—for example, an expression may be a tuple consisting of a register followed by a list of one or more assembly instructions. The addition tuples to our language reflects a design decision in which compilation is realized by passing expressions in high-level programs through intermediate forms containing tuples.

EXP ::= Addr |
        SUM EXP EXP |
        [register, assembly_seq]

PROG ::= ASSIGN Addr EXP |
         assembly_seq

Our goal is to create a transformation sequence capable of rewriting terms corresponding to high-level programs into terms representing assembly instruction sequences. In order to make our discussion more concrete, let us consider the following program as input to our transformation sequence.

initial program: ASSIGN 100 SUM SUM 101 102 103

Our plan is to transform this program into assembly instructions in the following fashion: First, we rewrite addresses to register load instructions. Then we rewrite each SUM to an appropriate add instruction. This step utilizes the [*register*, *machine_instr_list*] expression. The idea is to store the results of the evaluation of any expression into a register and explicitly keep track of that register by making it the first element of a tuple. For example, in the term [$r1$, *a_seq*], the value in register $r1$ represents the sum computed by *a_seq*. And finally, when the expression has been fully processed, we rewrite the ASSIGN term to a store instruction.

In formalizing these ideas, we make the following assumptions and notational simplifications:

1. We assume that at transformation time, the function *reg*() will provide the name of an unused register. (This allows us to avoid the details of register allocation in this presentation.) Further, we assume there are enough available registers to hold the needed intermediate values.
2. We assume that we have a concatenation function, +, allowing us to add statements to a statement list.

The following rewrites convert a statement in the abstract language into the machine instructions needed to execute the statement.

Rule 1: Addr → [z, "LD z Addr"]   where z = reg()

Rule 2: SUM [reg1, stmtlist1] [reg2, stmtlist2] →   where z = reg()
        [z, [stmtlist1 + stmtlist2 + "ADD z reg1 reg2"]]

Rule 3: ASSIGN Addr [reg stmtlist] →
        [stmtlist + "ST Addr reg"]

Transformation Rule 1 states that if we have an expression that is an address *Addr*, we can replace this with a tuple consisting of a register followed by a single machine instruction. Note that the sum computed by the machine instruction list is stored in the register z. Transformation Rule 2 states that if we have an expression consisting of a SUM followed by two tuples, each consisting of a register and a list of statements, we replace the entire term with a tuple having a register and a list of statements. This list of statements returned is the concatenation of the two statement lists and an ADD instruction. Again, the newly introduced register z holds the sum computed by the machine instruction list. Transformation Rule 3 states that if we have a program consisting of the terminal symbol ASSIGN followed by an address followed by a tuple, we can replace it with a list of statements.

Below is a trace highlighting of some of the intermediate forms produced when the above transformation rules are applied using an inside-out strategy to our initial program.

```
1  ASSIGN 100 SUM SUM 101 102 103
2  ASSIGN 100 SUM SUM [R3, LD R3 101][R2, LD R2 102]
                     [R1, LD R1 103]
3  ASSIGN 100 SUM [R4, LD R3 101 + LD R2 102 + ADD R4 R3 R2]
                  [R1, LD R1 103]
4  ASSIGN 100 [R5, LD R3 101 + LD R2 102 + ADD R4 R3 R2
                  + LD R1 103 + ADD R5 R4 R1]
5  [LD R3 101 + LD R2 102 + ADD R4 R3 R2 + LD R1 103
                  + ADD R5 R4 R1 + ST 100 R5]
```

Form 1 is the initial string. In a more standard notation, this could have the form $d := (a + b) + c$. The terms 100, 101, 102, and 103 are addresses of the variables $a, b, c,$ and d. Form 2 is the result of applying Transformation Rule 1 to the addresses 101, 102, and 103. Forms 3 and 4 result from the application of Transformation Rule 2. Form 5 is the result of applying the last transformation. Boyle et al. [5] describes another approach to this type of problem.

5.   TOP as a Program Development Method

In Example 2 above, we demonstrated the refinement of a program from a simple high-level language into low-level assembly code. This type of approach can generalized and used to solve the problem of transforming high-level specifications of program behavior into lower level, executable programs. When discussing the transformation of specifications, programs, and the like, we say *program* when referring to any term along the transformation sequence (e.g., intermediate forms as well as initial and final endpoints). Correctness is typically an invariant property spanning the entire transformation sequence. Informally we say that an intermediate form of a program is correct if it has the same semantics as the initial program. The correctness property is the dominant influence in TOP. It requires transformational changes to be understood with respect to the entire program. It also encourages encapsulation of changes as well as separation of concerns.

A typical TOP development cycle begins with a (correct) formal specification, which we will generically call a program. Then a set of transformation rules are constructed, and the application of these rules is guided by a strategy. In this context, we consider a program to be a *specification* if it satisfies any of the following properties:

1. It describes an algorithm in abstract terms (for which no compiler or interpreter exists).
2. It describes an algorithm in a clear, but unnecessarily inefficient manner (e.g., an exponential time algorithm describing a problem that can be solved in polynomial time).
3. It describes a non-computable function.

In contrast, we consider a program to be an *implementation* if it describes an efficient algorithm and is either expressed in a language for which a compiler exists or is expressed in a language that can be directly executed (i.e., machine code) by the targeted processor. Our goal is to define a transformation sequence that, when applied to a specification, will produce an implementation.

It is a violation of the TOP philosophy to apply a transformation rule that produces an incorrect intermediate form that must then be repaired by later transformational steps. This requirement of only producing correct intermediate forms of programs encourages a more global perspective in which software development steps are viewed in relation to the program as a whole. This global perspective allows certain types of complexity to be managed in manner that would otherwise not be possible.

5.1 Contrasting TOP with Component-Based Software Development

The construction of a jigsaw puzzle provides a useful metaphor for contrasting the differences between TOP development and a more traditional, component-based approach. Fig. 4 illustrates how component-based software development might proceed.

Initially, the system is decomposed into a collection of components taking into account an understanding of the entire system. Interfaces between components are specified. Later, when implementing the interfaces, a component-centric perspective is taken. The focus typically shifts to the interface requirements between components. After the components have been developed, they must then be assembled to produce a software system. The interfaces between components frequently change during the course of the development as requirements change or better abstractions are discovered. When the system design changes in this fashion, great care must be taken to ensure that all interfaces between components are consistent and reflect the current structural decomposition. Assuring such consistency requires a global perspective.

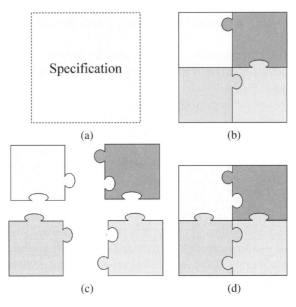

FIG. 4. Component-based development.

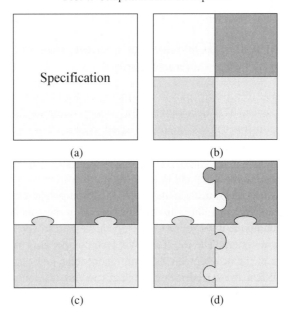

FIG. 5. Transformation-oriented development.

In contrast, TOP development strongly encourages such a global perspective, as shown in Fig. 5. Each transformational step produces a program at a lower level of abstraction. The product of each transformational step is a correct program. To refactor or reconfigure interfaces requires that the transformation rules be written with the proper perspective.

5.2   History of TOP

The seeds of transformation-oriented programming can be traced back to the 1970s where a landmark paper by Burstall and Darlington [6] outlined an approach in which a correct but inefficient specification could be transformed (in a semi-rigorous manner) into an efficient, albeit significantly more complex, implementation. Since then, advances in transformation-oriented programming have been sporadic. Research in this area has been triggered by several events such as discovery of new ideas, availability of more powerful computational environments, and increasing demand for highly dependable systems.

Currently, the TOP paradigm is being applied to a wide variety of problem domains within software engineering including synthesis [57], reverse engineering [2, 55], and various forms of optimization [52]. The goal in synthesis is to take a program at one level of abstraction and transform it into a program at a lower level of abstraction (where the term "lower" refers to the conceptual distance between a program and its binary executable). In Visser [54], a taxonomy of application areas is given in which transformation goals fall into two broad categories: *translation* and *rephrasing*. Translation takes a source program belonging to one language (e.g., specification language) and transforms it into a target program belonging to another language (e.g., a high-level programming language). A rephrasing takes a source program belong to one language and transforms it into a target program belonging to the same language. Given these definitions, synthesis (both refinement and compilation) as well as reverse engineering falls under the category of translation, while optimization falls under the category of rephrasing.

Reverse engineering is essentially the opposite of synthesis. Here the goal is to raise the level of abstraction rather than lower it. Reverse engineering has been used during software maintenance to provide specifications for legacy systems that require new functionality, for example the ability to handle calendar years beyond 1999 (i.e., the Y2K problem).

The goal in optimization is to improve the time and/or space requirements that a program needs in order to execute. Function inlining, variable inlining, and common subexpression elimination are well-known optimization techniques that have been implemented using transformations.

5.3   Transformation Systems General Architecture

A *program transformation system* is an environment that supports transformation-oriented programming. Such an environment typically includes:

1. a component, such as a parser, capable of defining elements in the domain of discourse (i.e., the programs we are interested in transforming);
2. a specialized *transformation language* containing appropriate primitives facilitating the development of transformation rules and strategies (We refer to programs written in this transformation language as *transformation programs*. The transformation language typically includes, as primitives, various term traversal operators, some form of matching, and iterators.);
3. an engine for executing transformation programs;
4. a means for displaying the results of transformation steps such as pretty-printing the initial, intermediate, and final forms of a program; and
5. a feedback system, such as a GUI containing a debugger, for facilitating the comprehension of transformation rules and how they are being applied by a particular strategy.

5.4   Syntax and Semantics of Transformation Rules

When designing a transformation system a number of issues must be addressed including the question, "What type of 'things' should the system transform?" Transformation systems commonly transform programs, strings, expressions, or even other transformation rules. We consider transformations on two types of structures, abstract syntax trees (ASTs) and syntax derivation trees (SDTs). ASTs can be described by an abstract syntax, and SDTs are described by BNF grammars. When the context is clear, we will refer to these structures as *terms*.

A transformation rule is a variation or extension of a rewrite rule. A rewrite rule consists of a left-hand side, called the *pattern*, and a right-hand side, called the *replacement*. A rewrite operator, denoted by the symbol $\rightarrow$, is used to connect a pattern with a replacement. Thus rewrite rules have the form:

pattern $\rightarrow$ *replacement*

The purpose of the pattern is to describe a particular term or type of term that one would like to transform. The purpose of the replacement is to define a term that will replace the pattern. Frequently this term is based on some manipulation of the accompanying pattern.

Patterns may contain variables. For example, we may have a rewrite rule of the form:

$$P(x) \rightarrow Q(b, x),$$

where b is a constant and x is a variable. If we are given the term $P(10)$, we can match this to the pattern by assigning the term "10" to the variable x. The pair $x/10$ is called a *substitution*. A substitution is applied to a term by replacing variables in the term with the pair of that variable in a substitution. The result of applying the substitution $x/10$ to the term $P(x)$ is $P(10)$. A set of substitutions is a unifier if, when the substitutions are applied to a pair of terms, the results are identical. When a substitution can be applied to a pattern p so that the result matches a term t, we say that t is an instance of p and that the rewrite rule applies to t.

Rewriting proceeds as follows. For a given term t, a determination is made to see if t is an instance of some pattern in a rewrite rule. If t is an instance of a pattern, the rule applies, and a corresponding instance of replacement is constructed by applying the unifier to the replacement. The result of this is used to replace t. In the example above, the result of applying $P(x) \rightarrow Q(a, x)$ to the term $P(10)$ is $Q(a, 10)$.

A pattern defines a set of terms. Determining whether a rewrite rule applies to a term t involves solving the set membership problem. Unification algorithms [35] can be used to solve the set membership problem. Higher-order, associative-commutative (AC) matching or unification as well as matching and unification modulo equational theories have also been used to further increase the power of patterns to describe sets [11]. In the case of first-order matching, the result of a successful match between a pattern and a term t is a substitution list in which variables occurring in the pattern are bound to subterms in t. This substitution is then applied to the replacement in order to produce the resultant term (i.e., the term that will be substituted in place of t). In the case of higher-order matching or AC-matching, the result will typically be a set of substitutions, in which case the result will a set of terms.

Rewrite rules can also be annotated with conditions. In this case, they are called conditional rewrites. A conditional rewrite is typically written as

pattern $\rightarrow$ *replacement if c*

where c denotes a Boolean formula. When a conditional rewrite is applied to a term t, a unification or match is attempted between the pattern and t, if this succeeds, the resulting substitution is applied to c after which c is evaluated. If c evaluates to true, then the conditional rewrite rule produces a transformational step, otherwise the term t is returned as the result of the rule application.

5.4.1   Example 3

The following example motivates the need for effective strategies for applying transformation rules. Consider a term language defining mathematical expressions. This language allows for integer values and expressions built from addition and multiplication. The following signature defines this language:

Signature
    Sorts: Integer, Expr
    Constructors
        num: Integer $\rightarrow$ Expr
        plus: Expr $*$ Expr $\rightarrow$ Expr
        mult: Expr $*$ Expr $\rightarrow$ Expr

If we assume first-order matching will be used during rule application, the distribution of multiplication over addition can be described by the following rewrite rules:

Rule1: mult $(x, \text{add } (y, z)) \rightarrow \text{add } (\text{mult } (x, y), \text{mult } (x, z))$
Rule2: mult $(\text{add } (y, z), x) \rightarrow \text{add } (\text{mult } (y, x), \text{mult } (z, x))$

Another possibility would be the following:

Rule1$'$: mult $(x, \text{add } (y, z)) \rightarrow \text{add } (\text{mult } (x, y), \text{mult } (x, z))$
Rule2$'$: mult $(x, y) \rightarrow \text{mult } (y, x)$

For the first set of rules, any arbitrary exhaustive rule application strategy (such as the fixed-point strategy given in the previous section) will succeed. However, in the second case we must be a little more careful when applying rules. The reason we need to be careful is that Rule2$'$ can be applied infinitely often to a term. A possible strategy for this second set of rules would be the following:

1. Apply Rule1$'$ to exhaustion.
2. Apply Rule2$'$ exactly once to every (sub)term.
3. If Rule1$'$ can be applied to any (sub)term, then goto step 1, else stop.

This example illustrates the difference between rules and strategies. Note that all rules are correctness preserving (in the sense that they preserve the numerical value of the expression) regardless of the strategy that is used to apply them.

6. HATS

The High-Assurance Transformation System (HATS) is a language-independent program transformation system whose development began in the late 1990s at Sandia National Laboratories [56]. The goal of HATS is to provide a transformation-oriented programming environment facilitating the development of transformation rules and strategies whose correctness can be formally verified. The following diagram (see Fig. 6) shows the HATS architecture.

In HATS, programs belonging to a particular problem domain are defined by a context-free grammar. Internally, HATS stores and manipulates these programs as

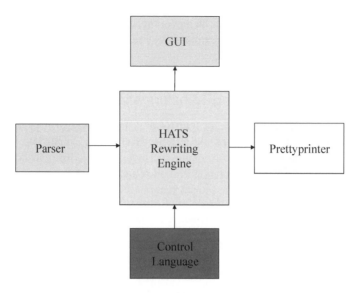

FIG. 6. HATS architecture.

syntax derivation trees. HATS provides a special purpose language for defining transformation rules and strategies. This language enables the description of the domain language in the standard manner [1]. A grammar $G = (V, T, P, S)$ is composed of a set of non-terminal symbols V, a set of terminal symbols T, a set of productions P, and a start symbol $S \in V$. Each production consists of a non-terminal symbol on the left-hand side and a sequence of terminal and non-terminal symbols on the right-hand side. A grammar derives a string by beginning with the start symbol and repeatedly replacing a nonterminal by the right-hand side of a production whose left-hand side matches that non-terminal. Given a context-free grammar G, the notation $A \overset{*}{\Longrightarrow} \beta$ denotes a derivation belonging to G. The expression $A[\beta]$ denotes the term whose start symbol (root of the SDT) is A and whose final form (leaf nodes of the SDT) are β.

Presently, an LR(k) parser[4] supporting Extended-BNFs is used to automatically convert an expression of the form $A[\beta]$ into a completed term. In this framework, nonterminal symbols in the grammar form the basis for defining variables that can be instantiated during matching. In particular, subscripted instances of nonterminal symbols of the context-free grammar are used to denote variables. For example, if E is a nonterminal symbol in our grammar, then $E_1, E_2, E_3, \ldots$ denote distinct vari-

---

[4]An LR(k) parser is for a grammar that can be parsed scanning left to right using k symbol look ahead. See Aho [1], pp. 215–247 for details.

ables of type E. Variables are quantified over the sublanguage of terms which they can derive according to the given grammar. As a result, they can only match with a term sharing the same root symbol.

6.1 Writing Transformation Rules

In HATS, a transformation rule, or transform, is a function that is parameterized on the term to which it is applied. At present, HATS uses a first-order matching algorithm to determine if a transform applies to a given term. A distinguishing feature of HATS is that the matching operation is explicit and is denoted by the symbol ==. The syntax we will use to describe transformation rules in this chapter is[5]

transform rule_name(variable){match_expression → replacement}

where *rule_name* denotes the name of the rule, *variable* denotes a term variable to which the rule will be applied, *match_expression* is a pattern that when matched returns an instance of *replacement*. The rule is preceded by the key word *transform*. The evaluation of a match expression produces a pair consisting of a Boolean value and a substitution list. If the Boolean value is true, the evaluation has succeeded and the substitution is applied to the replacement, which then rewrites the original term. If the Boolean value is false, the transform returns the input term.

6.1.1 Example 4

In this example, we show how the rules for distributing multiplication over addition can be expressed in HATS. Because HATS is SDT-based, we must define our language in terms of a BNF grammar (rather than a signature). The BNF and transformation rules are:

```
factor ::= plus( factor, factor )
         | mult( factor, factor )
         | integer
transform Rule1 (factor0)
{ factor0 == factor[ mult( factor1, plus( factor2, factor3 )) ]
    →
    factor[ plus( mult( factor1, factor2 ), mult( factor1, factor3 )) ]
}
```

---

[5]The actual syntax in HATS is somewhat different. For an example of actual HATS syntax, see Winter [56].

transform Rule2 (factor$_0$)
{ factor$_0$ == factor[mult(plus(factor$_1$, factor$_2$), factor$_3$))]
$\rightarrow$
factor[plus(mult(factor$_1$, factor$_3$), mult(factor$_2$, factor$_3$))]
}

Note that both Rule1 and Rule2 are of the same type in the sense that they can only produce transformational steps when applied to SDTs having the nonterminal symbol *factor* as the root symbol.[6] HATS provides the vertical bar symbol, "|", as a composition mechanism enabling rules of the same type to be conditionally grouped.[7] Using the vertical bar, the above rules may be also be written within a single transform as follows:

transform distribute_mult1 (factor$_0$)
{ factor$_0$ == factor[mult(factor$_1$, plus(factor$_2$, factor$_3$))]
$\rightarrow$
factor[plus(mult(factor$_1$, factor$_2$), mult(factor$_1$, factor$_3$))]
| factor$_0$ == factor[mult(plus(factor$_1$, factor$_2$), factor$_3$))]
$\rightarrow$
factor[plus(mult(factor$_1$, factor$_3$), mult(factor$_2$, factor$_3$))]
}

Due to the fact that matching is explicit in HATS, match expressions can be elegantly combined with other match expressions or modified through Boolean connectives. This has the effect of embedding application conditions within the match expression, and this gives HATS the ability to express conditional rewrites. Utilizing this feature of HATS enables us to alternatively express the distribution of multiplication over addition as follows:

transform distribute_mult2 (factor$_0$)
{ factor$_0$ == factor[mult(factor$_1$, plus(factor$_2$, factor$_3$))]
or
factor$_0$ == factor[mult(plus(factor$_2$, factor$_3$), factor$_1$))]
$\rightarrow$
factor[plus(mult(factor$_1$, factor$_2$), mult(factor$_1$, factor$_3$))]
}

---

[6]In this example the point is moot since the grammar only contains a single nonterminal symbol.

[7]Technically speaking, the semantics of the vertical bar is similar but not equivalent to the sequential composition of Rules 1 and 2. However, this difference does not come into play in this example.

int x;	int x;	int x;	int x;
bool y;	bool y;	bool y;	bool y;
x=6;	INT=INT;	INT=INT;	INT=INT;
x=x*x;	INT=INT*INT;	INT=INT;	INT=INT;
y=true;	BOOL=BOOL;	BOOL=BOOL;	BOOL=BOOL;
x=y;	INT=BOOL;	INT=BOOL;	ABORT;
y=x and y;	BOOL=INT and BOOL;	BOOL=ERROR_VALUE;	ABORT;
Form 1	Form 2	Form 3	Form 4

FIG. 7. Simple type checking.

6.2 Dynamic Transformations

There are situations in which it is not possible to tell *a priori* what a transformation rule should be, but it is possible to tell the form of the rule. In this section, we describe one of HATS' more advanced capabilities, rules for creating transformation rules.

When manipulating large terms, two or more data elements that are related with respect to a particular perspective may be scattered within the structure of the term. In the example below, we consider a Java program. We are interested in verifying the correctness of type assignments in the program.[8] In the example shown in Fig. 7, type information derived from declarations, constants, and expressions and is propagated across assignments.

Consider the code fragment in Form 1 of Fig. 7. If we wanted to use a transformational approach to check whether the code fragment is type correct, we might proceed as follows. First, rewrite all occurrences of variables in statements with their declared types and all constants to their types. This would result in the intermediate form in Form 2. Second, apply rules that transform expressions into their types. For example, an expression that adds two integers is of type integer. In this stage, we also introduce a new type called ERROR_VALUE that is used to denote the type of an expression that is type incorrect. The results of these transformations are displayed in Form 3.

Finally, construct transformation rules that capture the notion of type correctness at the statement-level. In our example, we define an assignment statement to be type correct if and only if the type of the variable assigned to (i.e., the left-hand side) is identical to the type of the value to be assigned (i.e., the expression on the right-hand side). We introduce a new type of statement called ABORT that we use to denote a statement that is type incorrect. Form 4 shows the results of applying these transformations.

---

[8]This example was inspired by a similar example given by Visser [53].

Performing simple type checking on programs in a transformational manner is conceptually straightforward. The major problem here is how the type of an identifier, which is found in the declaration, can be distributed throughout the program. We will refer to this problem as the *distributed data* problem. The root of the distributed data problem lies in the fact that one part of the program (e.g., the occurrence of an identifier in an expression) needs information that occurs in another part of the program. The syntactic distance between the declaration of an identifier and its first use can be arbitrarily large. This makes it impossible to use standard first-order matching to capture, within a single match, the declaration of an identifier and its first use.[9] Somehow we need to achieve the transmission of data between transformation rules.

In the example above, we simply wrote transformation rules that rewrote all occurrences of x and y to the types INT and BOOL, respectively. That is, we "hardwired" the type relationships within the transformation rules. These transformation rules are straightforward, and their correctness is easily shown. However, our goal is to write a general set of rules that is capable of type checking all programs. The distributed data problem arises precisely because we do not know the declarations that are in the code fragment at the time that we are writing our transformation rules.

HATS makes use of meta-transformation rules called *dynamic transformation rules*. A dynamic transformation rule takes a term as input and returns a set of transformation rules as its result. In contrast, a transformation rule takes a term as input and returns a term as its output. In HATS, the basic syntax of a dynamic transformation rule is:

```
dynamic rule_name (variable)
{ match_expression
    →
  transform (variable) {match_expression → term}
}
```

Let us examine how the distributed data problem can be solved using dynamic transformations. At this point, we include the BNF grammar describing our mini-programming language.

Given the grammar in Fig. 8, a dynamic transformation that solves the distributed data problem can be written in HATS as follows:

---

[9]If we contemplate extending the capabilities of our matching algorithm, we run into other problems like nested scopes containing multiple declarations of the same identifier. Another possibility is to somehow "carry" the information found in the declaration to the places in the program where the information is needed. In an imperative or functional paradigm, parameter passing is a key mechanism that is used to transmit information. Global variables can also be used, but it is widely accepted that these should be used sparingly as the concept of a global variable violates referential transparency, making it more difficult to reason about and maintain the program.

prog	::=	decl_list ; stmt_list ;
decl_list	::=	decl ; decl_list I decl
decl	::=	type id
stmt_list	::=	stmt ; stmt_list I stmt
stmt	::=	assign I ABORT
assign	::=	type_term = expr
expr	::=	expr b_op term I term
term	::=	boolean I (expr) I not(expr) I E
b_op	::=	or I and
E	::=	E + T I T
T	::=	T * F I F
F	::=	(expr) I int I type_term
type_term	::=	type I id
id	::=	ident
type	::=	type_name
int	::=	integer_value
boolean	::=	boolean_value

FIG. 8. BNF grammar of mini-programming language.

dynamic distribute_type_info ($decl_0$)
{ $decl_0$ == decl[$type_1$ id_1]
   $\rightarrow$
  transform ($type\_term_0$)
           { $type\_term_0$ == type_term[id_1] $\rightarrow$ type_term[$type_1$]}
}

When this dynamic transformation is applied to our sample program, it will produce the following sequence of (anonymous) transformation rules:

    transform ($type\_term_0$) { $type\_term_0$ == type_term[x] $\rightarrow$ type_term[int]}
    transform ($type\_term_0$) { $type\_term_0$ == type_term[y] $\rightarrow$ type_term[bool]}

Given these rules, we can easily transmit the type information of an identifier to places in the program where it is needed (e.g., a fixed point application of the above transformation rules to the statement list portion of the program). Furthermore, given the semantics of dynamic transformations, it is easy to conclude that the distributed data problem has been solved correctly.

7. Embedded Systems

Advances in computer technology are rapidly increasing the computational power that can be brought to bear within embedded systems. Chip designs are now reaching the point where the computational power they provide makes it possible to include dependability as a primary design objective, which in turn has opened the door for the consideration of such systems in high-consequence applications. The bottleneck facing high-consequence embedded system developers is their ability to provide sufficient evidence that an embedded design satisfies a given set of stringent dependability requirements.

Embedded systems are being developed to solve increasingly complex problems. For practical reasons, designers must give serious consideration to incorporating or leveraging existing research results and technologies such as robust programming languages and COTS products. When this is done judiciously, it becomes possible to develop dependable systems within reasonable time frames and cost constraints.

In this section we consider the adaptation of the Java Virtual Machine (JVM) to a particular class of embedded system designs. The specification of the JVM provides it with the ability to dynamically load and link classfiles during execution. This feature enables an application to begin execution before all of its classfiles have been loaded. Such eager execution is highly beneficial for applications having classfiles distributed across the Internet. However, the price that must be paid for this functionality is that many attributes of an application which are typically considered to be static (i.e., they can be resolved at compile-time) are now dynamic (i.e., their resolution must occur at runtime).

In many embedded applications, the eager execution capability provided by the JVM is not useful or even desirable. For example, downloading classfiles over the Internet during execution may present an unacceptable risk for a high-consequence application. Thus, the design for such an embedded system allows for the (more traditional) separation of the static and dynamic aspects of the JVM. As shown in Fig. 9, the goal of the classloader (the static portion of the JVM) is to take a set of classfiles as input and output an intermediate form in which all static aspects of the classfiles have be resolved.

Because the goal of the classloader is to manipulate a formally defined input (i.e., a set of classfiles), the problem is an ideal candidate for TOP. Furthermore, due to the size of the input space, testing, when used exclusively, is not an effective method for providing strong evidence in the correctness of the classloader. Thus, in order to achieve high-assurance other forms of evidence must be provided.

In this section, we demonstrate how program transformation can be used to positively impact an embedded system design having the architecture described above. In particular, we describe how the static functionality of the Java Virtual Machine (JVM) can be realized through TOP.

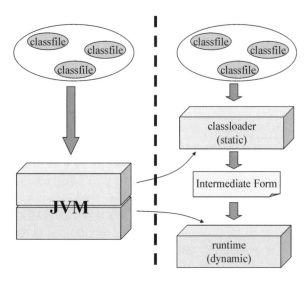

FIG. 9. Partitioning the JVM.

7.1   The SSP Project

At Sandia National Laboratories, an effort is underway to develop a system called the Sandia Secure Processor (SSP). This system consists of the *SSP-classloader* function that is implemented in software and the *SSP-runtime* function that is implemented in hardware. The intent is to develop a general-purpose computational infrastructure suitable for use in high-consequence embedded systems. Because of this, considerable resources are dedicated to providing strong evidence that all aspects of the SSP, both the classloader and the runtime, have been designed and implemented correctly.

In typical stand-alone embedded applications, all classes can be made available to the JVM before there is a need to invoke the application's `main` method. Because of this, loading, verification, most of preparation, and resolution can be done statically. The SSP has been suitably designed to enable a clean separation of the static and dynamic aspects of the preparation step thereby allowing the static portion to be shifted to the classloader and the dynamic portion to be shifted to the runtime.

The SSP is based on the JVM with three significant restrictions. First, threads are not supported. Second, strings and real numbers are not supported. Finally, dynamic loading is not supported. The classloader completes execution before the SSP runtime begins. This separation allows the development of a microprocessor implementing only the runtime function of the SSP, which results in a reduction of the size

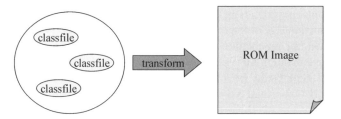

FIG. 10. Transforming classfiles into a ROM image.

of the microprocessor gate count, a reduction in microprocessor complexity, and an increase in execution speed.

7.2   The SSP-classloader

The specification of the JVM states that classes should be made available to a running program via a loading and linking sequence. The loading step consists of importing a classfile into the JVM. A classfile is the binary form of a class and is typically generated by a Java compiler. The linking phase can be broken down into three steps: (1) verification, (2) preparation, and (3) resolution. Verification ensures that a class is well formed. Preparation involves allocating the appropriate amounts of memory for classes and objects and assigning default values to these memory locations. Resolution is the act of transforming symbolic references into direct references with respect to a given hardware architecture.

The job of the SSP-classloader is to correctly translate Java classfiles into a form suitable for execution by the SSP-runtime. This translation produces an intermediate form that we call a *ROM image* (Fig. 10), and concerns itself with many issues such as:

1. Resolving symbolic references to physical addresses or direct and indirect offsets. This resolution is intimately linked to the architecture of the hardware.[10]
2. Correctly capturing the inheritance semantics of Java for applications consisting of multiple classfiles.
3. Providing suitable information for method invocation and return.
4. Constructing method tables.

The correctness of the classloader is the attribute that is of primary importance. Other attributes such as spatial and temporal efficiency are a distant second. Given

[10]One of the unique aspects of this project has been the close relationship between the classloader development team and the SSP development team. Both teams have frequent contact and are willing to negotiate design complexity issues in favor of increasing the analyzability of the overall system.

these constraints, program transformation provides a technology well suited for realizing the functionality of the classloader in an offline manner. While it is true that a more efficient implementation of the classloader can be constructed, for example, by simply implementing the SSP-classloader in C, the verification of such a classloader would undoubtedly be intractable. In contrast, program transformation lays the groundwork that provides the possibility of formally verifying the correctness of the classloader.

7.2.1 The SSP-runtime

The SSP-runtime is the hardware component of the SSP. It is charged with the responsibility of correctly executing bytecodes as well as handling any runtime requirements, such as exceptions, that result from their execution. The execution of the SSP with a given ROM image should produce the same behavior as the execution of a correct JVM implementation given the corresponding set of class files. This can be stated more precisely as follows:

- Let *App* denote the set of classfiles in a Java application.
- Let *SSP-classloader* and *SSP-runtime* denote the classloader and runtime functions of the SSP.
- Let *JVM* denote a Java Virtual Machine.
- Let *JVM(App)* denote the execution of *App* by *JVM*.
- Then $SSP\text{-}runtime(SSP\text{-}classloader(App)) = JVM(App)$.

Below is a partial list of requirements the SSP-runtime design should satisfy:

1. There must be the option of building the processor using radiation-hardened technology for military applications.
2. An open-source for the system must be available allowing detailed design analysis and testing of all aspects of the system down to the gate level.
3. Certification evidence should be provided by formal mathematical proofs of correctness to the extent possible, and strongly convincing evidence must be provided in all other cases where mathematical proofs have not been achieved.
4. A security policy must be strictly enforced ensuring that any program is either rejected as incorrect by compile-time or run-time checks, or its behavior must be understandable by reasoning based entirely on the language semantics, independent of the implementation. In particular, no violation of this policy may be permitted regardless of whether it results from an inadvertent error or a malevolent attack.
5. The processor should support an I/O interface such that the impact of I/O on computation is separated to as large an extent as possible. For example, I/O

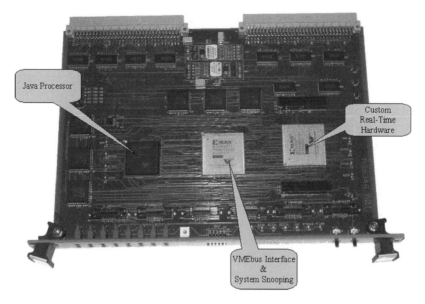

Fig. 11. 8031 system.

implementation via interrupts may dramatically impact computation time and is thus a poor design choice.

6. The processor should be compatible with Java technology (e.g., development environments, compilers, and byte-code verifiers).

At Sandia National Laboratories, an initial version of the SSP-runtime has been designed in VHDL. All indications are that it will be less than 40K gates and capable of operating near 75 MHz. Most importantly however is that the simplifications have reduced by at least an order of magnitude the number of test vectors required to fully verify the correct operation of the digital logic.

Current plans for fabrication are to use the design as a processor core in a system-on-a-chip that is based on a previously designed system. The system, shown in Fig. 11, was fabricated in CMOS6 technology and used a core based on Intel's 8031. The total number of gates in that system was approximately 120 K gates, of which the processor core consumed roughly 25 K gates. The total die size was 378 × 347 mils, and was packaged in a 208 BGA ceramic package.

The core logic of the new VHDL design synthesizes to approximately 37 K gates. The radiation hardened CMOS6R process will be used for initial fabrication. Tuning it for the desired radiation hardness characteristics in that technology will allow a maximum clock rate of 35 MHz. It is still unclear the number of bond pads that will be required as the testing methodology for the die is still being developed. It is expected that enhancements made to the surrounding logic coupled with a number of static memories to be included on the die would yield a final equivalent number of gates that approaches 200 K gates.

A second-generation part is intended to target the Silicon On Insulator (SOI) technology. Its smaller geometry will allow for the resultant maximum clock rate of 50 MHz.

7.3   A Transformation-Based Classloader

In this section we describe a TOP solution to the classloader problem. As a precondition we assume that classfiles can be represented by terms according to a given grammar description. The structure of these classfile terms closely matches the structure of classfiles as described in the JVM specification [30]. However, there are a few differences: (1) constant pool entries are explicitly indexed, (2) constant pool entries are modified so that they have a more homogeneous structure, and (3) constant pool indexes throughout the classfile are also correspondingly altered except for indexes that occur within bytecodes (e.g., checkcast, getfield). These alterations will be discussed in more detail in the following sections. The important point to remember is that the classfile is translated to a term (i.e., a parse tree) whose structure is similar, but not identical, to the term structure described in the JVM specification.

Under these conditions, the goal is to develop a set of transformation rules that when guided by an appropriate strategy will transform a collection of classfiles belonging to a Java application into a ROM image. A prototype transformation-based classloader has been implemented and the lessons learned have been used to extend and enhance the capabilities of our transformation system.

It is difficult to construct a suitable term language that describes the structure of Java classfiles, the structure of the ROM Image, and necessary intermediate forms. The capabilities of the transformation system (e.g., higher-order matching, AC-unification, dynamic transformations) as well as the transformational approach envisioned by the development team affect the design of the intermediate forms needed. There are many aspects that come into play here such as how the system matches terms, constructs replacement terms, as well as controls the application of transformation rules. One of the areas that we are actively researching is the application of various software engineering techniques such as UML class diagrams and OO analysis to help us in the construction of term languages [12].

7.3.1   *Constant Pool Resolution*

We will use the term *resolution* to refer to the various translations needed to convert a set of classfiles into a ROM image. Classfiles are assumed to come from trusted sources and are loaded offline. Thus, much of the information contained in a classfile can be discarded. The ROM image of a classfile consists predominantly of a constant pool and method areas.

The heart of resolution performed by the classloader is the construction of the ROM image constant pool. For a given classfile, constant pool resolution is accomplished by transforming the classfile through a sequence of canonical forms, each of which has some abstract property that can be utilized by a later transformational stage. The following canonical forms are used.

Canonical Form 1: Removal of indirection. A useful intermediate form when creating a ROM image is to remove all indirection in the constant pool. Initially, various types of information within a Java classfile are expressed as indexes into the constant pool. For example, bytecodes within methods can have constant pool indexes as arguments, and the name and type of a field element are expressed in terms of constant pool indexes. Furthermore, constant pools themselves store much of their information internally through indirection. For example, a class element entry contains a `name_index` rather than the name of the class. The constant pool entry at `name_index` is a string (i.e., a `constant_utf8_info` entry) whose value is the name of the class.

Canonical Form 2: Relevant constant pool construction. Since the SSP does not support Java string types, the string entries serve no useful purpose. Thus, `constant_utf8_info` and `constant_name_and_type_info` entries can be removed. We call the form that remains the *relevant constant pool*.

Canonical Form 3: Offset indexing. In this form, an offset is computed for each relevant constant pool entry. The reason for this is that the SSP accesses constant pool entries via offsets rather than abstract indexes. In contrast, Java classfiles access constant pool entries via abstract indexes. The difference between an offset and an abstract index is that an offset allows entries to have varying sizes (e.g., a 2 word entry versus a 1 word entry) while an abstract index considers all entries to have equal size.

Canonical Form 4: Resolution of fields. All field entries must be resolved either to absolute addresses (for static fields) or to offsets (for instance fields). Both of these resolutions require global information. For example, the absolute address of a static field depends on how many such addresses have been assigned during the resolution of other constant pools. The assignment of offsets to instance fields requires knowledge of where within the inheritance hierarchy this field declaration falls.

Canonical Form 5: Resolution of classes. Resolved class entries consist of an address to the class's method area structure and the object size for that class (e.g., how many instance fields an object will have).

Canonical Form 6: Resolution of methods. Java supports three types of methods: virtual, static, and special. Within the ROM image, resolved constant pool entries for static and special methods occupy two words of memory and contain the following information: (1) the memory size of the method's local variables, (2) the memory size of the methods parameters, (3) the location of the start of the method's bytecodes, and (4) the address of the constant pool structure associated with the method. In this chapter, we make the simplification that a virtual method element also occupies two words of memory. In the actual ROM image for the SSP, a virtual method occupies only one word.

The following sections describe in detail how transformations are used to realize the constant pool resolution steps for removal of indirection, construction of a relevant constant pool, and offset indexing.

7.4   Removal of Indirection

In this section we begin with a concrete example that shows how indirection can be removed from the entries in a constant pool that has been modified to improve its readability by humans. (See Appendices A, B, and C for a more complete example). With respect to an SSP constant pool, we have taken some liberties with how we present constant pool data. For example, we assume that abstract indexes for the constant pool have been made explicit.

Consider the following constant pool entries describing the field x of type integer belonging the to the class *animal*, shown in Fig. 12. This constant pool has six entries. Entry 4 in the table that describes x. This entry contains two pieces of information: the `class_index`, which leads to the class, and the `name_and_type index`, which leads to the name and type of the variable. The `class_index` refers to the second entry in the constant pool. This entry contains the index of a constant pool entry that contains a class name, namely the first entry. The first entry is a constant string of type `constant_utf8_info` and contains the string `animal`. The `name_and_type_index` of entry 4, through double indirection, arrive at the variable name x and the type `I`, contained in the final two table entries shown here.

The first task is to remove one level of indirection in this table. For example, we can take the `name_index` in the second entry and replace it with the value `animal`. The type of the entry in the constant pool changes. For example, the second entry should have type `constant_utf8_info` after the index is replaced by the string value. In the following tables, we keep the original type names and infer the actual type from the context. The removal of one level of indirection from each constant pool entry yields the table shown in Fig. 13.

The removal of one more level of indirection yields the table shown in Fig. 14.

Index	Original type	Contents
1	constant_utf8_info	animal
2	constant_class_info	name_index = 1
3	constant_name_and_type_info	name_index = 5
		descriptor_index = 6
4	constant_fieldref_info	class_index = 2
		name_and_type_index = 3
5	constant_utf8_info	x
6	constant_utf8_info	I

FIG. 12. Unresolved constant pool entries.

Index	Original type	Contents
1	constant_utf8_info	animal
2	constant_class_info	animal
3	constant_name_and_type_info	x
		I
4	constant_fieldref_info	class_index = 1
		name_index = 5
		descriptor_index = 6
5	constant_utf8_info	x
6	constant_utf8_info	I

FIG. 13. Partially resolved constant pool entries.

Index	Original type	Contents
1	constant_utf8_info	animal
2	constant_class_info	animal
3	constant_name_and_type_info	x
		I
4	constant_fieldref_info	animal
		x
		I
5	constant_utf8_info	x
6	constant_utf8_info	I

FIG. 14. Resolved constant pool entries.

In order to put a classfile in Canonical Form 1, we need to construct transformation rules that perform the operations shown above. We begin by considering how the removal of indirection can be expressed for constant-pool-like structures where each entry is either a data element or an index. Let *CP* denote an array corresponding to our constant pool. Abstractly, the removal of one level of indirection from an entry *k* would be achieved by simply replacing the current value of entry *k* (say, an index) with the entry in *CP* that is indexed by entry *k*. Transformationally this concept can be expressed in a rewrite rule-like style as:

$$CP[k] \rightarrow CP[CP[k]] \text{ when } CP[k] \text{ is an index}$$

More concretely, let us assume that *CP* is denoted by a list of tuples of the form: (*index, data*), where the first element of the tuple denotes the position of the tuple in the list, and data may be an index or a string (e.g., a *utf8*). For example, suppose we were given a constant pool called *CP* with the following form:

(1, 3)
(2, 4)
(3, "hello")
(4, "world")

The following dynamic transformation rule captures the removal of indirection concept.

dynamic remove_indirection (entry$_1$)
{entry$_1$ == entry[(index$_1$, data$_1$)]
    $\rightarrow$
    transform (entry$_2$) {entry$_2$ == entry[(index$_2$, index$_1$)]
                                    $\rightarrow$ entry[(index$_2$, data$_1$)]}
}

This dynamic transformation rule, when instantiated with respect to a particular value for *entry$_1$*, will create a transformation rule that rewrites indirect references to *entry$_1$* with the actual data corresponding to the reference. If we apply the above dynamic transformation rule to *CP*, the system will (internally) generate the following set of transformation rules, one rule for each entry in *CP*:

transform (entry$_2$) { entry$_2$ == entry[(index$_2$, 1)] $\rightarrow$ entry[(index$_2$, 3)]}
transform (entry$_2$) { entry$_2$ == entry[(index$_2$, 2)] $\rightarrow$ entry[(index$_2$, 4)]}
transform (entry$_2$) { entry$_2$ == entry[(index$_2$, 3)]
                                    $\rightarrow$ entry[(index$_2$, "hello")]}
transform (entry$_2$) { entry$_2$ == entry[(index$_2$, 4)]
                                    $\rightarrow$ entry[(index$_2$, "world")]}

If we now apply the above transformation rules to *CP* we will get:

(1, "hello")
(2, "world")
(3, "hello")
(4, "world")

Because the first two transformation rules above are never applied, one might conclude that they are not needed. In general, this is not the case. The reason the rules did not apply is because the level of indirection in the example given was only one level deep. Consider the addition of (5, 1) and (6, 2) to *CP*. The dynamic transformation rule generates two additional rules:

transform ($entry_2$) { $entry_2$ == entry[($index_2$, 5)] → entry[($index_2$, 1)]}
transform ($entry_2$) { $entry_2$ == entry[($index_2$, 6)] → entry[($index_2$, 2)]}

When this set of six rules is applied to the new *CP*, the last two rules are not used, but the first two are used. In general, it is not possible to determine in advance which rules will be applied.

This example demonstrates how the removal of indirection might be realized in a transformational manner. In order for this idea to be applied to the removal-of-indirection problem in the SSP classloader, a term language supporting suitable intermediate classfile forms must be designed. Below is an example of a partially completed context-free grammar describing such a term language. The grammar fragment below is intentionally ambiguous. HATS can parse such grammars so long as the transformation rules themselves do not define any terms in an ambiguous manner.

ClassFile ::=   magic
                minor_version
                major_version
                constant_pool_count
                constant_pool
                access_flags
                this_class
                super_class
                interface_count
                interfaces
                fields_count
                fields
                methods_count
                methods
                attributes_count
                attributes

```
constant_pool ::= cp_info_list
cp_info_list   ::= cp_info cp_info_list |  ()   the () denotes the ∈-production
cp_info        ::= access base_entry   |  base_entry
access         ::= index               |  offset index

base_entry ::= constant_class_info
             | constant_utf8_info
             | constant_fieldref_info
             | constant_methodref_info
             | constant_name_and_type_info
             | constant_integer_info

constant_name_and_type_info ::=  info2
constant_fieldref_info        ::=  info2
constant_methodref_info       ::=  info2
constant_class_info           ::=  info1
constant_integer_info         ::=  bytes
constant_utf8_info            ::=  info1

info1          ::=  index | utf8
info2          ::=  index | class name_and_type | name descriptor
class          ::=  name
name           ::=  info1
name_and_type ::=  info2
descriptor     ::=  info1
```

This is similar to the structure of classfiles specified in the JVM specification [30]. The major differences are:

1. a constant pool entry can be a base entry, or it can be a base entry preceded by access data (e.g., an index);
2. access data can be an abstract index (as defined by in JVM specification) or an offset address and an abstract index;
3. entities such as name, class, and descriptor are of type info1 and the name_and_type entry is of type info2;
4. info1 can be either an index or a utf8 value; and
5. info2 can be an (a) index, (b) a class and name_type, or (c) a name and descriptor.

While the construction of the term language shown above is not particularly complex, the structure and abstractions of such a grammar can profoundly influence how the developer thinks and expresses transformational ideas, both at the rule level and the strategy level. Grammars define how information can be represented. The nonter-

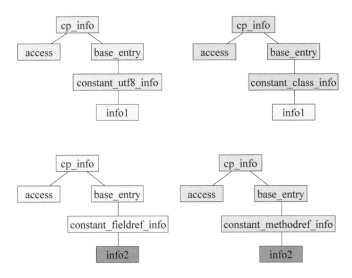

FIG. 15. Parse trees for constant pool entries.

minal symbols in a well-designed grammar describe important semantic concepts in the language. Similarly, important relationships and groupings between concepts can also be captured. We believe that it is well worth the effort to construct grammars in which the right semantic relationships are elegantly captured at the syntactic level.

In order to help us design a transformation strategy for removing indirection, let us look at the structure of some constant pool entries. Figs. 15 and 16 show the parse trees (i.e., terms) that describe five types of constant pool entries: `uft8` entries, `class` entries, `field` entries, `method` entries, and `name_and_type` entries.

Each constant pool entry type is ultimately defined with respect to either an `info1` or an `info2` element. This is an important structural design decision that permits writing transformation rules that rewrite `info1` and `info2`. To see how this might be done, let us now look more closely at the structure of `info1` and `info2` shown in Fig. 17.

As indicated by the grammar, `info1` can be either an `index` or a `utf8` value. Similarly, `info2` can be an `index`, a `name` and `descriptor`, or a `class` followed a `name_and_type` value. In turn, `name`, `descriptor`, `classes`, and `name_and_type` are all defined in terms of `info1`. Given these structural relationships, we can resolve indirection by: (1) rewriting all `info2` index terms to an `info2` name and `descriptor` term or to an `info2` class and `name_and_type` term; and (2) rewriting all `info1` index terms to `info1` `utft8` terms. Such rewriting will remove all `info1` and `info2` indexes.

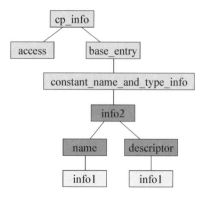

FIG. 16. Detailed parse tree of dual index entry.

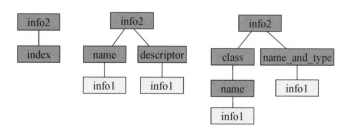

FIG. 17. The structure of info1 and info2.

Figs. 18 and 19 show how this approach would resolve a `constant_method-ref_info` element.

We need to construct transformation rules that rewrite `info2` and `info1` indexes to their proper non-index terms. Notice that a `class index` references a `class` entry, and a `class` entry is an `index` to a `utf8` element. Thus, we have two levels of indirection in this case. The dynamic transformation rule shown below constructs transformation rules that resolve both types of indirection occurring in `info1` terms.

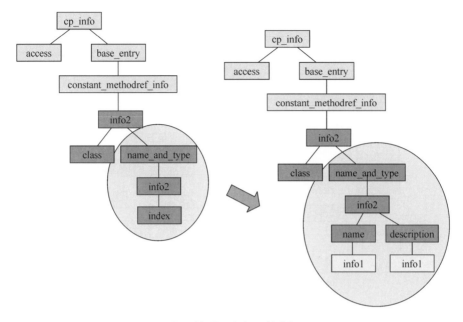

FIG. 18. Resolution of info2.

This dynamic transformation also constructs transformation rules that resolve the indirection that arises in `info2` terms.

dynamic resolve_info (cp_info$_0$)
{ (* this section constructs transformation rules for info1 indexes *)
   (cp_info$_0$ == cp_info[index$_1$ constant_utf8_info$_1$]
    and
    constant_utf8_info$_1$ == constant_utf8_info[info1$_1$]
)
or
   (cp_info$_0$ == cp_info[index$_1$ constant_class_info$_1$]
    and
    constant_class_info$_1$ == constant_class_info[info1$_1$]
)
→
   transform (info1$_0$) {info1$_0$ == info1[index$_1$] → info1$_1$ }
|
   (* this section constructs transformation rules for info2 indexes *)
   cp_info$_0$ == cp_info[index$_1$ constant_name_and_type_info$_1$]

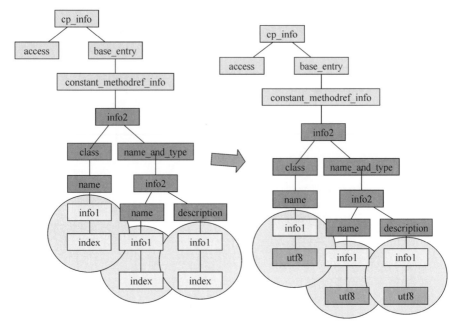

FIG. 19. Resolution of info1.

and
$$\text{constant\_name\_and\_type\_info}_1 == \text{constant\_name\_and\_type\_info}[\text{ info2}_1]$$
$\rightarrow$

    transform (info2$_0$) {info2$_0$ == info2[index$_1$] $\rightarrow$ info2$_1$ }
}

A feature of HATS seen in the above transformation rule is that match expressions can be disjunctions of other match expressions. Disjunctions come into play when information is common across the replacement of a number of transformation rules. In such cases, match expressions can be factored out of multiple rules and formed into a disjunction. For example, consider n rules having distinct match expressions but producing the same replacement term. Without the ability to express disjunction one would have to write n distinct rules:

    Rule 1: match_expr_1 $\rightarrow$ X
    Rule 2: match_expr_2 $\rightarrow$ X
    ...
    Rule n: match_expr_n $\rightarrow$ X

However, with disjunction, these rules can be factored into a single rule:

Rule 1: match_expr_1 or match_expr_2 or ... or match_expr_n $\rightarrow$ X

The dynamic transformation, *resolve_info*, when applied to a classfile, will create the set of transformation rules, $T1$, needed for removal of indirection. What remains is for these rules to be applied by an appropriate strategy. Recall that our goal is to remove all indirection (i.e., all indexes) through the entire classfile. Obviously a single pass is not sufficient; thus, an exhaustive application strategy is used. The transformation rule shown below defines a strategy that is capable of removing the indirection within classfiles.

In the resolve strategy, the expression *eval(post_order, resolve_info, ClassFile$_0$)* applies the dynamic rule *resolve_info* in order to produce a set of transformation rules which can then be applied to the entire classfile in order to remove indirection.

The transformation rule below defines a strategy for applying the resolve rule.

```
transform resolve (ClassFile₀)
{ ClassFile₁ == fix( post_order, ClassFile₀,
                     eval( post_order, resolve_info, ClassFile₀ ))
   →
  ClassFile₁
}
```

The current version of HATS provides three universal iteration operators: *first*, *once*, and *fix*. All iterators take three arguments: (1) the order that a term is to be traversed (*pre-order* or *post-order*), (2) the term to be traversed, and (3) the transformation rules to be attempted at every point in the traversal. The *first* operator traverses the term in the order specified and continues until the transformation rule is successfully applied for the first time. If the rule does not apply at all then when first reaches the end of its traversal it returns the original term (i.e., it leaves the input term unaltered). The *once* operator traverses the term in the order specified and attempts to apply the transformation rule to every point in the term. When the end of the traversal is reached, the resulting term is returned. And finally, the *fix* operator continues to traverse the term in the order specified until the transformation rule can no longer be applied. Note that this may require multiple traversals and can continue indefinitely in cases where the transformation rule is non-terminating.

Presently, the concept of a strategy and how it can be defined within HATS is undergoing a major revision, both at the theoretical level as well as the notational level. Our intention is to provide the user with more general capabilities for defining general strategies such as the recursive closures in Stratego as well as some of the concepts defined in the Rho-calculus.

It is worth mentioning that constant pool indexes throughout the entire classfile will be resolved using the above strategy. With the exception of indexes that occur within bytecodes (e.g., checkcast, getfield), a global resolution is exactly what our design calls for. In the approach presented, index resolution will not apply within the context of bytecodes because terms describing indexes within bytecodes differ from terms describing indexes in the remainder of the classfile. This restriction was stated at the beginning of the section. It is relatively easy to relax this restriction and require the selection of index resolution to be controlled by the strategy.

7.5 Relevant Constant Pool Construction

Continuing on with our example, we now show the relevant constant pool can be extracted from the present form of the constant pool. Recall that the constant pool with indirection removed has the form shown in Fig. 20.

The constant pool with only relevant entries is shown in Fig. 21.

An important observation at this point is that the abstract indexes (i.e., 2 and 4) no longer correspond to the position of the entry in the constant pool. This however does not present a problem because at the beginning of this example the abstract indexes were made explicit (i.e., part of the constant pool entry).

Here, the goal is to discard all constant_utf8_info and constant_name_ and_type_info entries. The transformation given below applies to all constant pool lists in which the first element is either a constant_utf8_info or constant_name_and_type_info. A successful application of the transformation will result in this first element being dropped from the list. A single traversal of the

Index	Original type	Contents
1	constant_utf8_info	animal
2	constant_class_info	animal
3	constant_name_and_type_info	x
		I
4	constant_fieldref_info	animal
		x
		I
5	constant_utf8_info	x
6	constant_utf8_info	I

FIG. 20. Fully populated constant pool.

Index	Original type	Contents
1		
2	constant_class_info	animal
3		
4	constant_fieldref_info	animal
		x
		I
5		
6		

FIG. 21. Relevant entries after resolution.

constant pool will produce the relevant constant pool. Note that because we have defined a constant pool entry list (i.e., cp_info_list) as a list whose last element is the empty string, we know that the final element of a cp_info_list will always be the empty string and therefore will not need to be removed.

transform relevant_cp (cp_info_list$_0$)
{ cp_info_list$_0$ == cp_info_list[index$_1$ constant_utf8_info$_1$ cp_info_list$_1$]
    or
  cp_info_list$_0$ == cp_info_list[index$_1$ constant_name_and_type_info$_1$
                        cp_info_list$_1$]
  $\rightarrow$
  cp_info_list$_1$
}
transform relevant (ClassFile$_0$)
{ ClassFile$_1$ == once(post_order, ClassFile$_0$, relevant_cp) $\rightarrow$ ClassFile$_1$ }

7.6   Offset Indexing

We continue with our example showing the result of adding offset information to our relevant constant pool. In this example, the offset for the first relevant constant pool entry is 4 words (i.e., the words at offset 0–3 in the constant pool are reserved for some other information). Furthermore, we are given that the class entry has a size of one word; hence the constant_fieldref_info entry has an offset of 5 words as shown in Fig. 22.

Expressing how offsets should be inserted into constant pool entries is simple, though the notation is somewhat verbose. Our approach is to define two transformation rules that accomplish simple rewrites and a third, strategic rule that controls their application. The *initial_offset* rule inserts, in the first element of the constant pool, an

Offset index	Original index	Original type	Contents
0004	2	`constant_class_info`	`animal`
0005	4	`constant_fieldref_info`	`animal x I`

FIG. 22. Relevant constant pool entries with physical offsets.

initial offset whose value is obtained from the function call *baseOffset( )*. The value of this base offset is defined by the specification of the structure of the ROM image. The *percolate_offset* rule adjusts and "percolates" the offset through the remaining entries in the constant pool according to the size of each entry.

transform initial_offset (cp_info$_0$)
{ cp_info$_0$ == cp_info[index$_1$ base_entry$_1$]
    and
        (* the function baseOffset is a library function *)
    { offset$_1$:= baseOffset() }
    $\rightarrow$
    cp_info[offset$_1$ index$_1$ base_entry$_1$]
}

Note that the *initial_offset* transformation makes use of a library call to the function *baseOffset* denoted by the expression:

{ offset$_1$:= baseOffset() }

Such functionality, supported by HATS, falls outside the realm of pure rewrite-based transformation. Nevertheless, it can be successfully applied in cases where one is willing to assume that the library function used is correct. A classic example where such functionality is highly beneficial is in situations (such as the upcoming transformation) where one wants to perform mathematical operations (e.g., addition and division). While it is possible to write transformation rules capable of performing such mathematical operations, doing this does not increase the understandability or correctness of the program.

The second transformation rule, *percolate_offset*, applies to adjacent constant pool entries where the first entry has an offset and the second entry does not. In such a situation, the offset for the second entry should be the value of the first offset plus 1 or 2 depending on the type of the first *base_entry*. If the first *base_entry* denotes a *class*, an *integer*, or a *fieldref*, then the offset for the second entry is equal to the offset for the first entry plus 1; otherwise, it is equal to the offset for the first entry plus 2.

transform percolate_offset (cp_info_list$_0$)
{ cp_info_list$_0$ == cp_info_list[offset$_1$ index$_1$ base_entry$_1$
                                    index$_2$ base_entry$_2$ cp_info_list$_1$]

and

  (base_entry$_1$ == base_entry[constant_class_info$_1$] or

    base_entry$_1$ == base_entry[constant_integer_info$_1$] or

    base_entry$_1$ == base_entry[constant_fieldref_info$_1$])

and

  (* the function u4_plus1 is a library function *)

  { offset$_2$:= u4_plus1(offset$_1$) }

$\rightarrow$

  cp_info_list[offset$_1$ index$_1$ base_entry$_1$

                offset$_2$ index$_2$ base_entry$_2$ cp_info_list$_1$]

| (* conclude base_entry$_1$ is a 2 word entry *)

  cp_info_list$_0$ == cp_info_list[offset$_1$ index$_1$ base_entry$_1$

                      index$_2$ base_entry$_2$ cp_info_list$_1$]

and

  (* the function u4_plus2 is a library function *)

  { offset$_2$:= u4_plus2(offset$_1$) }

$\rightarrow$

  cp_info_list[offset$_1$ index$_1$ base_entry$_1$

                offset$_2$ index$_2$ base_entry$_2$ cp_info_list$_1$]

}

The strategic transformation rule, *calculate_offsets*, is responsible for applying the *initial_offset* rule to the first entry in the constant pool followed by an application of the *percolate_offset* rule to every pair of constant pool entries beginning with the first two entries and proceeding in an ordered fashion from there. The application of both of the above transformation rules is controlled by the strategy *calculate_offsets*. In this rule, the word *first* indicates that the rule is to be applied to the first match only. After one application succeeds, HATS discontinues its attempt to apply the rule. The word *once* indicates that HATS will traverse the entire term one time, applying the transformation everywhere it matches.

transform calculate_offsets (cp_info_list$_0$)

{ cp_info_list$_1$ == first(post_order, cp_info_list$_0$, initial_offset)

  and

  cp_info_list$_2$ == once(pre_order, cp_info_list$_1$, percolate_offset)

  $\rightarrow$

  cp_info_list$_2$

}

8. Future Work: Verification

Earlier in this chapter we mentioned that one of the attractive features of TOP is that one can provide strong evidence that the output term of a transformation sequence is correct with respect to its input term. The ideal situation arises when transformation rules and strategies are so simple that the correctness of all rules and strategies can be (1) informally validated in situations where validation is considered to constitute acceptably strong evidence, or (2) automatically verified using theorem provers in situations where mathematical certainty constitutes strong evidence. In this section we discuss current work towards verification of the SSP classloader. It is our intent to complete the formal verification of the classloader in the near future.

In a TOP paradigm, problems are solved by transformation sequences, which are typically constructed in the following manner. First, an overall *transformation-oriented design* (TOP design) is developed in which a number of canonical forms are identified. Then an ordering of these canonical forms is determined. Finally, transformation rules and strategies are developed. We use the term *TOP implementation* when referring to the transformation rules and strategies that implement a TOP design. Because of the influence the structure of the term language can have over a TOP implementation, it is generally advisable to develop the term language concurrently (or iteratively) with the transformation rules and strategies when possible.

The two objectives of verification in a TOP framework are design verification and implementation verification. The objective of design verification is to show that passing an input term through the various canonical forms identified in the design produces an output term that solves the problem. The objective of implementation verification is to show that the design is correctly implemented, i.e., that the transformation rules and strategies are able to pass any input term through the various canonical forms identified in the design.

In this section, we consider a fragment of the TOP design for the classloader. In particular we will restrict our attention to the first three canonical forms of the design described in Section 7.3.1. We will refer to this fragment of the design as our *partial classloader design*. The partial classloader design is implemented by the following transformation rules and strategies discussed earlier: *resolve_info, resolve, relevant_cp, relevant, initial_offset, percolate_offset, calculate_offsets.*

The sequential application of *resolve, relevant*, and *calculate_offsets* to a classfile will produce a classfile that is in Canonical Form 3. In the following sections we sketch how one might go about verifying the correctness of the partial classloader design as well as its implementation.

8.1 Design Verification: Eval and BCE

The approach to verification described below is based on viewing the Java Virtual Machine in terms of a semantic function that defines the meaning of each bytecode relative to a set of classfiles and a current state. We extend this idea to a framework in which a number of such semantic functions can be defined. In this framework, semantic functions are linked. The functionality common between them is explicitly identified and sharable. Our goal is to demonstrate an equivalence, modulo transformation, between the semantic function defining the JVM and the semantic function defining the SSP.

Let **Eval** be a class of semantic functions that take as arguments a set of bytecode class files $\mathfrak{C}$ and a program state s and return as output the next program state s'. The program state records the values in program memory (the heap, frame, and opstack), registers, and the next bytecode instruction to be executed. Let $Eval_{JVM} \in$ **Eval** denote the semantic function that, given a set of classfiles $\mathfrak{C}_0$ and a state, computes the next state in accordance with the JVM specification. Similarly, let $Eval_{SSP} \in$ **Eval** denote the semantic function that, given a transformed set of classfiles $\mathfrak{C}_n = T(\mathfrak{C}_0)$ (where T denotes the transformation implementation of the classloader) and a state, computes the next state in accordance with the SSP specification. We want to show that these two functions with their respective inputs compute the same values. This problem can be decomposed into a sequence of equivalences as follows. For each (intermediate) canonical form i produced by the classloader, we define a semantic function $Eval_i$. To show that $Eval_{JVM}(\mathfrak{C}_0, s) = Eval_{SSP}(\mathfrak{C}_n, s)$, we will demonstrate that

$$Eval_{JVM}(\mathfrak{C}_0, s) = Eval_1(\mathfrak{C}_1, s) = Eval_2(\mathfrak{C}_2, s) = \cdots = Eval_{SSP}(\mathfrak{C}_n, s)$$

Decomposing $Eval_{JVM}(\mathfrak{C}_0, s) = Eval_{SSP}(\mathfrak{C}_n, s)$ into a set of equivalences allows the proof to be constructed incrementally, reducing the complexity of the proof.

Let $s' = Eval_{JVM}(\mathfrak{C}_0, s)$ for input state s. In order for $Eval_{JVM}$ to correctly compute s', it must effect the actions required by the JVM specification for the particular bytecode instruction to be executed in s. We define two sets of functions, $\mathfrak{F}^a$ and $\mathfrak{F}^b$ as follows. Let $\mathfrak{F}^b$ be the set of functions that define the semantics of Java bytecodes. In other words, for each bytecode there exists one function in $\mathfrak{F}^b$ defining its semantics. Let $\mathfrak{F}^a$ be the set of auxiliary functions that may be used by the functions in $\mathfrak{F}^b$.

In the partial classloader example that we are considering, $\mathfrak{F}^a = \{ info, access \}$. The function $info$ returns the resolved information for a constant pool index. For a standard classfile, this function traces through the indirection and returns the actual value required for computation. On the other hand, the function $access$, when given an index into the constant pool, simply returns the corresponding constant pool entry without tracing indirection.

In this discussion, we assume that the functions in $\mathfrak{F}^b$ may only access the constant pool through the functions in $\mathfrak{F}^a$. This means that the information associated with an entry necessary for properly executing bytecodes can only be obtained via the function *info*. Other information such as tags on constant pool entries and indexes are not needed other than to determine the information in an entry, and hence can be removed from $\mathfrak{C}_n$.

DEFINITION 1. An interpretation $I = \mathfrak{F}^a \cup \mathfrak{F}^b$ is the set of functions needed to compute a successor state given a set of classfiles and an initial state.

DEFINITION 2. Let $I_{JVM} = (\mathfrak{F}^a_{JVM} \cup \mathfrak{F}^b_{JVM})$ be the interpretation corresponding to the JVM.

DEFINITION 3. Let $I_{SSP} = (\mathfrak{F}^a_{SSP} \cup \mathfrak{F}^b_{SSP})$ be the interpretation corresponding to the SSP.

DEFINITION 4. Let $\mathcal{BCE}$ be a (byte code evaluator) function that takes an interpretation and produces a function $Eval_I \in \textbf{Eval}$. In particular, $Eval_{JVM} = \mathcal{BCE}(I_{JVM})$, and $Eval_{SSP} = \mathcal{BCE}(I_{SSP})$.

When defining the semantic functions $Eval_{JVM}$ and $Eval_{SSP}$, we require that $\mathfrak{F}^b_{SSP} = \mathfrak{F}^b_{JVM}$. Thus, all differences between these two semantic functions must be localized in $\mathfrak{F}^a$. Therefore what must be investigated is the relationship between the functions in $\mathfrak{F}^a_{JVM}$ and $\mathfrak{F}^a_{SSP}$ relative to the classloader.

Note that every function $Eval_i$ in the sequence from $Eval_{JVM}$ to $Eval_{SSP}$ is parameterized on classfiles of a distinct type. Let $\mathfrak{C}_{i-1}$ denote a set of classfiles having a type appropriate for $Eval_{i-1}$. The set of classfiles $\mathfrak{C}_i$ appropriate for $Eval_i$ is then derived from $\mathfrak{C}_{i-1}$ via a transformation strategy T_i capable of transforming $\mathfrak{C}_{i-1}$ to $\mathfrak{C}_i$. If we define M_i to be the mapping of functions in $\mathfrak{F}_{i-1}$ to the corresponding functions in $\mathfrak{F}_i$, then in order to show that $Eval_{i-1}(\mathfrak{C}_{i-1}, s) = Eval_i(\mathfrak{C}_i, s)$, it is necessary to show the following:

$$[\mathcal{BCE}(I_i)](s, \mathfrak{C}_i) = [\mathcal{BCE}(M_i(I_i))](T_i(s, \mathfrak{C}_i))$$

which is true if

$$\forall(f_i \in \mathfrak{F}^a_{i-1})\exists(f_j \in \mathfrak{F}^a_i): \ f_j = M_i(f_i),$$

$$\forall(f_i \in \mathfrak{F}^a_i): \ f_i(\mathfrak{C}_i) = M_i(f_i)(T_i(\mathfrak{C}_i)).$$

From this we see that the various interpretations of $\mathcal{BCE}$ form the basis for formally defining the meaning of the canonical forms in our design as well as all intermediate forms of classfiles that are produced by the classloader. At one end of the spectrum, $\mathcal{BCE}$ produces a function capable of executing bytecodes with respect to "pure" Java classfiles. At the other end of the spectrum, $\mathcal{BCE}$ produces a function capable of executing bytecodes with respect to ROM image classfiles. For all interpretations, the functions produced by $\mathcal{BCE}$ compute the same results when applied to the appropriate classfiles. Thus, the goal of a transformation step is to produce classfiles that preserve bytecode equivalence.

Below we sketch various interpretations of $\mathfrak{F}^a = \{$ *info, access* $\}$. We represent a constant pool as a list of constant pool entries, i.e., we abstract the constant pool to the extent that we can focus on the semantics of resolution and ignore the technical details of data representation. Furthermore, we abstractly define a constant pool entry as a list of data elements where the elements may be indexes or strings. In this setting, the information associated with a constant pool entry is a list of strings where each a string is ultimately the value of a `utf8` entry. For example, in its unresolved form, a `constant_fieldref_info` entry is a list of two indexes (an index to a `constant_class_info` entry, and an index to a `constant_name_and_type_info` entry). In contrast, the information in a resolved `constant_fieldref_info` entry will be a list containing (1) a string denoting the name of a class, (2) a string denoting the name of the field, and (3) a string denoting the type of the field (i.e., the field descriptor).

Given this model of the constant pool and its entries, we now formally define the auxiliary functions *info* and *access*. We encapsulate each interpretation of the auxiliary functions $\mathfrak{F}^a$ in a structure where functions within the structure can be externally referenced using the traditional dot notation. Within a structure for a given interpretation, we define *info* and *access* in an equational manner using a syntax similar to the programming language ML. For the sake of readability, we pass a minimal number of parameters to each function.[11]

Below we define three interpretations for *info* and *access*. While the definitions of these interpretations is not completely formal, we hope that they are rigorous enough to convince the reader that their complete formalization would not be particularly difficult.

(* ——————————————————————————————————— *)
$\mathcal{I}_0$:

info(Index(i)::es) = info(access(i, constant_pool)) @ info(es)
info(String(s)::es) = String(s)::info(es)
info([]) = []

---

[11] The drawback of minimizing parameters is that we must assume that certain information such as the constant pool is globally available to auxiliary functions whenever needed. This is a small technical problem that can be easily fixed in a more complete treatment of the definitions.

access(1, entry::entry_list) = entry
access(index, entry::entry_list) = access(index-1, entry_list)
access(index, []) = undefined

(* ———————————————————————————————— *)
$\mathcal{I}_1$:

info(Index(i)::es) = $\mathcal{I}_0$.info(Index(i)) @ info(es)
info(String(s)::es) = String(s)::info(es)
info([]) = []

access(j, element::entry_list) = if element = (j, entry) then entry
                                            else access(j, entry_list)
access(j, []) = $\mathcal{I}_0$.access(j, constant_pool)

(* ———————————————————————————————— *)
$\mathcal{I}_2$:

info(Index(i)::es) = $\mathcal{I}_1$.info(Index(i)) @ info(es)
info(String(s)::es) = String(s)::info(es)
info([]) = []

access(j, element::entry_list) = if element = (j, k, entry) then entry
                                            else access(j, entry_list)
access(j, []) = $\mathcal{I}_1$.access(j, constant_pool)
(* ———————————————————————————————— *)

In interpretation $\mathcal{I}_0$, constant pool entries are abstractly referenced by their position in the list, and the information associated with a constant pool entry is obtained by resolving indexes within an entry until all that remains is a list of string values. The interpretation $\mathcal{I}_1$, is stacked on top of the definition of $\mathcal{I}_0$. $\mathcal{I}_1$ assumes that constant pool entries are tuples of the form (*index, entry*), where *index* is the abstract reference of the entry and the second element is a fully resolved entry as defined in $\mathcal{I}_0$. Note that if a particular element of the expected form cannot be found, the search is repeated using the functionality defined in $\mathcal{I}_0$. Similarly, if the information in an entry is not in its expected (i.e., resolved) form, a resolution call is made to the info function in $\mathcal{I}_0$.

In a similar fashion, the interpretation $\mathcal{I}_2$, is stacked on top of $\mathcal{I}_1$. The interpretation $\mathcal{I}_2$ differs from $\mathcal{I}_1$ only in that $\mathcal{I}_2$ expects constant pool entries to be triples of the form (*offset, index, entry*) where *offset* is the physical offset of the constant pool entry within memory. In $\mathcal{I}_2$ constant pool entries are accessed by their offset rather than their (abstract) index.

In the interpretations $\mathcal{I}_0$, $\mathcal{I}_1$, and $\mathcal{I}_2$, if one strips away all references to previously defined interpretations, one is left with semantic functions that are suitable for constant pools that are in the appropriate canonical forms. The goal of transformation is to produce such canonical forms. Stacking of interpretations is needed to account for the incremental nature of transformation (intermediate forms are produced that are not canonical). Stacking of interpretations gives a well defined semantics to intermediate forms.

8.2   Basis for Verifying the Partial Classloader Design

Informally, the correctness of the partial classloader design can be argued as follows:

1. The representation of information in a direct fashion in constant pool entries is a refinement of the representation of the same information via indirection.
2. Explicit indexing enables entries to be removed from the constant pool while preserving abstract indexing.
3. All constant pool entries that are not referenced anywhere in the classfile can be removed from the constant pool.
4. Offsets can be computed for the remaining entries according to their specified sizes.

Let T_1, T_2, and T_3 respectively denote the following transformations:

1. Given a Java classfile cf, $T_1(cf)$ is a classfile in Canonical Form 1.
2. Given a classfile cf' in Canonical Form 1, $T_2(cf')$ is a classfile in Canonical Form 2.
3. Given a classfile cf'' in Canonical Form 2, $T_3(cf'')$ is a classfile in Canonical Form 3.

From a formal standpoint, we want to show the following:

THEOREM 5. $\forall cf,\ state\colon \mathcal{BCE}[I_1](state, cf) = \mathcal{BCE}[I_2](state, T_1(cf))$.

The proof of this is based on the assumption that information from an constant pool entry can only be obtained by calling the *info* function.

THEOREM 6. $\forall cf,\ state\colon \mathcal{BCE}[I_2](state, T_1(cf)) = \mathcal{BCE}[I_2](state, T_2(T_1(cf)))$.

The proof of this is based on the fact that no bytecode has an index corresponding to entries that are not relevant.

THEOREM 7. $\forall cf$, *state*: $\mathcal{BCE}[I_2](state, T_1(T_2((cf))) = \mathcal{BCE}[I_3](T_3(T_2(T_1(cf))))$.

The proof of this is based on the fact that the sizes of constant pool entries in the ROM image are specified by the SSP.

8.3   Implementation Verification

In general, interpretations can be viewed as the pre- and post-conditions of transformation sequences that take a term from one canonical form to the next. Given an interpretation $\mathcal{I}_1$ for a canonical form $C\mathcal{F}_1$ and an interpretation $\mathcal{I}_2$ for a canonical form $C\mathcal{F}_2$, one must demonstrate that the transformation rules and strategies are able to transform any term in $C\mathcal{F}_1$ to a corresponding term in $C\mathcal{F}_2$. In this setting, the interpretations $\mathcal{I}_1$ and $\mathcal{I}_2$ determine how terms in $C\mathcal{F}_1$ correspond to terms in $C\mathcal{F}_2$.

For example, to show that the dynamic transformation rule *resolve_cp* together with the strategy *resolve* correctly transform an indexed classfile into canonical form 1 (as defined in our partial classloader design) we need to show that all index data are correctly replaced by string data throughout the classfile. Informally we argue that one can use the semantics of dynamic transformation rules to show that *resolve_cp* will produce transformation rules that, when applied, correctly replace constant pool index data found throughout the classfile with data that is presently associated with the constant pool entry having that index. Furthermore, it can be argued that an exhaustive application of these transformations (as is done by the *resolve* strategy) will remove all indirection from the constant pool.

9.   Summary and Conclusion

In this chapter, we described high-consequence systems and argued that the ability to provide high assurance is one of the major risks faced in their development. Sufficient failures of high-consequence systems have been documented to support the allocation of resources in order to develop high-assurance systems. However, the willingness of management to devote sufficient resources is often clouded by short-term objectives such as return on investment. Another reason why management fails to allocate sufficient resources stems from a perception problem. It is difficult for humans to fully comprehend extremely large or extremely small numbers such as those used to define the reliability requirements for high-consequence systems. One might wonder if it matters (or how much it matters) that the system built has a reliability of 1-in-10^8 rather than 1-in-10^9.

Increasing the rigor in software development leads to the construction of more robust systems. The up-front costs associated with increased rigor often appear to be noticeably higher than the up-front costs associated with more traditional software development practices. However, increased expenditures early in a project are frequently rewarded by substantial savings later in the project (e.g., during the testing and maintenance phases). Furthermore, when developing a family of products, the cost of rigor can often be amortized over the product family, reducing the costs associated with rigor further.

In order to add rigor to software development, we proposed transformation-oriented programming (TOP) as a development paradigm. The approaches taken in TOP are based on equational reasoning. As such TOP lays the groundwork for the employment of formal verification to various development aspects, making TOP a suitable candidate for high-assurance software development. In TOP, the solution of a problem is captured by a TOP design and is realized by a TOP implementation. Transformation-oriented designs focus on passing an artifact (e.g., a formal specification) through a number of canonical forms. Transformation rules and strategies are realizations of transformation-oriented designs. We described in general terms a transformation system for implementing transformation-based designs, then we described the notation and capabilities of a specific transformation system called HATS. The remainder of the chapter was devoted to a TOP-based design and implementation of the static functionality of the Java Virtual Machine (JVM).

Appendix A: A Small Java Program

Jim McCoy developed the example below while he was working on the SSP project.

```
// animal class example for inheritance
// jamccoy 7/20/99
public class animal
{
  private int Location;
  protected int Feet;
  protected int Position;
  public static int START = 10;
  public static int FORWARD = 11;
  public static int BACKWARD = 12;
  public static int STANDING = 11;
  public static final int SITTING = 12;
  public static final int LAYING = 13;
// constructors
```

```
animal()
{
  Feet = 1;
  Location = START;
  Position = STANDING;
}
animal(int NumFeet)
{
  Feet = NumFeet;
  Location = START;
  Position = STANDING;
}
// the default way for all animals to stand
public void stand()
{
  Position = STANDING;
} // end of stand
  // since Location is private even animal's children can't see it so we
  // need a way for children to initialize it
public void setLoc(int NewLoc)
{
  if (NewLoc >= −25 && NewLoc <= 25)   // make sure it is safe
  {
  Location = NewLoc;
  }
  else
  {
  Location = −50;    // otherwise put them in a known location
  }
} // end of setLoc
  // the default way for animals to walk
  // an animal object can modify Location directly but since Location is
  // private none of animal's children can see it or modify it directly
  // this method provides a common interface for everything that is like
  // an animal
public void walk(int Distance, int Direction)
{
  if (Position == STANDING && Feet >= 2)    // make sure the conditions are
  { // correct
  if (Direction == FORWARD)    // and handle the different
```

```
  Location += Distance;     // situations correctly
  else if (Direction == BACKWARD)
  Location –= Distance;
  else
  Location = START;     // provide a default when things
} // aren't the way they should be
} // end of walk
  // the default way for animals to count their feet
public int countFeet()
{
  return Feet;
} // end of countFeet
  // the default way to find out what position an animal is in
public int getPos()
{
  return Position;
} // end of getPos
} // end of animal
```

Appendix B: Java Classfile

Here we present the constant pool entries corresponding to the animal class in a human-readable form.

```
animal
0001
java/lang/Object
0003
Location
I
Feet
Position
START
FORWARD
BACKWARD
STANDING
SITTING
ConstantValue
0000000C
LAYING
```

```
0000000D
<init>
()V
Code
0012 0013
0004 0015
0007 0006
0002 0017
0009 0006
0002 0019
0005 0006
0002 001B
000C 0006
0002 001D
0008 0006
0002 001F
LineNumberTable
LocalVariableTable
this
Lanimal;
(I)V
NumFeet
stand
setLoc
NewLoc
walk
(II)V
000A 0006
0002 002C
000B 0006
0002 002E
Distance
Direction
countFeet
()I
getPos
<clinit>
SourceFile
animal.java
FastJavac3.0
```

Appendix C: Resolved Classfile

This is the result of the three constant pool transformation steps we discussed. The numbers in the first column are hexadecimal offset values beginning with 4 as the base offset. The numbers in the second column are the hexadecimal abstract indexes that are originally used to reference constant pool entries.

```
0004 0002   = animal
0005 0004   = java/lang/Object
0006 000F   = 0000000C
0007 0011   = 0000000D
0008 0016   = java/lang/Object <init> ()V
000A 0018   = animal Feet I
000B 001A   = animal START I
000C 001C   = animal Location I
000D 001E   = animal STANDING I
000E 0020   = animal Position I
000F 002D   = animal FORWARD I
0010 002F   = animal BACKWARD I
```

REFERENCES

[1] Aho A., Sethi R., Ullman J., *Compilers, Principles, Techniques, and Tools*, Addison-Wesley, Reading, MA, 1988.

[2] Baxter I., Mehlich M., *Reverse Engineering is Reverse Forward Engineering. Working Conference on Reverse Engineering*, IEEE Press, New York, 1997.

[3] Beck K., *eXtreme Programming Explained*, Addison-Wesley, Boston, MA, 2000.

[4] Berard B., Bidoit M., Finkel A., Laroussinie F., Petit A., Pertucci P., Schnoebelen Ph., McKenzie P., *Systems and Software Verification, Model-Checking Techniques and Tools*, Springer, Berlin, 2001.

[5] Boyle J., Resler R., Winter V., "Do you trust your compiler?", *IEEE Computer* **32** (5) (1999) 65–73.

[6] Burstall R., Darlington J., "A transformation system for developing recursive programs", *Journal of the ACM* **24** (1) (1977) 44–67.

[7] Butler R., Finelli G., "The infeasibility of quantifying the reliability of life-critical real-time software", *IEEE Transactions on Software Engineering* **19** (1) (1993) 3–12.

[8] Butlin R., "Ariane explosion—positive aspects", *The Risks Digest* **18** (5) (1996), http://catless.ncl.ac.uk/Risks.

[9] Caldwell J., "Formal methods technology transfer: A view from NASA", *Formal Methods in System Design* **12** (1998) 125–137.

[10] Chiles J., *Inviting Disaster Lessons from the Edge of Technology*, Harper Business, New York, 2001.

[11] Cirstea H., Kirchner C., Introduction to the rewriting calculus, INRIA Research Report RR-3818, December 1999.

[12] Davis J., Gacek A., Vharma R., Winter V., Constructing transformable context-free grammars, Submitted to 3rd ACM SIGPLAN Workshop on Rule-Based Programming, October 5, 2002.

[13] Dorner D., *The Logic of Failure*, Perseus Books, Cambridge, MA, 1989.

[14] Elrad T., Filman R., Bader A., "Aspect oriented programming", *Communications of the ACM* **44** (10) (2001) 29–32.

[15] Flener P., *Logic Program Synthesis from Incomplete Information*, Kluwer Academic Publishers, Norwell, MA, 1995, pp. 3–53.

[16] Gannon J., Purtilo J., Zelkowitz M., *Software Specification A Comparison of Formal Methods*, Ablex Publishing Company, Norwood, NJ, 1995.

[17] Genesereth M., Nilsson N., *Logical Foundations of Artificial Intelligence*, Morgan Kaufmann, Los Altos, CA, 1987.

[18] Ghezzi C., Jazayeri M., Mandrioli D., *Fundamentals of Software Engineering*, Prentice-Hall, Englewood Cliffs, NJ, 1991.

[19] Green C., "Applications of theorem proving", *IJCAI* **69** (1969) 219–239.

[20] Green C., "Resolution in knowledge based program synthesis", *IJCAI* **79** (1979) 342–344.

[21] Havelund K., Lowry M., Penix J., "Formal analysis of a space craft controller using SPIN", in: *4th International SPIN Workshop, Paris, France*, November 1998.

[22] Havelund K., Lowry M., Park S., Pecheur C., Penix J., Visser W., White J., "Formal analysis of the remote agent before and after flight", in: *Proceedings of the 5th NASA Langley Formal Methods Workshop, Williamsburg, VA*, June 2000.

[23] Hinchey M., Bowen J., *Applications of Formal Methods*, Prentice-Hall, London, 1995.

[24] Holloway C.M., "Why engineers should consider formal methods", in: *Proceedings of the 16th Digital Avionics Systems Conference*, October 1997.

[25] Holzmann G., *Design and Validation of Computer Protocols*, Prentice-Hall, Englewood Cliffs, NJ, 1991.

[26] Jones C., *Systematic Software Development using VDM*, 2nd edn., Prentice-Hall, New York, 1990.

[27] Jones M., "What happened on Mars?", http://www.cs.cmu.edu/afs/cs/user/raj/www/mars.html, 1997.

[28] Kiczales G., Lamping J., Mendhekar A., Maeda C., Lopes C.V., Loingtier J., Irwin J., *Aspect-Oriented Programming*, in: *Lecture Notes in Comput. Sci.*, Vol. 1241, Springer-Verlag, Berlin, 1997.

[29] Leveson N., *Safeware: System Safety and Computers*, Addison-Wesley, Reading, MA, 1995.

[30] Lindholm T., Yellin F., *The Java Virtual Machine Specification*, 2nd edn., Addison-Wesley, Reading, MA, 1999.

[31] Lowry M., Philpot A., Pressburger T., Underwood I., "A formal approach to domain-oriented software design environments", in: *KBSE*, 1994.

[32] Mann C., "Why software is so bad...and what's being done to fix it?", *Technology Review* (July/August 2002), http://www.technologyreview.com/articles/mann0702.asp.

[33] Manna Z., Waldinger R., "A deductive approach to program synthesis", *ACM Transactions on Programming Languages and Systems* **2** (1) (1980) 90–121.

[34] Manna Z., Waldinger R., "Fundamentals of Deductive Program Synthesis", *IEEE Transactions on Software Engineering* **18** (8) (1992) 674–704.

[35] Martelli A., Montanari U., "An efficient unification algorithm", *ACM Transactions on Programming Languages and Systems* **4** (2) (1982) 258–282.

[36] McConnell S., "Daily build and smoke test", *Best Practices IEEE Software* **13** (4) (1996), http://www.construx.com/stevemcc/.

[37] McDonald J., Anton J., SPECWARE—Producing software correct by construction, Kestrel Institute Technical Report KES.U.01.3., March 2001.

[38] McMillan K., *Symbolic Model Checking*, Kluwer Academic Publishers, Dordrecht, 1993.

[39] Moore J., *Piton: A Mechanically Verified Assembly-Level Language*, Kluwer Academic Publishers, Dordrecht, 1996.

[40] Mukherjee P., Wichmann B.A., STV: A case study in VDM, Technical report DITC 219/93, National Physical Laboratory, Teddington, UK, May 1993.

[41] Nissanke N., *Formal Specification Techniques and Applications*, Springer, London, 1999.

[42] Parnas D., "Using mathematical models in the inspection of critical software", in: M. Hinchey, J. Bowen (Eds.), *Applications of Formal Methods*, Prentice-Hall, London, 1995.

[43] Pettorossi A., Proietti M., "Transformation of logic programs: Foundations and techniques", *Journal of Logic Programming* **19** (20) (1994) 261–320.

[44] Reeves G., "What really happened on Mars?", http://research.microsoft.com/~mbj/ Mars_Pathfinder/Authoritative_Account.html, 1998.

[45] RTI Health, Social, and Economics Research, The Economic Impacts of Inadequate Infrastructure for Software Testing, Final Report, Prepared for National Institute of Standards and Technology, Acquisition and Assistance Division, Gathersburg, MD, May 2002.

[46] Rushby J., Formal methods and their role in the certification of critical systems, Technical Report CSL-95-1, SRI International.

[47] Sebesta R., *Concepts of Programming Languages*, 5th edn., Addison-Wesley, Boston, 2002.

[48] Shankar N., Owre S., Rushby J., The PVS proof checker, A Reference Manual, Technical Report SRI-CLS-92-12, SRI International, Menlo Park, CA, February 1993.

[49] Smith D., "KIDS: A semiautomatic program development system", *IEEE Transactions on Software Engineering* **16** (9) (1990) 1024–1043.

[50] Srivas M., Miller S., "Formal verification of the AAMP5 microprocessor", in: M. Hinchey, J. Bowen (Eds.), *Applications of Formal Methods*, Prentice-Hall, London, 1995.

[51] Sterling L., Shapiro E., *The Art of Prolog*, 2nd edn., MIT Press, Cambridge, MA, 1994.

[52] Visser E., Benaissa Z., Tolmach A., "Building program optimizers with rewriting strategies", in: *Proceedings of the 3rd ACM SIGPLAN International Conference on Functional Programming (ICFP'98)*, ACM Press, New York, September 1998, pp. 13–26.

[53] Visser E., "Strategic pattern matching", in: *Rewriting Techniques and Applications (RTA'99), Trento, Italy*, in: *Lecture Notes in Comput. Sci.*, Vol. 1631, 1999, pp. 30–44.

[54] Visser E., "A survey of rewriting strategies in program transformation systems", in: B. Gramlich, S. Lucas (Eds.), *Workshop on Reduction Strategies in Rewriting and Programming (WRS'01)*, in: *Electronic Notes in Theoretical Computer Science*, Vol. 57/2, Elsevier Science Publishers, Amsterdam, 2001.

[55] Ward M., "Abstracting a specification from code", *Journal of Software Maintenance: Research and Practice* **5** (1993) 101–122.

[56] Winter V., "An overview of HATS: A language independent high assurance transformation system", in: *Proceedings of the IEEE Symposium on Application-Specific Systems and Software Engineering Technology (ASSET), March 24–27*, 1999.

[57] Winter V., Kapur D., Berg R., "A refinement-based approach to developing software controllers for train systems", in: *Proceedings of the 2nd International Conference on High Integrity Software (HIS)*, November 1999.

[58] Zachary G., *Show-Stopper!: The Breakneck Race to Create Windows Nt and the Next Generation at Microsoft*, Free Press, 1994.

Bounded Model Checking[1]

ARMIN BIERE

Institute of Computer Systems
ETH Zurich, 8092 Zurich
Switzerland
biere@inf.ethz.ch

ALESSANDRO CIMATTI

Istituto per la Ricerca Scientifica e Technologica (IRST)
via Sommarive 18, 38055 Povo (TN)
Italy
cimatti@irst.itc.it

EDMUND M. CLARKE AND OFER STRICHMAN

Computer Science Department
Carnegie Mellon University
5000 Forbes Avenue
Pittsburgh, PA 15213
USA
{emc,ofers}@cs.cmu.edu

YUNSHAN ZHU

ATG, Synopsys, Inc.
700 East Middlefield Road
Mountain View, CA 94043
USA
yunshan@synopsys.com

[1] This research was sponsored by the Semiconductor Research Corporation (SRC) under contract no. 99-TJ-684, the National Science Foundation (NSF) under grant no. CCR-9803774, the Army Research Office (ARO) under grant DAAD19-01-1-0485, the Office of Naval Research (ONR), and the Naval Research Laboratory (NRL) under contract no. N00014-01-1-0796. The views and conclusions contained in this document are those of the author and should not be interpreted as representing the official policies, either expressed or implied, of SRC, ARO, NSF, ONR, NRL, the U.S. government or any other entity.

117

Abstract

Symbolic model checking with Binary Decision Diagrams (BDDs) has been successfully used in the last decade for formally verifying finite state systems such
as sequential circuits and protocols. Since its introduction in the beginning of
the 90's, it has been integrated in the quality assurance process of several major hardware companies. The main bottleneck of this method is that BDDs may
grow exponentially, and hence the amount of available memory restricts the size
of circuits that can be verified efficiently. In this article we survey a technique
called Bounded Model Checking (BMC), which uses a propositional SAT solver
rather than BDD manipulation techniques. Since its introduction in 1999, BMC
has been well received by the industry. It can find many logical errors in complex systems that can not be handled by competing techniques, and is therefore
widely perceived as a complementary technique to BDD-based model checking.
This observation is supported by several independent comparisons that have been
published in the last few years.

1. Introduction

Techniques for automatic formal verification of finite state transition systems have
developed in the last 12 years to the point where major chip design companies are beginning to integrate them in their normal quality assurance process. The most widely
used of these methods is called *Model Checking* [11,12]. In model checking, the
design to be verified is modeled as a finite state machine, and the specification is
formalized by writing *temporal logic* properties. The reachable states of the design
are then traversed in order to verify the properties. In case the property fails, a counterexample is generated in the form of a sequence of states. In general, properties
are classified to 'safety' and 'liveness' properties. While the former declares what
should not happen (or equivalently, what should always happen), the latter declares

what should eventually happen. A counterexample to safety properties is a trace of states, where the last state contradicts the property. A counterexample to liveness properties, in its simplest form, is a path to a loop that does not contain the desired state. Such a loop represents an infinite path that never reaches the specified state.

It is impossible to know whether the specification of a system is correct or complete—How can you know if what you wrote fully captures what you meant? As a result, there is no such thing as a 'correct system;' it is only possible to check whether a system satisfies its specification or not. Moreover, even the most advanced model checkers are unable to verify all the desired properties of a system in a reasonable amount of time, due to the immense state-spaces of such systems. Model checking is often used for finding logical errors ('falsification') rather than for proving that they do not exist ('verification'). Users of model checking tools typically consider it as complementary to the more traditional methods of testing and simulation, and not as an alternative. These tools are capable of finding errors that are not likely to be found by simulation. The reason for this is that unlike simulators, which examine a relatively small set of test cases, model checkers consider all possible behaviors or executions of the system. Also, the process of writing the temporal properties in a formal language can be very beneficial by itself, as it clarifies potential ambiguities in the specification.

The term Model Checking was coined by Clarke and Emerson [11] in the early eighties. The first model checking algorithms explicitly enumerated the reachable states of the system in order to check the correctness of a given specification. This restricted the capacity of model checkers to systems with a few million states. Since the number of states can grow exponentially in the number of variables, early implementations were only able to handle small designs and did not scale to examples with industrial complexity.

It was the introduction of *symbolic model checking* [9,15] that made the first breakthrough towards wide usage of these techniques. In symbolic model checking, sets of states are represented implicitly using Boolean functions. For example, assume that the behavior of some system is determined by the two variables v_1 and v_2, and that $(11, 01, 10)$ are the three combinations of values that can be assigned to these variables in any execution of this system. Rather than keeping and manipulating this explicit list of states (as was done in explicit model checking), it is more efficient to handle a Boolean function that represents this set, e.g., $v_1 \lor v_2$. Manipulating Boolean formulas can be done efficiently with Reduced Ordered Binary Decision Diagrams [8] (ROBDD, or BDD for short), a compact, canonical graph representation of Boolean functions. The process works roughly as follows:[2] The set of initial

---

[2]The exact details of this procedure depends on the property that is being verified. Here we describe the procedure for testing simple 'invariant' properties, which state that some proposition p has to hold invariantly in all reachable states. There is more than one way to perform this check.

states is represented as a BDD. The procedure then starts an iterative process, where at each step i, the set of states that can first be reached in i steps from an initial state are added to the BDD. At each such step, the set of new states is intersected with the set of states that satisfy the negation of the property. If the resulting set is non-empty, it means that an error has been detected. This process terminates when the set of newly added states is empty or a an error is found. The first case indicates that the property holds, because no reachable state contradicts it. In the latter case, the model checker prints a counterexample. Note that termination is guaranteed, since there are only finitely many states.

The combination of symbolic model checking with BDDs [15,20], pushed the barrier to systems with 10^{20} states and more [9]. Combining certain, mostly manual, abstraction techniques into this process pushed the bound even further. For the first time a significant number of realistic systems could be verified, which resulted in a gradual adoption of these procedures to the industry. Companies like Intel and IBM started developing their own in-house model checkers, first as experimental projects, and later as one more component in their overall quality verification process of their chip designs. Intel has invested significantly in this technology especially after the famous Pentium bug a few years ago.

The bottleneck of these methods is the amount of memory that is required for storing and manipulating BDDs. The Boolean functions required to represent the set of states can grow exponentially. Although numerous techniques such as decomposition, abstraction and various reductions have been proposed through the years to tackle this problem, full verification of many designs is still beyond the capacity of BDD based symbolic model checkers.

The technique that we describe in this article, called *Bounded Model Checking* (BMC), was first proposed by Biere et al. in 1999 [5]. It does not solve the complexity problem of model checking, since it still relies on an exponential procedure and hence is limited in its capacity. But experiments have shown that it can solve many cases that cannot be solved by BDD-based techniques. The converse is also true: there are problems that are better solved by BDD-based techniques. BMC also has the disadvantage of not being able to prove the absence of errors, in most realistic cases, as we will later explain. Therefore BMC joins the arsenal of automatic verification tools but does not replace any of them.

The basic idea in BMC is to search for a counterexample in executions whose length is bounded by some integer k. If no bug is found then one increases k until either a bug is found, the problem becomes intractable, or some pre-known upper bound is reached (this bound is called the *Completeness Threshold* of the design. We will elaborate on this point in Section 5). The BMC problem can be efficiently reduced to a propositional satisfiability problem, and can therefore be solved by SAT methods rather than BDDs. SAT procedures do not suffer from the space explosion problem of BDD-based methods. Modern SAT solvers can handle propositional satisfiability problems with hundreds of thousands of variables or more.

Thus, although BMC aims at solving the same problem as traditional BDD-based symbolic model checking, it has two unique characteristics: first, the user has to provide a bound on the number of cycles that should be explored, which implies that the method is incomplete if the bound is not high enough. Second, it uses SAT techniques rather than BDDs. Experiments with this idea showed that if k is small enough (typically not more than 60 to 80 cycles, depending on the model itself and the SAT solver), it outperforms BDD-based techniques. Also, experiments have shown that there is little correlation between what problems are hard for SAT and what problems are hard for BDD based techniques. Therefore, the classes of problems that are known to be hard for BDDs, can many times be solved with SAT. If the SAT checkers are tuned to take advantage of the unique structure of the formulas resulting from BMC, this method improves even further [27]. A research published by Intel [14] showed that BMC has advantages in both capacity and productivity over BDD-based symbolic model checkers, when applied to typical designs taken from Pentium-4™. The improved productivity results from the fact that normally BDD based techniques need more manual guidance in order to optimize their performance. These and other published results with similar conclusions led most relevant companies, only three years after the introduction of BMC, to adopt it as a complementary technique to BDD-based symbolic model checking.

The rest of the article is structured as follows. In the next section we give a technical introduction to model checking and to the temporal logic that is used for expressing the properties. In Section 3 we describe the bounded model checking problem. In the following section we describe the reduction of the BMC problem to Boolean satisfiability, including a detailed example. In Section 5 we describe several methods for achieving completeness with BMC. In Section 6 we describe some of the essential techniques underlying modern SAT solvers, and in Section 7 we quote several experiments carried out by different groups, both from academia and industry, that compare these techniques to state of the art BDD-based techniques. We survey related work and detail our conclusions from the experiments in Section 8.

2. Model Checking

Model checking as a verification technique has three fundamental features. First, it is automatic; It does not rely on complicated interaction with the user for incremental property proving. If a property does not hold, the model checker generates a counterexample trace automatically. Second, the systems being checked are assumed to be finite.[3] Typical examples of finite systems, for which model checking has successfully been applied, are digital sequential circuits and communication protocols. Finally, temporal logic is used for specifying the system properties. Thus, model checking can be summarized as an algorithmic technique for checking temporal properties of finite systems.

As the reader may have deduced from the terminology we used in the introduction, we do not distinguish between the terms *design*, *system*, and *model*. An engineer working on real designs has to use a syntactic representation in a programming or hardware description language. Since we are only considering finite systems, the semantics of the engineer's design is usually some sort of a finite automaton. Independent of the concrete design language, this finite automaton can be represented by a *Kripke structure*, which is the standard representation of models in the model checking literature. It has its origin in modal logics, the generalization of temporal logics.

Formally, a Kripke structure M is a quadruple $M = (S, I, T, L)$ where S is the set of states, $I \subseteq S$ is the set of initial states, $T \subseteq S \times S$ is the transition relation and $L : S \to P(A)$ is the labeling function, where A is the set of atomic propositions, and $P(A)$ denotes the powerset over A. Labeling is a way to attach observations to the system: for a state $s \in S$ the set $L(s)$ is made of the atomic propositions that *hold* in s.

The notion of a Kripke structure is only a vehicle for illustrating the algorithms. It captures the semantics of the system under investigation. For a concrete design language, the process of extracting a Kripke structure from a given syntactic representation may not be that easy. In particular, the size of the system description and the size of the state space can be very different. For example, if we model a sequential circuit with a netlist of gates and flip-flops then the state space can be exponentially larger than the system description. A circuit implementing an n-bit counter illustrates this ratio: it can easily be implemented with $O(n)$ gates and $O(n)$ flip-flops, though the state space of this counter is 2^n. The exponential growth in the number of states poses the main challenge to model checking. This is also known as the *state explosion problem*.

The next step is to define the sequential behavior of a Kripke structure M. For this purpose we use *paths*. Each path π in M is a sequence $\pi = (s_0, s_1, \ldots)$ of states, given in an order that respects the transition relation of M. That is, $T(s_i, s_{i+1})$ for all $0 \leqslant i < |\pi| - 1$. If $I(s_0)$, i.e., s_0 is an initial state, then we say that the path is *initialized*. The length $|\pi|$ of π can either be finite or infinite. Note that in general some of the states may not be reachable, i.e., no initialized path leads to them. For $i <$

---

[3]There is an ongoing interest in generalizing model checking algorithms to infinite systems, for example, by including real-time, or using abstraction techniques. In this article we will restrict the discussion to finite systems.

	process A		**process** B
	forever		**forever**
A.pc = 0	**wait for** B.pc = 0	B.pc = 0	**wait for** A.pc = 0
A.pc = 1	*access shared resource*	B.pc = 1	*access shared resource*
	end forever		**end forever**
	end process		**end process**

FIG. 1. Pseudo code for two processes A and B competing for a shared resource.

$|\pi|$ we denote by $\pi(i)$ the ith state s_i in the sequence and by $\pi_i = (s_i, s_{i+1}, \ldots)$ the suffix of π starting with state s_i. To simplify some technical arguments we assume that the set of initial states is non-empty. For the same reason we assume that the transition relation is *total*, i.e., each state has a successor state: for all $s \in S$ there exists $t \in S$ with $T(s, t)$.

As an example, consider the mutual exclusion problem of two processes competing for a shared resource. Pseudo code for this example can be found in Fig. 1. We assume that the processes are executed on a single computing unit in an interleaved manner. The **wait** statement puts a process into sleep. When all processes are asleep the scheduler tries to find a waiting condition which holds and reactivates the corresponding process. If all the waiting conditions are false the system stalls.

On an abstract level, each process has two program counter positions 0 and 1 with 1 representing the critical section. A process may only access the shared resource in the critical section of its program. A state of the system is a pair of program counters and can be encoded as a binary vector $s \in S = \{0, 1\}^2$ of length two. Thus $S = \{0, 1\}^2$ is the set of states of the system. We assume that both processes start at program counter position 0, which implies that the set of initial states I consists of the single state represented by the Boolean vector 00. The transition relation consists of several possible transitions, according to the following two rules: the next state s' is the initial state 00 unless the current state is already the initial state; The initial state can transition forth and back to both 01 and 10. Thus, the transition relation $T \subseteq S^2 = \{0, 1\}^4$ can be represented as the following set of bit strings:

$$\{0100, 1000, 1100, 0001, 0010\}.$$

A graphical representation of this example in form of a Kripke structure is shown in Fig. 2. The initial state has an incoming edge without a source. The other edges correspond to one of the five transitions. Note that unreachable states, such as state 11 in this example, can only be removed after a *reachability analysis* has marked all reachable states. Accordingly the sequence $11, 00, 10, \ldots$ is a valid path of the Kripke structure, but it is not initialized, since initialized paths start with the state 00. An example of an initialized path is the sequence $00, 01, 00, 10, 00, 01, \ldots$ where each process takes its turn to enter the critical region after the other process has left it.

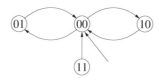

FIG. 2. A Kripke structure for two processes that preserve mutual exclusion.

Our example system is *safe* in the sense that the two processes obey the mutual exclusion property: at most one process can be in its critical region. A negative formulation of this property is that the state in which both processes are in their critical region is not reachable. Thus a simple model checking algorithm to check safety properties is to build the state transition graph and enumerate all reachable states through a graph search, starting from the set of initial states. Each visited state is analyzed in order to check whether it violates the safety property.

Now, assume that we add a faulty transition from 10 to 11. A depth first search, starting from the initial state 00 visiting 10 and then reaching 11 will show that the *bad* state 11 is reachable and thus the safety property fails. This path is a counterexample to the safety property that can help the user to debug the system.

What we have discussed so far is a typical *explicit* model checking algorithm for simple safety properties. It can be refined by building the Kripke structure on-the-fly: only after a state of the system is visited for the first time, the set of transitions is generated leaving this state. Once a bad state is found, the process terminates. This technique is particularly useful if the number of reachable states is much smaller than $|S|$, the number of all states, which is often the case in practice.

Recall that safety properties describe invariants of a system, that is, that something bad does not happen. As we have seen, these properties can be checked by reachability analysis, i.e., by searching through the states graph and checking that each visited state does not violate the invariant. Also recall that in addition to safety properties, it is sometimes desirable to use liveness properties in order to check whether something good will eventually happen. In the mutual exclusion example, a natural question would be to ask whether each process will eventually enter its critical region. For the first process this means that the state 01 is eventually reached. More complicated liveness properties can specify repeatedly inevitable behavior, such as 'a request always has to be acknowledged.' To capture this nesting and mutual dependency of properties, temporal logic is used as a specification language.

Temporal logic is an extension of classical logic. In this article we concentrate on Propositional Linear Temporal Logic (PLTL, or LTL for short) as an extension of propositional logic. From propositional logic LTL inherits Boolean variables and Boolean operators such as negation ¬, conjunction ∧, implication →, etc. In addition

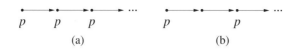

FIG. 3. Validity of next time operator in the formula $\mathbf{X}p$ along a path.

to the Boolean connectives, LTL has temporal operators. First, there is the *next time* operator $\mathbf{X}$. The formula $\mathbf{X}p$ specifies that property p holds at the next time step.

In Fig. 3(a) a path is shown for which $\mathbf{X}p$ holds. Each state is labeled with the atomic properties that hold in it. Fig. 3(b) depicts a path for which $\mathbf{X}p$ does not hold, because p holds in the first state but not in the next, second state. Now we can use this operator to build larger temporal formulas. For instance, $p \wedge \mathbf{X}\neg p$ holds iff p holds in the first state and p does not hold in the second. As usual $\neg$ is the Boolean negation operator. This formula is true for the path on Fig. 3(b) and fails for the path on Fig. 3(a). By nesting the operator $\mathbf{X}$ we can specify the behavior of the system up to a certain depth. For instance, the formula $\mathbf{X}\mathbf{X}p$ holds for both paths.

The next class of temporal operators that we discuss, allows specifying repeated unbounded behavior along an infinite path. The *Globally* operator $\mathbf{G}$ is used for safety properties. A formula $\mathbf{G}p$ *holds* along a path if p holds in all states of the path. Thus, it fails for the path in Fig. 3(b), since p does not hold in the second state. The safety property for our earlier example, the Kripke structure of Fig. 2, can be specified as $\mathbf{G}\neg(c_1 \wedge c_2)$, where c_i labels the states where process i is in its critical section. It literally can be translated into English as follows: for all states it is not the case that both c_1 and c_2 are true.

If *all* initialized paths of a Kripke structure satisfy a property, we say that the property holds for the Kripke structure. For instance, by making the state 11 in Fig. 2 an initial state, each path starting at 11 would be initialized and would violate $\mathbf{G}\neg(c_1 \wedge c_2)$ already in its first state. However since in our model 11 is not an initial state the property holds for the Kripke structure.

Finally we look at liveness properties. The simplest liveness operator is $\mathbf{F}$, the *Finally* operator. The formula $\mathbf{F}p$ holds along a path if p holds somewhere on the path. Equivalently, it fails to hold if p stays unsatisfied along the whole path. For instance, $\mathbf{F}p$ trivially holds in both paths of Fig. 3 since p is already satisfied in the first state. Similarly $\mathbf{F}\neg p$ holds for the path in Fig. 3(b), because p does not hold in the second state.

The liveness property for Fig. 2, which says that the first process will eventually reach its critical section, can be formalized as $\mathbf{F}c_1$. Since the system may loop between the initial state and the state 10 on the right, never reaching 01, this property does not hold. The initialized infinite path that starts with 00 and then alternates between 00 and 10 is a counterexample.

Now we can start to build more sophisticated specifications. The request/acknowledge property mentioned above is formulated as $\mathbf{G}(r \rightarrow \mathbf{F}a)$, where r and a are atomic propositions labeling states where a request and an acknowledge occurs, respectively. The same idea can be used to specify that a certain sequence of actions a_1, a_2, a_3 has to follow a guard $g : \mathbf{G}(g \rightarrow \mathbf{F}(a_1 \wedge \mathbf{F}(a_2 \wedge \mathbf{F}a_3)))$. Note that there may be an arbitrary, finite time interval (possibly empty) between the actions.

In this informal introduction to temporal logic, we will avoid a detailed explanation of the binary temporal operators *Until* (**U**) and *Release* (**R**). The reader is referred to [12] for more details. Also note that in the literature one can find an alternative notation for temporal operators, such as $\bigcirc p$ for $\mathbf{X}p$, $\Diamond p$ for $\mathbf{F}p$ and $\square p$ for $\mathbf{G}p$.

The formal semantics of temporal formulas is defined with respect to paths of a Kripke structure. Let π be an infinite path of a Kripke structure M and let f be a temporal formula. We define recursively when f holds on π, written $\pi \models f$:

$$\begin{array}{lll}
\pi \models p & \text{iff} & p \in L\big(\pi(0)\big), \\
\pi \models \neg f & \text{iff} & \pi \not\models f, \\
\pi \models f \wedge g & \text{iff} & \pi \models f \text{ and } \pi \models g, \\
\pi \models \mathbf{X}f & \text{iff} & \pi_1 \models f, \\
\pi \models \mathbf{G}f & \text{iff} & \pi_i \models f \quad \text{for all } i \geqslant 0, \\
\pi \models \mathbf{F}f & \text{iff} & \pi_i \models f \quad \text{for some } i \geqslant 0, \\
\pi \models f \, \mathbf{U}g & \text{iff} & \pi_i \models g \quad \text{for some } i \geqslant 0 \text{ and } \pi_j \models f \text{ for all } 0 \leqslant j < i, \\
\pi \models f \, \mathbf{R}g & \text{iff} & \pi_i \models g \quad \text{if for all } j < i, \; \pi_j \not\models f.
\end{array}$$

The semantics of the other Boolean operators such as disjunction and implication can be inferred from the above definition. As mentioned above we say that a temporal formula f holds for a Kripke structure M, written $M \models f$, iff $\pi \models f$ for all initialized paths π of M. Finally, we say that two temporal formulas f and g are *equivalent*, written $f \equiv g$ iff $M \models f \leftrightarrow M \models g$ for all Kripke structures M. With this notion, the semantics imply that $\neg \mathbf{F} \neg p \equiv \mathbf{G}p$. Thus, $\mathbf{F}$ and $\mathbf{G}$ are dual operators.

The standard technique for model checking LTL [19] is to compute the product of the Kripke structure with an automaton that represents the negation of the property (this automaton captures exactly the execution sequences that violate the LTL formula). Emptiness of the product automaton is an evidence of the correctness of the property. More details about this procedure can be found in [12].

3. Bounded Model Checking

The original motivation of bounded model checking was to leverage the success of SAT in solving Boolean formulas to model checking. During the last few years there has been a tremendous increase in reasoning power of SAT solvers. They can now handle instances with hundreds of thousands of variables and millions of clauses (we will elaborate more on how these solvers work in Section 6). Symbolic model checkers with BDDs, on the other hand, can check systems with no more than a few hundred latches. Though clearly the number of latches and the number of variables cannot be compared directly, it seemed plausible that solving model checking with SAT could benefit the former.

A similar approach has been taken in tackling the planning problem in Artificial Intelligence [18]. Classical planning problems seek for a plan, i.e., a sequence of steps, to perform some task (e.g., position cubes one above the other in descending size under certain constraints on the intermediate states). As in BMC, the search for a plan is restricted to paths with some predetermined bound. The possible plans in a given bound are described by a SAT instance, which is polynomial in the original planning problem and the bound. Compared to model checking, deterministic planning is only concerned with simple safety properties: whether and how the goal state can be reached. In model checking we want to check liveness properties and nested temporal properties as well.

Since LTL formulas are defined over *all* paths, finding counterexamples corresponds to the question whether there *exists* a trace that contradicts them. If we find such a trace, we call it a *witness* for the property. For example, a counterexample to $M \models \mathbf{G}p$ corresponds to the question whether there exists a witness to $\mathbf{F}\neg p$. For clarity of presentation we will use *path quantifiers* $\mathbf{E}$ and $\mathbf{A}$ to denote whether the LTL formula is expected to be correct over all paths or only over some path. In other words, $M \models \mathbf{A}f$ means that M satisfies f over all initialized paths, and $M \models \mathbf{E}f$ means that there exists an initialized path in M that satisfies f. We will assume that the formula is given in *negation normal form* (NNF), in which negations are only allowed to occur in front of atomic propositions. Every LTL formula can be transformed to this form by using the duality of LTL operators and De-Morgan's laws.

The basic idea of bounded model checking, as was explained before, is to consider only a finite prefix of a path that may be a witness to an existential model checking problem. We restrict the length of the prefix by some bound k. In practice, we progressively increase the bound, looking for witnesses in longer and longer traces.

A crucial observation is that, though the prefix of a path is finite, it still might represent an infinite path if there is a *back loop* from the last state of the prefix to any of the previous states, as in Fig. 4(b). If there is no such back loop, as in Fig. 4(a), then the prefix does not say anything about the infinite behavior of the path beyond state s_k. For instance, only a prefix with a back loop can represent a witness for $\mathbf{G}p$. Even if p holds along all the states from s_0 to s_k, but there is no back loop from s_k

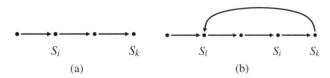

$$S_i \qquad\qquad S_k \qquad\qquad S_l \qquad\qquad S_i \quad S_k$$

(a)   (b)

FIG. 4. The two cases for a *bounded* path. (a) No loop, (b) (k, l)-loop.

to a previous state, we cannot conclude that we have found a witness for **G**p, since p might not hold at s_{k+1}.

DEFINITION 1. For $l \leqslant k$ we call a path π a (k, l)-loop if $T(\pi(k), \pi(l))$ and $\pi = u \cdot v^\omega$ with $u = (\pi(0), \ldots, \pi(l-1))$ and $v = (\pi(l), \ldots, \pi(k))$.[4] We call π a k-loop if there exists $k \geqslant l \geqslant 0$ for which π is a (k, l)-loop.

We will use the notion of k-loops in order to define the *bounded semantics* of model checking, i.e., semantics of model checking under bounded traces. The bounded semantics is an approximation to the unbounded semantics, which will allow us to define the bounded model checking problem. In the next section we will give a translation of a bounded model checking problem into a satisfiability problem.

In the bounded semantics we only consider a finite prefix of a path. In particular, we only use the first $k + 1$ states $(s_0, \ldots, s_k)$ of a path to determine the validity of a formula along that path. If a path is a k-loop then we simply maintain the original LTL semantics, since all the information about this (infinite) path is contained in the prefix of length k.

DEFINITION 2 (*Bounded semantics for a loop*). Let $k \geqslant 0$ and π be a k-loop. Then an LTL formula f is valid along the path π with bound k (in symbols $\pi \models_k f$) iff $\pi \models f$.

We now consider the case where π is not a k-loop. The formula $f := \mathbf{F}p$ is valid along π in the *unbounded* semantics if we can find an index $i \geqslant 0$ such that p is valid along the suffix π_i of π. In the bounded semantics the $(k + 1)$th state $\pi(k)$ does not have a successor. Therefore, unlike the unbounded case, we cannot define the bounded semantics recursively over *suffixes* (e.g., π_i) of π. We therefore introduce the notation $\pi \models_k^i f$, where i is the current position in the prefix of π, which means that the suffix π_i of π satisfies f, i.e., $\pi \models_k^i f$ implies $\pi_i \models f$.

DEFINITION 3 (*Bounded semantics without a loop*). Let $k \geqslant 0$, and let π be a path that is *not* a k-loop. Then an LTL formula f is *valid along π with bound k* (in

---

[4]The notation v^ω represents an infinite repetition of v.

symbols $\pi \models_k f$) iff $\pi \models_k^0 f$ where

$$\pi \models_k^i p \quad \text{iff} \quad p \in L\big(\pi(i)\big),$$

$$\pi \models_k^i f \wedge g \quad \text{iff} \quad \pi \models_k^i f \text{ and } \pi \models_k^i g,$$

$$\pi \models_k^i \mathbf{G} f \quad \text{is always false,}$$

$$\pi \models_k^i \mathbf{X} f \quad \text{iff} \quad i < k \text{ and } \pi \models_k^{i+1} f,$$

$$\pi \models_k^i f \mathbf{U} g \quad \text{iff} \quad \exists j,\ i \leqslant j \leqslant k,\ \pi \models_k^j g \text{ and } \forall n,\ i \leqslant n < j,\ \pi \models_k^n f,$$

$$\pi \models_k^i f \mathbf{R} g \quad \text{iff} \quad \exists j,\ i \leqslant j \leqslant k,\ \pi \models_k^j f \text{ and } \forall n,\ i \leqslant n < j,\ \pi \models_k^n g,$$

$$\pi \models_k^i \neg p \quad \text{iff} \quad p \notin L\big(\pi(i)\big),$$

$$\pi \models_k^i f \vee g \quad \text{iff} \quad \pi \models_k^i f \text{ or } \pi \models_k^i g,$$

$$\pi \models_k^i \mathbf{F} f \quad \text{iff} \quad \exists j,\ i \leqslant j \leqslant k,\ \pi \models_k^j f.$$

Note that if π is not a k-loop, then we say that $\mathbf{G} f$ is not valid along π in the bounded semantics with bound k since f might not hold along π_{k+1}. These constraints imply that for the bounded semantics the duality between $\mathbf{G}$ and $\mathbf{F}$ ($\neg \mathbf{F} f \equiv \mathbf{G} \neg f$) no longer holds.

Now we describe how the existential model checking problem ($M \models \mathbf{E} f$) can be reduced to a *bounded* existential model checking problem ($M \models_k \mathbf{E} f$). The basis for this reduction lies in the following two lemmas.

LEMMA 1. *Let f be an LTL formula and π a path, then $\pi \models_k f \Rightarrow \pi \models f$.*

LEMMA 2. *Let f be an LTL formula and M a Kripke structure. If $M \models \mathbf{E} f$ then there exists $k \geqslant 0$ with $M \models_k \mathbf{E} f$.*

Based on Lemmas 1 and 2, we can now state the main theorem of this section. Informally, Theorem 1 says that if we take a sufficiently high bound, then the bounded and unbounded semantics are equivalent.

THEOREM 1. *Let f be an LTL formula and M be a Kripke structure. Then $M \models \mathbf{E} f$ iff there exists $k \geqslant 0$ s.t. $M \models_k \mathbf{E} f$.*

4. Reducing Bounded Model Checking to SAT

In the previous section we defined the semantics for bounded model checking. We now show how to reduce bounded model checking to propositional satisfiability.

This reduction enables us to use efficient propositional SAT solvers to perform model checking.

Given a Kripke structure M, an LTL formula f and a bound k, we will construct a propositional formula $[\![M, f]\!]_k$. Let $s_0, \ldots, s_k$ be a finite sequence of states on a path π. Each s_i represents a state at time step i and consists of an assignment of truth values to the set of state variables. The formula $[\![M, f]\!]_k$ encodes constraints on $s_0, \ldots, s_k$ such that $[\![M, f]\!]_k$ is satisfiable iff π is a witness for f. The definition of formula $[\![M, f]\!]_k$ will be presented as three separate components. We first define a propositional formula $[\![M]\!]_k$ that constrains $s_0, \ldots, s_k$ to be a valid path starting from an initial state. We then define the *loop condition*, which is a propositional formula that is evaluated to true only if the path π contains a loop. Finally, we define a propositional formula that constrains π to satisfy f.

DEFINITION 4 (*Unfolding of the transition relation*). For a Kripke structure $M, k \geqslant 0$

$$[\![M]\!]_k := I(s_0) \wedge \bigwedge_{i=0}^{k-1} T(s_i, s_{i+1}).$$

The translation of an LTL formula depends on the shape of the path π. We define the propositional formula $_lL_k$ to be true if and only if there is a transition from state s_k to state s_l. By definition, $_lL_k$ is equal to $T(s_k, s_l)$. We use $_lL_k$ to define the loop condition L_k:

DEFINITION 5 (*Loop condition*). The loop condition L_k is true if and only if there exists a back loop from state s_k to a previous state or to itself: $L_k := \bigvee_{l=0}^{k} {}_lL_k$.

Depending on whether a path is a k-loop (see Fig. 4), we have two different translations of a temporal formula f. First we consider the case where the path is a k-loop. We give a recursive translation of an LTL formula f for a k-loop path π. The translation of f recurses over its subterms and the states in π. The intermediate formula $_l[\![\cdot]\!]_k^i$ depends on three parameters: l, k and i. We use l for the start position of the loop, k for the bound, and i for the current position in π.

DEFINITION 6 (*Successor in a loop*). Let k, l and i be non-negative integers s.t. $l, i \leqslant k$. Define the successor $\mathrm{succ}(i)$ of i in a (k, l)-loop as $\mathrm{succ}(i) := i + 1$ for $i < k$ and $\mathrm{succ}(i) := l$ for $i = k$.

DEFINITION 7 (*Translation of an LTL formula for a loop*). Let f be an LTL formula, $k, l, i \geqslant 0$, with $l, i \leqslant k$.

$$_l[\![p]\!]_k^i := p(s_i),$$
$$_l[\![\neg p]\!]_k^i := \neg p(s_i),$$
$$_l[\![f \vee g]\!]_k^i := {_l[\![f]\!]_k^i} \vee {_l[\![g]\!]_k^i},$$
$$_l[\![f \wedge g]\!]_k^i := {_l[\![f]\!]_k^i} \wedge {_l[\![g]\!]_k^i},$$
$$_l[\![\mathbf{G}f]\!]_k^i := {_l[\![f]\!]_k^i} \wedge {_l[\![\mathbf{G}f]\!]_k^{\mathrm{succ}(i)}},$$
$$_l[\![\mathbf{F}f]\!]_k^i := {_l[\![f]\!]_k^i} \vee {_l[\![\mathbf{F}f]\!]_k^{\mathrm{succ}(i)}},$$
$$_l[\![f \mathbf{U}g]\!]_k^i := {_l[\![g]\!]_k^i} \vee \left({_l[\![f]\!]_k^i} \wedge {_l[\![f \mathbf{U}g]\!]_k^{\mathrm{succ}(i)}}\right),$$
$$_l[\![f \mathbf{R}g]\!]_k^i := {_l[\![g]\!]_k^i} \wedge \left({_l[\![f]\!]_k^i} \vee {_l[\![f \mathbf{R}g]\!]_k^{\mathrm{succ}(i)}}\right),$$
$$_l[\![\mathbf{X}f]\!]_k^i := {_l[\![f]\!]_k^{\mathrm{succ}(i)}}.$$

The translation in Definition 7 is linear with respect to the size of f and bound k if subterms are shared. A common technique for sharing subterms in propositional logic is to introduce new Boolean variables for subterms. Consider, for example, the formula $(a \wedge b) \vee (c \rightarrow (a \wedge b))$. We introduce a new variable x for the subterm $a \wedge b$, and transform the original formula into $(x \vee (c \rightarrow x)) \wedge (x \leftrightarrow (a \wedge b))$. The transformation clearly preserves satisfiability.

For the translation presented in Definition 7, a new propositional variable is introduced for each intermediate formula $_l[\![h]\!]_k^i$, where h is a subterm of the LTL formula f and i ranges from 0 to k. The total number of new variables is $O(|f| \times k)$, where $|f|$ denotes the size of f. The size of the propositional formula $_l[\![f]\!]_k^0$ is also $O(|f| \times k)$.

For the case where π is not a k-loop, the translation can be treated as a special case of the k-loop translation. For Kripke structures with total transition relations, every finite path π can be extended to an infinite one. Since the property of the path beyond state s_k is unknown, we make a conservative approximation and assume all properties beyond s_k are false.

DEFINITION 8 (*Translation of an LTL formula without a loop*).
Inductive case: $\forall i \leqslant k$

$$[\![p]\!]_k^i := p(s_i),$$
$$[\![\neg p]\!]_k^i := \neg p(s_i),$$
$$[\![f \vee g]\!]_k^i := [\![f]\!]_k^i \vee [\![g]\!]_k^i,$$
$$[\![f \wedge g]\!]_k^i := [\![f]\!]_k^i \wedge [\![g]\!]_k^i,$$

$$[\![\mathbf{G}f]\!]_k^i := [\![f]\!]_k^i \wedge [\![\mathbf{G}f]\!]_k^{i+1},$$
$$[\![\mathbf{F}f]\!]_k^i := [\![f]\!]_k^i \vee [\![\mathbf{F}f]\!]_k^{i+1},$$
$$[\![f\,\mathbf{U}g]\!]_k^i := [\![g]\!]_k^i \vee \left([\![f]\!]_k^i \wedge [\![f\,\mathbf{U}g]\!]_k^{i+1}\right),$$
$$[\![f\,\mathbf{R}g]\!]_k^i := [\![g]\!]_k^i \wedge \left([\![f]\!]_k^i \vee [\![f\,\mathbf{R}g]\!]_k^{i+1}\right),$$
$$[\![\mathbf{X}f]\!]_k^i := [\![f]\!]_k^{i+1}.$$

Base case:

$$[\![f]\!]_k^{k+1} := 0.$$

Combining all components, the encoding of a bounded model checking problem in propositional logic is defined as follows.

DEFINITION 9 (*General translation*). Let f be an LTL formula, M a Kripke structure and $k \geqslant 0$

$$[\![M,f]\!]_k := [\![M]\!]_k \wedge \left((\neg L_k \wedge [\![f]\!]_k^0) \vee \bigvee_{l=0}^{k} ({}_l L_k \wedge {}_l[\![f]\!]_k^0) \right).$$

The left side of the disjunction is the case where there is no back loop and the translation without a loop is used. The right side represent all possible starting points l of a loop, and the translation for a (k, l)-loop is conjoined with the corresponding ${}_l L_k$ loop condition. The size of $[\![M, f]\!]_k$ is $O(|f| \times k \times |M|)$, where $|M|$ represents the size of the syntactic description of the initial state I and the transition relation T.

The translation scheme guarantees the following theorem, which we state without proof:

THEOREM 2. $[\![M, f]\!]_k$ *is satisfiable iff* $M \models_k \mathbf{E}f$.

Thus, the reduction of bounded model checking to SAT is sound and complete with respect to the bounded semantics.

EXAMPLE 1. Let us consider the mutual exclusion example in Fig. 2. Each state s of the system M is represented by two bit variables. We use $s[1]$ for the high bit and $s[0]$ for the low bit.

The initial state is represented as follows,

$$I(s) := \neg s[1] \wedge \neg s[0].$$

The transition relation is represented as follows,

$$T(s, s') := \left(\neg s[1] \wedge \left(s[0] \leftrightarrow \neg s'[0]\right)\right) \vee \left(\neg s[0] \wedge \left(s[1] \leftrightarrow \neg s'[1]\right)\right)$$
$$\vee \left(s[0] \wedge s[1] \wedge \neg s'[1] \wedge \neg s'[0]\right).$$

We now add a faulty transition from state 10 to state 11. We denote by T_f the new faulty transition relation.

$$T_f(s, s') := T(s, s') \vee \left(s[1] \wedge \neg s[0] \wedge s'[1] \wedge s'[0]\right).$$

Consider the safety property that at most one process can be in the critical region at any time. The property can be represented as $\mathbf{G} \neg p$, where p is $s[1] \wedge s[0]$. Using BMC, we attempt to find a counterexample of the property, or, in other words, look for a witness for $\mathbf{F} p$. The existence of such a witness indicates that the mutual exclusion property is violated by M. If, on the other hand, no such witness can be found, it means that this property holds up to the given bound.

Let us consider a case where the bound $k = 2$. Unrolling the transition relation results in the following formula:

$$[\![M]\!]_2 := I(s_0) \wedge T_f(s_0, s_1) \wedge T_f(s_1, s_2).$$

The loop condition is:

$$L_2 := \bigvee_{l=0}^{2} T_f(s_2, s_l).$$

The translation for paths without loops is:

$$[\![\mathbf{F}p]\!]_2^0 := p(s_0) \vee [\![\mathbf{F}p]\!]_2^1, \qquad [\![\mathbf{F}p]\!]_2^1 := p(s_1) \vee [\![\mathbf{F}p]\!]_2^2,$$
$$[\![\mathbf{F}p]\!]_2^2 := p(s_2) \vee [\![\mathbf{F}p]\!]_2^3, \qquad [\![\mathbf{F}p]\!]_2^3 := 0.$$

We can introduce a new variable for each intermediate formula $[\![\mathbf{F}p]\!]_2^i$. Alternatively, we can substitute all intermediate terms and obtain the following formula.

$$[\![\mathbf{F}p]\!]_2^0 := p(s_0) \vee p(s_1) \vee p(s_2).$$

The translation with loops can be done similarly. Putting everything together we get the following Boolean formula:

$$[\![M, \mathbf{F}p]\!]_2 := [\![M]\!]_2 \wedge \left(\left(\neg L_2 \wedge [\![\mathbf{F}p]\!]_2^0\right) \vee \bigvee_{l=0}^{2} \left({}_l L_2 \wedge_l [\![\mathbf{F}p]\!]_2^0\right) \right). \tag{1}$$

Since a finite path to a bad state is sufficient for falsifying a safety property, the loop condition in the above formula may be omitted. This will result in the following formula:

$$[\![M, \mathbf{F}p]\!]_2 := [\![M]\!]_2 \wedge [\![\mathbf{F}p]\!]_2^0$$

$$= I(s_0) \wedge T_f(s_0, s_1) \wedge T_f(s_1, s_2) \wedge \big(p(s_0) \vee p(s_1) \vee p(s_2)\big).$$

The assignment 00, 10, 11 satisfies $[\![M, \mathbf{F}p]\!]_2$. This assignment corresponds to a path from the initial state to the state 11 that violates the mutual exclusion property.

5. Techniques for Completeness

Given a model checking problem $M \models \mathbf{E}f$, a typical application of BMC starts at bound 0 and increments the bound until a witness is found. This represents a partial decision procedure for model checking problems. If $M \models \mathbf{E}f$, a witness of finite length k exists, and the procedure terminates at length k. If $M \not\models \mathbf{E}f$, however, the outlined procedure does not terminate. Although the strength of BMC is in detection of errors, it is desirable to build a complete decision procedure based on BMC for obvious reasons. For example, BMC may be used to clear a module level proof obligation which may be as assumption for another module. A missed counterexample in a single module may have the unpleasant consequence of breaking the entire proof. In such compositional reasoning environments, completeness becomes particularly important.

In this section, we will highlight three techniques for achieving completeness with BMC. For unnested properties such as $\mathbf{G}p$ and $\mathbf{F}p$, we determine in Section 5.1 the maximum bound k that the BMC formula should be checked with in order to guarantee that the property holds. This upper bound is called the Completeness Threshold. For liveness properties, we show an alternative path to completeness in Section 5.2. The alternative method is based on a semi-decision procedure for $\mathbf{AF}p$ combined with a semi decision procedure for $\mathbf{EG}p$. Finally, in Section 5.3, we show how for safety properties completeness can be achieved with induction based on strengthening inductive invariants.

5.1 The Completeness Threshold

For every finite state system M, a property p, and a given translation scheme, there exists a number $\mathcal{CT}$, such that the absence of errors up to cycle $\mathcal{CT}$ proves that $M \models p$. We call $\mathcal{CT}$ the *Completeness Threshold* of M with respect to p and the translation scheme.

The completeness threshold for $\mathbf{G}p$ formulas is simply the minimal number of steps required to reach all states. We call this the *reachability diameter* and formally define it as follows:

DEFINITION 10 (*Reachability diameter*). The reachability diameter $\mathrm{rd}(M)$ is the minimal number of steps required for reaching all reachable states:

$$\mathrm{rd}(M) := \min\left\{ i \mid \forall s_0, \ldots, s_n, \exists s_0', \ldots, s_t', t \leqslant i, \right.$$

$$I(s_0) \wedge \bigwedge_{j=0}^{n-1} T(s_j, s_{j+1}) \rightarrow$$

$$\left. \left(I(s_0') \wedge \bigwedge_{j=0}^{t-1} T(s_j', s_{j+1}') \wedge s_t' = s_n \right) \right\}. \tag{2}$$

Formula (2) simply states that every state that is reachable in n steps (left side of the implication) can also be reached in i steps (right side of the implication). In other words, $\mathrm{rd}(M)$ is the longest 'shortest path' from an initial state to any reachable state. This definition leaves open the question of how large should n be. One option is to simply take the worst case, i.e., $n = 2^{|V|}$, where V is the set of variables defining the states of M. A better option is to take $n = i + 1$ and check whether every state that can be reached in $i + 1$ steps, can be reached sooner:

$$\mathrm{rd}(M) := \min\left\{ i \mid \forall s_0, \ldots, s_{i+1}, \exists s_0', \ldots, s_i', \right.$$

$$I(s_0) \wedge \bigwedge_{j=0}^{i} T(s_j, s_{j+1}) \rightarrow$$

$$\left. \left(I(s_0') \wedge \bigwedge_{j=0}^{i-1} T(s_j', s_{j+1}') \wedge \bigvee_{j=0}^{i} s_j' = s_{i+1} \right) \right\}. \tag{3}$$

In formula (3), the sub formula to the left of the implication represent an $i + 1$ long path, and the sub-formula to the right of the implication represents an i long path. The disjunction in the end of the right-hand side forces the $i + 1$ state in the longer path to be equal to one of the states in the shorter path.

Both Eqs. (2) and (3) include an alternation of quantifiers, and are hence hard to solve for realistic models. As an alternative, it is possible to compute an over approximation of $\mathrm{rd}(M)$ with a SAT instance. This approximation was first defined in [5] as the *recurrence diameter*, and we now adapt it to the reachability diameter:

DEFINITION 11 (*Recurrence diameter for reachability*). The recurrence diameter for reachability with respect to a model M, denoted by $\mathrm{rdr}(M)$, is the longest loop-free path in M starting from an initial state:

$$\text{rdr}(M) := \max\left\{i \;\middle|\; \exists s_0 \dots s_i, \; I(s_0) \wedge \bigwedge_{j=0}^{i-1} T(s_j, s_{j+1}) \wedge \bigwedge_{j=0}^{i-1} \bigwedge_{k=j+1}^{i} s_j \neq s_k \right\}.$$
(4)

rdr(M) is clearly an over-approximation of rd(M), because every shortest path is a loop-free path.

The question of how to compute $\mathcal{CT}$ for other temporal properties is still open. Most safety properties used in practice can be reduced to some $\mathbf{G}p$ formula, by computing p over a product of M and some automaton, which is derived from the original property. Therefore computing $\mathcal{CT}$ for these properties is reduced to the problem of computing $\mathcal{CT}$ of the new model with respect to a $\mathbf{G}p$ property.

5.2   Liveness

In the discussion of bounded model checking so far, we have focused on existentially quantified temporal logic formulas. To verify an existential LTL formula against a Kripke structure, one needs to find a witness. As explained before, this is possible because if a witness exists, it can be characterized by a finite sequence of states. In the case of liveness, the dual is also true: if a proof of liveness exists, the proof can be established by examining all finite sequences of length k starting from initial states (note that for a proof we need to consider all paths rather than search for a single witness).

DEFINITION 12 (*Translation for liveness properties*).

$$[\![M, \mathbf{AF}p]\!]_k := I(s_0) \wedge \bigwedge_{i=0}^{k-1} T(s_i, s_{i+1}) \rightarrow \bigvee_{i=0}^{k} p(s_i).$$
(5)

THEOREM 3. $M \models \mathbf{AF}p$ *iff* $\exists k \; [\![M, \mathbf{AF}p]\!]_k$ *is valid.*

According to Theorem 3, we need to search for a k that makes the negation of $[\![M, \mathbf{AF}p]\!]_k$ unsatisfiable. Based on this theorem, we obtain a semi-decision procedure for $M \models \mathbf{AF}p$. The procedure terminates if the liveness property holds. The bound k needed for a proof represents the length of the longest sequence from an initial state without hitting a state where p holds. Based on bounded model checking, we have a semi-decision procedure for $M \models \mathbf{EG}\neg p$, or equivalently, $M \not\models \mathbf{AF}p$. Since we know that either $\mathbf{AF}p$ or $\mathbf{EG}\neg p$ must hold for M, one of the semi-decision procedures must terminate. Combining the two, we obtain a complete decision procedure for liveness.

5.3   Induction

Techniques based on induction can be used to make BMC complete for safety properties [25]. Proving $M \models \mathbf{AG}p$ by induction typically involves finding (manually) a strengthening *inductive invariant*. An inductive invariant is an expression that on the one hand is inductive (i.e., its correctness in previous steps implies its correctness in the current step), and on the other hand it implies the property. Proofs based on inductive invariants have three steps: the base case, the induction step and the strengthening step. Given a bound n, which we refer to as the induction depth, we first prove that the inductive invariant ϕ holds in the first n steps, by checking that formula (6) is unsatisfiable.

$$\exists s_0, \ldots, s_n, \ I(s_0) \wedge \bigwedge_{i=0}^{n-1} T(s_i, s_{i+1}) \wedge \bigvee_{i=0}^{n} \neg\phi(s_i). \tag{6}$$

Next, we prove the induction step, by showing that formula (7) is unsatisfiable:

$$\exists s_0, \ldots, s_{n+1}, \ \bigwedge_{i=0}^{n} \big(\phi(s_i) \wedge T(s_i, s_{i+1})\big) \wedge \neg\phi(s_{n+1}). \tag{7}$$

Finally, we establish that the strengthening inductive invariant implies the property for an arbitrary i:

$$\forall s_i, \ \phi(s_i) \rightarrow p(s_i). \tag{8}$$

If we use the property p as the inductive invariant, the strengthening step holds trivially and the base step is the same as searching for a counterexample to $\mathbf{G}p$.

In a further refinement of formula (7) suggested by Sheeran et al. [25], paths in M are restricted to contain distinct states. The restriction preserves completeness of bounded model checking for safety properties: if a bad state is reachable, it is reachable via a path with no duplicate states, or, in other words, via a loop-free path. The inductive step is now represented by formula (9):

$$\exists s_0, \ldots, s_{n+1}, \ \bigwedge_{j=0}^{n} \bigwedge_{k=j+1}^{n+1} (s_j \neq s_k) \wedge \bigwedge_{i=0}^{n} \big(\phi(s_i) \wedge T(s_i, s_{i+1})\big) \wedge \neg\phi(s_{n+1}). \tag{9}$$

The restriction to loop-free paths constrains the formula further and hence prunes the search space of the SAT procedure and consequently improves its efficiency. On the other hand, the propositional encoding of distinct state restriction is quadratic with respect to the bound k. When k is large, the restriction may significantly increase the size of the propositional formula. The practical effectiveness of this restriction is to be further studied.

6. Propositional SAT Solvers

In this section we briefly outline the principles followed by modern propositional SAT-solvers. Our description follows closely the ones in [30] and [27].

Given a propositional formula f, a SAT solver finds an assignment to the variables of f that satisfy it, if such an assignment exists, or return 'unsatisfiable' otherwise. Normally SAT solvers accept formulas in Conjunctive Normal Form (CNF), i.e., a conjunction of clauses, each contains a disjunction of literals and negated literals. Thus, to satisfy a CNF formula, the assignment has to satisfy at least one literal in each clause. Every propositional formula can be translated to this form. With a naive translation, the size of the CNF formula can be exponential in the size of the original formula. This problem can be avoided by adding $O(|f|)$ auxiliary Boolean variables, where $|f|$ is the number of sub expressions in f.

Most of the modern SAT-checkers are variations of the well-known Davis–Putnam procedure [17] and its improvement by Davis, Loveland and Logemann (known as DPLL) [16]. The procedure is based on a backtracking search algorithm that, at each node in the search tree, decides on an *assignment* (i.e., both a variable and a Boolean value, which determines the next sub tree to be traversed) and computes its immediate implications by iteratively applying the 'unit clause' rule. For example, if the decision is $x_1 = 1$, then the clause $(\neg x_1 \vee x_2)$ immediately implies that $x_2 = 1$. This, in turn, can imply other assignments. Iterated application of the unit clause rule is commonly referred to as Boolean Constraint Propagation (BCP). A common result of BCP is that a clause is found to be unsatisfiable, a case in which the procedure must backtrack and change one of the previous decisions. For example, if the formula also contains the clause $(\neg x_1 \vee \neg x_2)$, then clearly the decision $x_1 = 1$ must be changed, and the implications of the new decision must be re-computed. Note that backtracking implicitly prunes parts of the search tree. If there are n unassigned variables in a point of backtracking, then a sub tree of size 2^n is pruned. Pruning is one of the main reasons for the impressive efficiency of these procedures.

Fig. 5 describes a template that most SAT solvers use. It is a simplified version of the template presented in [30]. At each *decision level* d in the search, a variable assignment $V_d = \{T, F\}$ is selected with the Decide() function. If all the variables are already decided (indicated by ALL-DECIDED), it implies that a satisfying

```
// Input arg: Current decision level d
// Return value:
//    SAT():      {SAT, UNSAT}
//    Decide():   {DECISION, ALL-DECIDED}
//    Deduce():   {OK, CONFLICT}
//    Diagnose():{SWAP, BACK-TRACK} also calculates β
```

```
SAT(d)
    {
l₁:     if (Decide(d) == ALL-DECIDED) return SAT;
l₂:     while (TRUE) {
l₃:       if (Deduce(d) != CONFLICT) {
l₄:         if (SAT(d+1) == SAT) return SAT;
l₅:         else if (β < d || d == 0)
l₆:           { Erase(d); return UNSAT; }
        }
l₇:       if (Diagnose(d) == BACK-TRACK) return UNSAT;
        }
    }
```

FIG. 5. Generic backtrack search SAT algorithm.

assignment has been found, and SAT returns SATISFIABLE. Otherwise, the *implied assignments* are identified with the Deduce() function, which corresponds to a straightforward BCP. If this process terminates with no conflict, the procedure is called recursively with a higher decision level. Otherwise, Diagnose() analyzes the conflict and decides on the next step. If V_d was assigned only one of the Boolean values, it swaps this value and the deduction process in line l_3 is repeated. If the swapped assignment also fails, it means that V_d is not responsible for the conflict. In this case Diagnose() identifies the assignments that led to the conflict and computes the decision level β (β is a global variable that can only be changed by Diagnose()) to which SAT() should backtrack to. The procedure will then backtrack $d - \beta$ times, each time Erase()-ing the current decision and its implied assignments, in line l_6.

The original Davis–Putnam procedure backtracked one step at a time (i.e., $\beta = d - 1$). Modern SAT checkers include *Non-chronological Backtracking* search strategies (i.e., $\beta = d - j$, $j \geqslant 1$), allowing them to skip a large number of irrelevant assignments. The introduction of non-chronological backtracking to SAT solvers in the mid 90's was one of the main breakthroughs that allowed these procedures for the first time to handle instances with tens of thousands of variables (this technique was used previously in general Constraint Solving Problem (CSP) tools. See [30] for more details).

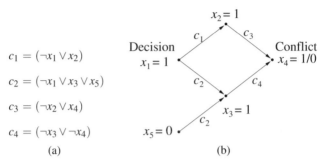

$$c_1 = (\neg x_1 \vee x_2)$$

$$c_2 = (\neg x_1 \vee x_3 \vee x_5)$$

$$c_3 = (\neg x_2 \vee x_4)$$

$$c_4 = (\neg x_3 \vee \neg x_4)$$

(a)   (b)

FIG. 6. A clause data base (a) and an implication graph (b) of the assignment $x_1 = 1$ shows how this assignment, together with assignments that were made in earlier decision levels, leads to a conflict.

The analysis of conflicts is also used for *learning*. The procedure adds constraints, in the form of new clauses (called *conflict clauses*) that prevent the repetition of bad assignments. This way the search procedure backtracks immediately if such an assignment is repeated. We explain the mechanism of deriving new conflict clauses by following a simplified version of an example given in the above reference.

EXAMPLE 2. Assume the clause data base includes the clauses listed in Fig. 6(a), the current truth assignment is $\{x_5 = 0\}$, and the current decision assignment is $x_1 = 1$. Then the resulting *implication graph* depicted in Fig. 6(b) describes the unit clause propagation process implied by this decision assignment.

Each node in this graph corresponds to a variable assignment. The incoming directed edges $(x_1, x_j) \ldots (x_i, x_j)$ labeled by clause c represent the fact that $x_1 \ldots x_i, x_j$ are c's literals and that the current value of $x_1, \ldots, x_i$ implies the value of x_j according to the unit clause rule. Thus, vertices that have no incoming edges correspond to decision assignments while the others correspond to implied assignments. The implication graph in this case ends with a conflict vertex. Indeed the assignment $x_1 = 1$ leads to a conflict in the value of x_4, which implies that either c_3 or c_4 cannot be satisfied. When such a conflict is identified, Diagnose() determines those assignments that are directly responsible for the conflict. In the above example these are $\{x_1 = 1, x_5 = 0\}$. The conjunction of these assignments therefore represents a sufficient condition for the conflict to arise. Consequently, the negation of this conjunction must be satisfied if the instance is satisfiable. We can therefore add the new conflict clause $\pi : (\neg x_1 \vee x_5)$ to the clause database, with the hope that it will speed up the search.

Another source of constant improvement in these tools is the development of new decision heuristics in DECIDE(), i.e., the strategy of picking the next variable and its value. The order can be static, i.e., predetermined by some criterion, or decided dynamically according to the current state of the search. For example, the DLIS strategy [29] picks an assignment that leads to the largest number of satisfied clauses. Although this strategy normally results in a good ordering, it has a very large overhead, since each decision requires a count of the currently unsatisfied clauses that contain each variable or its negation. A recently suggested strategy, called Variable State Independent Decaying Sum (VSIDS) [22], avoids this overhead by ignoring whether the clause is currently satisfiable or not. It counts (once) the number of times each variable appears in the formula, and then updates this number once new conflict clauses are added to the formula. By giving more weight to variables in newly added conflict clauses, it makes the decision *conflict-driven*, i.e., it gives higher priority to solving conflicts that were recently identified. This procedure turned out to be an order of magnitude faster, on average, compared to DLIS.

7. Experiments

Since the introduction of BMC several independent groups published experimental results, comparing BMC to various BDD based symbolic model checkers. In this section we quote some of the experiments conducted by the verification groups at IBM, Intel and Compaq, as well as our own experiments. All of these experiments basically reach the same conclusion: SAT based Bounded Model Checking is typically faster in finding bugs compared to BDDs. The deeper the bug is (i.e., the longer the shortest path leading to it is), the less advantage BMC has. With state of the art SAT solvers and typical hardware designs, it usually cannot reach bugs beyond 80 cycles in a reasonable amount of time, although there are exceptions, as the experiments conducted in Compaq show (see Fig. 10 below). In any case, BMC can solve many of the problems that cannot be solved by BDD based model checkers.

The experiments were conducted with different SAT solvers and compared against different model checkers. The introduction of the SAT solver CHAFF in mid 2001 changed the picture entirely, as on average it is almost an order of magnitude faster than previous SAT solvers. This means that experiments conducted before that time are skewed towards BDDs, compared to what these experiments would reveal today.

The first batch is summarized in Fig. 7. It shows the results of verifying a 16×16 shift and add multiplier, as was first presented in [4]. This is a known hard problem for BDDs. The property is the following: the output of the sequential multiplier is the same as the output of a combinational multiplier applied to the same input words. The property was verified for each of the 16 output bits separately, as shown in the table. For verifying bit i, it is sufficient to set the bound k to $i + 1$. This is the reason that the SAT instance becomes harder as the bit index increases. As a BDD model

Bit	k	SMV$_2$	MB	PROVER	MB
0	1	25	79	< 1	1
1	2	25	79	< 1	1
2	3	26	80	< 1	1
3	4	27	82	1	2
4	5	33	92	1	2
5	6	67	102	1	2
6	7	258	172	2	2
7	8	1741	492	7	3
8	9		> 1GB	29	3
9	10			58	3
10	11			91	3
11	12			125	3
12	13			156	4
13	14			186	4
14	15			226	4
15	16			183	5

FIG. 7. Results in seconds and Mega-Byte of memory when verifying a 16 × 16 bit sequential shift and add multiplier with overflow flag and 16 output bits.

Model	k	RULEBASE$_1$	RULEBASE$_2$	GRASP	GRASP (tuned)	CHAFF
Design 1	18	7	6	282	3	2.2
Design 2	5	70	8	1.1	0.8	< 1
Design 3	14	597	375	76	3	< 1
Design 4	24	690	261	510	12	3.7
Design 5	12	803	184	24	2	< 1
Design 6	22	*	356	*	18	12.2
Design 7	9	*	2671	10	2	< 1
Design 8	35	*	*	6317	20	85
Design 9	38	*	*	9035	25	131.6
Design 10	31	*	*	*	312	380.5
Design 11	32	152	60	*	*	34.7
Design 12	31	1419	1126	*	*	194.3
Design 13	14	*	3626	*	*	9.8

FIG. 8. The IBM® benchmark: verifying various hardware designs with an in-house BDD model checker (RULEBASE) and the SAT solver GRASP with and without special tuning. The last column presents the results achieved with the newer SAT solver CHAFF on the same benchmark examples. Results are given in seconds.

checker, we used B. Yang's version of SMV, which is denoted in the table as SMV$_2$. The variable ordering for SMV was chosen manually such that the bits of registers are interleaved. Dynamic reordering did not improve these results.

A second batch of comparisons was published in [27]. It presents a comparison between RULEBASE, IBM's BDD based symbolic model checker, and several SAT solvers, when applied to 13 hardware designs with known bugs. The columns RULE-BASE$_1$ and RULEBASE$_2$ represent results achieved by RULEBASE under two different configurations. The first is the default configuration, with dynamic reordering. The second is the same configuration without reordering, but the initial order is taken from the order that was calculated with RULEBASE$_1$. These two configurations represent a typical scenario of Model Checking with RULEBASE. Each time reordering is activated, the initial order is potentially improved and saved in a special order file for future runs. The column 'GRASP' contains results of solving the corresponding BMC formulas with the SAT solver GRASP. The following column, 'GRASP (tuned)', contains results of solving the same instances with a version of GRASP that is tuned for BMC, as explained in the above reference. The last column was not part of the original presentation in [27]; rather it was added for this article. It contains results achieved by CHAFF on the same benchmarks, without any special tuning (CHAFF was released after the above reference was published). The fact that CHAFF can solve all instances, while GRASP, which was considered as the state of the art solver before CHAFF, cannot solve it even with special tuning, demonstrates the great progress of SAT solvers and the influence of this progress on BMC.

Model	k	FORECAST (BDD)	THUNDER (SAT)
Circuit 1	5	114	2.4
Circuit 2	7	2	0.8
Circuit 3	7	106	2
Circuit 4	11	6189	1.9
Circuit 5	11	4196	10
Circuit 6	10	2354	5.5
Circuit 7	20	2795	236
Circuit 8	28	*	45.6
Circuit 9	28	*	39.9
Circuit 10	8	2487	5
Circuit 11	8	2940	5
Circuit 12	10	5524	378
Circuit 13	37	*	195.1
Circuit 14	41	*	*
Circuit 15	12	*	1070
Circuit 16	40	*	*
Circuit 17	60	*	*

FIG. 9. The Intel® benchmark: verifying various circuit designs with an in-house BDD model checker (FORECAST) and an in-house SAT solver (THUNDER). Results are given in seconds.

k	SMV	PROVER
25	62280	85
26	32940	19
34	11290	586
38	18600	39
53	54360	1995
56	44640	2337
76	27130	619
144	44550	10820

FIG. 10. The Compaq® benchmark: verifying an Alpha microprocessor with BDDs (SMV) and SAT (PROVER). Results are given in seconds.

The next benchmark examples was published in [14] by the formal methods group of Intel. They compared the run time of their BDD model checker FORECAST and their bounded model checker THUNDER (based on a SAT solver called SIMO) when applied to 17 different circuit designs. The table in Fig. 9 summarizes the results of their comparison when the two tools are run under their default configuration.[5]

Finally, Compaq published another batch of results obtained with industrial examples [6]. They used bounded model checking with the PROVER SAT solver for finding bugs in the memory system of an advanced Alpha microprocessor. Their conclusion was similar to the previous published comparative research: SAT based bounded model checking can solve in a short amount of time examples that cannot be solved with a BDD based model checker. Their results are summarized in Fig. 10.

8. Related Work and Conclusions

Verification techniques based on satisfiability checking have been used since the early 90's by G. Stålmarck and his company Prover Technologies [31]. The method is based on the patented SAT solver PROVER [26], that is very effective in tackling structured problems that arise from real-world designs. The work in [31] focuses on checking correctness of designs by means of inductive reasoning, as was explained in Section 5.3. Impressive results have been achieved in terms of integration of this technique within the development process in several domains (see e.g., [7]).

The initial successes of BMC drew attention from the verification community. It has been introduced in several model checkers (e.g., NuSMV [10]), and a number of advances have been achieved in several directions, which we briefly describe now.

[5]Other tables in the above reference show that with manual intervention in choosing the variable order the results can change in favor of FORECAST.

In [27], Strichman showed that it is possible to tune SAT solvers by exploiting the structure of the problem being encoded in order to increase efficiency. Notable contributions in [27] and [28] are the use of problem-dependent variable ordering and splitting heuristics in the SAT solver, pruning the search space by exploiting the regular structure of BMC formulas, reusing learned information between the various SAT instances and more. These improvements were the basis for the tuned SAT solver presented in Fig. 8. The work in [32] pushes this idea further. It relies on an incremental SAT solver, rather than on generating a new SAT instance for each attempted bound. At each step, they add and remove clauses from a single SAT instance, and this way retain the learned information from the previous instances, as was independently suggested in [28].

A related development was the extension of Bounded Model Checking to Timed Systems [2]. For this purpose they use MATHSAT [1], a SAT solver extended to deal with linear constraints over real variables. The encoding style extends the encoding for the untimed case, and uses constraints over real variables to represent the aspects related to time.

The success of SAT in solving large problems led several groups to combine SAT in various ways with other techniques used in verification, not just as part of BMC. We will mention here two of these works. McMillan [21] recently introduced a SAT-based *unbounded* CTL model checker. It is based on an quantifier elimination procedure similar to [23,24]. While the top level algorithm is basically the same as used in BDD-based CTL model checking, sets of states are represented as CNF formulas rather than with BDDs. This required a modification of the SAT solver in order to be able to perform the key operation of quantifier elimination. His experimental results show that this technique can compete with BDD based model checkers and in some cases outperform it. Compared to BMC, it has the obvious advantage of reaching a fixpoint after $rd(M)$ steps, rather than after $rdr(M)$ steps (see Section 5.1), which is only an over approximation of $rd(M)$. Currently there is no available data comparing this technique to BMC.

SAT-based techniques have also been used in the framework of abstraction/ refinement [13]. While a BDD based model checker is used to prove the abstract model, SAT solvers are used to check whether the counterexamples constructed in the abstract space are real or spurious, and also to derive a refinement to the abstraction being applied. This procedure relies on the speed of SAT to check whether a given trace (i.e., with a known length, as in BMC) is real. On the other hand it enjoys the completeness guaranteed by using BDD based model checkers.

A recently published work by Baumgartener et al. [3] holds a large promise for making BMC complete for a large class of hardware designs. They perform a structural analysis of the design in order to derive an over approximation of the reachability diameter, thus achieving completeness. The experiments show that the reachability diameter of realistic designs can be reached, and hence the property can be proved. This work was published only recently, and its effect is not yet clear. The authors of [3] showed that for a large class of netlists, it is possible to find smaller reachability diameters than those that are defined by formula (4). This requires a fairly simple analysis of the netlist structure, identifying frequently occurring components like memory registers, queue registers, etc., and identifying its Strongly Connected Components (SCC). The overall reachability diameter is then defined recursively on the reachability diameters of its individual SCCs. Their experiments showed that many netlists have reachability diameters as small as 20, which means that they can be easily proved with BMC. It is perhaps too early to judge to what degree this improvement will make BMC viable for verification, rather than for falsification alone.

Despite its recent introduction, Bounded Model Checking is now widely accepted as an effective technique that complements BDD-based model checking. A typical methodology applied in the industry today is to use both BMC and BDD based model checkers as complementary methods. In some cases both tools are run in parallel, and the first tool that finds a solution, terminates the other process. In other cases BMC is used first to find quickly the more shallow bugs, and when this becomes too hard, an attempt to prove that the property is correct is being made with a BDD based tool. In any case, it is clear that together with the advancements in the more traditional BDD based symbolic model checkers, formal verification of finite models has made a big step forward in the last few years.

References

[1] Audemard G., Bertoli P., Cimatti A., Kornilowicz A., Sebastiani R., "A SAT based approach for solving formulas over boolean and linear mathematical propositions", in: *18th Internat. Conference of Automated Deduction (CADE'02), Copenhagen*, in: *Lecture Notes in Artif. Intell.*, Springer-Verlag, Berlin, 2002.

[2] Audemard G., Cimatti A., Kornilowicz A., Sebastiani R., "Bounded model checking for timed systems", in: *22nd Joint International Conference on Formal Techniques for Networked and Distributed Systems (FORTE 2002), Houston, TX*, in: *Lecture Notes in Comput. Sci.*, Springer-Verlag, Berlin, 2002.

[3] Baumgartner J., Kuehlmann A., Abraham J., "Property checking via structural analysis", in: *Proc. 14th Internat. Conference on Computer Aided Verification (CAV'02)*, in: *Lecture Notes in Comput. Sci.*, Vol. 2404, 2002, pp. 151–165.

[4] Biere A., Cimatti A., Clarke E.M., Fujita M., Zhu Y., "Symbolic model checking using SAT procedures instead of BDDs", in: *Design Automation Conference (DAC'99)*, 1999.

[5] Biere A., Cimatti A., Clarke E., Zhu Y., "Symbolic model checking without BDDs", in: *Proc. of the Workshop on Tools and Algorithms for the Construction and Analysis of Systems (TACAS'99)*, in: *Lecture Notes in Comput. Sci.*, Springer-Verlag, Berlin, 1999.

[6] Bjesse P., Leonard T., Mokkedem A., "Finding bugs in an alpha microprocessor using satisfiability solvers", in: Berry G., Comon H., Finkel A. (Eds.), *Proc. 12th Internat. Conference on Computer Aided Verification (CAV'01)*, in: *Lecture Notes in Comput. Sci.*, Springer-Verlag, Berlin, 2001.

[7] Boralv A., Stalmarck G., "Prover technology in railways", in: *Industrial-Strength Formal Methods*, Academic Press, New York, 1998.

[8] Bryant R.E., "Graph-based algorithms for Boolean function manipulation", *IEEE Transactions on Computers* **C-35** (12) (1986) 1035–1044.

[9] Burch J.R., Clarke E.M., McMillan K.L., Dill D.L., Hwang L.J., "Symbolic model checking: 10^{20} states and beyond", *Information and Computation* **98** (2) (1992) 142–170.

[10] Cimatti A., Clarke E.M., Giunchiglia E., Giunchiglia F., Pistore M., Roveri M., Sebastiani R., Tacchella A., "NuSMV 2: An OpenSource tool for symbolic model checking", in: *Proc. 14th Internat. Conference on Computer Aided Verification (CAV'02)*, in: *Lecture Notes in Comput. Sci.*, Vol. 2404, 2002, pp. 359–364.

[11] Clarke E.M., Emerson A., "Synthesis of synchronization skeletons for branching time temporal logic", in: *Logic of Programs: Workshop, Yorktown Heights*, in: *Lecture Notes in Comput. Sci.*, Vol. 131, Springer-Verlag, Berlin, 1981, pp. 52–71.

[12] Clarke E.M., Grumberg O., Peled D., *Model Checking*, MIT Press, Cambridge, MA, 1999.

[13] Clarke E.M., Gupta A., Kukula J., Strichman O., "SAT based abstraction-refinement using ILP and machine learning techniques", in: *Proc. 14th Internat. Conference on Computer Aided Verification (CAV'02)*, in: *Lecture Notes in Comput. Sci.*, Vol. 2404, Springer-Verlag, Berlin, 2002, pp. 265–279.

[14] Copty F., Fix L., Fraer R., Giunchiglia E., Kamhi G., Tacchella A., Vardi M.Y., "Benefits of bounded model checking at an industrial setting", in: *Proc. 12th Internat. Conference on Computer Aided Verification (CAV'01)*, in: *Lecture Notes in Comput. Sci.*, Springer-Verlag, Berlin, 2001, pp. 436–453.

[15] Coudert O., Madre J.C., "A unified framework for the formal verification of sequential circuits", in: *Proc. IEEE International Conference on Computer-Aided Design*, 1990.

[16] Davis M., Logemann G., Loveland D., "A machine program for theorem-proving", *Communications of the ACM* **5** (1962) 394–397.

[17] Davis M., Putnam H., "A computing procedure for quantification theory", *Journal of the ACM* **7** (1960) 201–215.

[18] Kautz H., Selman B., "Pushing the envelope: planning, propositional logic, and stochastic search", in: *Proc. AAAI'96, Portland, OR*, 1996.

[19] Lichtenstein O., Pnueli A., "Checking that finite state concurrent programs satisfy their linear specification", in: *Proceedings of the 12th Annual ACM Symposium on Principles of Programming Languages*, 1985, pp. 97–107.

[20] McMillan K.L., *Symbolic Model Checking*, Kluwer Academic Publishers, Boston, 1993.

[21] McMillan K.L., "Applying SAT methods in unbounded symbolic model checking", in: *Proc. 14th Internat. Conference on Computer Aided Verification (CAV'02)*, in: *Lecture Notes in Comput. Sci.*, Vol. 2404, Springer-Verlag, Berlin, 2002, pp. 250–264.

[22] Moskewicz M., Madigan C., Zhao Y., Zhang L., Malik S., "Chaff: Engineering an efficient SAT solver", in: *Proc. Design Automation Conference 2001 (DAC'01)*, 2001.

[23] Plaisted D., Method for design verification of hardware and non-hardware systems, United States Patent, 6,131,078, October, 2000.

[24] Plaisted D., Biere A., Zhu Y., "A satisfiability procedure for quantified boolean formulae", *Discrete Applied Mathematics* (2002), accepted for publication.

[25] Sheeran M., Singh S., Stalmarck G., "Checking safety properties using induction and a SAT-solver", in: Hunt W.A., Johnson S.D. (Eds.), *Proc. Internat. Conf. on Formal Methods in Computer-Aided Design (FMCAD 2000)*, 2000.

[26] Sheeran M., Stalmarck G., "A tutorial on Stalmarck's method", *Formal Methods in System Design* **16** (1) (2000).

[27] Shtrichman O., "Tuning SAT checkers for bounded model checking", in: Emerson E.A., Sistla A.P. (Eds.), *Proc. 12th Internat. Conference on Computer Aided Verification (CAV'00)*, in: *Lecture Notes in Comput. Sci.*, Springer-Verlag, Berlin, 2000.

[28] Shtrichman O., "Prunning techniques for the SAT-based bounded model checking problem", in: *Proceedings of the 11th Advanced Research Working Conference on Correct Hardware Design and Verification Methods (CHARME'01), Edinburgh*, 2001.

[29] Silva J.P.M., "The impact of branching heuristics in propositional satisfiability algorithms", in: *9th Portuguese Conference on Artificial Intelligence (EPIA)*, 1999.

[30] Silva J.P.M., Sakallah K.A., GRASP—a new search algorithm for satisfiability, Technical Report TR-CSE-292996, University of Michigan, 1996.

[31] Stålmarck G., Säflund M., "Modelling and verifying systems and software in propositional logic", in: *Proc. SAFECOMP'90*, 1990.

[32] Whittemore J., Kim J., Sakallah K.A., "Satire: A new incremental satisfiability engine", in: *Design Automation Conference (DAC'01)*, 2001, pp. 542–545.

Advances in GUI Testing

ATIF M. MEMON

*Department of Computer Science
University of Maryland and Fraunhofer Center
for Experimental Software Engineering
College Park, MD 20742
USA
atif@cs.umd.edu*

Abstract

Graphical user interfaces are by far the most popular means used to interact with software today. Unfortunately, the state-of-the-practice in GUI testing has not kept pace with the rapidly evolving GUI technology. In practice, GUI testing is largely manual, often resulting in inadequate testing. There have been several research efforts to improve GUI testing. This chapter presents some of the recent advances in GUI testing and provides guidelines on how to combine them.

ADVANCES IN COMPUTERS, VOL. 58
ISSN: 0065-2458

149

1. Introduction

Graphical user interfaces (GUIs) have become nearly ubiquitous as a means of interacting with software systems. GUIs make software easy to use and, recognizing the importance of user-friendly software, today's software developers are dedicating an increasingly large portion of software code to implementing GUIs. GUIs constitute as much as 45–60% of the total software code [25,31,33,35,36].

A GUI is the front-end to underlying code (Fig. 1), and a software user interacts with the software using the GUI. The user performs *events* such as mouse movements, object manipulation, menu selections, and opening and closing of windows. The GUI, in turn, interacts with the underlying code through messages and/or method calls.

The widespread use of GUIs is leading to the construction of increasingly complex GUIs. Their use in safety-critical systems is also growing [56]. Many modern aircrafts, cars, trains, medical equipment provide information to their pilots/drivers/users in the form of a GUI. Human lives may be lost if these GUIs do not function correctly.

There are several different practices used to determine the correctness of GUIs. A popular method is to maintain checklists (usually organization specific) to conduct manual inspections[1] of the GUI. Another well-studied and applied method is to conduct usability evaluations [7,12,16,17,19,22,23,26,47,48] of the GUI. Yet another, albeit less popular, method is to use model-based approaches to check the structure and correctness of the GUI.

A popular method to check conventional software for errors is by testing the software. Automated testing of conventional software has achieved considerable success in the past two decades [8,15,37,42–45,49,58]. Adrion et al. [1] and Zhu et al. [59] provide an excellent survey of popular techniques for testing conventional software.

This chapter presents the recent advances in GUI testing, focusing primarily on automated techniques. In particular, the use of the following approaches is presented: (1) record/playback tools, (2) finite state machines, (3) variable finite state machines, (4) complete interaction sequences, (5) genetic algorithms, (6) Latin square methods, and (7) AI planning. Most of these techniques create an explicit/implicit model of the

---

[1] http://www.csst-technologies.com/guichk.htm.

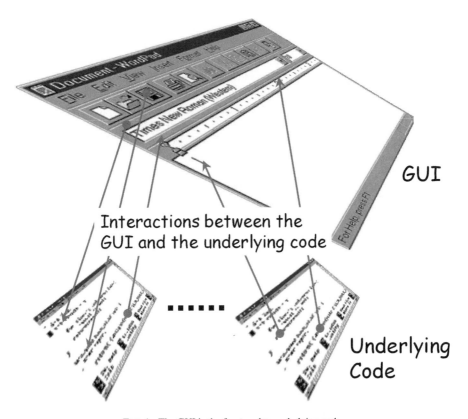

FIG. 1. The GUI is the front-end to underlying code.

GUI for test case generation. These models and the test case generation techniques will be presented. An important aspect that is beyond the scope of this work is checking the correctness of the model. Model checking [9] can be used to detect defects in the model before it is actually used for testing. This chapter addresses the detection of faults in the actual implementation of the GUI assuming a correct model.

1.1   What is GUI Testing?

Before we discuss the techniques used to test GUIs, we must first understand why GUI testing should be addressed as a separate testing problem and what is required of GUI testing, i.e., its goals.

When testing the underlying code, the code for the GUI may also be tested. However, it is important to separate the testing of the GUI from that of the underlying code. Multiple GUIs and multiple versions of GUIs are increasingly being used as front-ends to the same underlying code. The increased use of mobile devices interacting with software places limitations on the capabilities of GUIs that are used with some of these devices [21]. Device restrictions such as display resolution may require that different interfaces be implemented to access the same underlying application, such as a web application. Also, security restrictions may require that restricted views of the same software be provided to users with different security privileges. For example, the GUI for the MS Windows 2000 control panel of a system administrator has many more features than that of an ordinary user. Finally, the increased use of customizable interfaces provides different views to the same underlying code. A common example is customizable tool-bars available in most of today's software. By separately testing the underlying code (employing code-based testing techniques) and separately testing each GUI (employing GUI testing techniques), the final software can be composed by plugging-in the appropriate GUI as demanded by the application.

In its very fundamental form, the goal of GUI testing is to determine whether the GUI executes as expected, as documented in the specifications, or as required by the intended user. This definition is very broad and may encompass factors such as testing the GUI's usability, correctness, and performance. Since GUI testing is a multifaceted problem, no one technique can be used for GUI testing; in fact, in practice, a collection of techniques is almost always used. The most popular are usability evaluation and testing. While the primary focus of this chapter is testing, the next section briefly describes usability evaluations to make the distinction between the two approaches clear.

1.2   Usability Evaluation

The human–computer interaction characteristics of a system are measured by performing usability evaluation, the goal being the identification of usability weaknesses in the interface. There are several usability evaluation techniques. However, while they differ in effort invested in usability evaluation and hence the amount of improvement to the GUI, the basic principle is to involve users. For example, users may examine/use the GUI from the following perspectives.

- The user examines a GUI and looks for areas of confusion, slow-down, and/or mistakes, hence performing *exploratory evaluation*. Users perform such evaluation with no particular preconceived notions about where the problems lie or what form they may take. The deliverable for an exploratory evaluation is a list of problem areas for further examination: "users were visibly confused when faced with page p; only half the users were able to complete task x; task z takes longer than it should." Exploratory evaluation can be used at any point in the development life cycle, but is most effective when implemented early and often.

• The user measures the performance characteristics of a system against predetermined goals, hence performing *threshold evaluation*. This is a pass/fail effort: "with this system, users were able to complete task x in y seconds, making an average of z mistakes. This does (or does not) meet the release criteria." Threshold evaluation typically accompanies a beta release.

• The user measures the usability characteristics of two approaches or designs to determine which better suits users' needs, hence performing *comparison evaluation*. This evaluation is usually done at the early prototyping stage.

The key difference between usability evaluation and testing is that they have different goals. Usability evaluation is used to check the human–computer interaction aspects of a GUI (e.g., user friendliness), whereas testing is targeted towards finding faults in the GUI.

1.3   Types of GUI Testing

One way to test a GUI is to test the written code used to implement the GUI. In practice, unit testing of GUI code is performed by testers/developers who write unit tests to test each GUI event handler (e.g., class, method) in a given state. This approach is useful for identifying problems early in the development process. Unit testing is gaining popularity with emerging development processes such as extreme programming, which advocate unit testing. An example of a tool used for unit testing of GUI code is *JFCUnit*.[2] JFCUnit is an extension to the JUnit framework that enables a developer to execute unit tests against code that presents a Java Swing-based interface.[3]

An example of a Java Swing-based GUI application under test (AUT) is shown in Fig. 2(a). This Java code, when executed, opens a single window entitled "Testing Example" (executing application shown in Fig. 2(b)). This is done by Lines 6, 7, and 8 of the main method that creates a new object AUT, which creates a frame and shows it (Lines 10, 11, 12). Once a programmer has written the AUT class, it must be tested. JFCUnit provides the necessary framework for writing such a test. Fig. 2(c) shows a part of one such test case. The test case first invokes the AUT's main method so that its GUI is launched (Line 11) waits for a while (Line 14) and then checks whether a window is open. In case the window is not opened, or multiple windows are open, then an error is returned (Lines 19, 20). JFCUnit is still in its infancy and is constantly being upgraded with better features.

---

[2]http://sourceforge.net/projects/jfcunit.
[3]A tutorial of Swing is available at http://java.sun.com/docs/books/tutorial/uiswing/.

```
1   import javax.swing.*;
2
3   public class AUT{
4     private JFrame mFrame;
5
6     public static void main(String[] args) {
7       new AUT();
8     }
9
10    private AUT(){
11      mFrame = new JFrame("Testing Example");
12      mFrame.show();
13    }
14  }
```

(a)

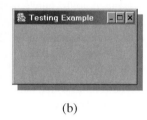

(b)

```
1   import junit.extensions.jfcunit.*;
2   import java.util.*;
3
4   public class tester extends JFCTestCase {
5     private JFCTestHelper testHelper;
6
7     public void testMain() {
8       Set windows;
9
10      // Invoke the AUT
11      AUT.main(new String[0]);
12
13      // Wait for AUT to launch
14      awtSleep();
15
16      windows = testHelper.getWindows();
17
18      // Check if a single window is open
19      assertEquals("Correct Number of Windows",
20              1, windows.size());
21    }
22  }
```

(c)

FIG. 2. A JFCUnit example.

Another popular way to test a GUI is to check the interaction of its events by performing sequences of events on the GUI. This type of testing is called *interaction testing* [54]. Although the use of GUIs continues to grow, GUI interaction testing

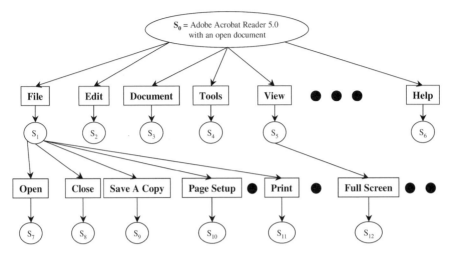

FIG. 3. Part of the search space for Adobe Acrobat Reader 5.0 GUI.

has remained a neglected research area. Adequately testing the interaction of events in a GUI is required to help ensure the safety, robustness and usability of an entire software system [34].

The GUI interaction testing problem can be viewed as a search problem with the state space of the GUI being the search space and the objective of the search to find errors. Since the number of events that a user may perform on the GUI at any given time is very large, the search space is extremely large (even infinite in most cases). Exhaustively traversing the search space is impractical in such cases. Fig. 3 shows a small part of the search space for the popular Adobe Acrobat Reader 5.0 GUI. As the figure shows, the user can start in a state S_0 and perform a number of events on the software, all leading to different states. The user can continue to perform different events in each state, hence traversing new states.

Since the entire search space of the GUI cannot be covered, any testing method must focus on a restricted set of interactions. Each of the approaches discussed in this chapter uses a unique technique to explore the restricted space. In the remainder of this chapter, the term "GUI testing" will be used for interaction testing.

2. GUI Testing Steps

Although GUIs have characteristics, such as user events for input and graphical output, that are different from those of conventional software and thus require the development of different testing techniques, the overall process of testing GUIs is similar to that of testing conventional software. The testing steps for conventional software, extended for GUIs, follow:

- *Determine what to test*
  During this first step of testing, *coverage criteria*, which are sets of rules used to determine what to test in a software, are employed. In GUIs, a coverage criterion may require that each event be executed to determine whether it behaves correctly.

- *Generate test input*
  The test input is an important part of the test case and is constructed from the software's specifications and/or from the structure of the software. For GUIs, the test input consists of events such as mouse clicks, menu selections, and object manipulation actions.

- *Generate expected output*
  Test oracles generate the expected output, which is used to determine whether or not the software executed correctly during testing. A *test oracle* is a mechanism that determines whether or not the output from the software is equivalent to the expected output. In GUIs, the expected output includes screen snapshots and positions and titles of windows.

- *Execute test cases and verify output*
  Test cases are executed on the software and its output is compared with the expected output. Execution of the GUI's test case is done by performing all the input events specified in the test case and comparing the GUI's output to the expected output as given by the test oracles.

- *Determine if the GUI was adequately tested*
  Once all the test cases have been executed on the implemented software, the software is analyzed to check which of its parts were actually tested. In GUIs, such an analysis is needed to identify the events and the resulting GUI states that were tested and those that were missed. Note that this step is important because it may not always be possible to test in a GUI implementation what is required by the coverage criteria.

After testing, problems are identified in the software and corrected. Modifications then lead to regression testing, i.e., re-testing of the changed software.

- *Perform regression testing*
  Regression testing is used to help ensure the correctness of the modified parts of the software as well as to establish confidence that changes have not adversely affected previously tested parts. A regression test suite is developed that consists of (1) a subset of the original test cases to retest parts of the original software that may have been affected by modifications, and (2) new test cases to

test affected parts of the software, not tested by the selected test cases. In GUIs, regression testing involves analyzing the changes to the layout of GUI objects, selecting test cases that should be rerun, as well as generating new test cases.

Any GUI testing method must perform all of the above steps. By far, the most commonly used tools for testing are record/playback tools [14,50], which are discussed next.

3. Record/Playback Tools

In their basic form, record/playback tools provide a mechanism to record a user's interaction with the GUI. The recorded sessions can later be replayed on the GUI (or its modified version) to recreate the same/similar sequences of user events, hence retesting the GUI.

Consider the simple GUI-based software shown in Fig. 4(a). The `MainWindow` contains only two buttons, namely `Edit` and `SaveFile`. `Edit` opens a new window entitled `Text Editor` used to edit a text file. `SaveFile` opens a window entitled `Save Modified File` only if the file has been modified. A simple interaction done on this software may be `Edit`, `TypeInText("Test")`, `Back to Main Menu`, `SaveFile`, `TypeFileName("new.txt")`, `Save`. This interaction may be stored as a sequence of system-level events shown in Fig. 4(b). Note that the session contains operating system-level mouse-clicks and keyboard events with hard-coded coordinates for buttons. Such a session can be played back by invoking operating-system calls, thereby mimicking the user and creating the same interaction with the GUI.

There are several disadvantages to using the above low-level approach. First, the test cases are system configuration dependent. For example, if the screen resolution changes, then the test cases cannot be rerun since the same coordinates may represent other events or no events at all. Second, the test cases are dependent on the GUI's layout. If the positions of the widgets change, then the test cases become useless.

To alleviate the above problems, several variations of the above low-level approach have been implemented. Instead of storing coordinates and system-level actions, events are stored in the test cases. The recording and playback mechanism is more sophisticated; recording extracts and stores the widget information rather than mouse coordinates, and playback searches for the correct widget and activates it. Fig. 4(c) shows the same test case as Fig. 4(b), except that the actions are represented in the form of widgets.

Other variations include synchronization with windows, GUI objects, etc. and storing partial state information of the GUI to be used as a test oracle at playback time.

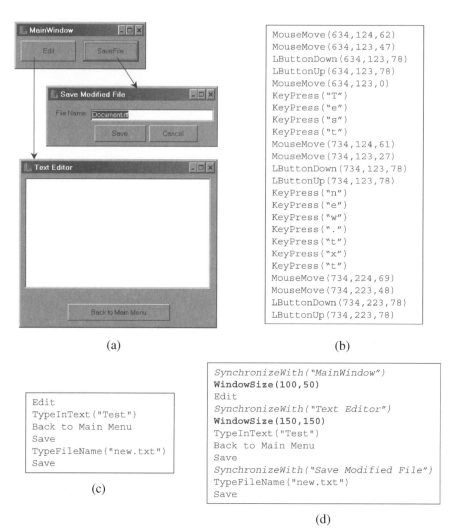

FIG. 4. Examples of record/playback sessions. Notations borrowed from a tool available at http://guitar.cs.umd.edu.

For example, Fig. 4(d) shows the same test case with windows synchronization primitives (italicized) and partial state information (boldfaced).

Even though record/playback tools are popular and effective at finding problems with GUIs, the process involved in using them is largely manual, making GUI testing slow and expensive. There have been several research efforts at developing tools and techniques for automating some aspects of GUI testing. The next section explains the challenges of developing such tools.

4. Challenges

Developing tools for GUI interaction testing offers a number of challenges. First, a **representation** of a GUI must be created that can be used across all the tools. A representation must be developed at a sufficiently high level of abstraction that it effectively captures the GUI events and their interactions and is general enough to be applicable to a wide variety of GUIs. Yet, the same representation must capture sufficient low level details of the GUI to enable a test oracle to verify the correctness of the GUI. An additional challenge for the representation is scalability; GUIs are large, containing huge bit-maps and a large number of events. If the representation is not scalable, then all phases of testing that employ it will also fail to scale.

For conventional software, **coverage** is evaluated using the amount and type of underlying code tested. Traditional coverage criteria may not work well for GUI testing, because what matters is not only how much of the code is tested, but whether the tested code corresponds to potentially problematic user interactions. Consider the example of a *Telnet* application's Edit menu shown in Fig. 5. Traditional code-based coverage criteria evaluate the amount of underlying code tested. GUIs and the underlying code are conceptually at different levels of abstraction. Therefore, it is difficult to obtain a mapping between GUI events and the underlying code. If code-based coverage criteria are used when testing GUIs, then problematic event interactions might be missed. For example, in the absence of sufficient memory, the events Edit + Copy generate a memory error but allow the user to continue after closing the error window. If the user continues to use the application, another Edit + Copy results in a system crash. If traditional code-based coverage criteria are employed, it may be difficult to test the code for such an interaction. This example illustrates that it is important to develop coverage criteria based on user events.

A third challenge is that even though the coverage criteria may help focus on specific parts of a GUI, it may be impractical to generate all possible **test cases** for these selected parts. A subset of these test cases must be generated for testing. The subset selection decision may have to be made by the test designer during test case generation. Another problem related to test case generation is called the *controllability problem*, i.e., bringing the GUI to a state in which a test case may be executed on it [3]. For each test case, appropriate events may need to be performed on the GUI to bring it to the desired state.

Fourth, **test oracles** for GUIs are different from those for conventional software. Test oracles determine whether or not the software executed correctly during test-

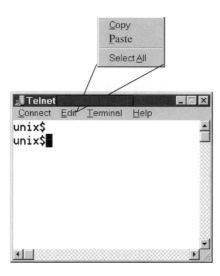

FIG. 5. A Telnet application's GUI.

ing. In conventional software testing, the test oracle is invoked after the end of test case execution, as shown in Fig. 6(a). The test case is executed by the software, and the final output is compared with the expected output. In contrast, GUI test case execution, shown in Fig. 6(b), requires that the test oracle invocation and test case execution be interleaved because an incorrect GUI state can lead to an unexpected screen. This screen may make further execution of the test case useless since events in the test case may not match any button on the GUI screen. Thus, execution of the test case should be terminated as soon as an error is detected. Also, if verification is not done after each step of test case execution, it may become difficult to pinpoint the actual cause of the error since in some cases the final output may be correct whereas the intermediate outputs may be incorrect. Consequently, in GUI test case execution, the inputs are given one step at a time, and the expected output is compared with the GUI's output after each step. This interleaving of verification and test case execution makes GUI testing more complex because (1) the expected output needs to be generated for each event, and (2) the correctness of the GUI is checked after each event is executed.

Finally, **regression testing** presents special challenges for GUIs. Both inputs and outputs to a GUI depend on positions of graphical elements on the screen. The input–output mapping may not remain constant across successive versions of the software [32]. Movement of buttons, changes in the bit-maps, and organization of menus may render older test cases useless. Moreover, the expected output used by the test oracles may become obsolete. Regression testing is especially important for

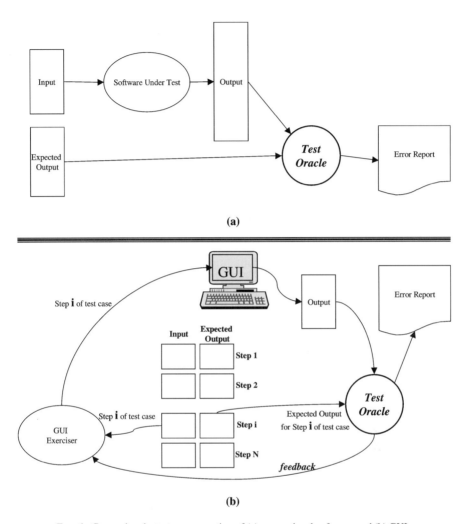

FIG. 6. Comparing the test case execution of (a) conventional software, and (b) GUIs.

GUIs as they are typically designed using *rapid prototyping* [32]. The GUI software is modified and tested on a continuous basis. Efficient regression testing mechanisms are needed to detect the frequent modifications to the GUI and adapt the old test cases.

Despite the above challenges, several techniques have been developed to perform interaction testing of GUIs. These techniques make two valuable contributions. One is the development of a representation of the GUI. The other one is the algorithm for test case generation. These techniques are discussed next.

5. State Machine Models

Several finite-state machine (FSM) models have been proposed to generate test cases for conventional software [2,4,5,10]. In this approach, the software's behavior is modeled as a FSM where each input triggers a transition in the FSM. A path in the FSM represents a test case, and the FSM's states are used to verify the software's state during test case execution. This approach has been used extensively for test generation of hardware circuits [13]. An advantage of this approach is that once the FSM is built, the test case generation process is automatic. It is relatively easy to model a GUI with a state machine model; each user event leads to a new state, and each transition models a user event. This simplistic approach has scaling problems for GUIs. Most approaches that employ FSMs to generate GUI test cases also make use of additional information to restrict the state space of the FSM.

5.1   Finite State Machines

In this section, we present details of the approach taken by Esmelioglu et al. [10]. who model the GUI as a finite state machine (FSM), represented by a directed graph. To aid in the testing process, they also create the model of a path through the FSM, the functional requirements, process flow, data model, context, transaction flow, and constraints. Subsequent paragraphs describe these aspects of the model and how they are used for test case generation.

Formally, a FSM can be represented as a quintuple $FSM = (S, I, O, T, \Phi)$, where S is the finite set of GUI states, I is the set of inputs, i.e., events that may be performed on the GUI, O is the finite set of outputs, T is the transition function $S \times I \rightarrow S$ that specifies the next state as a function of the current state and input event, Φ is the output function $S \times I \rightarrow O$ that specifies the resulting output from a transition.

Fig. 7 shows the FSM of the GUI shown in Fig. 4(a). S_0 is the start state. The user may perform SaveFile to remain in the same state or Edit to transit to a new state S_1. If no editing is done, then the user returns to S_0 by performing Back to Main Menu. If however, some text has been modified, then the GUI transits to S_1', where modifications can continue. If the user chooses to go back to the main menu, then the file is "dirty", hence the state S_0' is reached. The event SaveFile will take the user to the Save dialog in which Save can be performed and return to S_0.

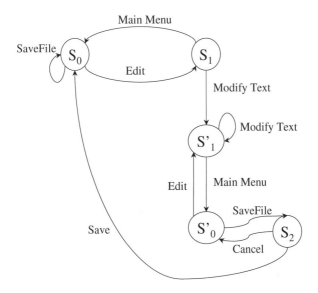

FIG. 7. The FSM of the GUI of Fig. 4(a).

DEFINITION. A *path* is a sequence of events that traverse through the FSM model defining a user scenario of the software.

The information along the vertices and edges along the path can be used during testing. For example, the edges may be used to determine the event that must be performed to transit the software from one state to the next, verify that the reached state is indeed correct, and that the software has responded correctly to an event. Once a path has been defined from the model, a test case is created for the path. The key idea is that when the test case is executed on the actual software, it follows the same sequence (or path) defined by the path derived from the model. The process of identifying paths, defining user scenarios, creating test cases may be repeated multiple number of times.

The software's behavior is modeled to help generate test cases. The model captures the *functional requirements* and *process flow*. The model contain functional description of the application as well as detailed data description. This model is used at two levels of abstraction: (1) a high-level to determine valid user scenarios, and (2) a low level to determine valid inputs and expected outputs.

Another important aspect of this work is the *data modeling* and maintaining the application *context* within the model. The authors make a distinction between hard and soft failures. Hard failures cause no change in the GUI's state. This feature enables the model to continue executing events that will cause hard failures so that all hard failures can be exhausted in one test case. Soft failures, however, cause a change in the GUI's state. During exhaustive testing, such failures may result in many permutations of events. A constraining strategy is used to narrow down the search.

Context is maintained in the model by embedding variables in the state machine. These variables can be changed, conditionally checked, and output at any point during test case execution. Moreover, these variables can be used to maintain context and generate data. For example, data values can be conditionally checked to verify the application's behavior. A variable called `clipboard` may be maintained to represent the state of the system's clipboard. When tests are being executed on the software, `clipboard` may be assigned `non-empty` after a `copy` or a `cut`. This assignment is used to define the current context for later use in determining the appropriate paths.

Since the authors tested a database application with a form-based GUI front-end, they also created a model of the *transaction flow* and the values of the data throughout this flow. The flow is used to generate database verification records. During test case execution, the data values are output to a forms processing script in the proper sequence creating the verification record. For verification, the database state is verified by querying the database. The output record is compared with the verification record; if it does not match then an error is logged.

Constraints play an important role in the testing process. Otherwise the number of permutations may lead to problems. Tests may be focused in several ways. First, the user scenarios provide a natural mechanism to generate focused test cases. Second, several constraints may be used to limit the scope of testing based on execution time, test case quality, as well as specific user functions. Finally, conditional expressions may be used in the FSM model to constrain the type of scenarios generated. For example, trivial cases may be filtered, cycles in the FSM may be removed, etc.

Test case generation from an FSM is very intuitive. The test designer may start at the start state, traverse edges of the FSM as desired and record the transitions as events. For example, in Fig. 7, a test case could be: `Edit`, `Modify Text`, `Main Menu`, `SaveFile`, and `Save`.

Although FSMs are easy to create, they suffer from some major problems. First, they do not scale for large GUIs. Moreover, the states may not have any relationship to the structure of the GUI. Hence they can be difficult to maintain. A new model called variable finite state machines (VFSMs), developed by Shehady et al. [46], presented next, attempts to rectify these problems.

5.2   Variable Finite State Machines

Shehady et al. use more sophisticated transition and output functions, and hence are able to describe the GUI in fewer number of states. Additionally, the VFSM's elements correspond closely to the structure of the GUI, making maintenance intuitive. Since the VFSMs are both smaller than FSMs and closely correspond to the GUIs elements, they are easier and cheaper to create and maintain.

The key difference between VFSMs and FSMs is that VFSMs allow a number of global variables, each of which takes values from a finite domain. Also, the value of the variable may be modified by a transition. The value of these variables is used to compute the next state and the output in response to an input. For example, the value of a variable may be used by the model to specify which transition should be taken for a particular input.

Formally, a VFSM is represented as a 7-tuple $VFSM = (S, I, O, T, \Phi, V, \Sigma)$, where S, I, O are similar to their counterparts in FSMs, $V = \{V_1, V_2, V_3, \ldots, V_n\}$ (each V_i is the set of values that the ith variable may assume) and n is the total number of variables in the VFSM. Let $D = S \times I \times V_1 \times V_2 \times \cdots \times V_n$ and $D_T \subseteq D$; T is the transition function $D_T \rightarrow S$ and Φ is a function $D_T \rightarrow O$. Hence the current state of each of the variables affects both the next state and the output of the VFSM. Σ is the set of variable transition functions. At each transition, Σ is used to determine whether any of the variables' values have been modified. Each variable has an initial state at startup.

The space of GUIs that can be modeled using VFSMs is the same as those that can be modeled using FSMs. A VFSM simply folds sequences of states into a variable, allowing the VFSM to model a state that can use previous inputs as a factor in how to respond to a current input. Variables reduce the size of the VFSM.

VFSMs can be converted into their equivalent FSMs for test case generation. VFSM is converted to an FSM. The key idea is to fold the information of V and Γ into S and T. Given a VFSM's S and $V = \{V_1, V_2, \ldots, V_n\}$, the new FSM's set of states S_{eq} is obtained as $S_{eq} = \{S_i \mid S_i \in S \times V_1 \times V_2 \times V_3 \times \cdots \times V_n\}$, i.e., this creates a set of states that combines the information of the states and the variables into one state. Similarly, the new FSM's transition function $T_{eq} : S_{eq} \times I \rightarrow S_{eq}$ may be created by combining the T and Γ functions of the VFSM. Since the range of T is S and the range of Γ is $V = \{V_1, V_2, \ldots, V_n\}$, S_{eq} is the Cartesian product of the two ranges; also T and S have the same domain. Once the FSM has been created, the test cases may be generated as described earlier for FSMs.

Fig. 8 shows the VFSM of the GUI shown in Fig. 4(a). Note that the FSM for the same GUI was shown earlier in Fig. 7. The structure of the VFSM is more intuitive than the FSM because it contains three vertices that correspond to the three windows in the GUI. The information of whether the file being edited is clean or dirty is maintained in a variable called V_{clean}. Edges of the VFSM are annotated with predicates (italicized) or assignments (boldfaced). Initially, V_{clean} is set to 0. Transitions are taken depending on the outcome of the predicates.

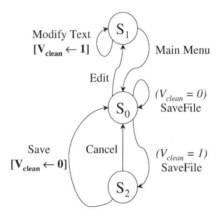

FIG. 8. The VFSM of the GUI of Fig. 4(a).

5.3   Complete Interaction Sequences (CIS)

Another approach to restrict the state space of a state machine is by employing software usage information. The method proposed by White et al. [55] solves the FSM's state explosion problem by focusing on a subset of interactions performed on the GUI. They key idea is to identify *responsibilities* for a GUI; a responsibility is a GUI activity that involves one or more GUI objects and has an observable effect on the surrounding environment of the GUI, which includes memory, peripheral devices, underlying software, and application software. For each responsibility, a *complete interaction sequence (CIS)*, which is a sequence of GUI objects and selections that will invoke the given responsibility, is identified. Parts of the CIS are then used for testing the GUI.

The GUI testing steps for CIS are as follows.

(1) Manually identify responsibilities in the GUI.
(2) For each responsibility, identify its corresponding CIS.
(3) Create an FSM for each CIS.
(4) Apply transformations to the FSM to obtain a *reduced FSM*. These transformations include the following.
    (a) Abstracting strongly connected components into a *superstate*.
    (b) Merging CIS states that have structural symmetry.
(5) Use the reduced FSM to test the CIS for correctness.

The two abstractions mentioned above (Steps (4a) and (4b)) are interesting from a modeling point of view. They are described in more detail next.

DEFINITION. A part of a FSM, called a *subFSM*, is a *strongly connected component* if for every pair (S_1, S_2), $S_1, S_2 \in S$, there exists a path from S_1 to S_2. Each such component is then replaced by a *superstate* and tested in isolation.

A subFSM has structural symmetry if the following conditions hold.

(1) it contains states S_1 and S_2 such that S_1 has one incoming transition, S_2 has one outgoing transition, and a number of paths reach S_2 from S_1;

(2) for each path in the subFSM, context (the path taken to get to S_1 from outside the subFSM) has no effect on the states/transitions or output;

(3) no transition or state encountered after S_2, is affected by paths taken inside the subFSM.

Such a subFSM can be reduced into a superstate and tested in isolation.

Given a GUI, the test designer first reduces the FSM after applying the above transformations, thereby reducing the total number of states in the FSM. This results in smaller number of paths in the FSM, hence reducing the number of test cases. Without any loss of generality, each FSM is assumed to have a distinct start state and distinct terminating state.

As mentioned earlier in previous sections, a test is a path through the FSM. The test designer then creates two types of tests: *design tests* that assume that the FSM is a faithful representation of the GUI's specifications, and *implementation tests* that for each CIS, assume that potential transitions not described in the design may also occur to and from all states of the given FSM.

For design tests, the test designer creates sufficient number of tests starting at the initial state and ending at the termination state so that the following conditions hold:

- all distinct paths in the reduced FSM are executed; each time a path enters a superstate corresponding to a component, an appropriate test path of the component is inserted into the test case at that point,

- all the design subtests of each component are included in at least one test, which may require additional tests of the reduced FSM to satisfy this constraint.

The key idea of conducting implementation testing is to check all GUI events in the CIS to determine whether they invoke any new transitions in the reduced FSM. To implement test the reduced FSM, the test designer must construct sufficient test sequences at the initial state and stopping at the terminal state so that the following conditions hold:

- all the paths of the reduced FSM are executed, and

- all the implementation tests for each remaining component are included at least once.

By using the CIS concept, the test designer can test a GUI from various perspectives, each defined by the CIS. These CIS can also be maintained in a library to be reused across various GUIs.

6. Behavioral Models

The notion of usage was introduced in the previous section, where a CIS was used to define an interaction. There is also a need to test the GUI from the perspective of different groups of users, e.g., experts and novice users. Unsophisticated and novice users often exercise GUI applications in ways that the designer, the developer, and the tester did not anticipate. An expert user or tester usually follows a predictable path through an application to accomplish a familiar task. The developer knows where to probe, to find the potentially problematic parts of an application. Consequently, applications are well tested for state transitions that work well for predicted usage patterns but become unstable when given to novice users. Novice users follow unexpected paths in the application, causing program failures. This notion is summarized in Fig. 9, where the solid arrows represent paths taken by the expert and tester. The dotted lines show the (often untested) paths taken by the novice, leading to system failures. Such failures are difficult to predict at design and testing time.

Kasik et al. [20] have developed a model of a novice user and have used it to generate test cases. Their key idea is to test the GUI for interactions that novice users may encounter in practice. The technique is based on genetic algorithms.

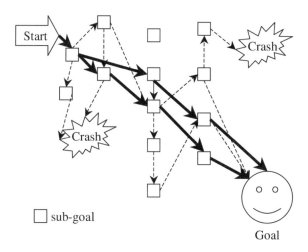

FIG. 9. Novice users may traverse indirect, untested paths (dotted lines) leading to software failures.

In its simplest form, a genetic algorithm manipulates a table of random numbers; each row of the table represents a gene. The individual elements of a row (gene) contain a numeric genetic code and are called *alleles*. Allele values start as numbers that define the initial genetic code. The genetic algorithm lets genes that contain "better" alleles survive to compete against new genes in subsequent generations.

The basic genetic algorithm is as follows:

- Initialize the alleles with valid numbers.
- Repeat the following until the desired goal is reached:
    - Generate a *score* for each gene in the table.
    - Reward the genes that produce the best results by replicating them and allowing them to live in a new generation. All others are discarded using a *death rate*.
    - Apply two operators, mutation and crossover, to create new genes.

For GUIs, the event sequence is represented by a gene, each element being an event. The primary task of setting up the genetic algorithm is to set the death rates, crossover styles, and mutation rates so that novice behavior is generated. Also, to use genetic algorithms to generate meaningful interactions mimicking novice users, a clear and accurate specification of both the user interface dialog and the program state information is needed. The state information controls the legality of specific dialog components and the names of a legal command during an interaction. Without access to the state information, the generator may produce many meaningless input events.

The best *reward system* would let the genes that generated the 'best' novice-like behavior survive by assigning a weighted score to user events. For example, one score can be given to a set of alleles that picks a list widget, a second to a set that types in specific characters, and a third to a set that provides input to a widget on the same window as the previous widget. Adjusting the weights allows the reward system to represent different types of novice user behavior.

The reward system can be based on the observation that a novice user learns how to use an application via controlled experiments. A novice starts one function in a dialog sequence and experiments with a number of different parameters. In this way, the novice uses localized parameter settings to understand the overall effect of a single function. This is only one of the possible characterizations of novice user behavior.

To implement this reward system, the weight for all user events is set to zero except one. A gene receives a positive score each time its allele values generate input for a widget (e.g., entering data into a text field, choosing an item from a list, selecting a radio button) that has the same window name as the last active window name. No additional score is generated to differentiate among the possible types of widgets on the window. The net result is that the longer a gene stays on the same window, the higher its score and better its odds of survival.

To simulate novice behavior, a tester:

- Begins with an expert generated test script.

- Inserts one or more DEVIATE commands into the script. DEVIATE departs from the existing script via the genetic algorithm and tries to return to the script.

- Tunes the genetic algorithm parameters to build a set of scripts that represent novice behavior.

This interface strategy lets the tester control when deviations occur because a DE-VIATE command can be inserted at arbitrary script locations. The script can then continue in either of *pullback* or *meander* mode. Pullback mode rewards genes for returning to the original script, while meander mode allows the activity to wander indefinitely. Even though pullback mode returns to the expert script, it will generally not generate the same results because additional functions are exercised.

Kasik et al. state that their technique my help uncover failures from novice usage earlier in the GUI development process if a model of the GUI can be created. This can result in considerable savings by cutting down on beta testing, a currently popular technique to test a software for novice behavior.

7. Statistical Methods

In its basic form, GUI interaction testing consists of testing for interactions between all GUI objects and their selections. White [54] identifies two ways in which GUI interactions can arise: statically and dynamically (or a combination of both). Static interactions are restricted to one screen whereas dynamic interactions move from one screen to another to perform events on GUI objects. White makes the assumption that it is enough to test pair-wise interactions of GUI events. Similar assumptions have led to success in finding errors efficiently for conventional software [6]. Consider the GUI window shown in Fig. 10. The total number of possible interactions on this window is $2 \times 2 \times 2 \times 1 = 8$. Using the pair-wise assumption, the total number of interactions can be cut down to $2 \times 2 = 4$.

White proposes the use of Latin squares to generate test cases that check the software for pair-wise interactions.

DEFINITION. A *Latin square*, of order n, is a matrix of n symbols in $n \times n$ cells, arranged in n rows and n columns, such that every symbol is exactly once in each row and once in each column.

FIG. 10.

DEFINITION. A pair of Latin squares $A = (a_{ij})$ and $B = (b_{ij})$ are *orthogonal* iff the ordered pairs (a_{ij}, b_{ij}) are distinct for all i and j.

Here are a pair of orthogonal Latin squares of order 3.

$$A = \begin{pmatrix} 1 & 2 & 3 \\ 2 & 3 & 1 \\ 3 & 1 & 2 \end{pmatrix}, \qquad B = \begin{pmatrix} 1 & 2 & 3 \\ 3 & 1 & 2 \\ 2 & 3 & 1 \end{pmatrix},$$

$$(A, B) = \begin{pmatrix} (1, 1) & (2, 2) & (3, 3) \\ (2, 3) & (3, 1) & (1, 2) \\ (3, 2) & (1, 3) & (2, 1) \end{pmatrix}.$$

A and B are clearly orthogonal Latin squares since, when superimposed, all ordered pairs from corresponding square entries are distinct.

Orthogonal Latin squares do not exist for all matrix sizes. There are no orthogonal Latin squares of order 2 because there are only two Latin squares of order 2 in the same symbols and they are not orthogonal. There are orthogonal Latin squares of order 3 as exemplified above. Orthogonal Latin squares of order 4 exist but are difficult to obtain. There are no orthogonal Latin squares of order 6 and 10.

Test case generation for GUIs starts by generating the elements of each factor by using mutually orthogonal Latin squares. The use of Latin squares will result in the minimum number of tests generated to solve the pair-wise interaction problem as long as the following conditions hold.

- $k - 2 \leqslant n - 1$ where n is the order of the Latin squares used and k is the number of factors, i.e., a GUI object from which selections are made,
- n is not equal to 6 or 10, or any other order for which $n - 1$ mutually orthogonal Latin squares do not exist.

Although the use of Latin squares allows the test designer to focus on pair-wise interactions of events, longer sequences must still be tested to uncover errors that require context of several events.

8. Hierarchical Techniques

Since GUI software is large, i.e., it may contain many events, some techniques have decomposed GUIs into smaller parts, the goal being to test these parts individually. In an approach presented by Memon et al. [29], the test designer identifies commonly used tasks for the GUI; these are then input to the test case generator. The generator employs the GUI representation and specifications to generate event sequences to achieve the tasks. The motivating idea behind this approach is that GUI test designers will often find it easier to specify typical user goals than to specify sequences of GUI events that users might perform to achieve those goals. The software underlying any GUI is designed with certain intended uses in mind; thus the test designer can describe those intended uses. Note that a similar approach is used to manually perform usability evaluation of the GUI [57]. However, it is difficult to manually obtain different ways in which a user might interact with the GUI to achieve typical goals. Users may interact in idiosyncratic ways, which the test designer might not anticipate. Additionally, there can be a large number of ways to achieve any given goal, and it would be very tedious for the GUI tester to specify even those event sequences that s/he can anticipate. The test case generator described in this section uses an automated technique to generate GUI test cases for commonly used tasks.

Note that test cases generated for commonly used tasks may not satisfy any of the structural coverage criteria defined by Memon et al. [30]. In fact, the underlying philosophies of testing software using its structure vs. commonly used tasks are fundamentally different. The former tests software for event sequences as dictated by the software's structure whereas the latter determines whether the software executes correctly for commonly used tasks. Both testing methods are valuable and may be used to uncover different types of errors. The structural coverage criteria may be used to determine the structural coverage of test cases generated for commonly used

TABLE I
ROLES OF THE TEST DESIGNER AND PATHS DURING TEST CASE GENERATION

Phase	Step	Test designer	PATHS
Setup	1		Derive planning operators from the GUI representation
	2	Define preconditions and effects of operators	
Plan generation	3	Identify a task T	
	4		Generate test cases for T

Iterate 3 and 4 for multiple scenarios.

tasks; missing event sequences may then be generated using a structural test case generation technique.

This approach uses AI planning to generate test cases for GUIs. The test designer provides a specification of initial and goal states for commonly used tasks. An automated planning system generates plans for each specified task. Each generated plan represents a test case that is a reasonable candidate for helping test the GUI, because it reflects an intended use of the system.

This technique of using planning for test case generation is called Planning Assisted Testing (PAT). The test case generator is called Planning Assisted Tester for grapHical user interface Systems (PATHS). The test case generation process is partitioned into two phases, the *setup* phase and *plan-generation* phase. In the first step of the setup phase, the GUI representation is employed to identify planning operators, which are used by the planner to generate test cases. By using knowledge of the GUI, the test designer defines the preconditions and effects of these operators. During the second or plan-generation phase, the test designer describes scenarios (tasks) by defining a set of initial and goal states for test case generation. Finally, PATHS generates a test suite for the tasks using the plans. The test designer can iterate through the plan-generation phase any number of times, defining more scenarios and generating more test cases. Table I summarizes the tasks assigned to the test designer and those performed by PATHS.

8.1 AI Plan Generation

Automated plan generation has been widely investigated and used within the field of artificial intelligence. Given an initial state, a goal state, a set of operators, and a set of objects, a planner returns a set of actions (instantiated operators) with ordering constraints to achieve the goal. Many different algorithms for plan generation have been proposed and developed. Weld presents an introduction to least commitment planning [52] and a survey of the recent advances in planning technology [53].

Formally, a planning problem $P(\Lambda, D, I, G)$ is a 4-tuple, where Λ is the set of operators, D is a finite set of objects, I is the initial state, and G is the goal state. Note that an operator definition may contain variables as parameters; typically an operator does not correspond to a single executable action but rather to a family of actions, one for each different instantiation of the variables. The solution to a planning problem is a plan: a tuple $\langle S, O, L, B \rangle$ where S is a set of plan steps (instances of operators, typically defined with sets of preconditions and effects), O is a set of ordering constraints on the elements of S, L is a set of causal links representing the causal structure of the plan, and B is a set of binding constraints on the variables of the operator instances in S. Each ordering constraint is of the form $S_i < S_j$ (read as "S_i before S_j") meaning that step S_i must occur sometime before step S_j (but not necessarily immediately before). Typically, the ordering constraints induce only a partial ordering on the steps in S. Causal links are triples $\langle S_i, c, S_j \rangle$, where S_i and S_j are elements of S and c represents a proposition that is the unification of an effect of S_i and a precondition of S_j. Note that corresponding to this causal link is an ordering constraint, i.e., $S_i < S_j$. The reason for tracking a causal link $\langle S_i, c, S_j \rangle$ is to ensure that no step "threatens" a required link, i.e., no step S_k that results in $\neg c$ can temporally intervene between steps S_i and S_j.

Fig. 11(a) shows an example plan for a problem in which memory (RAM) and a network interface card (NIC) need to be installed in a computer system (PC). The initial and goal states describe the problem to be solved. Plan steps (shown as boxes) represent the actions that must be carried out to reach the goal state from the initial. For ease of understanding, partial state descriptions (italicized text) are also shown in the figure. Note that the plan shown is a partial-order plan, i.e., the RAM and NIC can be installed in any order once the PC is open. Fig. 11(b) shows the four operators used by the planner to construct the plan. Each operator is defined in terms of preconditions and effects. Preconditions are the necessary conditions that must be true before the operator could be applied. Effects are the result of the operator application. Fig. 11(c) shows the details of the `installNIC` operator. This operator can only be applied (i.e., the NIC can only be installed) when a NIC is available (*haveNIC*), the PC is open (~*PCclosed*), and there is no NIC already installed (~*installedNIC*). Once all these conditions are satisfied, the `installNIC` operator can be applied resulting in an installed NIC (*installedNIC*).

As mentioned above, most AI planners produce *partially-ordered* plans, in which only some steps are ordered with respect to one another. A total-order plan can be derived from a partial-order plan by adding ordering constraints, induced by removing threats. Each total-order plan obtained in such a way is called a linearization of the partial-order plan. A partial-order plan is a solution to a planning problem if

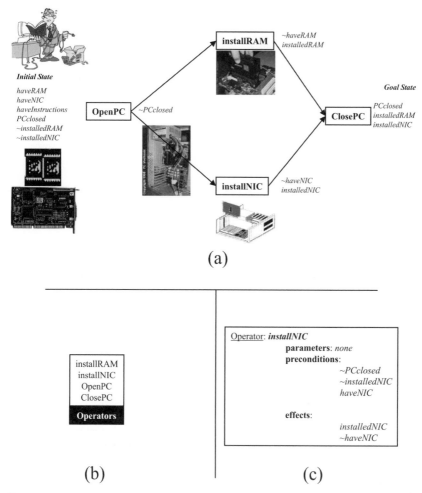

FIG. 11. (a) A plan to install ram and a network interface card in the computer, (b) the operators used in the plan, and (c) detailed definition of the installNIC operator.

and only if every consistent linearization of the partial-order plan meets the solution conditions.

Fig. 12(a) shows another partial-order plan, this one for a GUI interaction. The nodes (labeled S_i, S_j, S_k, and S_l) represent the plan steps (instantiated operators) and the edges represent the causal links. The bindings are shown as parameters of the operators. Fig. 12(b) lists the ordering constraints, all directly induced by

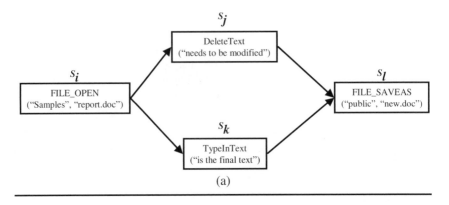

(a)

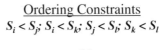

Ordering Constraints
$S_i < S_j;\ S_i < S_k;\ S_j < S_l;\ S_k < S_l$

(b)

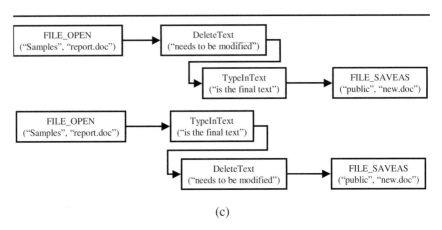

(c)

FIG. 12. (a) A partial-order plan, (b) the ordering constraints in the plan, and (c) the two linearizations.

the causal links in this example. In general, plans may include additional ordering constraints. The ordering constraints specify that the DeleteText() and Type-InText() actions can be performed in either order, but they must precede the FILE_SAVEAS() action and must be performed after the FILE_OPEN() action. Two legal orders shown in Fig. 12(c) are obtained.

8.1.1   Action Representation

The output of the planner is a set of actions with certain constraints on the relation-ships among them. An action is an instance of an operator with its variables bound to values. One well-known action representation uses the STRIPS[4] language [11] that specifies operators in terms of parameterized preconditions and effects. STRIPS was developed more than twenty years ago and has limited expressive power. For in-stance, no conditional or universally quantified effects are allowed. Although, in prin-ciple, sets of STRIPS operators could be defined to encode conditional effects, such encodings lead to an exponential number of operators, making even small planning problems intractable. A more powerful representation is ADL [38,39], which allows conditional and universally quantified effects in the operators. This facility makes it possible to define operators in a more intuitive manner. A more recent representation is the Planning Domain Definition Language[5] (PDDL). The goals of designing the PDDL language were to encourage empirical evaluation of planner performance and the development of standard sets of planning problems. The language has roughly the expressiveness of ADL for propositions.

8.1.2   Plan Generation as a Search Problem

The roots of AI planning lie in problem solving by using search. This search can either be through a space of domain states or plans. A *state space search* starts at the initial state, and applies operators one at a time until it reaches a state contain-ing all the requirements of the goal. This approach—as is the case with all search problems—requires good heuristics to avoid exploring too much of the huge search space. State space planners typically produce totally-ordered plans. A *plan space planner* searches through a space of plans. It starts with a simple incomplete plan that contains a representation of only the initial and goal states. It then refines that plan iteratively until it obtains a complete plan that solves the problem. The inter-mediate plans are called "partial plans". Typical refinements include adding a step, imposing an ordering that puts one step before another, and instantiating a previ-ously unbound variable. Plan space planners produce *partial-order plans*, introduc-ing ordering constraints into plans only when necessary. A solution to the planning problem is any linearization of the complete plan that is consistent with the ordering constraints specified there. A partial order plan is a solution to a planning problem if and only if every consistent linearization of the partial order plan meets the solu-tion conditions. Usually, the performance of plan space planners is better than that of state space planners because the branching factor is smaller (but cf. Veloso and

---

[4]STRIPS is an acronym for STanford Research Institute Problem Solver.
[5]Entire documentation available at http://www.cs.yale.edu/pub/mcdermott/software/pddl.tar.gz.

Stone [51]). Again, however, heuristic search strategies have an important effect on efficiency.

A popular example of a plan space planner is UCPOP [40]. UCPOP and other earlier planning systems rely on graph search requiring unification of unbound variables. Unification considerably slows down the planning process. Consequently, these planners are useful for solving small problems and studying the behavior of different search strategies [41]. Results of experiments conducted by Memon et al. have in fact shown that these planners are much faster than their modern counterparts in finding short plans in domains containing a large number of objects [27].

The remainder of this section presents the design of PATHS. In particular, the derivation of planning operators and how AI planning techniques are used to generate test cases is described. An algorithm that performs a restricted form of hierarchical planning is presented that employs new hierarchical operators and leads to an improvement in planning efficiency and to the generation of multiple alternative test cases. The algorithm has been implemented in PATHS, and Memon et al. [29] present the results of experiments in which test cases for the example WordPad system were generated using PATHS.

8.2   Creating the GUI Model

The state of a GUI is not static; events performed on the GUI change its state. Events are modeled as state transducers.

DEFINITION. The *events* $E = \{e_1, e_2, \ldots, e_n\}$ associated with a GUI are functions from one state of the GUI to another state of the GUI.

Since events may be performed on different types of objects, in different contexts, yielding different behavior, they are parameterized with objects and property values. For example, an event `set-background-color(w, x)` may be defined in terms of a `window` w and `color` x; w and x may take specific values in the context of a particular GUI execution. As shown in Fig. 13, whenever the event `set-background-color(w19, yellow)` is executed in a state in which window w19 is open, the background color of w19 should become `yellow` (or stay `yellow` if it already was), and no other properties of the GUI should change. This example illustrates that, typically, events can only be executed in some states; `set-background-color(w19, yellow)` cannot be executed when window w19 is not open.

It is of course infeasible to give exhaustive specifications of the state mapping for each event: in principle, as there is no limit to the number of objects a GUI can

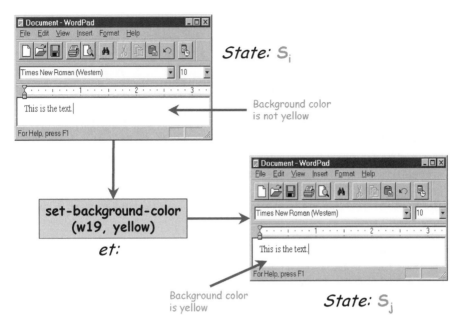

FIG. 13. An event changes the state of the GUI.

contain at any point in time, there can be infinitely many states of the GUI.[6] Hence, GUI events are represented using *operators*, which specify their preconditions and effects:

DEFINITION. An **operator** is a 3-tuple <Name, Preconditions, Effects> where:

- Name identifies an event and its parameters.
- Preconditions is a set of positive ground literals[7] $p(arg_1, \ldots, arg_n)$, where p is an n-ary property (i.e., $p \in P$). $Pre(Op)$ represents the set of preconditions for operator Op. An operator is applicable in any state S_i in which all the literals in $Pre(Op)$ are true.

---

[6]Of course in practice, there are memory limits on the machine on which the GUI is running, and hence only finitely many states are actually possible, but the number of possible states will be extremely large.

[7]A literal is a sentence without conjunction, disjunction or implication; a literal is ground when all of its arguments are bound; and a positive literal is one that is not negated. It is straightforward to generalize the account given here to handle partially instantiated literals. However, it needlessly complicates the presentation.

- `Effects` is also a set of positive or negative ground literals $p(arg_1, \ldots, arg_n)$, where p is an n-ary property (i.e., $p \in P$). $Eff(Op)$ represents the set of effects for operator Op. In the resulting state S_j, all of the positive literals in $Eff(Op)$ will be true, as will all the literals that were true in S_i except for those that appear as negative literals in $Eff(Op)$.

For example, the following operator represents the `set-background-color` event discussed earlier:

Name: `set-background-color(wX: window, Col: Color)`
Preconditions: `is-current(wX)`, `background-color(wX, oldCol)`, `oldCol` $\neq$ `Col`
Effects: `background-color(wX, Col)`

Going back to the example of the GUI in Fig. 13 in which the following properties are true before the event is performed: `window(w19)`, `background-color(w19, blue)`, `is-current(w19)`. Application of the above operator, with variables bound as `set-background-color(w19, yellow)`, would lead to the following state: `window(w19)`, `background-color(w19, yellow)`, `is-current(w19)`, i.e., the background color of window `w19` would change from `blue` to `yellow`.

The above scheme for encoding operators is the same as what is standardly used in the AI planning literature [39,52,53]; the persistence assumption built into the method for computing the result state is called the "STRIPS assumption." A complete formal semantics for operators making the STRIPS assumption has been developed by Lifschitz [24].

One final point to note about the representation of effects is the inability to efficiently express complex events when restricted to using only sets of literals. Although in principle, multiple operators could be used to represent almost any event, complex events may require the definition of an exponential number of operators, making planning inefficient. In practice, a more powerful representation that allows conditional and universally quantified effects is employed. For example, the operator for the `Paste` event would have different effects depending on whether the clipboard was empty or full. Instead of defining two operators for these two scenarios, a conditional effect could be used instead. In cases where even conditional and quantified effects are inefficient, *procedural attachments*, i.e., arbitrary pieces of code that perform the computation, are embedded in the effects of the operator [18]. One common example is the representation of computations. A calculator GUI that takes as input two numbers, performs computations (such as addition, subtraction) on the numbers, and displays the results in a text field will need to be represented using different operators, one for each distinct pair of numbers. By using a procedural at-

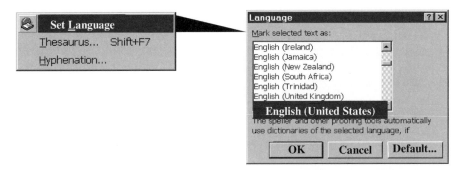

FIG. 14. The event `Set Language` opens a modal window.

tachment, the entire computation may be handled by a piece of code, embedded in a single operator.

Since today's GUIs are large and contain a large number of events, any scalable representation must decompose a GUI into manageable parts. As mentioned previously, GUIs are hierarchical, and this hierarchy may be exploited to identify groups of GUI events that can be analyzed in isolation. One hierarchy of the GUI and the one used in this research is obtained by examining the structure of *modal windows* in the GUI.

DEFINITION. A *modal window* is a GUI window that, once invoked, monopolizes the GUI interaction, restricting the focus of the user to a specific range of events within the window, until the window is explicitly terminated.

The language selection window is an example of a modal window in MS Word. As Fig. 14 shows, when the user performs the event `Set Language`, a window entitled `Language` opens and the user spends time selecting the language, and finally explicitly terminates the interaction by either performing `OK` or `Cancel`.

Other windows in the GUI are called *modeless windows* that do not restrict the user's focus; they merely expand the set of GUI events available to the user. For example, in the MS Word software, performing the event `Replace` opens a modeless window entitled `Replace` (Fig. 15).

At all times during interaction with the GUI, the user interacts with events within a modal dialog. This modal dialog consists of a modal window X and a set of modeless windows that have been invoked, either directly or indirectly by X. The modal dialog remains in place until X is explicitly terminated. Intuitively, the events within the modal dialog form a *GUI component*.

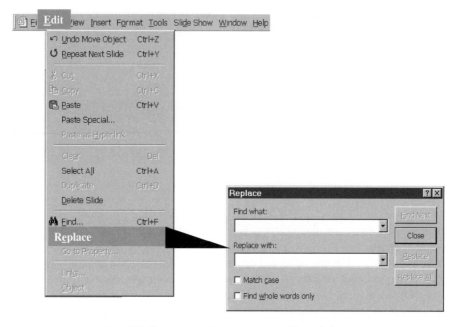

FIG. 15. The event Replace opens a modeless window.

DEFINITION. A *GUI component C* is an ordered pair $(\mathcal{RF}, \mathcal{UF})$, where $\mathcal{RF}$ represents a modal window in terms of its events and $\mathcal{UF}$ is a set whose elements represent modeless windows also in terms of their events. Each element of $\mathcal{UF}$ is invoked either by an event in $\mathcal{UF}$ or $\mathcal{RF}$.

Note that, by definition, events within a component do not interleave with events in other components without the components being explicitly invoked or terminated.

Since components are defined in terms of modal windows, a classification of GUI events is used to identify components. The classification of GUI events is as follows:

Restricted-focus events open *modal windows*. Set Language in Fig. 14 is a restricted-focus event.

Unrestricted-focus events open *modeless windows*. For example, Replace in Fig. 15 is an unrestricted-focus event.

Termination events close modal windows; common examples include OK and Cancel (Fig. 14).

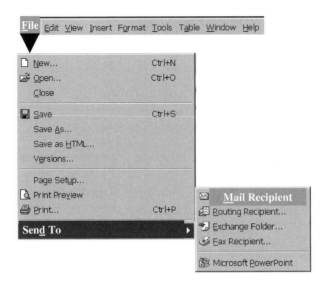

FIG. 16. Menu-open events: `File` and `Send To`.

The GUI contains other types of events that do not open or close windows but make other GUI events available. These events are used to open menus that contain several events.

Menu-open events are used to open menus. They expand the set of GUI events available to the user. Menu-open events do not interact with the underlying software. Note that the only difference between menu-open events and unrestricted-focus events is that the latter open windows that must be explicitly terminated. The most common example of menu-open events are generated by buttons that open pull-down menus. For example, in Fig. 16, `File` and `SentTo` are menu-open events.

Finally, the remaining events in the GUI are used to interact with the underlying software.

System-interaction events interact with the underlying software to perform some action; common examples include the `Copy` event used for copying objects to the clipboard (see Fig. 17).

Table II lists some of the components of WordPad. Each row represents a component and each column shows the different types of events available within each component. `Main` is the component that is available when WordPad is invoked.

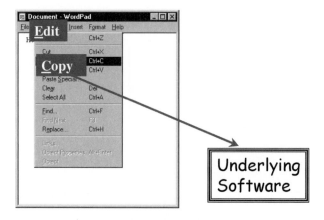

FIG. 17. A system-interaction event: Copy.

TABLE II
TYPES OF EVENTS IN SOME COMPONENTS OF MS WORDPAD

Component name	Event type					Sum
	Menu open	System interaction	Restricted focus	Unrestricted focus	Termination	
Main	7	27	19	2	1	56
FileOpen	0	8	0	0	2	10
FileSave	0	8	0	0	2	10
Print	0	9	1	0	2	12
Properties	0	11	0	0	2	13
PageSetup	0	8	1	0	2	11
FormatFont	0	7	0	0	2	9
Sum	7	78	21	21	3	121

Other components' names indicate their functionality. For example, FileOpen is the component of WordPad used to open files.

As described in Section 8.1, setting up a planning problem requires performing two related activities: (1) defining planning operators in terms of preconditions and effects, and (2) describing tasks in the form of initial and goal states. This section provides details of these two activities in the context of using planning for test case generation.

8.3   Modeling Planning Operators

For a given GUI, the simplest approach to obtain planning operators would be to identify one operator for each GUI event (Open, File, Cut, Paste, etc.) directly from the GUI representation, ignoring the GUI's component hierarchy. For the remainder of this chapter, these operators, presented earlier in Section 8.2, are called *primitive operators*. When developing the GUI representation, the test designer defines the preconditions and effects for all these operators. Although conceptually simple, this approach is inefficient for generating test cases for GUIs as it results in a large number of operators.

An alternative modeling scheme, and the one used in this test case generator, uses the component hierarchy and creates high-level operators that are decomposable into sequences of lower level ones. These high-level operators are called *system-interaction operators* and *component operators*. The goal of creating these high-level operators is to control the size of the planning problem by dividing it into several smaller planning problems. Intuitively, the system-interaction operators fold a sequence of menu-open or unrestricted-focus events and a system-interaction event into a single operator, whereas component operators encapsulate the events of the component by treating the interaction within that component as a separate planning problem. Component operators need to be decomposed into low-level plans by an explicit call to the planner. Details of these operators are presented next.

The first type of high-level operators are called system-interaction operators.

DEFINITION. A *system-interaction operator* is a single operator that represents a sequence of zero or more menu-open and unrestricted-focus events followed by a system-interaction event.

Consider a small part of the WordPad GUI: one pull-down menu with one option (Edit) which can be opened to give more options, i.e., Cut and Paste. The events available to the user are Edit, Cut and Paste. Edit is a menu-open event, and Cut and Paste are system-interaction events. Using this information the following two system-interaction operators are obtained.

```
EDIT_CUT = <Edit, Cut>
EDIT_PASTE = <Edit, Paste>
```

The above is an example of an *operator-event mapping* that relates system-interaction operators to GUI events. The operator-event mappings fold the menu-open and unrestricted focus events into the system-interaction operator, thereby reducing the total number of operators made available to the planner, resulting in planning efficiency. These mappings are used to replace the system-interaction operators by their corresponding GUI events when generating the final test case.

In the above example, the events `Edit`, `Cut` and `Paste` are hidden from the planner, and only the system-interaction operators, namely, `EDIT_CUT` and `EDIT_PASTE`, are made available to the planner. This abstraction prevents generation of test cases in which `Edit` is used in isolation, i.e., the model forces the use of `Edit` either with `Cut` or with `Paste`, thereby restricting attention to meaningful interactions with the underlying software.[8]

The second type of high-level operators are called *component operators*.

DEFINITION. A *component operator* encapsulates the events of the underlying component by creating a new planning problem and its solution represents the events a user might generate during the focused interaction.

The component operators employ the component hierarchy of the GUI so that test cases can be generated for each component, thereby resulting in greater efficiency. For example, consider a small part of the WordPad's GUI shown in Fig. 18(a): a `File` menu with two restricted-focus events, namely `Open` and `SaveAs`. Both these events invoke two components called `Open` and `SaveAs`, respectively. The events in both windows are quite similar. For `Open` the user can exit after pressing `Open` or `Cancel`; for `SaveAs` the user can exit after pressing `Save` or `Cancel`. For simplicity, assume that the complete set of events available is `Open`, `SaveAs`, `Open.Select`, `Open.Up`, `Open.Cancel`, `Open.Open`, `SaveAs.Select`, `SaveAs.Up`, `SaveAs.Cancel` and `SaveAs.Save`. (Note that the component name is used to disambiguate events.) Once the user selects `Open`, the focus is restricted to `Open.Select`, `Open.Up`, `Open.Cancel` and `Open.Open`. Similarly, when the user selects `SaveAs`, the focus is restricted to `SaveAs.Select`, `SaveAs.Up`, `SaveAs.Cancel` and `SaveAs.Save`. Two component operators called `File_Open` and `File_SaveAs` are obtained.

The component operator is a complex structure since it contains all the necessary elements of a planning problem, including the initial and goal states, the set of objects, and the set of operators. The *prefix* of the component operator is the sequence of menu-open and unrestricted-focus events that lead to the restricted-focus event, which invokes the component in question. This sequence of events is stored in the operator-event mappings. For the example of Fig. 18(a), the following two operator-event mappings are obtained, one for each component operator:

```
File_Open = <File, Open>, and
File_SaveAs = <File, SaveAs>.
```

---

[8]Test cases in which `Edit` stands in isolation can be created by (1) testing `Edit` separately, or (2) inserting `Edit` at random places in the generated test cases.

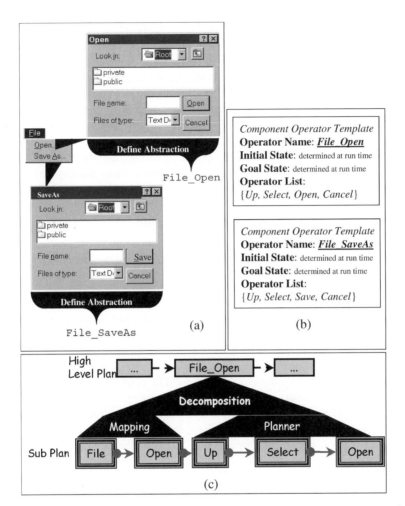

FIG. 18. (a) Open and SaveAs windows as component operators, (b) component operator templates, and (c) decomposition of the component operator using operator-event mappings and making a separate call to the planner to yield a sub-plan.

The *suffix* of the component operator represents the modal dialog. A component operator definition template is created for each component operator. This template contains all the essential elements of the planning problem, i.e., the set of operators that are available during the interaction with the component and initial and goal states, both determined dynamically at the point before the call. The component operator definition template created for each operator is shown in Fig. 18(b).

The component operator is decomposed in two steps: (1) using the operator-events mappings to obtain the component operator prefix, and (2) explicitly calling the planner to obtain the component operator suffix. Both the prefix and suffix are then substituted back into the high-level plan. At the highest level of abstraction, the planner will use the component operators, i.e., `File_Open` and `File_SaveAs`, to construct plans. For example, in Fig. 18(c), the high-level plan contains `File_Open`. Decomposing `File_Open` requires (1) retrieving the corresponding GUI events from the stored operator-event mappings (`File`, `Open`), and (2) invoking the planner, which returns the sub-plan (`Up`, `Select`, `Open`). `File_Open` is then replaced by the sequence (`File`, `Open`, `Up`, `Select`, `Open`). Since the higher-level planning problem has already been solved before invoking the planner for the component operator, the preconditions and effects of the high-level component operator are used to determine the initial and goal states of the sub-plan.

8.4   Modeling the Initial and Goal State and Generating Test Cases

Once all the operators have been identified and defined, the test designer begins the generation of particular test cases by identifying a task, consisting of an initial state and a goal state. The test designer then codes these initial and goal states. Recall that GUI states are represented by a set of properties of GUI objects. Fig. 19 shows an example of a task for WordPad. Fig. 19(a) shows the `initial state`: a collection of files stored in a directory hierarchy. The contents of the files are shown in boxes, and the directory structure is shown in an `Exploring` window. Assume that the initial state contains a description of the directory structure, the location of the files, and the contents of each file. Using these files and WordPad's GUI, a goal of creating the new document shown in Fig. 19(b) and then storing it in file *new.doc* in the `/root/public` directory is defined. Fig. 19(b) shows this `goal state` that contains, in addition to the old files, a new file stored in `/root/public` directory. Note that *new.doc* can be obtained in numerous ways, e.g., by loading file `Document.doc`, deleting the extra text and typing in the word `final`, by loading file `doc2.doc` and inserting text, or by creating the document from scratch by typing in the text. The code for the initial state and the changes needed to achieve the goal states is shown in Fig. 20. Once the task has been specified, the system automatically generates a set of test cases that achieve the goal.

8.5   Generating Plans

The test designer begins the generation of particular test cases by inputting the defined operators into PATHS and then identifying a task, such as the one shown

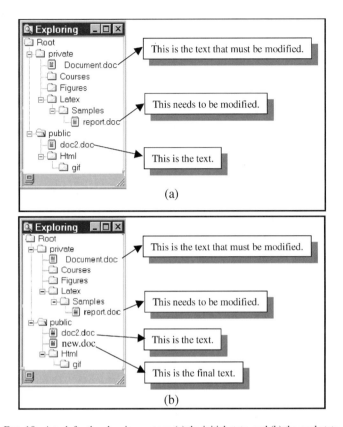

FIG. 19. A task for the planning system; (a) the initial state, and (b) the goal state.

in Fig. 19, that is defined in terms of an initial state and a goal state. PATHS automatically generates a set of test cases that achieve the goal. An example of a plan
is shown in Fig. 21. (Note that TypeInText() is a keyboard event.) This plan
is a high-level plan that must be translated into primitive GUI events. The translation process makes use of the operator-event mappings stored during the modeling
process. One such translation is shown in Fig. 22. This figure shows the component
operators contained in the high-level plan are decomposed by (1) inserting the expansion from the operator-event mappings, and (2) making an additional call to the
planner. Since the maximum time is spent in generating the high-level plan, it is desirable to generate a family of test cases from this single plan. This goal is achieved
by generating alternative sub-plans at lower levels. One of the main advantages of
using the planner in this application is to automatically generate alternative plans (or

Initial State:
```
isCurrent(root)
contains(root private)
contains(private Figures)
contains(private Latex)
contains(Latex Samples)
contains(private Courses)
contains(private Thesis)
contains(root public)
contains(public html)
contains(html gif)
containsfile(gif doc2.doc)
containsfile(private
            Document.doc)
containsfile(Samples
report.doc)
currentFont(Times Normal
            12pt)
in(doc2.doc This)
in(doc2.doc is)
in(doc2.doc the)
in(doc2.doc text.)
isText(This)
isText(is)
isText(the)
isText(text)
after(This is)
after(is the)
after(the text.)
```

```
font(This Times Normal 12pt)
font(is Times Normal 12pt)
font(the Times Normal 12pt)
font(text. Times Normal
            12pt)
```
....

Similar descriptions for
Document.doc *and* **report.doc**

Goal State:
```
containsfile(public new.doc)
in(new.doc This)
in(new.doc is)
in(new.doc the)
in(new.doc final)
in(new.doc text.)
after(This is)
after(is the)
after(the final)
after(final text.)
font(This Times Normal 12pt)
font(is Times Normal 12pt)
font(the Times Normal 12pt)
font(final Times Normal
            12pt)
font(text. Times Normal
            12pt)
```
....

FIG. 20. Initial State and the changes needed to reach the goal state.

sub-plans) for the same goal (or sub-goal). Generating alternative plans is important to model the various ways in which different users might interact with the GUI, even if they are all trying to achieve the same goal. AI planning systems typically generate only a single plan; the assumption made there is that the heuristic search control rules will ensure that the first plan found is a high quality plan. PATHS generates alternative plans in the following two ways.

1. Generating multiple linearizations of the partial-order plans. Recall from an earlier discussion (Section 8.1) that the ordering constraints O only induce a partial ordering, so the set of solutions are all linearizations of S (plan steps) consistent with O. Any linear order consistent with the partial order is a test

FIG. 21. A plan consisting of component operators and a GUI event.

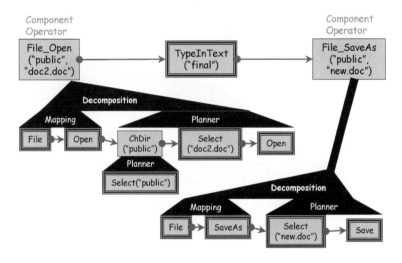

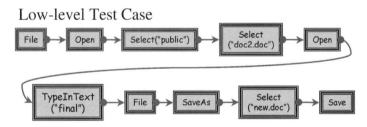

FIG. 22. Expanding the higher level plan.

case. All possible linear orders of a partial-order plan result in a family of test cases. Multiple linearizations for a partial-order plan were shown earlier in Fig. 12.

2. Repeating the planning process, forcing the planner to generate a different test case at each iteration.

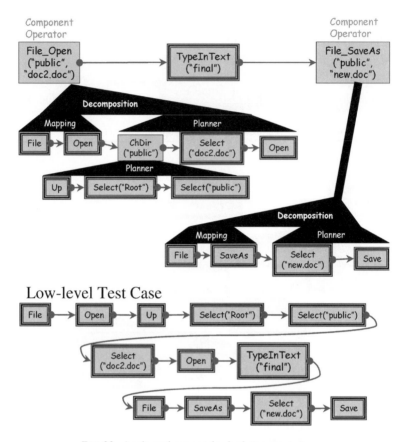

FIG. 23. An alternative expansion leads to a new test case.

The sub-plans are generated much faster than generating the high-level plan and can be substituted into the high-level plan to obtain alternative test cases. One such alternative low-level test case generated for the same task is shown in Fig. 23. Note the use of nested invocations to the planner during component-operator decomposition.

8.6 Algorithm for Generating Test Cases

The test case generation algorithm is shown in Fig. 24. The operators are assumed to be available before making a call to this algorithm, i.e., steps 1–3 of the test case

<pre>   Lines
Algorithm :: GenTestCases(
  Λ = Operator Set;   1
  D = Set of Objects;   2
  I = Initial State;   3
  G = Goal State;   4
  T = Threshold) {   5

  planList ← { };   6
  c ← 0;   7
  /* Successive calls to the planner (Φ),
     modifying the operators before each call */
  WHILE ((p == Φ(Λ, D, I, G)) ! = NO_PLAN)   8
    && (c < T) DO {   9
    InsertInList(p, planList);   10
    Λ ← RecordPlan(Λ, p);   11
    c + +}   12

  linearPlans ← { };   /* No linear plans yet */   13
  /* Linearize all partial order plans */
  FORALL e ∈ planList DO {   14
    L ← Linearize(e);   15
    InsertInList(L, linearPlans)}   16

  testCases ← linearPlans;   17
  /* decomposing the testCases */
  FORALL tc ∈ testCases DO {   18
    FORALL C ∈ Steps(tc) DO {   19
      IF (C == systemInteractionOperator) THEN {   20
        newC ← lookup(Mappings, C);   21
        REPLACE C WITH newC IN tc}   22
      ELSEIF (C == componentOperator) THEN {   23
        ΛC ← OperatorSet(C);   24
        GC ← Goal(C);   25
        IC ← Initial(C);   26
        DC ← ObjectSet(C);   27
        /* Generate the lower level test cases */
        newC ← APPEND(lookup(Mappings, C), GenTestCases(ΛC, DC, IC, GC, T));   28

        FORALL nc ∈ newC DO {   29
          copyOftc ← tc;   30
          REPLACE C WITH nc IN copyOftc;   31
          APPEND copyOftc TO testCases}}}}   32
  RETURN(testCases)}   33
</pre>

FIG. 24. The complete algorithm for generating test cases.

generation process shown in Table I must be completed before making a call to this algorithm. The parameters (`lines 1..5`) include all the components of a planning problem and a threshold (**T**) that controls the looping in the algorithm. The loop (`lines 8..12`) contains the explicit call to the planner (Φ). The returned plan **p** is recorded with the operator set, so that the planner can return an alternative plan in the next iteration (`line 11`). At the end of this loop, **planList** contains all the partial-order plans. Each partial-order plan is then linearized (`lines 13..16`), leading to multiple linear plans. Initially the test cases are high-level linear plans (`line 17`). The decomposition process leads to lower level test cases. The high-level operators in the plan need to be expanded/decomposed to get lower level test cases. If the step is a system-interaction operator, then the operator-event mappings are used to expand it (`lines 20..22`). However, if the step is a component operator, then it is decomposed to a lower level test case by (1) obtaining the GUI events from the operator-event mappings, (2) calling the planner to obtain the sub-plan, and (3) substituting both these results into the higher level plan. Extraction functions are used to access the planning problem's components (`lines 24..27`). The lowest level test cases, consisting of GUI events, are returned as a result of the algorithm (`line 33`).

9. Discussion

All (or a combination of some) of the techniques presented in this chapter may be used for GUI testing. However, test planning becomes challenging when mixing and matching testing techniques. What is needed is a set of guidelines that may be used to assist in test planning.

Ideally, a comparison of the presented techniques along several dimensions is required to present these guidelines. These dimensions include the resource requirements (time, effort, cost, etc.) and fault-detection effectiveness of each technique on a standard set of programs. However, no formal empirical study comparing and evaluating these techniques exists.

Experience and familiarity with these techniques may still be used to sketch a set of guidelines for practitioners. These guidelines have been developed keeping in mind the coverage criteria presented by Memon et al. [30]. The guidelines are presented next:

1. Unit test each event in the GUI by performing each event at least once. This is the least expensive type of testing and may be done manually. Errors in the implementation of individual events may be exposed during this step.

2. Interactions between events may be tested by using the Orthogonal Latin Squares technique. This step may expose additional errors due to event interactions.
3. Longer event sequences may need to be tested. Specific interactions may be tested by using Complete Interaction Sequences. The cost of this type of testing may be controlled by restricting the number of interactions during testing.
4. While the above steps are important to expose faults in the GUI implementation, the techniques used for the steps are influenced by the test designer. To complement the above steps, the AI planning technique and state machine models may be used to generate long sequences of events automatically. Although the setup cost of these techniques may be high, a large number of test cases may be obtained once a model has been created. Moreover, the test oracle is obtained automatically [28].
5. Finally, once the GUI has been tested for predictable event sequences and/or predictable tasks, the sequences taken by novice users may be checked by using the Genetic Algorithms technique. The advantage of using this technique at the end is that much of the testing information collected during the earlier steps may be reused. For example, event sequences obtained from planning and state machine models may be used as a starting point for genetic algorithms.

Not all of the above steps may be performed because of practical limitations. Most test designers may choose to perform the first three (cheapest) steps.

10. Summary

- Graphical user interfaces (GUIs) have become critical parts of today's software. Their correct operation is imperative to the correctness and safety of the overall software.
- There are several ways to check a GUI for correctness; the most popular being manual inspections, usability evaluations, and testing.
  - *Inspections*: checklists are used to manually examine specific features of the GUI for correctness.
  - *Usability evaluations*: usability weaknesses in the interface are identified by users who examine the GUI from several different perspectives.
  - *Testing*: test cases are created and executed (either manually or automatically) to find errors in the GUI.
- There are several different approaches to test GUIs: unit testing and interaction testing.

- *Unit testing*: tools such as *JFCUnit* are employed by code developers to write unit tests for event handlers, e.g., methods, classes.
- *Interaction testing*: the interaction between GUI events is checked by executing sequences of events on the GUI.
- The following ways are used to perform interaction testing.
  - *Finite state machines*: the GUI's behavior is modeled as a FSM where each input event triggers a transition in the FSM. A path in the FSM represents a test case, and the FSM's states are used to verify the GUI's state during test case execution. Once the FSM is built, the test case generation process is automatic.
  - *Variable finite state machines*: VFSMs are extensions of FSMs; the key difference being that VFSMs allow a number of global variables, each of which takes values from a finite domain. Also, the value of the variable may be modified by a transition. The value of these variables is used to compute the next state and the output in response to an input. For example, the value of a variable may be used by the model to specify which transition should be taken for a particular input.
  - *Complete interaction sequences*: FSMs for large GUIs may be too large for practical use. CISs solve this problem by focusing on a subset of interactions performed on the GUI. They key idea is to identify *responsibilities* for a GUI; a responsibility is a GUI activity that involves one or more GUI objects and has an observable effect on the surrounding environment of the GUI, which includes memory, peripheral devices, underlying software, and application software. For each responsibility, a *complete interaction sequence* (*CIS*), which is a sequence of GUI objects and selections that will invoke the given responsibility, is identified. Parts of the CIS are then used for testing the GUI.
  - *Genetic algorithms*: Genetic algorithms have been used to test the GUI for interactions that novice users may encounter in practice. This comes from a need to test the GUI from the perspective of different groups of users, e.g., experts and novice users. Unsophisticated and novice users often exercise GUI applications in ways that the designer, the developer, and the tester did not anticipate. An expert user or tester usually follows a predictable path through an application to accomplish a familiar task. The developer knows where to probe, to find the potentially problematic parts of an application. Consequently, applications are well tested for state transitions that work well for predicted usage patterns but become unstable when given to novice users. Novice users follow unexpected paths in the application, causing program failures. Such failures are difficult to predict at design and testing time.

- *Orthogonal Latin squares*: A *Latin square*, of order n, is a matrix of n symbols in $n \times n$ cells, arranged in n rows and n columns, such that every symbol exactly once in each row and once in each column. A pair of Latin squares $A = (a_{ij})$ and $B = (b_{ij})$ are *orthogonal* iff the ordered pairs (a_{ij}, b_{ij}) are distinct for all i and j. The use of orthogonal Latin squares is based on the assumption that it is enough to test pair-wise interactions of GUI events.

- *AI planning*: The test designer provides a specification of initial and goal states for commonly used tasks. An automated planning system generates plans for each specified task. Each generated plan represents a test case that is a reasonable candidate for helping test the GUI, because it reflects an intended use of the system. The motivating idea behind this approach is that GUI test designers will often find it easier to specify typical user goals than to specify sequences of GUI events that users might perform to achieve those goals. The software underlying any GUI is designed with certain intended uses in mind; thus the test designer can describe those intended uses. However, it is difficult to manually obtain different ways in which a user might interact with the GUI to achieve typical goals. Users may interact in idiosyncratic ways, which the test designer might not anticipate. Additionally, there can be a large number of ways to achieve any given goal, and it would be very tedious for the GUI tester to specify even those event sequences that s/he can anticipate. The planning based test case generator uses an hierarchical planning to generate GUI test cases for commonly used tasks.

- Although there are no empirical studies comparing the techniques presented in this chapter, experience with these techniques has been used to develop guidelines useful for test planning.

REFERENCES

[1] Adrion W.R., Branstad M.A., Cherniavsky J.C., "Validation, verification, and testing of computer software", *ACM Computing Surveys (CSUR)* **14** (2) (1982) 159–192.

[2] Bernhard P.J., "A reduced test suite for protocol conformance testing", *ACM Transactions on Software Engineering and Methodology* **3** (3) (1994) 201–220.

[3] Chays D., Dan S., Frankl P.G., Vokolos F.I., Weyuker E.J., "A framework for testing database applications", in: *Proceedings of the 2000 International Symposium on Software Testing and Analysis (ISSTA)*, 2000, pp. 147–157.

[4] Chow T.S., "Testing software design modeled by finite-state machines", *IEEE Trans. on Software Engineering SE-4* **3** (1978) 178–187.

[5] Clarke J.M., "Automated test generation from a behavioral model", in: *Proceedings of Pacific Northwest Software Quality Conference*, IEEE Press, New York, 1998.

[6] Cohen D.M., Dalal S.R., Kajla A., Patton G.C., "The automatic efficient test generator (AETG) system", in: *Proceedings of the 5th International Symposium on Software
Reliability Engineering*, IEEE Computer Society Press, 1994, pp. 303–309.

[7] Corry M.D., Frick T.W., "User-centered design and usability testing of a Web site: An il-
lustrative case study", *Educational Technology Research and Development* **45** (4) (1997)
65–75.

[8] Dillon L.K., Ramakrishna Y.S., "Generating oracles from your favorite temporal logic
specifications", in: *Proceedings of the 4th ACM SIGSOFT Symposium on the Foundations of Software Engineering*, in: *ACM Software Engineering Notes*, Vol. 21, ACM
Press, New York, 1996, pp. 106–117.

[9] Dwyer M.B., Carr V., Hines L., "Model checking graphical user interfaces using abstractions", in: Jazayeri M., Schauer H. (Eds.), *ESEC/FSE'97*, in: *Lecture Notes in Computer
Science*, Vol. 1301, Springer/ACM Press, 1997, pp. 244–261.

[10] Esmelioglu S., Apfelbaum L., "Automated test generation, execution, and reporting", in:
Proceedings of Pacific Northwest Software Quality Conference, IEEE Press, 1997.

[11] Fikes R., Nilsson N., "STRIPS: A new approach to the application of theorem proving to
problem solving", *Artificial Intelligence* **2** (1971) 189–208.

[12] Grady H.M., "Web site design: A case study in usability testing using paper prototypes",
in: *Approaches to Prototyping, IEEE IPCC 2000/ACM 18th International Conference on
Systems Documentation*, 2000, pp. 39–46.

[13] Cho H., Hachtel G.D., Somenzi F., "Redundancy identification/removal and test generation for sequential circuits using implicit state enumeration", *IEEE Transactions on
Computer-Aided Design of Integrated Circuits and Systems* **12** (7) (1993) 935–945.

[14] Hammontree M.L., Hendrickson J.J., Hensley B.W., "Integrated data capture and analysis tools for research and testing an graphical user interfaces", in: *Proceedings of the
Conference on Human Factors in Computing Systems, New York, NY*, 1992, pp. 431–
432.

[15] Harrold M.J., Soffa M.L., "Interprocedual data flow testing", in: *Proceedings of the
ACM SIGSOFT'89 3rd Symposium on Testing, Analysis, and Verification (TAV3)*, 1989,
pp. 158–167.

[16] Hong J.I., Landay J.A., "WebQuilt: a framework for capturing and visualizing the web
experience", in: *Proceedings of the 10th International World Wide Web Conference on
World Wide Web*, 2001, pp. 712–724.

[17] Ivory M.Y., Hearst M.A., "The state of the art in automating usability evaluation of user
interfaces", *ACM Computing Surveys (CSUR)* **33** (4) (2001) 470–516.

[18] Jónsson A.K., Ginsberg M.L., "Procedural reasoning in constraint satisfaction", in:
Aiello L.C., Doyle J., Shapiro S. (Eds.), *Proceedings of the 5th International Confer-
ence on Principles of Knowledge Representation and Reasoning*, Morgan Kaufmann,
San Francisco, 1996, pp. 160–173.

[19] Kaasgaard K., Myhlendorph T., Snitker T., Sorensen H.-E., "Remote usability testing
of a web site information architecture: 'testing for a dollar a day' ", in: *Remote Interaction and Evaluation Proceedings of IFIP INTERACT'99: Human–Computer Interaction*,
1999, pp. 443–450.

[20] Kasik D.J., George H.G., "Toward automatic generation of novice user test scripts", in: *Proceedings of the Conference on Human Factors in Computing Systems: Common Ground*, ACM Press, New York, 1996, pp. 244–251.

[21] Kirda E., "Web engineering device independent web services", in: *Proceedings of the 23rd International Conference on Software Engineering, Doctoral Symposium, Toronto, Canada*, 2001.

[22] Kotelly C.B., "World wide web as usability tester, collector, recruiter", in: *Proceedings of ACM CHI 97 Conference on Human Factors in Computing Systems, Short Talks: Usability*, Vol. 2, 1997, pp. 285–286.

[23] Levi M.D., Conrad F.G., "Usability testing of World Wide Web sites: A CHI 97 workshop", *ACM SIGCHI Bulletin* **29** (4) (1997) 40–43.

[24] Lifschitz V., "On the semantics of STRIPS", in: Georgeff M.P., Lansky A.L. (Eds.), *Reasoning about Actions and Plans: Proceedings of the 1986 Workshop, Timberline, Oregon*, Morgan Kaufmann, 1986, pp. 1–9.

[25] Mahajan R., Shneiderman B., Visual and textual consistency checking tools for graphical user interfaces, Technical Report CS-TR-3639, University of Maryland, College Park, May 1996.

[26] Marold K.A., Larsen G., Shaw K., Robertus P., "Usability testing for a computer skills WBT (web based training) program", in: Prasad J. (Ed.), *Proceedings of the 1999 ACM SIGCPR Conference (SIGCPR-99)*, ACM Press, New York, 1999, p. 304.

[27] Memon A.M., Pollack M., Soffa M.L., Comparing causal-link and propositional planners: Tradeoffs between plan length and domain size, Technical Report 99-06, University of Pittsburgh, Pittsburgh, 1999.

[28] Memon A.M., Pollack M.E., Soffa M.L., "Automated test oracles for GUIs", in: *Proceedings of the ACM SIGSOFT 8th International Symposium on the Foundations of Software Engineering (FSE-8), New York*, 2000, pp. 30–39.

[29] Memon A.M., Pollack M.E., Soffa M.L., "Hierarchical GUI test case generation using automated planning", *IEEE Transactions on Software Engineering* **27** (2) (2001) 144–155.

[30] Memon A.M., Soffa M.L., Pollack M.E., "Coverage criteria for GUI testing", in: *Proceedings of the 8th European Software Engineering Conference (ESEC) and 9th ACM SIGSOFT International Symposium on the Foundations of Software Engineering (FSE-9)*, 2001, pp. 256–267.

[31] Myers B.A., in: *State of the Art in User Interface Software Tools*, Vol. 4, Ablex Publishing, 1993, pp. 110–150.

[32] Myers B.A., Why are human–computer interfaces difficult to design and implement?, Technical Report CS-93-183, Carnegie Mellon University, School of Computer Science, July 1993.

[33] Myers B.A., "User interface software tools", *ACM Transactions on Computer–Human Interaction* **2** (1) (1995) 64–103.

[34] Myers B.A., Hollan J.D., Cruz I.F., "Strategic directions in human–computer interaction", *ACM Computing Surveys* **28** (4) (1996) 794–809.

[35] Myers B.A., Olsen Jr. D.R., "User interface tools", in: *Proceedings of ACM CHI'94 Conference on Human Factors in Computing Systems, Tutorials*, Vol. 2, 1994, pp. 421–422.

[36] Myers B.A., Olsen D.R. Jr., Bonar J.G., "User interface tools", in: *Proceedings of ACM INTERCHI'93, Conference on Human Factors in Computing Systems—Adjunct Proceedings, Tutorials*, 1993, p. 239.

[37] Osterweil L., Clarke L.A. Directions for U.S. research and development efforts on software testing and analysis, Technical Report UM-CS-1990-073, University of Massachusetts, Amherst, Computer Science, March 1990.

[38] Pednault E.P.D., Toward a mathematical theory of plan synthesis, PhD thesis, Dept. of Electrical Engineering, Stanford University, Stanford, CA, December 1986.

[39] Pednault E.P.D., "ADL: Exploring the middle ground between STRIPS and the situation calculus", in: *Proceedings of KR'89, Toronto, Canada*, 1989, pp. 324–331.

[40] Penberthy J.S., Weld D.S., "UCPOP: A sound, complete, partial order planner for ADL", in: Nebel B., Rich C., Swartout W. (Eds.), *Proceedings of the 3rd International Conference on Principles of Knowledge Representation and Reasoning, Cambridge, MA*, Morgan Kaufmann, 1992, pp. 103–114.

[41] Pollack M.E., Joslin D., Paolucci M., "Flaw selection strategies for partial-order planning", *Journal of Artificial Intelligence Research* **6** (6) (1997) 223–262.

[42] Richardson D.J., "TAOS: Testing with analysis and oracle support", in: Ostrand T. (Ed.), *Proceedings of the 1994 International Symposium on Software Testing and Analysis (ISSTA): August 17–19, 1994, Seattle, Washington*, ACM SIGSOFT, ACM Press, New York, 1994, pp. 138–153.

[43] Rosenblum D.S., Weyuker E.J., "Using coverage information to predict the cost-effectiveness of regression testing strategies", *IEEE Transactions on Software Engineering* **23** (3) (1997) 146–156.

[44] Rothermel G., Harrold M.J., "Empirical studies of a safe regression test selection technique", *IEEE Transactions on Software Engineering* **24** (6) (1998) 401–419.

[45] Rothermel G., Harrold M.J., Ostrin J., Hong C., "An empirical study of the effects of minimization on the fault detection capabilities of test suites", in: *Proceedings International Conference on Software Maintenance*, 1998, pp. 34–43.

[46] Shehady R.K., Siewiorek D.P., "A method to automate user interface testing using variable finite state machines", in: *Proceedings of the 27th Annual International Symposium on Fault-Tolerant Computing (FTCS'97), Washington–Brussels–Tokyo*, IEEE Press, 1997, pp. 80–88.

[47] Spool J.M., Scanlon T., Snyder C., Schroeder W., "Measuring website usability", in: *Proceedings of ACM CHI 98 Conference on Human Factors in Computing Systems (Summary)*, Vol. 2, Special Interest Groups (SIGs), 1998, p. 390.

[48] Szczur M., "Usability testing—on a budget: A NASA usability test case study", *Behaviour and Information Technology* **13** (1,2) (1994) 106–118.

[49] Taylor R.N., Levine D.L., Kelly C.D., "Structural testing of concurrent programs", *IEEE Transactions on Software Engineering* **18** (3) (1992) 206–215.

[50] The L., "Stress tests for GUI programs", *Datamation* **38** (18) (1992) 37.

[51] Veloso M., Stone P., "FLECS: Planning with a flexible commitment strategy", *Journal of Artificial Intelligence Research* **3** (1995) 25–52.

[52] Weld D.S., "An introduction to least commitment planning", *AI Magazine* **15** (4) (1994) 27–61.

[53] Weld D.S., "Recent advances in AI planning", *AI Magazine* **20** (1) (1999) 55–64.

[54] White L., "Regression testing of GUI event interactions", in: *Proceedings of the International Conference on Software Maintenance, Washington*, 1996, pp. 350–358.

[55] White L., Almezen H., "Generating test cases for GUI responsibilities using complete interaction sequences", in: *Proceedings of the International Symposium on Software Reliability Engineering*, 2000, pp. 110–121.

[56] Wick D.T., Shehad N.M., Hajare A.R., "Testing the human computer interface for the telerobotic assembly of the space station", in: *Proceedings of the 5th International Conference on Human–Computer Interaction, Special Applications*, Vol. 1, 1993, pp. 213–218.

[57] Wong A.Y.K., Donkers A.M., Dillon R.F., Tombaugh J.W., "Usability testing: Is the whole test greater than the sum of its parts?", in: *Proceedings of ACM CHI'92 Conference on Human Factors in Computing Systems—Posters and Short Talks, Posters: Helping Users, Programmers, and Designers*, 1992, p. 38.

[58] Yang C.-S., Souter A., Pollock L., "All-du-path coverage for parallel programs", *Proceedings of the ACM SIGSOFT International Symposium on Software Testing and Analysis (ISSTA-98), New York, ACM Software Engineering Notes* **23** (2) (1998) 153–162.

[59] Zhu H., Hall P., May J., "Software unit test coverage and adequacy", *ACM Computing Surveys* **29** (4) (1997) 366–427.

Software Inspections

MARC ROPER, ALASTAIR DUNSMORE AND
MURRAY WOOD

Department of Computer and Information Science
University of Strathclyde, Livingstone Tower
Glasgow G1 1XH, Scotland
UK

Abstract

Since their introduction in the mid 1970s software inspections have become established as an effective means of finding defects. Inspections are a simple technique—essentially a group of people read a document (which might be code or design), and then get together to draw up an agreed list of defects. The appeal of the technique is not only in its effectiveness and simplicity, but also in its wide range of applicability. Any form of document produced at any stage in the lifecycle can be inspected with the minimum of support. Over the years, people have questioned the organisation and execution of inspections and suggested alternative process models. There has also been a shift away from the meeting, and towards the individual, as the prime detector of defects. This has led to an increase in the importance of support mechanisms (in the form of "reading techniques") for the individual. The period has also seen dramatic changes in the way that software is developed (primarily the introduction of object-orientation) and inspections have had to adapt to these changes. Finally, tool support is becoming more prevalent and has opened up the possibility of providing even more support to the individual and exploring new inspection processes.

1. Introduction

Software Inspection is a defect-detection technique that essentially involves distributing a document to a number of individuals, allowing them time to study it, and then bringing them together to collect their observations. Given the context of its application it is a remarkably simple approach that acknowledges the fact that people are fairly good at spotting errors in the work of others (most people have experienced the impact that a "fresh pair of eyes" can have on their buggy code—typically a form of exasperated elation coupled with a gasp of "Why didn't I see that?"). But this is trivialising the large amount of effort that has gone into refining and improving the technique, and Software Inspection has, over the last twenty-five years, established itself as an effective and efficient technique for finding defects. The effectiveness of inspections has been established through a large number of controlled experiments and industrial case studies and over the years numerous efforts have been made to optimise the process and increase its effectiveness. The aim of this chapter is to review the progress that has been made in this area and describe the current state of the technique.

Inspections, as originally defined by Fagan [20], usually involve four or more people and are made up of several phases: an introduction, where participants are presented with a general overview of the area being addressed; preparation, where individual participants try to understand the artefacts under inspection; group inspection, where participants get together as a group and attempt to find as many defects as possible; rework, where defects found are dealt with by the designer or implementor of the artefacts; and follow-up, where all issues and concerns are verified as being dealt with.

One of the most appealing aspects of inspections to emerge was their flexibility. Inspections can be carried out at many of the stages in the software development process—in addition to being used for code documents, inspections are applied to a wide range of other documents including software requirements, design documents, test plans, and test cases [4,21,57,67]. As well as expanding the scope of documentation covered by inspection, the application of the technique and the supporting materials have been refined and honed and there is active interest in continually developing the concept, and much research has been carried out in the area of software inspection since Fagan's original description in 1976. There have been many variations proposed on the traditional inspection process that he first described. Tools have been created to help inspectors find more defects and co-ordinate their efforts in more cost-effective ways. Defect detection aids (e.g., reading techniques) have been defined for different software development artefacts (requirements, code, etc.).

This chapter provides an introduction to inspection by describing Fagan's original inspection process and the numerous variations of this that have been developed over the years. It shows how the focus of detecting defects has moved away from being a group activity to one that is carried out by the individual inspector. This refocus makes the reading technique used by the inspector to help prepare and find defects within an inspection artefact one of the key parts of the inspection process. An overview is presented of the various reading techniques currently available for individual inspectors. This is followed by a review of current work in the area of object-oriented inspection. The chapter concludes with a review of the developments in tools to support the inspection activity.

2. The Beginnings of the Inspection Process

Fagan originally defined his inspection process in 1976 [20], later updating it in 1986 [21]. Inspections, as originally discussed by Fagan [20], are a *"formal, efficient,*

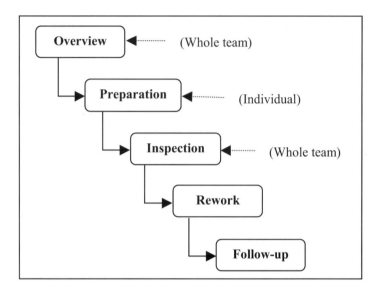

FIG. 1. The five steps in Fagan's original inspection process.

and economical method of finding errors in design and code." Fagan went on to define an error, or as is now commonly termed, a defect, as *"any condition that causes a malfunction or that precludes the attainment of expected or previously specified results."* As an example, a deviation between a specification and the corresponding code document is a defect.

In Fagan's original description of inspection, there should, under ideal conditions, be four people in an inspection team, each having a specific role. These roles include the Moderator (a competent programmer, sometimes from a different project, to manage the inspection team and offer guidance), Designer (person who produced the program design), Coder/Implementor (person who translated the design into code), and Tester (person responsible for testing the product). In Fagan's original inspection process he defines five main steps (shown in Fig. 1):

(1) *Overview*—The designer uses this phase to present all the participants involved in the inspection with a general overview of the area being addressed, followed by more specific information on the artefact to be inspected. For code inspections, the overview phase is considered optional.

(2) *Preparation*—This phase is carried out individually. Participants should understand the artefact under inspection using the appropriate documentation (requirements, design, etc.). The inspection team are aided in this process by the use of ranked distributions of error types based on recent inspections, as

well as checklists containing clues on finding these errors. The main emphasis of this phase is on understanding rather than defect detection.

(3) *Inspection*—All participants in the inspection group get together. The moderator controls the meeting, making sure that it stays focused, so that it does not get out of hand or stray off course. All related documentation should be available during the inspection. With the design of the artefact under inspection understood (in the previous preparation phase), the main objective in this phase is to find defects. This occurs as the "reader," chosen by the moderator (usually the coder) takes the team through the inspection artefact. Once a defect is found, no attempt should be made by the inspectors to find a solution. Defects are noted by one of the group members given the task of being meeting scribe (either the tester or someone with no other task).

(4) *Rework*—All the defects noted in the inspection report from the previous phase are resolved by the designer or implementer.

(5) *Follow-up*—All issues and concerns are verified as being followed-up. If more than 5% of the material inspected has in some form had to be reworked, the inspection team should regroup and carry out a full re-inspection of the material.

There have been many reports on the successes achieved through the use of inspections. Fagan [21] commented that inspection was detecting between 60 to 90% of defects and that the feedback obtained from the inspections was proving useful in helping programmers avoid making the same mistakes. Ackerman et al. [1] reported that inspections were two to ten times more efficient at defect removal than testing. Russell [60], based on 2.5 million lines of high-level code, found that if inspection was correctly implemented, then approximately one defect was found for every man-hour invested, leading to savings of nearly 33 hours of maintenance due to every hour spent on inspection. Russell claims this was two to four times faster than detecting defects by testing. Reports by Weller [70], Grady and Slack [25], have also supported the use of inspection, detailing improvements to the process and suggestions for achieving widespread use. In addition to these findings there is general acceptance of the benefits that inspection can bring: the ability to catch many defect types, its complementary nature to testing, the beneficial learning and training effects, and its applicability to all stages of the lifecycle, have seen it become established as a standard of good software engineering practice.

3. Variations on the Original Process

Since Fagan's original inspection process, there have been many variations attempting to improve the performance of inspections as a result of real or perceived inefficiencies in Fagan's original proposal. These alterations tend to focus on two main areas: the meeting stage and the preparation stage. Over the years some doubt has arisen over the efficacy of the meeting phase and the alleged synergy that makes it a powerful defect detection activity. In contrast, the role of the individual has increased and efforts have been made to reliably capture the benefits of having a diverse and talented team of inspectors available. This section presents, in approximate chronological order, the major process alterations that have been suggested over the years.

3.1   Active Design Reviews

Active Design Reviews [52] were originally created to ensure complete coverage of design documents and advocate several small, focused inspection meetings rather than one large meeting involving a lot of people. Additionally, the overall process is less rigorously specified than that proposed by Fagan. In each of these smaller meetings, inspectors are assigned different and specific roles to look for different types of defect, and are selected according to their particular skills. This role is emphasised by requiring the inspector to complete a questionnaire specific to their particular error type during the checking (preparation) phase. Following on from this is the discussion phase where the authors read the questionnaire and discuss issues raised with the reviewers. A meeting is held for each reviewer responsibility and to further ensure complete coverage of the document, some reviewers will be looking at the document as a whole.

3.2   *N*-Fold Inspections

N-Fold Inspections [61] involve performing not one but many parallel inspections by different teams on the same artefact. The assumption is that a single inspection team will only find a fraction of the defects, and that multiple teams will not significantly duplicate each other's efforts, and hence an increase in defect detection will be seen when the results are combined. The number of teams involved in the inspection is increased until the costs of employing another inspection team outweigh the benefits (i.e., a significant number of unique defects are not being detected). The value of N is going to vary between organisations and will typically take some effort to establish. The technique was originally conceived for application to user requirements documents. The cost of repairing defects in these documents later in the lifecycle can be dramatic, and so the potential savings that can be made at the requirements stage are great (this justifies the potentially high cost of the approach). However, in principle there is no reason why the technique could not be applied to any type of document.

3.3   Phased Inspections

Phased Inspections [35] divide the normal inspection into several smaller phases. Each phase focuses on one specific type of defect (compared to more traditional inspections, which look for all types of defect in one big inspection) or a particular property such as portability or reusability. One or more inspectors may carry out these phases, and individual inspectors are assigned to check properties related to their areas of expertise. If only one inspector is employed then they strictly apply a checklist to judge the compliance of the product. Phases are carried out in sequence, meaning that the next phase is not started until the previous one has been completed and satisfied all the questions on the checklist. Properties that cannot be easily captured by simple checklist questions are tackled by several inspectors who examine the document independently and then meet to create one definitive defect list.

3.4   To Meet or not to Meet

In Fagan's original inspection process [20], the preparation phase was used by inspectors to obtain an understanding of the inspection artefact and the inspection phase was used by the inspectors as a group to carry out defect detection. A series of empirical studies investigating the group aspect of the inspection process have cast doubt on its relevance as a focus for defect detection. Votta [69] suggests that inspection meetings are no longer required since the number of extra defects discovered in the meeting over those found in the individual phase is relatively small (average 4%), and they are not cost effective due to the time delay in preparing, organising, and holding the inspection meetings. Meetings should be replaced by either small deposition meetings (used to collect reviewers' findings and comments), or defect lists should be collected by other verbal or written media (e.g., electronic mail, telephone). Land et al. [41] found that the strength of inspection meetings is not in finding defects, but discriminating between true defects and false positives (potential defects which turn out not to be actual defects). They found that only a small number of extra defects were found by inspectors when working in a group. Porter and Johnson [54] found that far more issues are generated by individual defect detection compared to group-based defect detection, but this comes at the cost of higher rates of false positives and defect duplication. The current goals of the group aspect of inspection are now for the inspectors to agree upon a final list of defects based upon those found individually, and to reduce the number of false positives in the final report [40]. The main focus for the preparation phase of inspection is now the detection of defects [40,55].

3.5   Gilb and Graham/Jones Inspection

In their authoritative text, Gilb and Graham [24] describe an inspection process that is similar to that of Fagan but which incorporates the defect prevention process described by Jones [31]. The essential difference is a shift in the major focus of defect detection from the meeting to the preparation phase. This preparation phase is known as the "checking" phase (and the author also contributes to this) when each individual works independently to discover defects and records them for presentation at the meeting. The meeting is essentially a *logging* session that ensures that the maximum number of potential defects noted by the individual checkers is recorded. The process then reverts to that described by Fagan.

3.6   Formal Technical Asynchronous Review Method (FTArm)

FTArm [29] is supported by the Collaborative Software Review System (CSRS). In the set up phase the document has to be prepared for inspection using CSRS by organizing it into a hypertext structure and entering it into a database. Following this is the private review phase (similar to preparation) during which the inspector reads each source node in turn and make annotations (which take the form of new nodes). These annotations can include issues indicating defects, comments or questions directed at the producer, and actions indicating a possible solution to a defect. When all nodes have been reviewed by each inspector, all annotations become public and inspectors can asynchronously examine each one and vote on its status. This phase is effectively the meeting phase (but no traditional meeting takes place) and tool support is essential for this activity to take place. When all nodes have been resolved, or if the moderator decides that further voting and on-line discussion will not be fruitful, the public (meeting) phase is declared complete. The moderator then summarises any unresolved issues and may decide to call a group meeting to handle these. After this point the inspection proceeds as normal.

3.7   Humphrey's Inspection Process

The initial and final phases of the inspection process described by Humphrey [28] are similar to that described by Fagan. However, there is considerable variation at the heart of the process. During the preparation stage, instead of familiarizing themselves with the documents and being prepared to put forward defects, the reviewers are required to produce a list of defects which are then analysed and collated by the producer prior to the meeting. The meeting itself is then centred around this defect list, where the producer addresses each defect in turn but may seek clarification from the reviewers. This result in an agreed defect list which is then addressed in the standard way.

3.8   Sample-Driven Inspections

Sample-Driven Inspections [66] is a method designed to reduce the effort during an inspection session by concentrating the inspection effort on the software artefacts that contain the most defects. The approach is a reaction to the fact that, effective though they are, inspections are a time-consuming activity and to review all the documents in an entire project is going to be expensive. The defect searching is divided into two parts. A pre-inspection occurs where samples of the artefacts are inspected to estimate which artefacts contain the most faults. Secondly, the main inspection is carried out on the selected artefacts.

3.9   Summary

These alternative processes have varied such elements as the number of steps in the inspection process, the number of inspectors, and the roles of inspectors. Although each variation has made alterations to the inspection process or altered characteristics of the phases, the inspection phases of preparation, inspection, and rework/follow-up from Fagan's original description have remained [39]. Although there have been a number of variations on the process proposed, the most common factor is the move away from the allegedly synergistic meeting as the primary defect detection phase to the preparation or checking phase. This shift has placed more emphasis on the performance of the individual and the material provided to support them.

Porter and Votta [53] found that defect detection results have less to do with the particular inspection process used, and have more to do with the techniques and technology supporting individual inspectors. Giving support to individual inspectors to find defects may increase their effectiveness. With the re-emphasis of the defect detection part of the inspection process on the individual preparation phase, there has been a shift in inspection research. Basili [3] pointed out that reading was by far the most important activity for successful individual defect detection and highlighted the lack of research examining the technologies that underlie the reading process. Adequate support for the defect detection activity of inspectors (i.e., reading strategies) has the potential to dramatically improve the effectiveness and efficiency of inspection [40]. The more the inspector can understand the material to be inspected, the greater the chance of finding defects [59]. The next section presents a summary of the reading techniques and looks at how they attempt to help the inspector find defects.

4.   Reading Techniques

With the emphasis of defect detection being placed on the preparation phase of inspection [40,55] and a realisation that reading is important for defect detection, there has been an increased emphasise on the development and evaluation of effective reading techniques. Laitenberger and DeBaud [39] described a reading technique as a "series of steps or procedures whose purpose is for an inspector to acquire a deep understanding of the inspected software product." One purpose of the reading technique is to support the individual and make the defect detection less reliant on the talents, enthusiasm and experience of the individual. Another purpose is to focus an individual's attention towards certain classes of defect or types of deficiency in the document. In Fagan's original inspection process he suggested the use of checklists [20], but since then a number of other approaches have been developed. This section describes some of the more prominent reading techniques currently available.

4.1   Ad-hoc

One of the simplest reading techniques (and probably more accurately defined as the absence of a technique), ad-hoc, provides no support for inspectors, i.e., no guidelines or direction. Inspectors have to rely on their own knowledge and experience, reading the inspection artefact, whether they are specifications or code, in their own preferred way. Although the ad-hoc approach offers no guidance to inspectors, it is considered to be a reading technique [39,56].

A strength of the ad-hoc technique is that more experienced inspectors have the freedom to use their knowledge and abilities to find defects, free from any technique overhead that may intrude upon their thinking. The main weakness of the ad-hoc technique is that with no support, the performance of the less experienced inspectors may suffer, since they do not have the experience to guide them.

4.2   Checklist

Checklists, which were first introduced in Fagan's early inspections, are straightforward to use and offer stronger guidance to inspectors than ad-hoc reading. They are based upon a series of specific questions that are intended to focus the inspector's attention towards common sources of defects. The questions in a checklist are there to guide the inspector through the document under inspection. To make it clear that a potential defect has been found, the questions are phrased in such a way that if the answer is 'No,' then a potential defect has been discovered. A typical code-oriented checklist might contain the following type of questions:

Are all variables initialised correctly?
Are all logical expressions correct?
Do procedure invocations match the definitions?
Are all parameters used with procedures?
And so on...

The precise questions will vary according to the document. For example, an object-oriented language checklist will refer to classes, methods, etc., whereas checklists for languages such as C or C++ might place more emphasis on the errors that can arise through incorrect use of pointers or de-referencing operators. For an example of such a checklist see Humphrey [28]. According to Gilb and Graham [24] and Humphrey [28], checklists should be based on localised historical information and should not be general checklists obtained from elsewhere as they can lose their relevance. This implies a need for constant data capture and analysis from inspection meetings in order to keep checklists relevant. Checklists, along with ad-hoc reading are still thought of as the most frequently used defect detection methods [24,55]. Checklists have been used to inspect many different documents, including design, specification, and code.

Although checklists have been well promoted [21,28], there are several weakness which have been identified. Laitenberger et al. [39] summarised a list of the weaknesses of the checklist technique from the literature. Firstly, that the questions are often too general or based upon checklists created from the defect experience of others. Similarly, Tervonen [65] commented that one of major problems facing checklists is their generality, that they are not sufficiently tailored to a particular development method or phase in a specific project. Second, instructions guiding inspectors on how to use a checklist are rarely available, i.e., it is often unclear when and based on what information an inspector is to answer a particular checklist question. Finally, the questions of a checklist are often limited to the detection of defects which belong to particular defect types. Since the defect types are based on past information [13], inspectors may fail to spot defect types not previously detected and, therefore may miss whole classes of defects (a problem only slightly reduced by the constant revision that should occur with checklists).

4.3   Step-wise Abstraction

The step-wise abstraction reading strategy offers more structured and focused instructions on how to read code. The technique was based on the step-wise abstraction technique of reading developed in the late 70's by Linger, Mills and Witt [45]. In step-wise abstraction, the aim is to start with the simplest components in the code, understand them, and abstract out a higher level description of their functionality [6]. This process is repeated, combining higher and higher levels of functionality, until a final description of the code is obtained. This final description is then compared with the original specification. This way any differences between the original specification and the derived specification highlight potential defects. Stepwise abstraction has been most commonly used as a code reading technique by the Cleanroom community [62] (the Cleanroom development method is a technical and organisational approach to developing software with certifiable reliability).

Based upon evidence from the literature, Laitenberger et al. [40] believed that inspectors utilising the step-wise abstraction technique were forced into a more rigorous examination of the code than using either the ad-hoc or checklist reading techniques.

4.4   Scenario-Based Reading

The scenario reading strategy was created by Porter et al. [57] to address a perceived lack of effectiveness in the use of ad-hoc and checklist methods for Software Requirements Specifications (SRS). The work builds on the inspection process from Active Design Reviews by Parnas and Weiss [52], who argued for the need for different and specific roles for inspectors to systematically inspect a document. Porter et al. described a scenario as a *"collection of procedures that operationalise strategies for detecting particular classes of defects."* Each inspector is given one scenario, which differs from the scenarios given to the other inspectors in the inspection team. Each scenario contains a set of questions and instructions informing the inspector how to perform the inspection of the SRS. Multiple inspectors are required to obtain a reasonable level of coverage from the document.

To illustrate this point, consider the checklists and scenarios described by Porter et al. [57]. The checklist entry for "Incorrect or Extra Functionality" contains the following points:

- *Are all the described functions necessary to meet the system objectives?*
- *Are all inputs to a function necessary to perform the required function?*
- *Are the inputs and outputs for all interfaces necessary?*
- *Are all the outputs produced by a function used by another function or transferred across an external interface?*

In contrast, the "Incorrect Functionality Scenario" contains points such as:

- *For each functional requirement identify all input/output data objects:*
  - *Are all values written to each output data object consistent with its intended function?*
  - *Identify at least one function that uses each output data object.*
    And:
- *Develop an invariant for each system mode (i.e., Under what conditions must the system exit or remain in a given mode?):*
  - *Can the system's initial conditions fail to satisfy the initial mode's invariant?*

- *Identify a sequence of events that allows the system to enter a mode without satisfying the mode's invariant.*
- *Identify a sequence of events that allows the system to enter a mode, but never leave (deadlock).*

These two are only samples from the two types of support documents but provide an illustration of the difference. The checklist is more passive and often relies on the vigilance or ingenuity of the inspector to spot defects. The scenario is more active and challenges the inspector to identify or find particular instances that are going to either cause problems or refute the presence of a defect.

The success of this technique relies heavily on the effectiveness of the designed scenarios. Several variations on the scenario approach have been developed, each varying the way the scenarios are created. In defect-based reading by Porter et al. [57], the scenarios are derived from defect classes with a set of questions the inspector has to answer. For scenario-based reading by Cheng and Jeffrey [12], the scenarios are based on Function Point Analysis (scenarios are developed around a software system defined in terms of its inputs, files, enquiries, and outputs). In perspective-based reading by Basili et al. [4], the inspection artefact is inspected from the perspective of different stakeholders. Each of these reading techniques provide a generic process for inspecting requirements documents, although the material generated by the processes for use in inspections are target specific (to a particular development environment).

The last of these techniques, perspective-based reading, has continued to be refined and has been implemented not just for requirements documents but for code documents as well.

4.5   Perspective-Based Reading

Perspective-based reading (PBR), first presented by Basili et al. [4], evolved from the work carried out on scenarios. PBR, compared to the Scenario technique, offers a more detailed set of instructions (scenarios) for inspectors. The PBR-scenarios are an algorithmic set of instructions informing inspectors how to read an artefact under inspection. Inspectors understand the artefact by constructing an appropriate abstraction defined by the scenario. Laitenberger and DeBaud [38] claim that a focused understanding of the document obtained through the use of PBR should be more effective than either an ad-hoc or a checklist based reading technique. Ad-hoc and checklist based reading techniques are thought of as non-systematic in nature [55]. They do not offer a set of concrete reading instructions, meaning that inspectors' experience has a significant impact on the number of defects found [38]. One of the aims of PBR is to enforce the independence of inspectors and encourage a diversity of views. It is also notable that most changes in the inspection process described earlier in this chapter also appear to be ways of trying to achieve different perspectives.

The PBR technique continues to be refined, giving better instructions on the creation and content of scenarios [36]. A PBR-scenario contains three parts. The first explains to inspectors their interest/perspective on the inspection artefact. The second part consists of a set of activities that inspectors have to perform. This allows them to extract the required information out of the inspection artefact. In the final part, inspectors then apply a series of questions to this information to verify its correctness. As an example, the tester scenario for the C programming language, created by Laitenberger et al. [40], contains the following instructions: The first part outlines the role of the tester (ensuring that the functionality of the code is correct). The second (activities) part requires the inspector to identify the functions, determine their inter-dependencies, and create a call-graph. Following this they are instructed to start with the functions at the leaves of the graph and determine test cases to verify the operation of the function by checking each branch and loop. Inspectors are then told to mentally execute these test cases and report any differences with respect to the specification as a defect. The final part consist of the following questions which they are told to ask themselves while following the instructions:

(1) *Do you have the necessary information to identify a test case (e.g., are all constant values and interfaces defined)?*
(2) *Are branch conditions used in a correct manner?*
(3) *Can you generate test cases for each branch and each loop? Can you traverse all branches by using specific test cases?*
(4) *Is allocation and de-allocation of memory used correctly?*

In an inspection, each inspector has a different scenario to allow the artefact to be looked at from different views (e.g., analyst, maintainer, tester). By following the scenario the inspectors should build up an understanding of the artefact. Although the early work on PBR was carried out on requirements documents [4], some of the more recent work has focused on C code documents [38,40].

An experiment by Laitenberger et al. [40], investigated the effectiveness and cost per defect ratio of PBR compared to checklists for C code documents. The results showed that two-person inspection teams were more effective using PBR than checklists. Applying PBR was found to increase subjects understanding of the code, but was found to require greater effort from inspectors. This improved understanding was also found to have helped to reduce the cost of defects for PBR compared to checklists during the meeting phase. With a greater understanding in the meeting, it took less effort on the inspectors' behalf to explain the de-

fect they had found to the other inspectors, as well as taking less effort to resolve false positives. It should be noted however, that the checklist used during
the experiment was a general one, based upon an existing checklist [50] and books
on C programming [16,33]. This goes against the currently available advice [24,
28], which states that checklists are most effective when based upon historical
data.

Biffle and Gutjhar [8] used the results from 196 student inspectors applying either
a checklist-based approach or one of three scenario [perspective]-based approaches
on a requirements document, to investigate the possible impact of varying team sizes
and inspection technique combinations. They found that for a team size of greater
than three, a mixture of reading techniques was the most effective approach to detecting defects (below this, the effective approach was for all inspectors to use the
best single technique). As intuitively expected, as team size grows, the efficiency of
inspection decreases. Since the work is based on student inspectors, they do not pro-
nounce on the ideal team size and combination, but instead provide a model that uses
context-dependent data to calculate these values.

Although most of the experiments investigating the effectiveness of using PBR
have been positive, there has recently been one experiment (based upon a lab package by Basili et al. [5]) investigating its effectiveness and efficiency with relation to
requirements documents [58]. The results contradicted the earlier work on PBR and
showed that there was no significant difference in the type of defects found by each
of the three perspectives used during the inspection.

4.6 Summary

Reading techniques have evolved from offering no support and minimal guidance
to inspectors into detailed task driven processes that encourage inspectors to attain a
good understanding of the artefact under inspection. More recent reading techniques
have also introduced the notion of inspecting artefacts from different views (perspectives). This allows inspectors to focus on different aspects and different defect types
in greater detail.

The increased understanding promoted by recent reading techniques is achieved
through clear, unambiguous instructions that guide the inspector in extracting and
querying the required information from the inspected artefact. It is the development
of this good understanding of the code that is key to a successful inspection. The main
drawbacks of these techniques are an increased pressure on the individual inspector
and the additional effort involved in the preparation and maintenance of support materials (such as checklists, perspectives and scenarios).

5. Adapting to a New Paradigm—Dealing with Object-Orientation

Although the most recent work on inspection reading techniques has focused on design and requirements documents, and one of the strengths of inspections is their flexible application to a variety of document types, in industry it is the inspection of code documents that is still predominant [39]. Laitenberger et al. [40] conclude that this makes the improvement of reading techniques for code documents a high priority. Until recently, most of the research carried out in connection with reading techniques, and inspection in general has related to procedural languages—the predominant paradigm used when inspections were originally proposed. The last ten years have seen the object-oriented paradigm growing in influence and use—particularly since the introduction of C++ and Java. Laitenberger et al. [36] commented that *"over the past decade object-oriented development methods have replaced conventional structured methods as the embodiment of software development, and are now the approach of choice in most new software development projects."* But in the area of software inspections the response to this development has been slow and consequently there is a significant lack of information indicating how inspections should be applied to object-oriented code.

The object-oriented paradigm has gained widespread acceptance [11] and, it has been argued, has delivered many benefits to the programmer such as better structured and more reliable software for complex systems, greater reusability, more extensibility, and easier maintainability [34]. With these claimed successes, there have also arisen new problems to be tackled. In 1994, Jones [30] listed some of the gaps in information about the object-oriented paradigm. One of those gaps was in the area of inspection. Jones noted that *"Since formal inspections are the most effective known way of eliminating software defects, software quality assurance personnel are anxiously awaiting some kind of guidance and quantitative data on the use of inspections with object-oriented projects."*

The lack of guidance on how to apply inspections to object-oriented code is disturbing—the impact of the paradigm on the inspection process and the effectiveness of the highly important reading techniques are unknown. This could result in inspections being performed in a far from efficient manner. This section looks at the impact that the object-oriented paradigm has on the code inspection activity and describes the developments that have taken place so far to address this.

5.1 Object-Oriented Problems and Pitfalls for Inspection

Object-oriented languages differ from procedural ones in a number of profound ways—the encapsulation of data and associated functionality, the common use of inheritance, and the concepts of polymorphism and dynamic binding—to name but a few. These factors influence the way that modules (classes) are created in object-oriented systems, which in turn influences the way that object-oriented systems are structured and execute. The key features of the object-oriented paradigm may have a significant impact on the ease of understanding of program code and failing to adapt to this paradigm may inhibit the effective application of inspections to object-oriented systems.

There is a significant body of literature developing that suggests that the characteristic features of the paradigm can make object-oriented code more difficult to understand compared to the procedural equivalent—an issue that has direct impact on code inspection. Much of this literature centres on experience gathered from the software maintenance domain. The problems encountered in maintenance can apply equally to the task of inspection—both require sections of code to be read and understood.

According to Gamma et al. [23], the structure of an object-oriented program at run-time is vastly different to that of its code structure, *"In fact, the two structures [run-time and compile-time] are largely independent. Trying to understand one from the other is like trying to understand the dynamism of living ecosystems from the static taxonomy of plants and animals, and vice-versa."* Whereas the compile-time structure code structure is static, the run-time structure consists of rapidly changing networks of communicating objects.

Dependencies exist in all code, but their number are increased by object-oriented languages [11,71]. Wilde and Huitt [71] described a dependency in a software system as *"A direct relationship between two entities in the system $X \to Y$ such that a programmer modifying X must be concerned about possible side effects in Y."* Wilde and Huitt suggested that using polymorphism and inheritance hierarchies dramatically increases the kinds of dependencies that need to be considered. Chen et al. [11] described three kinds of dependencies found in object-oriented languages, message dependence (relationship between a method and its callers), class dependence (inheritance, aggregation and association relationships) and declaration dependence (relationship between classes (types) and objects (variables)).

Dynamic binding is a specific example of a characteristic of object-oriented programs that increases the complexities and dependencies in a program. This concept, closely associated with polymorphism, involves not knowing the type of a particular object referenced by a variable, as this is only determined at run time [10,48]. When a method invocation occurs, only at run time can the type of an object be correctly identified. All the associations created through the use of polymorphism and dynamic binding usually mean that more than one class needs to be looked at (especially in the case of a class which is part of a deep inheritance hierarchy) in order to fully understand how one small fragment of code works. Wilde and Huitt suggested that tracing

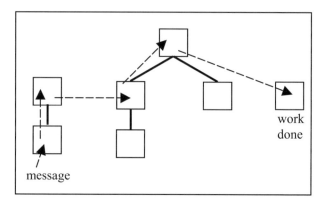

FIG. 2. Chain of message invocations. (Reproduced from [17] with kind permission of the ACM.)

these dependencies is vital for effective software maintenance [71]. Lejter et al. [43] claimed that dynamic binding (along with inheritance) made object-oriented programs much more difficult to maintain and understand. This view is also supported by Crocker and von Mayrhauser [14].

The structure of object-oriented programs differs from that of conventional programs [71]. Method sizes may be very small as a natural consequence of good object-oriented design [44,72]. Daly et al. [15] found that unconstrained use of inheritance may result in understanding difficulties. When investigating the difficulties experienced programmers encountered learning and using the Smalltalk programming language, Nielsen and Richards [51] found that the distributed nature of the code caused problems when attempting to understand a system. Together with inheritance, this distribution may result in traversing up and down inheritance hierarchies and across class boundaries in an attempt to locate where the work is carried out and build up a complete understanding of the task. This problem is illustrated in Fig. 2.

Many of the problems that have been mentioned have also created difficulty for other areas of software engineering outside of software maintenance, such as comprehension [42], component reuse [22], testing [32,49], and visualisation [42]. Each area has had to re-evaluate how it achieves its objectives, and in many cases redesign its processes. Binder [9], in his review of testing for object-oriented software, highlighted that most believe the feature set of object-oriented software will require the development of new approaches to be able to achieve adequate levels of testing.

5.2 Current State of Object-Oriented Inspection

With the rise in popularity of object-orientation, the research community has turned to adapting inspections to this new paradigm and its particular artefacts. As will be seen in this section, the work carried out so far has focused on the inspection of object-oriented requirements and design documents. Although some initial work has been positive, there has been a lack of research regarding how the key features of the object-oriented paradigm may impact on the inspection of object-oriented code.

Travassos et al. [67] found that there was a lack of guidance on how to inspect object-oriented design documents and carried out a preliminary investigation. The main focus was on designs described by UML diagrams. They developed a technique called Traceability-Based Reading (TBR) that evolved from the experience gathered from the development of reading techniques for requirements documents [57]. TBR is a two-step process. The first step involves the correctness and consistency checks on requirements documents that have traditionally occurred. This is described as horizontal reading and takes the form of comparing requirements documents with the likes of use-case diagrams or scenario descriptions (i.e., documents capturing a similar level of abstraction). The second step is described as vertical reading, and differs from the traditional process, in that requirements documents are compared with design documents (such as class diagrams, object interaction diagrams or state machine diagrams) to ensure consistency.

An experiment carried out using TBR found encouraging, but not conclusive results. Horizontal and vertical reading were found on average to highlight different types of defect. Vertical reading found slightly more defects concerning omission and inconsistency (between diagrams and requirements), whereas horizontal reading found more defects concerning ambiguity and inconsistency (between diagrams). An important finding was that the technique forced more focus on semantic information (an understanding of the meaning of the document), similar to the focus encouraged by the scenarios of PBR. In its current state, the technique relies too much on syntactic information, making sure that certain words and attributes in one diagram appear in their correct location elsewhere. Another drawback is that the technique was found to be time consuming.

Laitenberger and Atkinson [36] presented an adaptation of Perspective-Based Reading (PBR) for any object-oriented development artefact. They provided a generally applicable definition of the technique, describing instructions on how to generate PBR-scenarios. An experiment [37] was carried out to investigate the effectiveness of PBR for UML design documents in comparison to checklists. The results of the experiment showed that PBR-scenarios help improve inspectors understanding of the inspection artefacts. This was found to reduce the cost of defects in the group phase (as a collation exercise) for PBR in comparison to checklists. The checklist structure was designed along the lines discussed by Chernak [13], but the checklist questions, due to the lack of other such checklists for object-oriented design documents that could be reused, were developed from scratch.

As can be seen, the majority of research carried out in the area of object-oriented inspection has so far been aimed at the development of reading techniques to help inspectors find defects in requirements and design documents. These techniques have tried to address a perceived lack of reading guidance, but have not fully investigated how the key features of the object-oriented paradigm impact upon code inspections.

5.3   Investigating the Inspection of Object-Oriented Code

Dunsmore et al. [17] carried out an empirical investigation into the issues arising when inspecting object-oriented code. They found that the characteristics of the 'hard to find' defects included use of class libraries, sending wrong messages to objects, inheritance, overriding and design mismatches. Many of the problem characteristics identified by the investigation were also highlighted by an industrial survey. The key features of object-orientation were found to have a significant impact on the ease of understanding of the resulting program by distributing closely related information throughout the code. To understand a piece of code, trails of method invocations had to be followed through many classes, moving both up and down the inheritance hierarchy. Soloway et al. [63] first observed this in the context of program comprehension, describing a 'delocalised plan' as "*where the code for one conceptualised plan is distributed non-contiguously in a program*". Soloway continues, "*Such code is hard to understand. Since only fragments of the plan are seen at a time by a reader, the reader makes inferences based only on what is locally apparent—and these inferences are quite error prone.*"

Dunsmore et al. [17] identified three significant issues requiring further research:

(1) *Chunking*—The many dependencies and links between classes make it very difficult to isolate even one or two classes for inspection, and delocalisation complicates this further. How you partition the code for inspection defines what an inspector gets to inspect. Two issues in this respect need to be addressed: (1) the identification of suitable chunks of code to inspect, and (2) decide how to break the chunk free of the rest of the system, minimising the number of dependencies and the amount of delocalisation.

(2) *Reading strategy*—How should object-oriented code be read, especially if systematic reading of code is impractical? Is there a reading strategy that could help inspectors deal with delocalisation? Can checklists or PBR be modified to address delocalisation or are new reading strategies required?

(3) *Localising the delocalisation*—A way has to be found to abstract the delocalised information for the inspector, providing the benefits of systematic reading without the unrealistic requirement that *everything* is read. Inspections

```
public void cancelReservation(Person u, GregorianCalendar d)
{
  Reservation r = new Reservation(u,d);
  for(int i=0; i<reservations.size(); i++)
  {
    if (reservations.removeElement(r))
      System.out.println("Reservation Cancelled");
    else
      System.out.println("Cancellation Failed");
  }
}
```

FIG. 3. Example of a delocalised defect. (Reproduced from [17] with kind permission of the ACM.)

have to be able to address the frequent references that object-oriented code makes to parts of the system that are outwith the current inspection focus.

5.4   Inadequacy of Current Inspection Approaches

There are various reading techniques available that can be used by individual inspectors during the inspection of code. How much do currently available reading techniques help inspectors deal with the issue of delocalisation?

Consider the example shown in Fig. 3. There are several flaws in the structure of the cancelReservation method. Given a person and a date, the method was supposed to remove the associated reservation that had previously been made for a particular video. The flaws in the method were:

- The use of a for loop when none was required.

- An assumption placed on comparisons made between the date held in d and the dates held in the reservations vector. The specification for the method stated that only the year, month and day were to be taken into account when comparing dates. However, the Vector method removeElement compares two objects using their equals method, meaning that in this case, the hour, minute and seconds values in both these objects were also considered in the comparison.

The ad-hoc reading technique offers no support to the inspector, who instead relies on their own knowledge and experience and reads the code in their own preferred way. It offers no guide to help focus an inspector on parts of the code or help them comprehend the code. Whether any of the delocalised information is traced depends solely on what the inspector does. This suggests that ad-hoc reading may have poor results when dealing with delocalised information, and depends heavily on the individual inspectors. It certainly provides no active support to address delocalisation.

Checklists offer more support than ad-hoc in the form of a series of questions, which must be answered by the inspector. One drawback of using a checklist is that it *"provides little support to help an inspector understand the inspected artefact"* [39]. It is unlikely that a checklist would highlight incorrect use of the date storage class GregorianCalendar in Fig. 3 as the code is, in itself, functionally correct but contains the hidden assumption relating to the number of fields used in the date comparison. Although Porter et al. [57] commented that checklists might be thought of as systematic because they define reviewers responsibilities and ways to identify faults, they argue that the generality of the questions and lack of concrete strategies for answering the questions makes checklists a non-systematic reading strategy. Checklists do not encourage inspectors to follow the trail of delocalisation, they encourage *localised, as-needed reading* (see following section).

In PBR each inspector is given one perspective. Multiple inspectors are required to obtain a 'reasonable' level of coverage of the document. Each perspective contains instructions on extracting the relevant information for examination (in respect to their perspective), and is followed by a series of questions to be answered based on the information collected. In this way, PBR encourages a better understanding of the code but, like checklists, it doesn't actively encourage inspectors to follow the delocalisation trail. However, it is conceivable that a perspective could be created with just this remit, although this idea has not yet been explored.

Another weakness of all three approaches—ad-hoc, checklist and PBR—is that none of them help reduce the amount of code that would have to be understood if delocalisation trails were followed. Following the trails is necessary for a sufficient understanding of the code to help identify delocalised defects. An inspection on 200 lines of object-oriented code could easily swell by an order of magnitude due to inter-class dependencies. All of the approaches assume that a manageable quantity of code (e.g., 100 lines per hour) can be easily isolated.

Thus the reading techniques ad-hoc, checklist and PBR are not designed to cope with defects where the information required to understand and identify them is delocalised. They neither encourage inspectors to follow the trails of delocalisation nor help reduce the amount of code to be read if the delocalisation trail is followed. New techniques and aids are needed to address these problems.

5.5   Techniques for Object-Oriented Code Inspection

To address the problems of reading strategy and delocalisation, Dunsmore et al. [18] developed and evaluated a systematic abstraction-driven reading technique. The systematic technique forced inspectors to follow the trail of delocalisation, building up their understanding of the code by reverse engineering an abstract specification of the method currently under inspection. These abstract specifications can then be referenced by current and future inspections and bypass the need to follow further trails of delocalised code—all the information necessary to understand the method should be contained within the specification. An evaluation of the systematic reading technique comparing it against the ad-hoc reading technique found that there was no significant difference between the number of defects found by ad-hoc subjects compared to systematic subjects. However, some interesting issues emerged.

Defects with delocalised characteristics still appeared difficult to find. Subjects using the systematic technique found all the defects, whereas those using the ad-hoc technique missed several delocalised defects. As a by-product the systematic technique produced abstractions that can be reused at a later date for re-inspection. By generating the abstractions subjects found that they obtained a greater understanding of the code. Subjects commented favourably on the more structured process and ordering of the code encouraged by the systematic technique, but found that the process of generating the abstractions required a lot of time. The systematic technique was found to help the weaker subjects, improving their defect detection ability, but was also found to inhibit the natural abilities of the stronger subjects. A potential weakness of the systematic technique was found to be its reliance on the static view of object-oriented code. The dynamic nature of object-oriented systems may hinder the effectiveness of such a static reading approach.

Following on from this, three reading techniques were developed and compared to investigate these issues [19]. The three techniques were: a checklist, a systematic reading technique, and a technique based upon use-cases. The checklist was updated to reflect the demands of object-oriented code. It included specific guidance on reading order (in an attempt to minimise the impact of delocalisation), and was based upon the defect data from earlier studies. The systematic reading technique was essentially a slight evolution from that explored in the first evaluation. The use-case technique involved developing scenarios (particular test cases) from use cases and following these through sequence diagrams until the class under inspection was encountered. At this point, focus is transferred to the code until an invocation is made to some external object, when focus is returned to the sequence diagram. The philosophy behind the technique is to explore the dynamic use of an object and determine its response to a variety of likely input scenarios.

An evaluation of the three reading techniques found a significant difference (at the 10% level) in the number of defects detected between the reading techniques. The delocalised defects that were seeded in the experiment were more evenly distributed within the results for all the techniques.

The checklist technique was found to have the best overall performance, although subjects using the systematic technique were more effective at finding delocalised defects. Subjects noted that the checklist technique was easy and straightforward to use.

Those who used the systematic technique stated that it encouraged a greater level of understanding. Subjects with different ability levels using the checklist performed reasonably well. The systematic technique was again found to help the defect detection ability of weaker subjects, but still seemed to constrain the ability of stronger subjects.

Weaker use-case subjects appeared to struggle (possibly due to the complexity of the technique). In general subjects found this technique very demanding but this may be a result of using students rather than subjects with more industrial experience.

5.6 Advice on Practical Object-Oriented Code Inspection

The work presented in this section has made an initial investigation into the issues facing the inspection of object-oriented code. The main indication is that for inspections to continue to be effective, they must take into account the effect of delocalised information and the difference between the static and dynamic representation of code.

Checklists, despite their criticisms in the literature, can be very effective at this task. They are relatively straightforward to use and have very few overheads. If checklists can be tailored to the development environment using historical defect data and include questions that specifically target object-oriented characteristics then they have the potential to be an effective aid to object-oriented inspections. However, it should be noted that this limits the checklist to recognised defect characteristics, and reduces the chances of finding new or unexpected defects. The questions used within the checklist should also try to encourage a deeper understanding of the code and, in particular, its relationship with the rest of the system. This would help avoid the more traditional 'lightweight' checklist questions that only superficially probe the code.

The systematic technique provided encouraging results concerning the detection of delocalised defects. The technique offers a potential long-term advantage through the creation of abstractions. However, it has a higher overhead than checklists and may fail to adequately deal with some localised defects. Although the generated abstractions require further evaluation to establish their most effective form and usefulness, the ordering of code for inspection and the use of stepwise abstraction to help with delocalisation are aspects of the technique that can be recommended.

Although the results for the use-case technique were weaker, it has several potential strengths. Inspectors read the code from a dynamic model viewpoint and the technique offers an independent source of comparison for the code with software requirements (in the form of use-cases, scenarios and sequence diagrams). The technique better focuses on inter-class relationships as well as state information and has the potential to deal with defects of omission. This was found to be the most demanding of all the reading techniques, and it may be that it is a technique that can only be used by those with more industrial experience. However, it should be remembered that due to the nature of the technique, some parts of a class may go unchecked because they do not participate in the use-case that is driving the current inspection. It may be necessary to compliment this reading technique with another to ensure complete coverage of a class.

Where practical, object-oriented inspections should be based on teams of inspectors using at least two different reading techniques. The checklist was found to have a strong overall performance, but the systematic technique was found to be more effective at finding delocalised defects. A problem with the checklist is that its performance can rely heavily on the relationship between the questions and the context it is used in, whereas other techniques have less reliance on context and may give a more consistent performance.

Using a combination of reading techniques is a view similar to the one advocated by the developers of the Perspective Based Reading (PBR) technique, where different perspectives are used to represent different stakeholders, e.g., tester or code analyst. Each of these perspectives is expected to highlight different types of defects. If a PBR approach was to be adopted, it is suggested that one of the perspectives should specifically focus on object-oriented issues. Combining reading techniques, such as those described in this section, offers a good degree of robustness and the potential to deal with many different defect types—the recurring defects, defects that require deeper insights, and defects associated with the features of object-orientation that distribute functionality throughout a system.

6. Tool Support for Inspection

6.1 Introduction

Over the last decade tool support for inspection has been an area of active and widespread research and development. Conventionally, software inspection is implemented as a manual, paper-based process but there is great potential to computerise almost all aspects of the process. The focus of early tools was on the support of single, usually proprietary processes [46]. In recent years, as the focus of manual, paper-based inspection has moved to individual reading, there has been a trend towards more general tool support managing documents, collecting data, supporting meetings and thus allowing the developer to concentrate on the key activity of defect detection.

There are differing views on the use or benefits of tool support. Code inspections are traditionally thought of as non-execution based, i.e., the inspector is never allowed to execute or compile the code during the inspection. This allows inspection to be applied to code documents long before tests are designed or even run [24]. It has also been found that if the code is executed and tested before an inspection, the motivation of the inspectors may be reduced and make the inspection process appear redundant [60,70]. Humphrey [28], in the Personal Software Process (PSP), states that as part of the process to ensure a quality product, inspections should take place before the first compile or test. Taking the opposite view, Gilb and Graham [24] and Strauss and Ebenau [64] consider sending code to a compiler as one of the many different entry criteria that have to be passed before an inspection can begin. The reason for the clean compilation check is that it is cheaper for the compiler (or other automatic tools) to find those kinds of defects, than the more expensive inspector.

This section discusses those aspects of inspection that are the focus of current tool support: document handling, meeting support, data collection and reading support. It then briefly describes the features of two representative tools that explicitly support those aspects. After that, two approaches that reflect a current emphasis in inspection tool development, namely the use of Groupware Support Systems and Web-based systems, are described. The section concludes with an example of a tool that explicitly supports defect detection during individual reading.

6.2   Document Handling

Supporting documents in an electronic format during inspection has a number of potential benefits. Since most documents are inevitably developed and stored on computers, it would seem natural to distribute and view them this way. The distribution of documents is considerably simplified (and is environmentally beneficial) and more complex documents (such as design diagrams which might span several pages or take the form of navigable hierarchies) are easier to view, explore and analyse. An additional benefit is the capability to cross-reference multiple documents and then provide automatic links between these documents.

One of the major challenges identified in inspecting object-oriented code was the problem of delocalisation—understanding information directly related to the object under inspection that was not local to that object. Tool support is seen as having an important role to play in addressing this—supporting controlled navigation to related code, design documentation, library code documentation, etc. If the use-case approach is taken to object-oriented code inspection then tool support has an important role to play in allowing the inspector to visualise the use-cases simultaneously with the code.

6.3   Meeting Support

Due to the recommended two-hour time limit on inspection meetings it may take several meetings before an inspection is complete. There is typically a large overhead in setting up a meeting: finding a time that is mutually agreeable, a suitable location, and so on. Depending on the company organization and project management style, there may also be an overhead in travelling to the meeting. For example, a project might be spread over different company sites, or a user from a different company might be involved in the inspection. One possible solution is to hold a distributed meeting where all meeting participants may communicate with each other electronically and the meeting itself is supported by software that enables decision making, records outcomes etc. Given that current thinking de-emphasises the role of the inspection meeting, a natural extension of this idea is to dispense with the traditional meeting phase and execute the inspection asynchronously. In this case individual inspectors work in their own time and, on completion, the author and moderator, perhaps with automated support, resolve the individual defect lists.

6.4   Data Collection

The use of tools also provides the opportunity to automatically capture data for use in analysing and improving the inspection process. This might include time spent during preparation, or in the meeting, exactly where time was spent, defects found and so on. It could also provide evidence that supports the tuning of checklists or PBR-scenarios based on the behaviour of the inspectors utilizing them. Manual collection of such data in an accurate and reliable fashion is notoriously difficult. This is particularly relevant for support materials such as checklists, which rely on the timely analysis of frequently occurring defects to maintain their effectiveness.

6.5   Reading Support

Although it is unlikely that automation will ever replace the human in this key phase of inspection, there are several ways in which tool support can assist the individual in preparation for, and during, the reading phase. Initially, a certain amount of automatic defect detection may be carried out addressing tasks that are fairly mundane for the human, e.g., removing syntax errors and detecting standards violations. This has the benefit of freeing the inspector to concentrate on the deeper, and potentially far more troublesome, semantic issues.

Checklists and PBR-scenarios should be visible and take the form of "active" on-line forms that have to be completed before the inspection can continue. Tool support should be provided to help create the models or test cases required by PBR-scenarios to reflect the deep understanding encouraged by the perspective. Supporting documents should be kept visible and clearly cross-referenced.

If electronic document support is available then an individual's comments (defects, questions, etc.) may take the form of annotations to the document. This allows for a more accurate correspondence between the defect description and its location as well as ensuring that all comments are recorded. Following on from this the comments from all individuals can then be simply gathered, collated and distributed for use before and during the meeting.

In addressing the challenges of object-oriented code inspection using the systematic, abstraction-driven reading strategy tools have a critical role to play both in visualizing abstractions and supporting their creation.

6.6   Current Tool Support

Macdonald and Miller [46] provide a thorough description and comparison of sixteen inspection tools developed during the 1990s. During this period there has been a move from focused support for specific standalone inspection processes, towards tools that provide generic support for a variety inspection process, general document types and enable inspections to be carried out asynchronously, distributed across multiple sites.

An example of the former is ICICLE (Intelligent Code Inspection in a C language Environment) [7]. ICICLE was designed to support the inspection of C/C+ code providing some automated support for defect detection based on the use of the UNIX tool 'lint' and its own rule-based system that was capable of detecting issues such as failure to de-allocate memory. It also include a feature to browse Unix manual pages and cross reference code over multiple files. ICICLE supported synchronous, same-room meetings where the "reader" controlled the rate of inspection on all machines. After the inspection ICICLE generated a list of defects summarized by type and severity together with basic process timing information.

Macdonald and Miller themselves developed ASSIST (Asynchronous/Synchronous Software Inspection Support Tool) [47] which is a good example of the kind of automated support that is currently available. ASSIST was designed to address a range of inspection processes and document types, and to reduce effort and improve inspector performance. A full range of inspection processes may be defined using the associated inspection process definition language. The system has flexible document support that allows the addition of new document types and their associated browsers. Individual inspectors may then annotate documents at varying degrees of detail. A checklist browser supports active checklists (which have to be completed by the individual) and the system cross-references items in the checklist with keywords in the document. The on-line meeting is controlled by the reader and may be distributed, synchronous or asynchronous. The system has an auto-collation facility that allows multiple defect lists to be combined.

Current thinking on inspection tools reflects the emphasis on the individual reading phase that is now apparent in manual, paper-based inspection. It is suggested that Groupware Support Systems or Web-based systems can provide the basis for effective generic support for the inspection process, management of documents, data collection, synchronous or asynchronous, distributed meetings together with basic support for the reading phase. In parallel with this specialised tools that specifically aid the individual reading phase are being proposed.

Halling et al. [26] suggest that GroupWare Support Systems (GSSs) provide the necessary infrastructure for automated support of the inspection process. GSS technology is widely used to communicate, cooperate, coordinate, solve problems or negotiate. Van Genuchten et al. [68] provide empirical evidence from a professional environment that a GSS can support and enforce the inspection process leading to improved effectiveness and efficiency compared to a manual process.

Halling et al. (see http://www.groupsystems.com) argue that a GSS such as Group-Systems actively supports inspection in the following ways. GSSs are tailorable to any inspection process and automatically support distributed and synchronous or asynchronous meetings. GSSs support a variety of communication models between inspectors ranging from the possibility of no communication to full communication (every participant receives all the annotations of all other team members). GSSs support extracting the semantic structure from (textual) documents. This enables checklist questions, for example, to be directly related to the relevant parts of the document (though there no is built-in support in these systems for reading strategies based on checklists or PBR-scenarios). Similarly defect data can be directly associated to the underlying semantic structure of the document. GSSs provide built-in support for data collection that includes information on process conformance, process effectiveness and inspector performance. Halling et al. also argue that the high degree of flexibility in a GSS means that the inspection process may be changed as a reaction to experiences or data gathered during an actual inspection run. The downside of these tools is the effort required to tailor the tool to the inspection process, an effort that, it is argued, is clearly less than developing a tool from scratch.

A third trend in general inspection process support is the use of Web-based tools. Harjumma et al. [27] have been at the forefront of Web-based inspection tools over the last five years. They argue that the Web provides a useful infrastructure for collaborative inspection tools due to its *"prevalence, platform independence and familiarity."* the fact that its browsers can cope with most document formats and that geographical distribution is a fundamental feature. They have developed Web-based inspection tools that support inspection and annotation of any HTML document, simultaneous viewing of checklists, and basic process statistics gathering. Current

Web-based tools provide no support for synchronous meetings and, according to Har-jumma et al. suffer from a lack of "*flexibility and interoperability*"—the capability to smoothly integrate different document and tool types into a web-based environment. Their current research is aimed at addressing these weaknesses based on the use of Mozilla as a generic application environment and XML as an underlying document format.

The final area of focus for current tool support is in actively helping the inspector to discover defects during the individual reading phase. It is extremely unlikely that tools will ever replace humans in this phase but there is plenty of scope for tool support to help humans acquire the deep understanding that is necessary for this task. CodeSurfer [2] is a good example of such a commercial tool. CodeSurfer uses a range of dependence graphs together with slicing and graph reachability algorithms to provide the following facilities to support the inspection of structured languages such as C:

- variable usage information—where variables are defined, used and modified, including via pointers,
- predecessors and successors—how does a variable acquire a certain value, or where is a value, generated at a certain point, used,
- slicing—what points in the program does a set of starting points depend on, what points in the program depend on a set of starting points,
- chopping—how does execution of one set of program points affect a second set of program points,
- model checker—supports a variety of 'canned' queries about possible paths through the software.

Although CodeSurfer has not been applied to object-oriented code the approach it embodies would seem to offer potential support for the delocalisation issues discussed earlier in this chapter. More generally, careful investigation is required to determine how such tools can be properly integrated with reading strategies based on the use of checklists or PBR-scenarios.

6.7 Tool Summary

Over the last decade there has been a significant amount of development of and experimentation on tools to support software inspection. Initially these tools were aimed at specific models of inspection. Over the years the focus has become more general, accommodating a variety of inspection processes and document types, and making use of communications technology to enable new models of distributed and asynchronous inspection. Current researchers advocate the use of more generalized software such as Groupware Support Systems or web infrastructure as the basis of inspection tools, ideally in conjunction with tools that actively support the core inspection activity of defect detection. An issue of some concern is that, despite the significant efforts that have been made in the area of tool support and the fairly compelling arguments for their usefulness, there is not much evidence of these tools being used to support inspection outside of the organizations responsible for their development. Finally, object-oriented technology currently dominates the construction of new software systems but there is no tool support that specifically addresses the kind of issue that can arise when inspecting object-oriented code.

7. Conclusions

Inspections are an effective method used to find defects in many different documents generated throughout the lifetime of a software project. Recently, the focus for detecting defects has moved away from the group inspection activity. Instead, the focus for detecting defects is the preparation phase, where the individual inspector reads the artefact in preparation for the group phase (which is now used for defect collation).

With the focus for detecting defects in inspection moved to the preparation phase, the reading technique used by the inspector to help prepare and find defects within an inspection artefact has become one of the key aspects of the inspection process. Adequate support for inspectors is necessary to help them be as efficient and as effective as possible.

Reading techniques have evolved from offering no support and minimal guidance to inspectors (e.g., ad-hoc and checklist) into detailed task driven processes that encourage inspectors to attain a good understanding of the artefact under inspection (e.g., scenarios and perspective-based reading). It is the development of this good understanding of the code that is key to helping inspectors increase their effectiveness.

Within the last decade, the object-oriented paradigm has grown both in influence and use. It has been shown that this presents significant challenges to the software inspector. The major issues to be addressed are delocalisation (the distribution of semantically related information over a wide range of classes), and chunking (the problem of extracting an "inspectable" block of code from a tightly coupled network of objects). In addition, the dynamics of object-oriented code are very different from its static representation. It has been shown that a checklist based upon a good set of historical data, and modified to acknowledge the chunking problem, can be an effective inspection aid. The systematic abstraction based approach may be effective with delocalised defects, and the use-case driven technique has the potential to deal with faults of omission and understanding the dynamics of the code. Overall, a combination of approaches is recommended in order to ensure a range of perspectives and a high degree of robustness.

Tool support has also changed considerably since the advent of inspections. Once the suitable technology was available the initial systems concentrated on providing support for proprietary processes. Since then, tools have continued to capitalise on technological advances, have increased in flexibility (in particular in their ability to handle a wide range of document types), have opened up new possibilities for models of inspection (such as distributed, asynchronous inspections).

REFERENCES

[1] Ackerman A.F., Buchwald L.S., Lewski F.H., "Software inspections: An effective verification process", *IEEE Software* **6** (3) (1989) 31–36.

[2] Anderson P., Teitelbaum T., "Software inspection using CodeSurfer", in: *Proceedings of the 1st Workshop on Inspection in Software Engineering (WISE'01), Paris*, 2001, http://www.cas.mcmaster.ca/wise/wise01/.

[3] Basili V.R., "Evolving and packaging reading technologies", *Journal of Systems and Software* **38** (1) (1997) 3–12.

[4] Basili V.R., Green S., Laitenberger O., Lanubile F., Shull F., Sørumgård S., Zelkowitz M., "The empirical investigation of perspective-based reading", *Empirical Software Engineering* **2** (1) (1996) 133–164.

[5] Basili V.R., Green S., Laitenberger O., Lanubile F., Shull F., Sørumgård S., Zelkowitz M., "Lab package for the empirical investigation of perspective-based reading", 1998. Available at http://www.cs.umd.edu/projects/SoftEng/ESEG/manual/pbr_package/manual.html.

[6] Basili V.R., Mills H.D., "Understanding and documenting programs", *IEEE Transactions on Software Engineering* **8** (3) (1982) 270–283.

[7] Bell Communications Research, *ICICLE User's Guide* (1993).

[8] Biffl S., Gutjahr W., "Influence of TEM size and defect detection technique on inspection effectiveness", in: *Proceedings of the 7th International Software Metrics Symposium (METRICS 2001)*, IEEE Press, 2001.

[9] Binder R.V., "Testing object-oriented software: a survey", in: *Software Testing, Verification and Validation*, Vol. 6, 1996, pp. 125–252.

[10] Booch G., *Object-Oriented Analysis and Design with Applications*, 2nd edn., Benjamin/Cummings Publishing Company, 1994.

[11] Chen X., Tsai W., Huang H., "Omega—an integrated environment for C++ program maintenance", *International Conference on Software Maintenance* (1996) 114–123.

[12] Cheng B., Jeffrey R., "Comparing inspection strategies for software requirements specifications", in: *Proceedings of the 1996 Australian Software Engineering Conference*, 1996, pp. 203–211.

[13] Chernak Y., "A statistical approach to the inspection checklist formal synthesis and improvement", *IEEE Transactions on Software Engineering* **22** (12) (1996) 866–874.

[14] Crocker R.T., von Mayrhauser A., "Maintenance support needs for object-oriented software", in: *Proceedings of COMPSAC'93*, 1993, pp. 63–69.

[15] Daly J., Brooks A., Miller J., Roper M., Wood M., "Evaluating inheritance depth on the maintainability of object-oriented software", *Empirical Software Engineering* **1** (2) (1996) 109–132.

[16] Deitel H., Deitel P., *C How to Program*, 2nd edn., Prentice-Hall, 1994.

[17] Dunsmore A., Roper M., Wood M., "Object-oriented inspection in the face of delocalisation", in: *Proceedings of the 22nd International Conference on Software Engineering*, ACM Press, New York, 2000, pp. 467–476.

[18] Dunsmore A., Roper M., Wood M., "Systematic object-oriented inspection—an empirical study", in: *Proceedings of the 23rd International Conference on Software Engineering*, IEEE Computer Society Press, 2001, pp. 135–144.

[19] Dunsmore A., Roper M., Wood M., "Further investigations into the development and evaluation of reading techniques for object-oriented inspection", in: *Proceedings of the 24th International Conference on Software Engineering*, ACM Press, New York, 2002, pp. 47–57.

[20] Fagan M.E., "Design and code inspections to reduce errors in program development", *IBM Systems Journal* **15** (3) (1976) 182–211.

[21] Fagan M.E., "Advances in software inspections", *IEEE Transactions in Software Engineering* **12** (7) (1986) 744–751.

[22] Fichman R.G., Kemerer C.F., "Object technology and reuse: lessons from early adopters", *IEEE Computer* **30** (10) (1997) 47–59.

[23] Gamma E., Helm R., Johnson R., Vlissides J., *Design Patterns: Elements of Reusable Object-Oriented Software*, Addison-Wesley, Reading, MA, 1994.

[24] Gilb T., Graham D., *Software Inspection*, Addison-Wesley, Reading, MA, 1993.

[25] Grady R.B., Van Slack T., "Key lessons in achieving widespread inspection use", *IEEE Software* **11** (4) (1994) 46–57.

[26] Halling M., Grunbacher P., Biffl S., "Groupware support for software requirements inspection", in: *Proceedings of the 1st Workshop on Inspection in Software Engineering (WISE'01)*, Paris, 2001, http://www.cas.mcmaster.ca/wise/wise01/.

[27] Harjumma L., Hedberg H., "Web-based software inspection tools—past, present and future", in: *Proceedings of the 20th IASTED International Multi-Conference Applied Informatics (AI 2002), Austria*, 2002.

[28] Humphrey W.H., *A Discipline for Software Engineering*, Addison-Wesley, Reading, MA, 1995.

[29] Johnson P., "An instrumented approach to improving software quality through formal technical review", in: *Proceedings of the 16th International Conference on Software Engineering*, 1994.

[30] Jones C., "Gaps in the object-oriented paradigm", *IEEE Computer* **27** (6) (1994).

[31] Jones C.L., "A process-integrated approach to defect prevention", *IBM Systems Journal* **24** (2) (1985) 150–167.

[32] Jüttner P., Kolb S., Zimmerer P., "Integrating and testing of object-oriented software", in: *Proceedings of EuroSTAR'94*, 1994, pp. 13/1–13/14.

[33] Kernighan B., Ritchie D., *Programming in C*, Hanser-Verlag, 1990.

[34] Khan E.H., Al-A'ali M., Girgis M.R., "Object-oriented programming for structured procedural programmers", *IEEE Computer* **28** (10) (1995) 48–57.

[35] Knight J.C., Myers E.A., "An improved inspection technique", *Communications of the ACM* **36** (11) (1993) 51–61.

[36] Laitenberger O., Atkinson C., "Generalising perspective-based inspection to handle object-oriented development artefacts", in: *Proceedings of the 21st International Conference on Software Engineering*, 1999, pp. 494–503.

[37] Laitenberger O., Atkinson C., Schlich M., El Emam K., "An experimental comparison of reading techniques for defect detection in UML design documents", *The Journal of Systems and Software* **53** (2) (2000) 183–204.

[38] Laitenberger O., DeBaud J.-M., "Perspective-based reading of code documents at Robert Bosch GmbH", *Information and Software Technology (Special Issue)* **39** (1997) 781–791.

[39] Laitenberger O., DeBaud J.-M., "An encompassing life-cycle centric survey of software inspection", *Journal of Systems and Software* **50** (1) (2000) 5–31.

[40] Laitenberger O., El-Emam K., Harbich T.G., "An internally replicated quasi-experiment comparison of checklist and perspective-based reading of code documents", *IEEE Transactions on Software Engineering* **27** (5) (2001) 387–421.

[41] Land L.P.W., Sauer C., Jeffery R., "Validating the defect detection performance advantage of group designs for software reviews: Report of a laboratory experiment using program code", in: *6th European Software Engineering Conference*, 1997, pp. 294–309.

[42] Lange D.B., Nakamura Y., "Object-oriented program tracing and visualisation", *IEEE Computer* **30** (5) (1997) 63–70.

[43] Lejter M., Meyers S., Reiss S.P., "Support for maintaining object-oriented programs", *IEEE Transactions on Software Engineering* **18** (12) (1992) 1045–1052.

[44] Lieberherr K.J., Holland I., "Assuring good style for object-oriented programs", *IEEE Software* **6** (5) (1989) 38–48.

[45] Linger R., Mills H., Witt B., *Structured Programming: Theory and Practice*, Addison-Wesley, Reading, MA, 1979.

[46] Macdonald F., Miller J., "A comparison of computer support systems for software inspection", *Automated Software Engineering* **6** (3) (1999) 291–313.

[47] Macdonald F., Miller J., "ASSIST—A tool to support software inspection", *Information and Software Technology* **41** (1999) 1045–1057.

[48] Macdonald F., Miller J., Brooks A., Roper M., Wood M., "Applying inspection to object-oriented software", in: *Software Testing, Verification and Reliability*, Vol. 6, 1996, pp. 61–82.

[49] Murphy G.C., Townsend P., Wong P.S., "Experiences with cluster and class testing", *Communications of the ACM* **37** (9) (1994) 39–47.

[50] National Aeronautics and Space Administration, "Software Formal Inspection Guidebook", Technical Report NASA-GB-A302, National Aeronautics and Space Administration, 1993, http://satc.gsfc.nasa.gov/fi/fipage.html.

[51] Nielsen J., Richards J., "Experience of learning and using Smalltalk", *IEEE Software* **6** (3) (1989) 73–77.

[52] Parnas D.L., Weiss D.M., "Active design reviews: principles and practice", in: *Proceedings of 8th International Conference on Software Engineering*, 1985, pp. 132–136.

[53] Porter A., Votta L., "What makes inspections work", *IEEE Software* **14** (6) (1997) 99–102.

[54] Porter A.A., Johnson P.M., "Assessing software review meetings: Results of a comparative analysis of two experimental studies", *IEEE Transactions on Software Engineering* **23** (3) (1997) 129–144.

[55] Porter A.A., Siy H.P., Toman C.A., Votta L.G., "An experiment to assess the cost-benefits of code inspections in large scale software development", *IEEE Transactions in Software Engineering* **23** (6) (1997) 329–346.

[56] Porter A.A., Siy H.P., Votta L.G., "A review of software inspections", *Advances in Computers* **42** (1996) 39–76.

[57] Porter A.A., Votta L.G., Basili V.R., "Comparing detection methods for software requirements inspections: A replicated experiment", *IEEE Transactions on Software Engineering* **21** (6) (1995) 563–575.

[58] Regnell B., Runeson P., Thelin T., "Are the perspectives really different? Further experimentation on scenario-based reading on requirements", *Empirical Software Engineering: An International Journal* **5** (4) (2000) 331–356.

[59] Rifkin S., Deimel L., "Applying program comprehension techniques to improve software inspections", in: *19th Annual NASA Software Engineering Laboratory Workshop, Maryland*, 1994.

[60] Russell G.W., "Experience with inspection in ultralarge-scale developments", *IEEE Software* **8** (1) (1991) 25–31.

[61] Schneider G.M., Martin J., Tsai W.T., "An experimental study of fault detection in user requirements documents", *ACM Transactions on Software Engineering and Methodology* **1** (2) (1992) 188–204.

[62] Selby R.W., Basili V.R., Baker F.T., "Cleanroom software development: An empirical evaluation", *IEEE Transactions on Software Engineering* **13** (9) (1987) 1027–1037.

[63] Soloway E., Pinto J., Letovsky S., Littman D., Lampert R., "Designing documentation to compensate for delocalised plans", *Communications of the ACM* **31** (11) (1988) 1259–1267.

[64] Strauss S.H., Ebenau R.G., *Software Inspection Process*, McGraw-Hill Systems Design and Implementation Series, 1993.

[65] Tervonen I., "Consistent support for software designers and inspectors", *Software Quality Journal* **5** (1996) 221–229.

[66] Thelin T., Petersson H., Wohlin C., "Sample-driven inspection", in: *Proceedings of the 1st Workshop on Inspection in Software Engineering*, Software Quality Research Lab, McMaster University, 2001, pp. 81–91.

[67] Travassos G.H., Shull F., Fredericks M., Basili V.R., "Detecting defects in object oriented designs: Using reading techniques to increase software quality", in: *Conference on Object-Oriented Programming, Systems, Languages, and Applications (OOPSLA)*, 1999.

[68] van Genuchten M., van Dijk C., Scholten H., Vogel D., "Using group support systems for software inspections", *IEEE Software* **18** (3) (2001).

[69] Votta L.G., "Does every inspection need a meeting?", *ACM Software Engineering Notes* **18** (5) (1993) 107–114.

[70] Weller E.F., "Lessons from three years of inspection data", *IEEE Software* **10** (5) (1993) 38–45.

[71] Wilde N., Huitt R., "Maintenance support for object-oriented programs", *IEEE Transactions on Software Engineering* **18** (12) (1992) 1038–1044.

[72] Wilde N., Matthews P., Huitt R., "Maintaining object-oriented software", *IEEE Software* **10** (1) (1993) 75–80.

Software Fault Tolerance
Forestalls Crashes: To Err Is Human;
To Forgive Is Fault Tolerant

LAWRENCE BERNSTEIN

Stevens Institute of Technology
Castle Point
Hoboken, NJ 07030
USA
lbernstein@ieee.org

Abstract

Software Fault Tolerance prevents ever-present defects in the software from hanging or crashing a system. The problem of preventing latent software faults from becoming system failures is the subject of this chapter. Software architectures, design techniques, static checks, dynamic tests, special libraries, and run-time routines help software engineers create fault tolerant software. The nature of software execution is chaotic because there are few ways to find singularities, and even those are rarely practiced. This leads to complex and untrustworthy software products.

The study of software fault tolerance starts with the goal of making software products available to users in the face of software errors. Availability is a mathematical concept; it is the Mean Time-To-Failure divided by the Mean Time-To-Failure plus the Mean Time-To-Repair. The idea is to make the Mean Time-To-Failure as large as possible and the Mean Time-To-Repair as small as possible. Continuing with Reliability Theory we can express the Mean Time-To-Failure as the reciprocal of the failure rate. Assuming an exponential reliability model the failure rate is the expected value of the reliability of the system. This chapter shows how these quantitative concepts can be used to make software engineering tradeoffs.

First, there is a historical perspective on, and problems with, the study of software fault tolerance. Then new approaches are presented with a theme of making it possible to trade-off software execution time, complexity, staff effort, and the effectives of the staff to achieve desired system availability.

1. Background

1.1 Fault Tolerant Computers

The 1990s were to be the decade of fault tolerant computing. Fault tolerant hardware was in the works and software fault tolerance was imminent. But it didn't happen. Hardware suppliers successfully convinced customers that highly reliable configurations with duplicate disks in RAID configurations as shown in Fig. 1 were good enough. The most popular computer suppliers did not have fault tolerant configurations to offer their customers. To keep their market share they convinced their customers that the incremental value of a hardware fault tolerant configuration did not warrant the extra costs. In addition, they radically reduced the costs of their high reliability configurations. Fault tolerant computers became twice as expensive as high reliable ones. Since the application software was not fault tolerant the incumbent suppliers argued the new computers were not cost effective. Except in some special cases their arguments carried the day. The incumbent suppliers eventually absorbed the new companies that made fault tolerant computers. In the 1990s, the Web Wave surged. Highly reliable server hardware configurations became the solution of choice. Software failures were not addressed. Software developers lost interest in fault tolerance until a rash of server failures, denial of service episodes, web outages and the September 11th attack occurred.

Software fault tolerance methods are often extrapolated from hardware fault tolerance concepts. This approach misses the mark because hardware fault tolerance is aimed at conquering manufacturing faults. Environmental and other faults are rarely

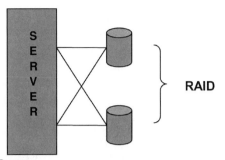

Storage Server:
- RAID: Redundant Array of Independent Disks
6-gigabytes/sec transfer
20 gigabytes/drive

- Disk files are mirrored.

- When a sector error occurs the RAID device driver falls over to the backup copy.

FIG. 1. High reliability Storage Server.

treated. Redundant hardware subsystems solved many single errors with extended operating systems programmed to recognize the hardware failure and launch the application on the working hardware. Design diversity was not a concept usually applied hardware fault tolerance. Software fault tolerant designers, however, adopt this approach by using N-version (also called multi-version) programming.

1.2   Why Software Is Different from Hardware

The N-version concept attempts to parallel in software the hardware fault tolerance concept of N-way redundant hardware. In an N-version software system, each module is made with up to N different implementations. Each version accomplishes the same task but in a different way. Each version then submits its answer to a decider that determines the correct answer and returns that as the result of the module. In practice, this means that more than one person must work a module to have different approaches. If each version but one succumbed to the same conceptual error, the one correct version would be cancelled out even though it alone was correct. This approach works only when it is possible to create uncorrelated yet equivalent designs and that the resulting programs do not share similar failure modes. Design diversity with independent failure modes are hard to achieve. Nancy Leveson points out, "... every experiment with [multi-version programming] that has checked for dependencies between software failures has found that independently written software routines do not fail in a statistically independent way" [17]. The techniques of N-version programming are well treated by Michael Lyu [19].

Lui Sha shows that "...the key to improving reliability is not the degree of diversity, per se. Rather the existence of simple and reliable components ensures the system's critical functions despite the failure of non-core software components." He continues to say, "...diversity with N-version programming does not usually improve reliability and points out that FAA DO 178B discourages its use" [28].

An alternative to N-version is the use of recovery blocks. Transactions are closely monitored so that if there is a failure during the execution of any transaction, the software can be rolled back to a previously sound point. Then special recovery software is executed based on the needs of the application. The failed transaction can be dropped allowing the system to execute other transactions, or the transaction may be retried and, if it is not successful within some number of attempts, the entire system may be halted. If the loss of any transaction is unacceptable, the database may be secured and the system halted. The database might be rebuilt by special recovery software and then the system could be restarted. Older recovery blocks executed several alternative paths serially until an acceptable solution emerged. Newer recovery block methods may allow concurrent execution of various alternatives. The N-version method was designed to be implemented using N-way hardware concurrently. In a serial retry system; the cost in time of trying multiple alternatives may be too expensive, especially for a real-time system. Conversely, concurrent systems require the expense of N-way hardware and a communications network to connect them. Software uses a module to decide. It may consider more than the absolute results to determine the action to take. Hardware uses strict comparison of results. The recovery block method requires that each module build a specific decider. This requires a lot of development work. The recovery block method creates a system that makes it is difficult to enter into an incorrect state, if and only if the programmer can design simple and bug free decision code. In comparison the N-version method may use a single decider.

Hardware faults are predominantly caused when component performance degrades. Design faults are found and fixed early. In a few cases hardware design failures appear in the final system. When they do, it is often left to the software to compensate for them. Software faults are different; they result from design shortcomings. Techniques for dealing with such shortcomings are detailed later in this chapter. Software manufacturing is the process of configuration management, trouble tracking and reproduction of software [26]. Errors in this process, unlike the hardware-manufacturing situation can be entirely prevented by appropriate tools, technician education and standards. Errors in software manufacturing are not part of software fault tolerance studies. For the purposes of this chapter, the software is assumed to be accurately reproduced and installed on the target host computer.

Software is characterized by branching, executing alternative series of commands based on input. This quality creates complexity. Even short programs can be very difficult to fully understand. Software branching can contain latent faults that only come to light long after a software product is introduced into the marketplace.

Typically, testing alone cannot fully verify that software is complete and correct. In addition to testing, other verification techniques and a structured and documented development process must be combined to assure a comprehensive validation approach.

In their work on "Quantitative Analysis of Faults and Failures in a Complex Software System" N.E. Fenton and N. Ohlsson describe a number of results from a study of faults and failures in two releases of a major commercial system. They tested a range of basic software engineering hypotheses relating to: the Pareto principle of distribution of faults and failures; the use of early fault data to predict later fault and failure data; metrics for fault prediction; and benchmarking fault data. They found very strong evidence that a small number of modules contain most of the faults discovered in pre-release testing, and that a very small number of modules contain most of the faults discovered in operation. However, in neither case is this explained by the size or complexity of the modules. They found no evidence relating module size to fault density, nor did they find evidence that popular complexity metrics are good predictors of either fault-prone or failure-prone modules. They confirmed that the number of faults discovered in pre-release testing is an order of magnitude greater than the number discovered in one year of operational use. They also discovered stable numbers of faults discovered at corresponding testing phases. Their most surprising and important result was strong evidence of a counter-intuitive relationship between pre and post release faults: those modules which are the most fault-prone pre-release are among the least fault-prone post-release, while conversely the modules which are most fault-prone post release are among the least fault-prone pre-release. This observation has serious ramifications for the commonly used *fault density* metric. Not only is it misleading to use it as a surrogate quality measure, but its previous extensive use in metrics studies is flawed.

Software is deceptively easy and fast to change the speed and ease. This can lead to the false impression that software faults can be easily corrected. Combined with a lack of understanding of software, it can lead engineering managers to believe that tightly controlled engineering is not as important for software projects as it is for hardware ones. In fact, the opposite is true. Because of its complexity, the development process for software should be tightly controlled as the development cycle nears project completion. The goal is to prevent problems that will be hard to find later.

Software may improve with age, as latent defects are discovered and removed. Repairs made to correct software defects, in fact, establish a new design. Seemingly insignificant changes in software code can create unexpected and very significant problems elsewhere. Musa's execution time model takes advantage of data gathered during software testing [23]. His approach extends the fundamental reliability exponential model that can be used at all stages of the software development process. Musa's approach is best used during a carefully designed set of longevity and stress tests. Test cases typically reflect samples of user operations. The key idea is to find how long a system will operate before it fails and the operational impact when it does fail. One way to estimate the intrinsic reliability of the software is to examine charts showing tests passed as a function of time. The more reliable the software the more this plot follows a typical human skills acquisition graph, with plateaus during which competence is acquired followed by sudden jumps in capability [5].

Software validation is a critical tool in assuring product quality for device software and for software automated operations. Software validation can increase the usability and reliability of the device, resulting in decreased failure rates, fewer recalls and corrective actions, less risk to patients and users, and reduced liability to manufacturers. Software validation can also reduce long term costs by making it easier and less costly to reliably modify software and revalidate software changes. Software maintenance represents as much as 50% of the total cost of software. An established comprehensive software validation process helps to reduce the long term software cost by reducing the cost of each subsequent software validation.

1.3   Software Errors (Bugs)

In contrast to hardware, software faults are most often caused by design shortcomings that occur when a software engineer either misunderstands a specification or simply makes a mistake. Design for reliability is rarely taught to Computer Science majors. Software faults are common for the simple reason that the complexity in modern systems is often pushed into the software part of the system. Then the software is pushed to and beyond its limits. I estimate that 60–90% of current computer errors are from software faults.

Software faults may also be triggered from hardware; these faults are usually transitory in nature, and can be masked using a combination of current software and hardware fault tolerance techniques. In the 1960s, I managed a software project that tracked missiles. As we prepared for the first missile test, managers argued about the wisdom of using special fault tolerant hardware and software subsystems called 'Mission Mode.' The problem was that these subsystems were not fully tested. One manager argued using the alternative the 'stop on error' approach there would be no chance to recover from an error. Another argued, "Untested software will not work."

Which would you pick? The executive in charge chose the logically correct 'Mission Mode' approach. The missile blew up. The computer skipped the instruction that updated the position of the electronically steered phase array radar. There was no inertia to keep the radar pointing in the general direction of the missile. A six-week investigated showed that the timing chains in the logic had negative timing margins when run in certain configurations peculiar to Mission Mode and with a particular combination of data. Even though there had been hundreds of tests run before the mission, the hardware executed the software in that configuration for the first time 30 seconds into the mission. During the investigation, the problem could not be reproduced and all missile testing stopped. Some wanted to proceed with more missions before the problem was solved, claiming that the problem was a random occurrence. Some twenty-five years later AT&T experienced a massive network failure caused by a similar problem in the fault recovery subsystem they were upgrading. This time there was a latent software fault in the update. It became a failure. There was not enough testing of the recovery subsystem before it was deployed. In both cases, the system failed because there was no limits placed on the results the software could produce. There were no boundary conditions set. Designers programmed with a point solution in mind and without bounding the domain of software execution. Testers were rushed to meet schedules and the planned fault recovery mechanisms did not work.

While software cannot be designed without bugs, it does not have to be as buggy as it is. For example, as early as 1977, a software based store and forward message switch was in its fourth year of operation and it handled all administrative messages for Indiana Bell without a single failure. This record was achieved after a very buggy start followed by a substantial investment in failure prevention and bug fixes. One particularly error-prone software subsystem was the pointers used to account for clashes in the hash function that indexed a message data file. The messages could remain in the file system for up to thirty days. There were many hash clashes due to the volume of messages and the similarity of their names. Once the obvious bugs were fixed the residual ones were hard to find. This led to unexpected behavior and system crashes. A firm requirement was not to lose any messages. Failures exhibited by latent faults can appear to be random and transient. But they are predictable if only we can get the initial conditions and transaction load that trigger them. They are sometimes called Heisenbugs. It was just too costly to find and fix all the Heisenbugs in the file index code, so the hash tables were rebuilt daily in the early hours of the morning when there was no message traffic. With fresh hash tables daily, the chances of triggering a fault was small especially after the bugs that were sensitive to the traffic mix were found and fixed. This experience shows that it is not necessary for software to be bug free.

Software runs as a finite state machine. Software manipulates variables that have states. Unfortunately flaws in the software that permit the variables to take on values outside of their intended operating limits often cause software failures. Software also fails when coded correctly, but the design is in error. Software can fail when the hardware or operating systems are changed in ways unanticipated by the designer. Also, software often fails when users overload it. In the final analysis, most failures are due to some human error. While human error is hard to predict, it is predictable. The work of John Musa, for example, which for years has dealt with the predictability of software faults, shows that the behavior of many software failures fit a mathematical model.

1.4 Application Concerns

When some service is especially critical or subject to hardware or network failure, the application designer needs to include software fault tolerance in its design. These are typical issues facing application designers:

- *Consistency*: In distributed environments, applications sometimes become inconsistent when code in a host is modified unilaterally. For example, the code in one software component may be updated and this change may require sending out new versions of the client application code. In turn, all dependent procedures must be re-compiled. In situations where a single transaction runs across several servers, a two-phase commit approach may be used to keep the distributed databases consistent. If the clients and servers are out of step there is a potential for a failure even though they have been designed and tested to work together. The software in the hosts need to exchange configuration data to make sure they are in lock step before every session.

- *Robust security*: Distributed application designers need to ensure that users cannot inadvertently or deliberately violate any security privileges.

- *Software component fail over*: The use of several machines and networks in distributed applications increases the probability that one or more could be broken. The designer must provide for automatic application recovery to bypass the outage and then to restore the complex of systems to its original configuration. This approach contains the failure and minimizes the execution states of the complex of systems.

BEA pioneered industrial strength two-phase commit middleware in their Tuxedo product that originated at Bell Laboratories. Applications developed using Oracle databases address many of the complex reliability and security considerations that affect partitioned, distributed applications. BEA's Application Infrastructure platform [3] implements each layer of the application infrastructure as a single, well-architect solution. The platform simplifies software engineering by providing an integrated framework for developing, debugging, testing, deploying and managing applications. The platform is

(a) Reliable—ensuring that applications never "break," even under the most demanding circumstances.
(b) Available—enabling applications that can run continuously $24 \times 7 \times 365$.
(c) Scalable—allowing companies to plan cost-effectively for any level of usage.
(d) Trusted—because in today's world of heightened security, an enterprise must maintain complete control of its data.

In information technology—communications no less than computing—software often is the machine. It's been said that it takes 100 million lines of code to make a typical phone call. The global telecommunications industry has roughly 100 billion lines of software code in products or in development. Any of these may be a bug. Across the board, there will be increasing demands for reliability on a level seldom-encountered outside telecommunications, defense and aerospace. Customers want future Internet services to be as reliable and predictable as services on yesterday' voice networks.

Software fault tolerance is at the heart of the building trustworthy software. Today Microsoft is embarking on a major Trustworthy Computing initiative. Bill Gates sent a memo to his entire workforce demanding, "... company wide emphasis on developing high-quality code that is available, reliable and secure-even if it comes at the expense of adding new features." [*Information Week* **873** (21 Jan. 2002) p. 28.] Trustworthy software is stable. It is sufficiently fault-tolerant that it does not crash at minor flaws and will shut down in an orderly way in the face of major trauma. Trustworthy software does what it is supposed to do and can repeat that action time after time, always producing the same kind of output from the same kind of input. The National Institute of Standards and Technology (NIST) defines trustworthiness as "software that can and must be trusted to work dependably in some critical function, and failure to do so may have catastrophic results, such as serious injury, loss of life or property, business failure or breach of security. Some examples include software used in safety systems of nuclear power plants, transportation systems, medical devices, electronic banking, automatic manufacturing, and military systems" [32].

1.5 Origins of Software Engineering

NATO convened a meeting in 1968 to confront a crisis that didn't make the headlines—"the software crisis." Experts from a dozen countries, representing industrial labs as well as universities, met in Garmisch, Germany, to grapple with two basic questions that are still with us: Why is it so hard to produce functionally correct and **reliable** software that meets users' needs and performance requirements and comes in on time and within a projected budget? And where should software producers be looking for solutions? The answers revolved around "software engineering," a term coined by the organizers of the Garmisch conference—somewhat controversial at the time, and wholly inspirational—to focus on a missing discipline with the potential to resolve the crisis. Software production should be "industrialized." Systems should be built from reliable components.

There are significant advances in Software Engineering. Programmers are better now, most code is written in high level languages, better tools exist, development is done on-line, better design models exist, and standards have been established in some key areas. A number of recently developed or recently successful innovations include libraries for fault tolerant computing, object-oriented programming, remote procedure calls that are the foundation for client–server applications, application programming interfaces, graphical user interfaces and development tools, prototyping, and source-level debugging. Components exist and are widely used. This belies the common wisdom that software components are rare. The C libraries with all their richness of fundamental or atomic functions provide 20% reuse in most industrial strength UNIX based applications. Software that makes a library of graphical elements, or a text-processing tool, available to multiple applications—with a major reservation is also in wide use. IBM and others are using software libraries providing generic fault avoidance and recovery.

2. Fault Tolerance Is Related to Reliability Theory

A fault is an erroneous state of software and fault tolerance is the ability of the software system to avoid execution the fault in a way that causes the system to fail. "The reliability of a system as a function of time $R(t)$, is the conditional probability that the system has (not failed) in the interval $[0, t]$, given that it was operational at time $t = 0$" [29]. Therefore it is essential to examine software reliability to understand software fault tolerance.

The most common reliability model is:

$$R(t) = e^{-\lambda t},$$

where λ is the failure rate. It is reasonable to assume that the failure rate is constant even though faults tend to be clustered in a few software components. The software execution is very sensitive to initial conditions and external data driving the software. What appear to be random failures are actually repeatable. The problem in finding

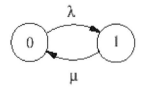

FIG. 2. Two-state reliability model.

and fixing these problems is the difficulty of doing the detective work needed to discover the particular initial conditions and data sequences that can trigger the fault so that it becomes a failure [23].

In a two-state continuous-time Markov chain the parameters to be estimated are failure rate λ and repair rate μ (see Fig. 2).

The Mean Time Between Failures (MTTF) $= 1/\lambda$.

The Mean Time To Repair (MTTR) $= 1/\mu$.

The steady-state availability is:

Availability $= \text{MTTF}/(\text{MTTF} + \text{MTTR}) = 1/[1 + \lambda/\mu]$.

The goal of Software Fault Tolerance is to make Availability $= 1$.

This can be approached by making λ very small and/or by making μ very large. The rest of this chapter describes how to accomplish both using a unified equation tying the practices, processes, algorithms and methods of software engineering together. With this unifying equation software engineering tradeoffs may be quantitatively made.

Software Fault Tolerance in the large focuses on failures of an entire system, whereas Software Fault Tolerance in the small, usually called transaction recovery, deals with recovery of an individual transaction or program thread. The system MTTF is usually greater for the system than for any transaction as individual transactions may fail without compromising other transactions. Telephone switching systems employ this strategy by aborting a specific call in favor of keeping the remaining calls up. Sometimes the integrity of the data is so important that the system tries to rerun a transaction or recover lost data as part of an error recovery strategy. This recovery software operates for one transaction while the rest of the transactions operate normally. If there are too many transaction failures the system may need to be restarted to clear a data problem or reinitialize control flows. This is a fault becoming a failure. The MTTR usually addresses the recovery of a transaction, but with the software rejuvenation technique [15], described in this paper, the re-initialization of the software execution states can be considered as part of the MTTR. With this function there may be no system failure, but transaction executions may be delayed.

2.1   Sha's Reliability Model

Professor Lui Sha's of University of Illinois at Urbana-Champaign created a model of reliability based on these postulates [28]:

(1) Complexity begets faults. For a given execution time software reliability decreases as complexity increases.
(2) Faults are not equal, some are easy to find and fix and others are Heisenbugs. Faults are not random.
(3) All budgets have limits so that there is not unlimited time or money to pay for exhaustive testing.

Sha chooses the MTTF $= E/kC$ and the reliability of the system is $R(t) = e^{-kCt/E}$, where k is a scaling constant, C is the complexity. Sha defines complexity as the effort needed to verify the reliability of a software system made up of both new and reused components, t is the continuous execution time for the program, E is the development effort that can be estimated by such tools as Checkpoint, COCOMO or Putnam's approach. Development effort is a function of the complexity of the software so the numerator and denominator of the exponent must be factored. $R(0) = 1$ because all the startup failures are assumed to be removed through classical unit, block and system testing.

Unfortunately we cannot use these equations to compute the reliability of a system from its components because failure modes may depend on a particular combination of the software components. Sha's approach works for a system as a whole. Until software components can be isolated and their execution characteristics made independent of one another the reliability of an entire system is **not** the product of the reliability of its component parts.

2.2   Effectiveness Extension of Reliability Model

An extension of the model adds an effectiveness factor to the denominator. This reflects the investment in software engineering tools, processes and code expansion that makes the work of one programmer more effective. Let ε be the expansion factor that expresses the ability to solve a program with fewer instructions with a new tool such as a compiler. It may be the ratio of the number of lines of code a compiler may expand into machine code. This idea of the improvement in productivity due to investment in the software tools has been explained in an earlier article [4]. Then the effectiveness equals the conciseness factor and the reliability equation becomes:

$$R = e^{-kCt/E\varepsilon}.$$

This equation expresses reliability of a software system in a unified form as related to software engineering parameters. The longer the software system runs the lower the reliability and the more likely a fault will be executed to become a failure. Reliability can be improved by investing in tools (ε), simplifying the design (C), or increasing the effort in development to do more inspections or testing than required by software effort estimation techniques. The estimation techniques provide a lower bound on the effort and time required for a successful software development program. These techniques are based on using historical project data to calibrate a model of the form:

$$\text{Effort} = a + b(\text{NCSLOC})^{\beta},$$

where a and b are calibration constants, NCSLOC is the number of new or changed source lines of code needed to develop the software system, β is an exponent expressing the diseconomies of scale for software projects and is greater than 1 [7].

An elaboration of the Sha model provides the foundation for a general theory of reliability-based software engineering. Various software engineering processes are combined to understand the reliability of the software; by increasing reliability, the software becomes more fault tolerant. Consider the reliability equation term by term: C, t, and E.

2.3 Complexity Factors (C)

2.3.1 Complexity

Sha states that the primary component of complexity is the effort needed to verify the reliability of a software system. Typically reused software has less complexity than newly developed software because it has been tested in the crucible of live operation [18]. But, this is just one of many aspects of software complexity. Among other aspects of software engineering complexity a function of [30]:

(a) The nature of the application characterized as
  (1) Real-time, where key tasks must be executed by a hard deadline or the system will become unstable. Other high complexity software must be aware of the details of the hardware operation. Operating systems, communication and other drivers are typical of this software. Embedded software must deal with all the states of the hardware. The hardest ones for the software engineer to cope with is the 'don't care states.'

(2) On-line transactions, where multiple transactions are run concurrently interacting with people or to with other hardware. Large database systems are typical of these applications.

(3) Report generation and script programming;

(b) the nature of the computations including the precision of the calculations;

(c) the size of the component;

(d) the steps needed to assure correctness of a component;

(e) the length of the program; and

(f) the program flow.

Sha's view is that the effort to verify the correctness of the component factor dominates the length factor. He assumes that reasonable design steps have been taken and the there are no singularities in the execution of the component. Cyclomatic metrics are used effectively to find components that are orders of magnitude more complex than others in the system. Trustworthy system design demands that these components be redesigned. In any event, by reducing complexity or equivalently simplifying the software, the reliability increases.

2.3.2   Trustworthy Software Is Reliable

First there must not be any degenerate situations in the implementation of the software. A few causes for such degeneration are:

(1) computational lags in controlling external equipment,

(2) round-off errors in computing control commands,

(3) truncation errors induced when equations are approximated,

(4) memory leaks that prevent other processes from executing memory,

(5) thrashing, and

(6) buffer overflows.

Reliable software is trustworthy software. It is easier to make simple software reliable than it is to make complex software reliable. Trustworthiness is the ideal. It is confounded by what insurance companies call "acts of God" in the environment, by human beings who misunderstand, ignore or circumvent system warnings, by chaotic software conditions that arise from untested areas, by the pressures of the marketplace to sell new versions of software that invalidate earlier versions, and by malevolent attacks from people. The interplay among these dimensions of instability is complicated.

Software system development is frequently focused solely on performance and functional technical requirements and does not adequately address the need for reliability or trustworthiness in the system. Not only must software designers consider how the software will perform they must account for consequences of failures. Trustworthiness encompasses this concern.

"Trustworthiness is a holistic property, encompassing security including confidentiality, integrity, and availability, correctness, reliability, privacy, safety and survivability. It is not sufficient to address only some of these diverse, dimensions, nor is it sufficient to simply assemble components that are themselves trustworthy. Integrating the components and understanding how the trustworthiness dimensions interact is a central challenge in building a trustworthy Networked Information System." This definition appeared in a fine article by Fred Schneider, Steven Bellovin and Alan S. Inouye in the November/December 2002 issue of IEEE Internet Computing, p. 64 [http://computer.org/internet/]. The article discusses many aspects of network operation but takes for granted the trustworthiness of the underlying software. Because of the increasing complexity and scope of software, its trustworthiness will become a dominant issue.

Modern society depends on large-scale software systems of astonishing complexity. Because the consequences of failure in such systems are so high, it is vital that they exhibit trustworthy behavior. Much effort has been expended in methods for reliability, safety and security analysis, as well as in methods to design, implement, test and evaluate these systems.

Yet the "best practice" results of this work are often not used in system development. A process is needed to integrate these methods within a trustworthiness framework, and to understand how best to ensure that they are applied in critical system development. It is critical that we focus attention on critical systems and to understand the societal and economic implications of potential failures.

Trustworthiness is already an issue in many vital systems, including those found in transportation, telecommunications, utilities, health care and financial services. Any lack of trustworthiness in such systems can adversely impact large segments of society, as shown by software-caused outages of telephone and Internet systems. It is difficult to estimate the considerable extent of losses experienced by individuals and companies that depend on these systems. This issue of system trustworthiness is not well understood by the public. One measure of the Trustworthiness of a system is its stability.

2.3.3 Software Stability Is Key to Simplicity

Internal software stability means that the software will respond with small outputs to small inputs. If the software response grows without bound, the system will usually crash or hang. These are the most egregious failures. All systems have latent faults that can cause system failures. The trick is to use feedback control to keep system execution away from these latent faults or singularities so that the faults do not become failures. Most instabilities internal to the software are caused by:

- buffer usage that increases to eventually dominate system performance,
- computations that cannot be completed before new data arrive,
- round-off errors that build,
- an algorithm that is embodied in the software is inherently flawed,
- memory leaks,
- register overflow,
- thrashing access to files on secondary storage,
- thrashing of routes in a network,
- broadcast storms.

There is only a weak theoretical model for software behavior. Chaotic conditions can arise over time outside the windows of testing parameters. There is little theory on dynamic analysis and performance under load. The question is how to compensate for destabilizing factors and catch problems early in the design process. The Federal Food and Drug Administration has issued a paper on general principles of software validation that remarks, "Software verification includes both static (paper review and automatic programs that process the source code such as Lint) and dynamic techniques. Dynamic analysis (i.e., testing) is concerned with demonstrating the software's run-time behavior in response to selected inputs and conditions. Due to the complexity of software, both static and dynamic analysis is needed to show that the software is correct, fully functional and free of avoidable defects."

2.3.4 Buffer Overflows

A significant issue facing software engineers is keeping buffers from overflowing. Buffers are used to allow computer processors to multithread processes and by TCP to exchange data between computers. When control programs are fast, buffer areas can be small, otherwise large buffers must be available so that they do not overflow and cause the software to stop exchanging data or to transfer to undefined locations causing the system to hang or crash and thus fail.

The exploitation of buffer overflow bugs in process stacks cause many security attacks. To deal with the problems there are new libraries that work with any existing pre-compiled executable and can be used system-wide.

The Microsoft® .NET Framework eliminates security risks due to buffer overflows; and shifts the burden from having to make critical security decisions—such as whether or not to run a particular application or what resources that application should be able to access—from end users to developers. With the ever-increasing complexity and functionality of software applications comes assaults. The managed code architecture of the .NET Framework provides one solution to the problem of software application security. It transparently controls the behavior of code even in the most adverse circumstances, so that the risks inherent in all types of applications—client- and server-side—are greatly reduced. A *common language runtime* (CLR) is the engine that runs and "manages" executing code enforcing .NET Framework's restrictions and prevents executing code from behaving unexpectedly. The CLR performs "just-in-time" compilation and inserts control code in the execution module. The .NET *Framework class libraries* are a collection of reusable classes, or types, that developers use to write programs that will execute in the common language runtime. An *assembly* is an executable compiled using one of the .NET Framework's many language compilers. Assemblies contain *metadata*, which the CLR uses to locate and load classes, lay out instances in memory, resolve method invocations and generate native code.

It sets runtime context boundaries. The *verification process* ensures the runtime safety of managed code. During JIT compilation, the CLR verifies all managed code to ensure memory type safety. This eliminates the risk of code executing or provoking "unexpected" actions that could bypass the common application flow and circumvent security checks. The verification process prevents common errors from occurring. It does not allow integer pointers to access arbitrary memory locations. It does not allow access to memory outside the object boundary or accessing method outside its class. It does not allow access to newly created objects before they have been initialized. It prevents buffer overflows. These common programming faults no longer pose a threat within the type safe, managed environment provided by the .NET Framework. .NET cannot be used to solve all problems and many applications cannot honor the .NET restrictions.

Another approach is to use special library processes to intercept all calls to other library functions known to be vulnerable. A safe version of the buffer management code then ensures that any buffer overflows are contained within the invoked stack frame. A second approach is to force verification of critical elements of stacks before use. Performance overhead of fault tolerant libraries implementing these safe approaches range from negligible to 15%. This method does not require any modification to the operating system and works with existing binary programs. It does not require access to the source code of defective programs, nor does it require recompilation or off-line processing of binaries. It can be implemented on a system-wide basis transparently. It is based on a middleware software layer that intercepts all function calls made to library functions that are known to be vulnerable. A substitute version of the corresponding function implements the original functionality, but in a manner that ensures that any buffer overflows are contained within the current stack frame, thus, preventing attackers from 'smashing' (overwriting) the return address and hijacking the control flow of a running program. It is a Linux dynamically loadable library called *libsafe*. Fig. 3 is a description of the library [2].

Overview

It is generally accepted that the best solution to buffer overflow and format string attacks is to fix the defective programs. However, fixing defective programs requires knowing that a particular program is defective. The true benefit of using libsafe and other alternative security measures is protection against future attacks on programs that are not yet known to be vulnerable. That is libsafe version 2.0 source code is under the GNU Lesser General Public License.

In contrast to most other solutions, libsafe is extremely easy to install and use. No source code, recompilation or special expertise is needed. And, the installation only takes a few minutes.

Libsafe does not support programs linked with libc5. If you find that a process protected by libsafe experienced a segmentation fault, use the *ldd* utility to determine if the process is linked with libc5. If that is the case, then you will either need to recompile/relink the application with libc6 (i.e., glibc) or to download a newer version that has been linked with libc6 although most applications are offered with a libc6 version.

NOTE: The latest release of libsafe is version 2.0-11, released on 02-28-02.

FIG. 3. Libsafe: Protecting critical elements of stacks.

Buffer overflow bugs can cause a large transfer of data to a buffer, overflowing it, and then overwriting the memory. A hacker can inject additional code into an unsuspecting process and hijack control of that process by overwriting return addresses on the process stack or by overwriting function pointers in the process memory. There are many error-prone functions in the Standard C Library. Here are a few examples of these functions:

Function	Potential problem
strcpy(char *dest, const char *src)	May overflow the destination buffer
gets(char *s)	May overflow the s buffer
realpath(char *path, char resolved path[])	May overflow the path buffer
scanf(const char *format, ...)	May overflow its arguments

Nicolas Wirth defines intermediate level languages such as C in his paper PL/360. These languages differ from Higher Level Languages in that they give programmers access to the machine registers and architecture when they need it. The compilers for these languages differ from assembly languages in that they provide compactness of expression. This ability along with the C libraries made C industrial strength. It is widely used today and laid the foundation for C++. One can even see the influence of C on Java [1].

The importance of C is that it led to remarkable improvement in software reliability and programmer productivity by a factor of 3 : 1 over assembler language development without giving up the key ability to solve complex software problems or meet harsh performance requirements in industrial strength production systems. Because of its inherent flexibility, C is vulnerable to misuse. Higher-level languages protect programmers from the architecture of the machine. If they need to gain significant performance improvement they must drop down to the machine level. This leads to a discontinuity in the development environment and makes it likely that more code than desired will be low-level code. It is very hard for skilled software engineers to switch between development paradigms. Furthermore, tools are needed to manage two and sometimes more languages and the issue of assembler vs. compiler permeates many design designs within the project. Control of software changes becomes more difficult too. Today's Java-hype as a total C++ replacement still is unproven. Java is a fine language, but when industrial strength programs are needed C++ with its ability to naturally drop down to C is the industrial software engineer's choice.

2.3.5 Small and Bounded Time Lags Are Critical

Sometimes software components embedded in a system must respond to the environment within some time interval. If the system fails because the time constraints are not satisfied the system is a real-time one. If the response time becomes unacceptably long the system is an on-line one. In either case successful performance of the software demands that the computations are completed in the required time. The feedback characteristics of these systems often dominate, as computation results must be available in sufficient time to affect some external process. Feedback operation and meeting deadlines are two key attributes of embedded software. Systems containing a computer as one of their elements belong to the class of sampled data systems. A typical feedback control system is shown in Fig. 4, where $x(n)$ is the physical input to the external equipment that is sampled and encoded with a certain number of bits or precision, $y(n)$ is the computer output from the computers control equations using the error from the previous sampled time as the input.

The objectives of the control equations are to:

- achieve a satisfactory level of reliability in system operation. The outputs of the system need to be bounded to match physical properties of the equipment being controlled,

- be easy to initialize and that the initial conditions lead to stable software execution,

- calculations should be easy to implement and quick to process,

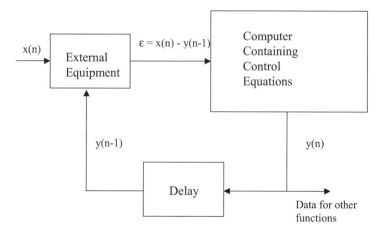

FIG. 4. Feedback control system.

- occupy a minimum amount of memory that suggests using recursive filters such as those use in the Transaction Control Protocol (TCP) computation of roundtrip time used for flow control in Internet applications,
- avoid duration-related memory leaks and fragmentation can degrade execution time, often causing reduced throughput and eventual system failure.

A case history of a mechanism all web users employ daily illustrates these points.

2.3.6 Case Study: TCP Timer for Resend

TCP uses an Automatic Request Response window with selective repeat to control the flow of packets between the sender and the receiver. The buffer size of the receiver and the bandwidth-delay product of the network typically limit the window size. Buffers may overflow. The lowest capacity link on the route becomes the bottleneck. The goal is to make the window as large as possible to gain the best network throughput consistent with not losing packets or driving the network into congestion that can lead to application failures. Fig. 5 shows a client accessing a web page across the Internet using TCP.

If one packet is lost TCP re-sends everything.

The problem is when do the senders resend packets. Resending too soon and too often causes congestion and resending too late causes inefficient network throughput. Therefore, the engineering compromise is to average the last 10 measurements of the round trip-time (RTT). Every TCP message is time stamped, the receiver measures the difference between the time the acknowledgement is received, and the time the

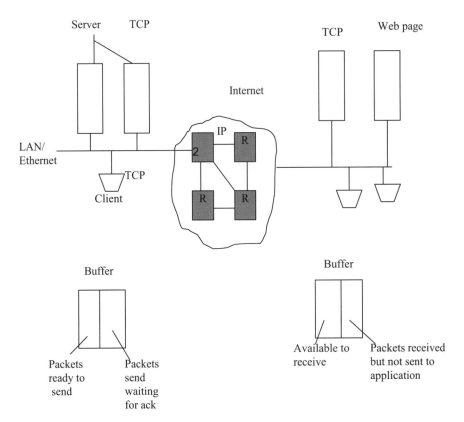

FIG. 5. TCP timer for resend.

message is sent.

$$\overline{RTT}(k) = 1/k \sum_{i=1}^{k} RTT(i),$$

where $\overline{RTT}(k)$ is the average roundtrip time.

$$\overline{RTT}(k+1) = 1/(k+1) \sum_{i=1}^{k+1} RTT(i)$$

$$= 1/(k+1) \left[RTT(k+1) + k/k \sum_{i=1}^{k} RTT(i) \right]$$

$$= k/(k+1)\overline{RTT}(k) + 1/(k+1)RTT(k+1).$$

Now using exponential filter smoothing

$$\widehat{RTT}(k+1) = \alpha\widehat{RTT}(k) + (1-\alpha)RTT(k+1),$$

$\alpha = 7/8$ for smoothing over the last 10 observations.

But with wild swings in RTT, TCP had too many retransmissions clogging up the links.

Designers wanted to use the standard deviation of the average RTT but they soon saw that they would be unable to complete the computations within the required time because of the need to take a square root. The time needed would lead to a computation lag destabilizing the system. So a measure of the variance is used, the mean variance that avoids square roots.

$$\widehat{DEV}(k+1) = \alpha\widehat{DEV}(k) + (1-\alpha)\left|RTT(k) - \overline{RTT}(k)\right|,$$

$$RTO(k+1) = \widehat{RTT}(k+1) + f\widehat{DEV}(k+1).$$

By trial and error it was found that the expected value of $f = 2$ that reflected on deviation for each direction was too tight a bound and many retransmissions occurred. The pragmatic use of $f = 4$ was used to keep the calculations simple.

If a timeout still occurs a binary exponential backoff is used for each timeout

$$RTO(j) = 2RTO(j-1),$$

where $j - 1$ is the number of timeouts in a row up to 16.

Here is a summary of fault tolerant design algorithms:

- Approximate an averaging process by a polynomial filter of length 10.
- Change the filter length from 0.9 to 7/8 to simplify the implementation and take advantage of binary arithmetic in the computer.
- Move from standard deviation to mean variance to eliminate square roots.
- Use 4, a binary number, for computing RTO settings.

Simplify the design by reducing complexity of equations, eliminating redundant functions and sections of code, and reducing the fan out of the modules. The fan out is the 'used by' view, which is the inverse of the 'uses.' A general approach is to use a concordance of the components 'make files.' Start with a visualization of the makefile calling trees to see the complexity.

- Eliminate 'gold plated' functions.
- Use Commercial Off-the-Shelf packages to replace custom modules.

- Renegotiate requirements with hard cost/value analysis. Costs may be development or equipment costs in the target machine.
- Use architectural, design and implementation patterns.
- Use well-known algorithms.

2.3.7 Refactoring to Simpler Software

Martin Fowler writes, "Refactoring is the process of changing a software system in such a way that it does not alter the external behavior of the code yet improves its internal structure. It is a disciplined way to clean up code that minimizes the chances of introducing bugs. In essence when you refactor you are improving the design of the code after it has been written" [10].

Refactoring is a powerful and very effective way to reduce complexity. The notion of 'if it works, don't fix it' is a poor approach to software design. Experts, the inventors of Unix, C and C++, practiced a 'make it work, make it work right and then make it work better philosophy.' One big obstacle is that software revision is very difficult without the originator's help because most code is obscure. Designers must work hard to get the logical organization right at every level. It is even harder with object-oriented code because the long-reaching effects of early decisions in bottom-up design demand greater insight than top-down design. Managers don't tout their product's internal simplicity and clarity. Efficiency, features, production schedule, all comes in for praise, but clarity—never! Yet only clear code can be modified. Preserving clarity through cycles of modification is even harder. During Norman Wilson's five-year tenure as the primary maintainer of research UNIX™, he wrote a negative amount of code. The system became more capable, more maintainable and more portable. Imagine a major software project *subtracting* code in the course of adding a feature! Allocating as much as twenty percent of the effort on a new release to refactoring pays large dividends by making the system perform better, avoiding failures induced by undesired interactions between modules and reducing the time and space constraints on new feature designs. The goal is to reduce the amount of processor time modules use and the amount of memory they occupy or I/O they trigger while holding their interfaces fixed. Other modules may be modified or new ones added to provide new features. This strategy naturally leads to more reliable systems. This approach is best demonstrated in the story of the development of 'diff,' one of the most used and least understood C function that can take the difference of arbitrary files. It is the backbone of most software change control and build systems.

2.3.8   The Tale of "diff": Real-World Refactoring

Once upon a time, there was a mathematical problem of finding the longest subsequence of lines common to two files.[1] "No sweat," thought the developer. A dynamic programming technique that takes time mn and space mn to compare an m-line file to an n-line file would do the trick. But space mn was unacceptable on the small machines of yesteryear. "OK, we'll fly seat of the pants," thought our hero. So he read both files until he found a line that disagreed, then figured he would somehow search back and forth in both until he got back in sync. 'Somehow' was the killer. Suppose the second line in one file agreed with the fourth line ahead in the other and vice versa. How to choose?

Then news came from afar in Princeton that the Wizard Hirschberger had seen a way to reduce space mn by a mathematical method to space m, while only doubling the time. "Good deal!" thought our guy. "Now we can afford to run it. It was slow, but it did work and gave an explainable 'right' answer in a clearly defined way."

But the people complained. When they moved a paragraph, it showed up as two changes, a deletion here and an addition there. So our hero made a "diff" that found moves. It was again seat of the pants, but it ran pretty well. Yet, sometimes, an evil occurred. If the people ran it on stuff where the same line occurred in many places, like assembly language or text processing, it discovered lots of deletions and additions that could be explained as moves. Our hero was filled with consternation.

Then along came a shining knight, Harold Stone, with a dynamic programming technique that reduced the running time from the product to the sum of the file lengths, except in unnatural cases. Now here was something fast enough to use on big files, efficient in space and time, mathematically justifiable as giving a good answer, and experimentally shown to be physiologically useful.

But then the people tinkered. Three times they altered output. They added features. They added stars! And the tinkering caused the code to increase and the manual to swell to half again its size. "Well," said our guy. "It is important to know when to stop."

2.3.9   Reuse 'as is'

Data collected on the reuse of 2954 modules of NASA programs [27] clearly demands the shocking conclusion that to reap the benefits of the extra original effort to make a module reusable, it must be reused essentially unchanged. No change costs five percent; the slightest change drives the cost up to sixty percent. The issues of who pays the differential and who pays for ongoing support remain serious barriers to reuse. Within an organization, however, success is possible. Before middleware

---

[1] With the permission of Doug McIlroy, inventor of diff.

platforms were available, most products contained only ten percent reused modules and none contained a hundred percent reused modules. After platforms became available some product was made entirely of reused modules.

In the category of currently intractable problems, it has been impossible to systematically reuse software across application domains. There is ongoing work in modeling application domains to capture the relationship between requirements and object types to reuse software architectures [13]. Also, reuse even in the same application domain is successful only when throughput and response time are not overriding concerns. Finally, it is not yet possible to maintain an asset base of software modules except when they are in packaged libraries and when they are utility functions.

Where reuse is successful, there is high level of management attention to detail and a willingness to invest in design for reusability. Software configuration management assumes that there is an existing base of software components from which the components of a specific system are chosen, assembled, tested and distributed to a user [16]. Even then, exhaustive re-testing is still required to root out what Jackson called "undesired interactions."

2.3.10   Boundary and Self-Checking Software

One of the fundamental challenges to those building fault tolerant software is bounding the results so that errors cannot propagate and become failures. In one case, mentioned in Section 1.2, an electronically steered radar was tracking a missile when it told by a computer to suddenly steer the radar beam down to the horizon when the missile was actually at 10,000 feet. The system lost track of the missile. For safety reasons the missile was destroyed when an onboard countdown timer timed out and triggered an explosion. The countdown timer was reset whenever a radar tracking pulse reflected off the missile. This was a pioneering use of electronically steered radars and the software developers could not imagine the radar beam shifting so wildly so quickly. After all, mechanically steered radars had inertia working for them. There were no bounds placed on the output commands for radar beam steering from the computer. Software engineers understand the need to bound outputs but they are often at a loss for just what bounds to use. Checking on the outputs and other internal states of the software during its execution is referred to as self-checking software.

Self-checking software is not a rigorously described method in the literature, but rather a more ad hoc method used in some important systems [20]. Self-checking software has been implemented in some extremely reliable and safety-critical systems already deployed in our society, including the Lucent ESS-5 phone switch and the Airbus A-340 airplanes [20].

Self-checking software often include some amount of check pointing and rollback recovery for fault-tolerant or safety critical systems. Other methods include separate tasks that "walk" the heap to find and correct data errors and there is always an option to use reliable but degraded performance algorithms. While self-checking may not be a rigorous methodology, it has shown to be surprisingly effective.

The obvious problem with self-checking software is its lack of rigor. Code coverage for a fault tolerant system is unreliable. Without the proper rigor and experiments comparing and improving self-checking software cannot effectively be done.

A breakthrough idea by Sha [28] uses well-tested high reliable components to bound the outputs of newer high performance replacements. He reports, "Once we ensure that the system states will remain admissible, we can safely conduct statistical performance evaluation of the high-performance controller... the high-assurance subsystem (used to bound the states)... protects... against latent faults in the high-performance control software that tests and evaluations fail to catch." I call this the 'Sha Tandem High-Assurance Paradigm.'

When systems share a common architecture, they are the same and can form the base for use of the Sha Tandem paradigm. Architecture is the body of instructions, written in a specific coding language, which controls the structure and interactions among the system modules. The properties of reliability, capacity, throughput, consistency and module compatibility are fixed at the architectural level.

The processing code governs how the modules work together to do the system functions. The communication architecture is code that governs the interactions among the processing modules with data and with other systems. The data architecture is code that controls how the data files are structured, filled with data, and accessed.

Once the architecture is established, functions may be assigned to processing modules, and the system may be built. Processing modules can vary greatly in size and scope, depending on the function each performs, and the same module may be configured differently across installations. This is called feature loading. In every case, however, the processing architecture, communication architecture and data architecture constitute the software architecture that is the system's unchanging 'fingerprint.'

When several sites use software systems with a common architecture, they are considered to be using the same software system even though they may do somewhat different things. Alternatively, two systems with differing architectures can perform the same function although they do not do it the same way. They would be different systems.

For example, in the late 1980s, Bell Laboratories needed to develop a system to control a very critical congestion situation. The system was called NEMOS and had distributed database architecture. It soon became apparent that the design problem was extremely complex and broke new theoretical ground. Since there was no history of similar development for a guide and the need was urgent, Bell Laboratories decided, for insurance, to develop a second system in parallel. It was also called NEMOS, but used instead integrated database architecture. The result was two systems with the same name, performing the same function. The system with the distributed database architecture failed, and the system with the integrated database architecture succeeded. They were two different systems.

No two iterations of a software system are the same, despite their shared architecture. When a system is installed at two or more sites, localization is always required. Tables are populated with data to configure the software to meet the needs of specific customer sites. The customer may have special needs that require more than minor table adjustments. Customization of some modules may be required. New modules may be added. Ongoing management of this kaleidoscope of systems is a major effort. The use of the Sha Tandem paradigm to bound nominal performance again can keep all sites at a high assurance level.

2.3.11   Trustworthiness in the Large

Some software practitioners [24] broaden the definition of trustworthiness to include confidentiality, authentication of users and authentication of the source and integrity of data. Technologies exist to further these ends. Cryptography is little used in commercial, personal computer and network environments. It is expensive and hard to use, and imposes significant performance burdens. Firewalls are a mechanism that is deployed at the boundary between a secure enclave and an insecure network, a somewhat effective and relatively inexpensive approach. Specifications for system functionality can constrain access to system resources and require authentication of users and their access requests. An interesting idea is to build networked computer systems that protect themselves with the same kind of herding or schooling behaviors exhibited in the natural world. The aggregate behavior of the system, not the functioning of specific single components according to their requirements, would achieve trustworthiness. For example, a system that relies on a consensus decision to change a routing table may be more resilient than one that does not, because an attacker would need to subvert not just an individual router but the entire consensus group. The best protection is increasing the overall quality of commercial software through formal engineering methods: high-level languages, coding standards, object-oriented design and testing based on various coverage metrics.

First Constraint: Control-free Interfaces.   Large distributed real-time systems can be built effectively by integrating a set of nearly autonomous components that communicate via stable control-free interfaces, called temporal firewalls. A temporal firewall provides an understandable abstraction of the subsystem behind the firewall, confines the impact of most changes to the encapsulated subsystem, and limits the potential of error propagation. "Reusing software components in mission-critical applications cannot succeed if the components do not provide clearly stated service guarantees [6]."

Second Constraint: Software Error Recovery.

If failure is unavoidable, then the software design must be constrained so that the system can recover in an orderly way. This is called exception handling. Each software process or object class should provide special code that recovers when triggered. A software fault-tolerant library with a watchdog daemon can be built into the system. When the watchdog detects a problem, it launches the recovery code peculiar to the application software. In call processing systems this usually means dropping the call but not crashing the system. In administrative applications where keeping the database is key, the recovery system may recover a transaction from a backup data file or log the event and rebuild the database from the last checkpoint. Designers are constrained to explicitly define the recovery method for each process and object class using a standard library.

Fault tolerance differs from exception handling. Fault tolerance attempts to provide services compliant with the specification after detecting a fault [20]. Exception handling contains a problem and eliminates it. Reliable software accomplishes its task under adverse conditions while robust software finds and isolates a problem. Both approaches are needed in trustworthy software.

Peter Weinberger of AWK fame[2] pointed out that there are process recovery features in UNIX: "A process can choose to catch signals. This mechanism gives the process a chance to react to certain kinds of internal and external events. A data filtering process can catch arithmetic errors (like overflow or divide by zero)... and by using *longjump( )* to re-initialize itself and continue." A parent process can restart a damaged process and avoid complicated recovery code.

The software architecture for the Safeguard anti-missile system included restarts. The operating system provided a 'mission mode' capability. It allowed the software engineer to tailor specific error recovery to a process and exit without crashing or hanging the computer. For example, the software that tracked Intercontinental Ballistic Missiles had error recovery code that dropped track and reinitialized the tracking data area when a 'divide by zero' trap alerted the operating system. The operating system transfered the computer to special 'on interrupt' code and then returned to normal processing. Since the fuel tank of an ICBM flies on a lower trajectory than its re-entry vehicle (RV) and breaks into pieces during atmospheric reentry, a vital questions facing the software engineers was, "could the system track the reentry vehicle through tank breakup? Would the RV be masked by the tank pieces? Would the

---

[2]Private communication.

system lose track of the reentry vehicle?" Once ballistic missiles and their fuel tanks reenter the atmosphere they slow down. Being heavier and specially designed the reentry vehicle continues to fly at high speed. The tank or its pieces slow down faster than the RV. The software uses measured position and the Doppler effect to predict the next position of an object it is tracking. Multiple radar returns from different objects close together confuse the software. During one test flight, the software was tracking the tank and the reentry vehicle as two separate objects. Once the tank hit the atmosphere it broke up and slowed. Additional software tracking channels were assigned and tank pieces were tracked. The re-entry vehicle flew through the dispersed tank debris. The software computed zero or negative velocity for several objects being tracked. The radar returns from the debris and the re-entry vehicle became confused. A design flaw, later corrected, did not bound and validate the computed velocity for an object in a track. More than 1000 'divide by zero' traps occurred in the tracking equations assigned to the tank and its pieces, but the system continued operating satisfactorily. The software continued to track the RV. An interceptor missile was launched and came with a lethal distance of the attacking RV. Since this tank breakup and subsequent fly through was not expected, the software was not tested for the high rate of 'divide by zero' traps before the test flight.

Third Constraint: Recovery Blocks.   The recovery block method is a simple method developed by Randell from what was observed as somewhat current practice at the time [20]. The recovery block operates with a program that confirms the results of various implementations of the same algorithm. In a system with recovery blocks, the system view is broken down into fault recoverable blocks. The entire system is constructed of these fault tolerant blocks. Each block contains at least a primary, secondary and exceptional case code along with an adjudicator. (It is important to note that this definition can be recursive, and that any component may be composed of another fault tolerant block composed of primary, secondary, exceptional case, and adjudicator components.) The adjudicator is the component that determines the correctness of the various blocks to try. The adjudicator should be kept somewhat simple in order to maintain execution speed and aide in correctness. Upon first entering a unit, the adjudicator first executes the primary alternate. (There may be N alternates in a unit which the adjudicator may try.) If the adjudicator determines that the primary block failed, it then tries to roll back the state of the system and tries the secondary alternate. If the adjudicator does not accept the results of any of the alternates, it then invokes the exception handler, which then indicates the fact that the software could not perform the requested operation. The challenge is to write a reliable adjudicator.

    The recovery block system is also complicated by the fact that it requires the ability to roll back the state of the system from trying an alternate. This may be accomplished in a variety of ways, including hardware support for these operations. This 'try and rollback' ability has the effect of making the software to appear extremely transactional. A transaction is constrained within a recovery block. The advantages of a system built with a transactional constraints is, that it tends to resist incorrect or unstable states. This property, in combination with check pointing and recovery helps build distributed hardware fault tolerant systems.

Fourth Constraint: Limit the Language Features Used and Inspect the Code.

Most communications software is developed in the C or C++ programming languages. Java is promising but still not industrial strength for many applications. Hatton's Safer C [14] describes the best way to use C and C++ in mission-critical applications. Hatton advocates constraining the use of the language features to achieve reliable software performance and then goes on to specify instruction by instruction how to do it. He says, "The use of C in safety-related or high-integrity systems is not recommended without severe and automatically enforceable constraints. However, if these are present using the formidable tool support (including the extensive C library), the best available evidence suggests that it is then possible to write software of *at least* as high intrinsic quality and consistency as with other commonly used languages."

C is an intermediate language, between high level and machine level. The power of C can be harnessed to assure that source code is well structured. One important constraint is to use function prototypes or special object classes for interfaces. Patterns also help assure consistency of execution.

Once you have the code it is important to read it. While formal code inspections have proven valuable in finding faults and improving the reliability of the software it can lead to an exodus of the very best developers. This happens when code inspections become perfunctory. A good practice is to inspect the code of programmers when they first join the project and then inspect their code again whenever they produce buggy code. Programming standards should at least cover:

(1) Defining variable names that make the code self-documenting.
(2) Commentary: Too many comments could mask the code and be hard to keep current. The comments be balanced and explain why a particular pattern of instructions is used rather than what they do.

Code Reviews are needed to determine:

(1) If wild transfers are possible by checking every entry and exit point.
(2) If boundary conditions are checked.
(3) Are there buffer overflows? Buffer overflows are still a serious problem, even with Java. Unconstrained pointers can result from poor array bounds leading to memory leaks.

(4) Do comments agree with code?
(5) Are variables, pointers and arrays initialized?
(6) Does every loop terminate?
(7) Are subscripts to see if we are within bounds?

EXAMPLE.
Array

$X[i]$ — i is defined as $16 \leqslant i \leqslant 37$

How many elements are there in the array? It is $(h - 1 + 1)$, but too often software designers forget to take into account the "1"

Best way to define i is $16 \leqslant i < 38$

Now the equation becomes $(h - 1)$, i.e. $(38 - 16) = 22$

Check if semantics and syntax of boundary conditions are specified properly.

Code Reading. Everybody on the team is involved in this process. Designers submit their unit tested code. The code is re-distributed until everyone has somebody else's code. Code is read and then they group meets to discuss what they have found. This process improves the coding ability of the group.

Code Review. The designer finds the most bugs. Test the code for syntax error, logic errors, and incompleteness error. Check the code against user requirements. Check the code against coding standards.[3] Don O'Neill, an expert in software process writes, "Analysis of the issues raised in the experiment to date has revealed common problems that reoccur from session to session. Organizations that want to reduce their software fault rates need to prevent these defects:

(1) Software product source code components not traced to requirements. As a result, the software product is not under intellectual control, verification procedures are imprecise, and changes cannot be managed.

(2) Software engineering practices for systematic design and structured programming is applied without sufficient rigor and discipline. As a result, high defect rates are experienced in logic, data, interfaces and functionality.

(3) Software product designs and source code are recorded in an ad hoc style. As a result, the understandability, adaptability and maintainability of the software product is directly impacted.

(4) The rules of construction for the application domain are not clearly stated, understood, and applied. As a result, common patterns and templates are not exploited in preparation for later reuse.

---

[3] See http://hometown.aol.com/ONeillDon/nsqe-results.html where there is an explanation of the code review process.

(5) The code and upload development paradigm is becoming predominant in emerging e-commerce applications. As a result, the enterprise code base services only the short term planning horizon where code rules and heroes flourish, but it mortgages the future where traceable baseline requirements, specification, and design artifacts are necessary foundations."

Read the following code segment. Note how it is self-documenting but it is not fault tolerant. Even though Qname and Qvalue are validated an input by a web client, there is the possibility that an unanticipated data value can be passed to the server. The last 'else' clause should have another else that reports an error condition and reinitializes the process so that it is ready for the next user. This code was taken from an undergraduate class in formal code reviews at Stevens Institute of Technology:

Code Extract:

```
while(values.hasMoreElements())
    {
    Qname = new String((String)values.nextElement());
    Qvalue = new String(req.getParameterValues(Qname)[0]);
if (("day".equals(Qname)) || ("month".equals(Qname)) ||
    ("year2".equals(Qname)))
        {
        date.addElement(Qvalue);
        }
else if (("death".equals(Qname)) || ("road_func".equals(Qname)) ||
        ("atmos_cond".equals(Qname)))
    {
    afields.addElement(Qname);   // accident category
    avals.addElement(Qvalue);
    }
else if (("restraint".equals(Qname)) || ("drug_invl".equals(Qname)) ||
        ("injury_severity".equals(Qname)) || ("police_report_alco".equals(Qname)) ||
        ("sex".equals(Qname)) || ("ejection".equals(Qname)))
    {
    pfields.addElement(Qname);   // person category
    pvals.addElement(Qvalue);
    }
else if (("make".equals(Qname)) || ("model".equals(Qname)) ||
        ("year".equals(Qname)) || ("rollover".equals(Qname)) ||
        ("no_of_occup".equals(Qname)) || ("death".equals(Qname)) ||
        ("reg_state".equals(Qname)) || ("impact1".equals(Qname)) ||
        ("fire".equals(Qname)))
```

```
    {
       vfields.addElement(Qname);    // vehicle category
       vvals.addElement(Qvalue);
    }
  else
    {
       dfields.addElement(Qname);    // driver category
       dvals.addElement(Qvalue);
    }
    }
```

Fifth Constraint: Limit Module Size and Initialize Memory. The optimum module size for the fewest defects is between 300 to 500 instructions. Smaller modules lead to too many interfaces and larger ones are too big for the designer to handle. Structural problems creep into large modules.

All memory should be explicitly initialized before it is used. Memory leak detection tools should be used to make sure that a software process does not grab all available memory for itself, leaving none for other processes. This creates gridlock as the system hangs in a wait state because it cannot process any new data.

Sixth Constraint: Reuse Modules Without Change. A study of 3000 reused modules by NASA as reported by Selby [27] showed that changes of as little as 10% led to substantial rework—as much as 60%—in the reused module. It is difficult for anyone unfamiliar with a module to alter it, and this often leads to redoing the software rather than reusing it. For that reason, it is best to reuse tested, error-free modules as they are with no changes.

In Summary. Formal methods specify or model the requirements mathematically, even though not all ambiguity can be eliminated with this method. Prototyping, simulation and modeling can also be used to complement mathematical requirements. Component isolation separates safety critical components; this modularity ensures that changes are contained. Information hiding similarly prevents one component's actions from affecting another's. Redundancy is used to prevent or recover from failure. Human factors design during the design phase is critical.

Use of high-level languages lessens programming errors by eliminating problematic programming practices. Reverse engineering recreates documentation for preexisting software and provides a basis for reuse. There are also software engineering practices that apply to the software assurance processes. Cost-modeling and risk assessment techniques aid the project management process. Inspections, reviews and audits can be applied to all software processes under the software quality assurance process. Software error measurement, and timing and sizing analysis techniques are useful during the software verification and validation process.

2.4   Time Factors (t)

2.4.1   Program Execution Time—Software Rejuvenation

Reliability is improved by limiting the execution domain state space. Today's software runs non-periodically, which allows internal states to develop chaotically too often without bound. Software rejuvenation is a concept that seeks to contain the execution domain by making it periodic. An application is gracefully terminated and immediately restarted at a known, clean, internal state. Failure is anticipated and avoided. Non-stationary, random processes are transformed into stationary ones. The software states would be re-initialized periodically, process by process, while the system continued to operate. Increasing the rejuvenation period reduces downtime but increases overhead. Rejuvenation does not remove bugs; it merely avoids them with incredibly good effect. Chandra Kintala of Bell Labs defines three software fault tolerance components. They may be used with any UNIX or NT application to let the application withstand faults. They are watchd, libft and repl.[4]

Watchd is a watchdog daemon process for detecting UNIX process failures (crashes and hangs) and restarting those processes. The fault tolerance mechanism is based on a cyclic protocol and the recovery mechanism is based on the primary copy approach. Libft is a C library for check pointing the internal state of an application process periodically on a backup node. It also provides recovery routines to restore the state of a process at the backup node and a location-dependent connection mechanism between server and client processes. With these checkpoint and recovery mechanisms, a server process can be dynamically migrated to a different node for load balancing and fault tolerance. To tolerate design and program faults, it provides fault tolerance programming constructs, such as, recovery blocks, N-version programming, and exception handling. It also provides fault tolerant I/O functions for safe I/O.

REPL is a file replication mechanism that replicates files located on one physical file system onto another physical file system at run time. It provides features for both synchronous as well as asynchronous run-time replication of file updates [15].

Windows has a special library WinFT that provides automatic detection and restarting of failed processes; diagnosing and rebooting of a malfunctioning or strangled OS; check pointing and recovery of critical volatile data; and preventive actions, such as software rejuvenation [8] (Fig. 6).

---

[4]Note that *watchd, libft* and *REPL* are registered trademarks of AT&T Corporation.

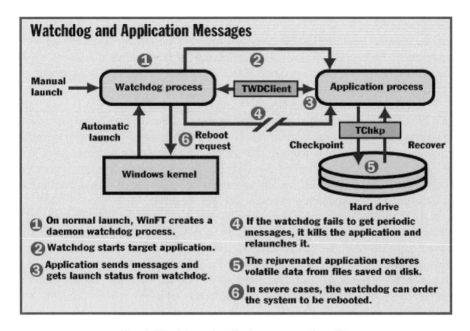

FIG. 6. Watchdog and application messages (from [8]).

By using a fixed or upper bound on the execution time and then restarting the reliability equation becomes:

$R(t) = e^{-ktC/E}$, where $0 < t < T$ and T is the upper bound of the rejuvenation interval. This limits the reliability to be no less than $e^{-kTC/E}$ for a fixed C and E.

Software rejuvenation was initially, developed by Bell Laboratories in the late 1970s for its billing systems and perfected by NASA.

The execution of a software process can show signs of wear after it executes for a long period. This process aging can be the effects of buffer overflows, memory leaks, unreleased file locks, data corruption or round-off errors. Process aging degrades the execution of the process and can often cause it to fail. This effect is different than the software aging problem identified by Parnas. He points out that application programs become less reliable and often fail due to a changing extended machine environment, new requirements and maintenance. In contrast process aging is related to application processes degrading after days and weeks of execution. Software fault tolerance techniques need to deal with **both** aging mechanisms.

With process aging the software works perfectly for a period with no risk of failure. It then enters a jeopardy period where it is vulnerable to executing the fault that now becomes a failure. As an example a process with a memory leak problem will not fail until the process memory request exceeds all allocated memory. For the time that the memory footprint for the process is growing the software is executing with no problem. Sometimes slower response times are noticed before the failure when the process enters the jeopardy state. Kintala calls the period that the software is working fine the 'base longevity interval.'

This story is in progress. The NASA mission to explore Pluto has a very long mission life of 12 years. A fault-tolerant environment incorporating on-board preventive maintenance is critical to maximize the reliability of a spacecraft in a deep-space mission. This is based on the inherent system redundancy (the dual processor strings that perform spacecraft and scientific functions). The two processor strings are scheduled with an on/off duty cycle periodically, to reduce the likelihood of system failure due to radiation damage and other reversible aging processes.

Since the software is reinitialized when a string is powered on, switching between strings results in software rejuvenation. This avoids failures caused by potential error conditions accrued in the system environment such as memory leakage, unreleased file locks and data corruption. The implementation of this idea involves deliberately stopping the running program and cleaning its internal state by flushing buffers, garbage collection, reinitializing the internal kernel tables or, more thoroughly, rebooting the computer.

Such preventive maintenance procedures may result in appreciable system downtime. However, by exploiting the inherent hardware redundancy in this Pluto mission example, the performance cost is minimal. One of the strings is always performing and starting it before the current active string is turned off can mask the overhead for a string's initialization. An essential issue in preventive maintenance is to determine the optimal interval between successive maintenance activities to balance the risk of system failure due to component fatigue or aging against that due to unsuccessful maintenance itself [31].

Continuing experimentation is being done, to refine this technique. It has, however, been in the literature for more than twenty years and its use in the industry is negligible. Most software practitioners are unaware of it.

2.5   Effort Factors (E)

2.5.1   Effort Estimates

Barry Boehm, Capers Jones and Larry Putnam have developed software estimation theory and models. The fundamental equation in Barry Boehm's COCOMO model is

$$SM = (2.94)(\text{Size})^E \left[\prod EM(n) \right],$$

where *SM* is the expected number of staff months required to build the system, size is thousands of new or changed source lines of code excluding commentary, $[\prod EM(n)]$ is the product of effort multipliers, one of the multipliers is complexity. The complexity multiplier rates a component based on the factors of Control Operations, Computational Operations, Device dependent operations, Data Management Operations and User Interface Management Operations. This effort multiplier varies from 0.73 for very low complexity and 1.74 for extra high complexity.

The effort term *E* in the Sha equation is equal to or greater than *PM*. For a given component once the average effort is estimated, reliability can be improved if the invested effort exceeds the nominal effort. If the invested development effort is less very unreliable software can be expected. The programmers can be made more effective by investing in tools and training. These factors are integrated into the COCOMO model.

2.5.2   Hire Good People and Keep Them

This is key. Every shop software claims to employ the 'best and the brightest.' Few really do. The book Peopleware is a necessary read for how to improve the software staff. Guru Programmers who are masters at their art are twenty to thirty times more productive than average programmers. Hiring the best tends to raise the level of the entire organization as methods and reasoning are taught to colleagues. It is vital to recognize the difference between vocational training and education. An educated staff can quickly adapt to new technologies and processes.

Practitioners are too poorly trained in known good methods. The New York Times has commented on the trend in the computer industry towards younger and less well educated practitioners. They are supposedly valued for their intuitive skills and aversion to structure. High school dropouts are hobbyists who learn skills not in a classroom but in pursuit of computer games, digital music, video editing, computer animation and film. On the job training consists of random mucking about, romantically excused by saying the industry moves too quickly for textbooks and knows precious few rules. Immaturity is prized. Some started as toddlers with parents' home computers and are admittedly deficient in human socialization and interactive skills due to that early and prolonged isolation. That a major software corporation offers quasi-certification of such people diminishes the value of genuine engineering. A Cisco Certified Internet work Expert certificate holder's starting salary *was* $75K, quite remarkable even in an inflated technology atmosphere [33]. By 2002 these same hot shots were looking for work.

2.5.3   Effectiveness of Programming Staff

Any software shop can make their people more effective as they set about improving the quality of their people. They can recognize that very large changes (more than

100 instructions) and very small changes (fewer than 5 instructions) are more error-prone than medium sized changes. This may have some relationship to the average size of human working memory, and our limited ability to attend to details.

Even when excellent methods are developed it is difficult to have the methodology promulgated and incorporated into school curricula for widespread study. An effective software shop invests in keeping their people current.

Do new methods ignore the dynamics of commercial software development? Successful corporations act in their own best interests. If basic engineering principles are ignored and trustworthiness is imperiled, there must be some stronger motivation in operation. Microsoft Windows is an example of planned obsolescence. Each new version is deliberately incompatible with the previous version in some commands, menus, formats and responses. Each new version requires extensive human re-learning and reconfiguration of interfacing systems. It creates a market for services and pressure to buy the most current version to remain compatible, which is profitable for Microsoft, but it is a chronic drain of time and money.

Sometimes it might be expedient to not invest in expensive security measures because the customer had not demanded it. It might be that customers are slowly becoming better-educated consumers, however. The lessons learned from a recent crippling of commercial web servers are that everyone is super-empowered, individuals and vandals alike, in a networked world. Many little encroachments on privacy add up to large losses of personal control that people find distressing. Nations may come to understand that government still matters because it is the only entity with the resources and the laws to ensure that personal rights are protected [11]. When there is such demand from people through their governments, basic engineering principles will probably be valued by software corporations.

Do practitioners accurately identify key problems? There is no cultural basis for sound engineering practice in the software industry. Even NASA, the very best software shop in the world and renown for its early successes has fallen into the trap of taking engineering shortcuts that have come back to haunt them.

On June 4, 1997, the Mars Pathfinder landed and for the next 3 months Sojourner surveyed the terrain. This very successful mission began, however, with Pathfinder experiencing mysterious system resets that took ingenious work on the part of the software design team at NASA's Jet Propulsion Laboratory to find and fix the defect. It turned out that the priorities assigned to tasks in the multitasking real-time system fell into a priority inversion because the load volume was heavier than the maximum that had been tested as shown in the next case study.

2.5.4   Case study: the Mars Explorer

Failures on Mars missions:

- communication problem between 2 teams, one using the metric system and the other using yards,
- a software bug caused the probe not to decelerate fast enough when entering the Mars atmosphere.
- the Mars lander stops sending images occasionally, and then reboots.

Explanation:

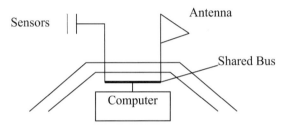

There is a conflict for accessing the resource: Bus
Priorities should be:

- Reboot,
- Send images,
- Gather data.

But due to a faulty use of preemptive multithreading, they were:

- Reboot,
- Gather data,
- Send images.

Priorities designed for the hardware, the application software and the driver that controlled the bus were inconsistent. A fail-safe watchdog counter rebooted the system after it had been inactive for some time. This is why the lander was rebooting after being silent for too long. This is a **fail-safe** system.

This problem is a typical deadlock that can happen when access to resources are not properly designed. The deadlock is similar to those experienced in multi-thread database systems.

Some Solutions.

- Design defensively: leave in the debug code, build fail-safe systems.

- Stress test: test the system beyond its limits established in the requirements. It is best to test to the breaking point. The difference between the breaking point and the maximum design load is the system margin. The stress tests for the Mars Explorer were actually thought to be the worst case. But because data gathering was so successful there was more data than expected. This resulted in the shared bus not being released.

- Explain all anomalies that show up during system test. Sometimes you must release the software for its intended use even though you have not been able to discover the cause of the anomaly. In these cases treat the release as "provisional" and continue to work on understanding the anomaly. In the case of the Mars Explorer, the anomaly was detected during the tests; however, it was believed to be a hardware problem and ignored.

- Hold architecture reviews and pay special attention to performance issues. Process scheduling algorithms need detailed analysis. All shared resources must be understood and interactions must be analyzed. Simulate use cases.

Fortunately, the software on the Pathfinder had debugging trace features left in place, so an exact replica of the software could be used on Earth with the confidence that the timing nature of the problem would not be contaminated. A fix was implemented using a priority inheritance protocol that was built into the operating system. As an aside, an early anti-missile test failed when the configuration used in the missile firing differed slightly from the one used in testing. Software developers insisted that the firing be done with the debug software in the configuration. The mission planners over ruled them since the debug software might halt the computer. Logic in this case failed because of the fragile nature of the software. A small difference in the real data from that used in all the tests caused mission failure.

Returning to the Mars Mission.   The actual data rates experienced during the mission were better than the test "worst case." NASA's test engineers did report one or two system resets during their testing, however they never successfully reproduced or explained these failures. Their observations were dismissed as aberrations.

There were two missed opportunities to catch this priority inversion. First, classically trained engineers stress a system until it breaks, then guarantee it for considerably less than the break point. A mere guess at what the break point might be, especially in a very new environment, is unacceptable. Had the software been sufficiently loaded to reveal the priority inversion, it could have been fixed without heroics. Over-engineering and over-testing are not sound practices that take the place of analysis and designs.

Human factors specialists are familiar with the pitfalls of 'wishing problems away' and are vigilant against it. Unexplained system failures cannot be ignored because of management pressures to pass the software to meet a date. Failures cannot be brushed away with the hope that they were so infrequent, maybe they will not happen again [21]. The Apollo missions owed their successes in large part to the excellent human factors work that was done to rehearse and anticipate every possible contingency in entirely new circumstances. Apparently, with a new generation of designers, that knowledge has been lost because it is rarely incorporated in university curricula. Moreover, these efforts are expensive. They can consume as much as 20% of resources and there are few financial consequences to failure. To get the contract be the low-cost bidder. The low-cost bidder too often minimizes reliability testing.

2.5.5   Object-Oriented Design Improves Effectiveness

Object oriented technology can help to fulfill early computer industry aspirations and lead to predictable system developments with high reliable software, fast time to market and solid performance [22].

The case history of one modern telephone software system makes the point. The project was to support the use of new, very fast broadband networks in the telephone company access network. Since this was clearly a large-scale development effort, the designers adopted the use of objects very early. The size of the project in its first release was 12,600 function points, 22 software modules with 47 interfaces, and 12 databases. This complexity was organized into 278 object classes and 1200 objects. The developers adhered to five overarching principles in making their design decisions:

(1) System synthesis, the melding of methods and business objects, began from the customer's, not the developers', viewpoint.

(2) Modular architecture separated data from applications.

(3) Effective data stewards were appointed with responsibility and authority for the object classes. They were charged with authority and responsibility of the reliability of the methods in the object class.

(4) Object oriented analysis included extensive domain analysis, rigorous requirements, business usage scenarios worked out with the user, formal external and internal interface agreements, and an integrated data model.

(5) Object oriented design used client/server architecture and industry wide standards.

(6) Code inspections were performed on selected modules. Cyclomatic metrics were computed for each module to find those that needed formal code inspections.

(7) System testers were granted the 'right of refusal.' They could reject any object library or application processes that in their judgment were not reliable. Designers had to do the redesign and still meet their schedule commitments. These redesigned modules were expected to be formally code inspected. Management resolved conflicts.

The most serious problem this project faced was the need to keep data consistent. Consistency drove accuracy. All former designs used convoluted error paths; these were error-prone and required more code and execution time than straightforward designs that included consistency checks in the object class methods.

Legacy systems provided and accepted data from the system. Data normalization techniques, with robust error processing isolated the new system from the legacy system. Here object oriented technology was a powerful tool for allowing quick system updates to accommodate new features and changes in business practices. It made reuse natural. System designers were able to accurately reflect business objectives in the object classes.

Until such robust object oriented design became a habit, an enforced object encapsulation strategy with centralized object libraries is vital. Skilled project managers must insist that all subsystems and modules use the same Operation, Administration and Management (OA&M) software. This achieves meaningful reuse and results in huge system cost savings in operation of the system itself.

2.5.6   Corroborating Object Experiences

That these results can be attributed to a disciplined use of object-oriented technology is corroborated by the experience of others. Swiss Bank Corporation designers told me that they obtained a fifty percent productivity improvement during re-engineering efforts that started in 1991. By 1994, they were installing their new object oriented system and said that reuse was the key to their success. The benefits of prototyping and adherence to clean object class definitions were particularly apparent. They managed risks by adhering to the standard enterprise object classes and linking them together. They anticipated some performance problems and these did occur, but the cost/performance improvement of new computer servers more than compensated for the ten percent performance overrun they saw.

AT&T developed more than fifty object-oriented systems using a unique 'objects *in memory* approach.' The objects were locked in memory while the system ran. One such system may be biggest and fastest object oriented network management system in the world. It uses 1 gigabyte of memory for its 15 million objects and thousands of transactions per second on a HP high-end workstation. It has been in production for three years with no significant problems. It replaced a vintage IBM-hosted facility provisioning system. This new approach can become widely used when logical memory is extended to 64 bit addressing and added to the natural structure of object-oriented databases. This will open virtual memory machines to objects and regain freedom from memory constraints enjoyed by application developers in the earlier transaction systems.

2.5.7 Objects in Large-Scale Projects

Large-scale evolving software presents a special challenge to object architects. Typically, an application consists of a network of objects connected through compatible interfaces. The need to meet new requirements and/or fix defects often results in new interfaces and object versions. When a new version of an object is created, it must be dynamically installed without causing disruption to existing software. Objects must be intelligent enough to handle the problems of dynamic reconfiguration, coordinate inter-module communication, and track the internal states of both the objects and the links. This increases the complexity of objects and can prevent them from being reused in different contexts. One solution is to not allow interface changes. This harsh rule often makes the application difficult to build because application level interfaces are imprecise due to time-outs and repeated transmissions triggered by buffer losses in asynchronous communication. Additionally, the interface specifications are vague and not amenable to analysis.

In this dynamic environment, however, there is a premium for keeping all the modules consistent. It is very difficult for designers, who are focused on the function of each module, to worry about the way all the pieces will fit together. As a result, the issue of interface consistency is often left to test teams, where it is inefficient and time consuming. Experience shows that it is three times more expensive for testers to find and fix problems than developers. So, the interfaces must change but in a controlled way. Object oriented technology opens the door to dynamic checking of interface states and internal consistency because for the first time it is possible for projects to create libraries of interface object classes to do this job. International standards bodies recognized this problem and developed the Common Object Request Broker Architecture (CORBA) standard to do distributed computing. CORBA is in its infancy, but industry cooperation is making CORBA the object middleware standard [12]. One problem is that CORBA locks the sender until the receiver receives and acknowledges the message, and CORBA does not support multi-cycle transactions. CORBA's object module is evolving and may become the standard of choice. The hope is that the object oriented CORBA will provide the fabric to let architects connect independently designed components together. Mediators add the dimension of a database storing the objects used in the communication interfaces. Network Programs, Inc. provided a multiple transaction capability for mapping applications to one another. Their adapter/collector technology is a robust way of connecting systems while avoiding undesired interactions. Meanwhile, Microsoft offers its own brand-specific object approach, Distributed Common Object Model (DCOM), which allows clients to access servers across a network and provides a binary interface for packaging and linking libraries or other applications. Since the situation is still fluid, most organizations are using both approaches in combination with in-house controls for their interface designs.

Java applets and CORBA are well suited to building distributed web applications. Browsers give access to network management data, and they allow networks to be managed remotely. To overcome delays due to network latency in the time it takes for a command to get to a network element, the *management by delegation* approach has become popular [34]. Data are stored in management information databases close to the network elements. They may be sent to the network elements as remote agents with their programs or they may be mapped to CORBA objects which can be located anywhere but must be statically mapped to the network element. Using Java applets, designers can overcome this limitation and dynamically reconfigure programs and their data objects. Java has a remote method invocation feature that is similar to CORBA but is restricted to only Java objects. Since CORBA can be used for many languages, it is the best choice for distributing the network management data. This client approaches are proving successful too.

3. Summary

Software Fault Tolerance can be aimed at either preventing a transaction failure to keep the system operating or at recovering the database for an entire system. In both cases the goal is to prevent a fault from becoming a failure.

Software fault tolerance can be measured in terms of system availability that is a function of reliability. The exponential reliability equation using an extension to Sha's Mean Time To Failure can be used to quantitatively analyze the utility various processes, tools, libraries, test methods, management controls and other quality assurances technologies. Collectively these technologies comprise the field of software engineering. The extended reliability equation provides a unifying equation to reliability-based software engineering. Now, it is possible to define the software fault tolerance requirements for a system and then make engineering tradeoffs to invest in the software engineering technology best able to achieve the required availability.

Citigal Labs measures software fault tolerance and software safety. Their web page summarizes the state-of-the art of software fault tolerance in 2002:

> "Traditionally, fault-tolerance has referred to building subsystems from redundant components that are placed in parallel" [9]. A prime example is the computer system for the space shuttle. On page 20 of his book, Peter Neuman states that [25]: "the on-board shuttle software runs on two pairs of primary computers, with one pair being in control as long as the simultaneous computations on both agree with each other, with control passing to the other pair in the case of a mismatch. All four primary computers run identical programs. To prevent catastrophic failures in which both pairs fail to perform (for example, if the software were wrong), the shuttle has a fifth computer that is programmed with different code by different programmers from a different company, but using the same specifications and the same compiler (HAL/S). Cutover to the backup computer would have to be done manually by the astronauts."

On the shuttle, we see a combination of redundant computers and redundant software versions; redundant software versions from the same specification are typically referred to as N-version programming. *N-version programming* is a fault-tolerance improvement paradigm that executes multiple versions (that were independently designed/written and implement the same software function) in parallel and then takes a vote among the results as to which output value is most frequent.

We use the term fault-tolerance in our research and commercial products at Citigal slightly differently. For us, software is deemed as fault-tolerant if and only if:

(1) the program is able to compute an *acceptable* result even if the program itself suffers from incorrect logic; and,

(2) the program, whether correct or incorrect, is able to compute an *acceptable* result even if the program itself receives *corrupted* incoming data during execution.

The key to our definition is what is considered "acceptable." This can include characteristics such as correctness and/or safety, and is based on the system. The interpretation for what constitutes software fault-tolerance according to our definition results from a combination of the principles of software safety and robust design.

Widely accepted software engineering design practices call for *robustness* and *graceful degradation* whenever a system gets into an undesirable state. Software fault tolerance is a related concept. The distinction between robustness and fault tolerance rests on whether the undesirable state is "expected" or "unexpected." Robustness deals primarily with problems that are expected to occur and must be protected against. By contrast, fault tolerance deals with unexpected problems. These must also be protected against. For example, if we are accessing in an integer to be used in a division operation, a robust design ensures that the division operation is not executed if the integer is zero. A fault-tolerant design accounts for unanticipated possibilities (e.g., if the integer is corrupted, a fault tolerant design might freeze the state of the program and not complete a division operation or it might require that the integer be reread). Here, we are interested in assessing fault-tolerance, which can be a side-benefit of robust design practices.

For critical software, there are three classes of output states that can be produced from a program execution: (1) correct, (2) incorrect, but acceptable, and non-hazardous, and (3) hazardous. Software fault-tolerance refers to the ability of the software to produce "acceptable" outputs regardless of the program states that are encountered during execution. Software safety refers to the ability of the software to produce "non-hazardous" outputs regardless of the program states that are encountered during execution. (What constitutes an output hazard is defined by the system level safety requirements.) Software safety then, according to our perspective on fault-tolerance, is a special type of software fault-tolerance.

Fault-tolerance refers to a class of outputs that can be tolerated, and software safety refers to a class of outputs that cannot be tolerated. For example, for an input value of 1 to the software, suppose that the correct output value is 100.0. But suppose that the numerical algorithms we use produce an output of 99.9. If the set of acceptable, non-hazardous values is {99.0, 101.0} and only this range, then this value is acceptable, and hence the software was fault-tolerant with respect to an inaccurate algorithm. Further suppose that the software, for some reason, may not receive the correct input value of 1 when it should, due to some external problem. Say the code instead receives a value of 0.0. Finally suppose that along with its low-accuracy numerical algorithm, the software produces an output value of 102.0, which is hazardous since it is out of the range of {99.0, 101.0}. Then we immediately gain knowledge that there is a potential safety problem."

ACKNOWLEDGEMENTS

The New Jersey Center for Software Engineering sponsored some of the work reported here. The Committee on National Software Studies (http://www.cnsoftware. org) provided data and contacts. Professor Sha's excellent paper triggered the reliability approach to software engineering. Professor Brian Randell's, winner of the 2002 IEEE Emanuel R. Piore Award for seminal contributions and leadership in computer system dependability research, established this filed of study. Les Hatton, Collin Tulley, Sam Keene leads discussions groups on software reliability and quality that were very helpful. Chandra Kintala and H. Yuang worked with me on these ideas for many years and made fundamental contributions to making software more reliable as they made my rejuvenation insights practical. Peter Neuman identified the risks of not attending to software reliability. Will Tracz encouraged me for many years.

Special thanks to my dear friend C.M. Yuhas of 'Have Laptop—Will Travel' for contributing material in this chapter.

REFERENCES

[1] AT&T Bell Laboratories, "Programming languages", in: *A History of Engineering and Science in the Bell System*, Vol. VII, 1984, pp. 379–380.
[2] Baratloo A., Singh N., Tsai T., "Transparent run-time defense against stack smashing attacks", in: *Proceedings of 2000 USENIX Annual Technical Conference, San Diego, CA*, 2000, pp. 18–23.
[3] BEA White Paper, "Managing complexity with application infrastructure", BEA Systems, San Jose, CA, http://www.bea.com.
[4] Bernstein L., "Software investment strategy", *Bell Labs Technical Journal* **2** (3) (1997) 233–243.
[5] Bernstein L., Yuhas C.M., "Testing network management software", *Journal of Network and Systems Management* **1** (1) (1993) 5–15.
[6] Beugnard A., "Making components contract aware", *Computer* **12** (7) (1999) 38–45.
[7] Boehm B., et al., Software estimation with COCOMO II, PTR.
[8] Carreira J., et al., "Fault tolerance for Windows applications", *Byte Magazine* (February 1997) 51–52.
[9] http://www.cigitallabs.com/resources/definitions/software_safety.html.
[10] Fowler M., *Refactoring-Improving the Design of Existing Code*, Addison-Wesley, 2000, p. xvi.
[11] Friedman T.L., "The Hackers' lessons", *The New York Times* **15** (2000) A27.
[12] Gaud S., "Object stamp of approval", *ComputerWorld* **31** (11) (1997) 1.
[13] Goma H., "Reusable software requirements and architecture for families of systems", *Journal of Systems & Software* **28** (3) (1995) 189–202.

[14] Hatton L., *Safer C: Developing Software for High-Integrity and Safety-Critical Systems*, in: *The McGraw-Hill International Series in Software Engineering*, 1997.

[15] Huang Y., Kintala C.M.R., "Software implemented fault tolerance: technologies and experience", in: Lyu M. (Ed.), *Proceedings of 23rd Internat. Symposium on Fault-Tolerant Computing, Toulouse, France, June 1993, Software Fault Tolerance*, John Wiley & Sons, 1995, pp. 2–9.

[16] Krishnamurthy B. (Ed.), *Practical Reusable UNIX Software*, John Wiley & Sons, New York, 1995, pp. 5–8.

[17] Leveson N.G., *Safeware-System Safety and Computers*, Addison-Wesley, 1995, p. 436.

[18] Lim W.C., "Effects of reuse on quality, productivity and economics", *IEEE Software* (1994) 23–29.

[19] Lyu M., *Handbook of Software Fault Tolerance*, chapter 2.

[20] Lyu M.R., *Software Fault Tolerance*, John Wiley and Sons, Chichester, 1995.

[21] March S., "Learning from Pathfinder's bumpy start", *Software Testing & Quality Engineering* **1** (5) (1999) 10–12.

[22] Marciniak J.J., *Encyclopedia of Software Engineering*, John Wiley and Sons, 2002, pp. 526–546.

[23] Musa J., Iannino A., Okumoto K., *Software Reliability: Measurement, Prediction, Application*, McGraw-Hill, 1987, Appendix E.

[24] National Research Council, *Information Systems Trustworthiness Interim Report*, National Academy Press, Washington, DC, 1997, pp. 18–29.

[25] Neuman P.G., *Computer Related Risks*, Addison-Wesley, 1995, pp. 20–21.

[26] "Software manufacturing", *UNIX Review* **7** (1989) 38–45.

[27] Selby R., "Empirically analyzing software reuse in a production environment", in: Tracz W. (Ed.), *Software Reuse: Emerging Technology*, IEEE Computer Society Press, 1988, pp. 176–189.

[28] Sha L., "Using simplicity to control complexity", *IEEE Software* **18** (4) (2001) 27.

[29] Siweiorek D., Swarz R., *The Theory and Practice of Reliable System Design*, Digital Press, Bedford, MA, 1982, p. 7.

[30] Stoyen A.D., "Fighting complexity in computer systems", *Computer* **30** (8) (1997) 47–48, http://computer.org/pubs/computer/computer.htm.

[31] Tai A.T., Chau S.N., Alkalaj L., Hecht H., "On-board preventive maintenance: Analysis of effectiveness and optimal duty period", in: *Proceedings of the 3rd International Workshop on Object-Oriented Real-time Dependable Systems (WORDS'97), Newport Beach, CA*, 1997, pp. 40–47.

[32] Wallace D.R., Ippolito L.M., "A framework for the development and assurance of high integrity software", *National Institute of Standards and Technology (NIST) Special Publication 500-223*, U.S. Dept. of Commerce, Dec. 1994, p. ix.

[33] Wallace M., "Who Needs a Diploma? Why the high-tech industry wants dropouts", *The New York Times Magazine* **5** (2000) 76–78.

[34] Yemini Y., Goldszmidt G., Yemini S., "Network management by delegation", in: I. Krishnan, W. Zimmer (Eds.), *Integrated Network Management, II*, Elsevier, New York, 1991, pp. 95–107.

Advances in the Provision of System and Software Security— Thirty Years of Progress

RAYFORD B. VAUGHN

Mississippi State University
P.O. Box 9637
Mississippi State, MS 39762
USA
vaughn@cse.msstate.edu

Abstract

This chapter addresses systems and software security in computing environments over the past thirty years. It is partially a historical treatment of the subject which outlines initial efforts to bound the security problem beginning early 1970 through today's state of security engineering practice. It includes an introduction to the topic, definitions and explanations necessary for background, design principles that were established by researchers and practiced today by security engineers. Government programs are described as they were initiated over time and their applicability to today's security engineering practice is discussed. Important law and Executive decisions are included which have had a direct impact on the state of computer security today. Lessons learned by practicing security engineers are included as a part of concluding remarks. Much progress has been accomplished in research and practice, yet systems today appear as vulnerable or perhaps more vulnerable than they were in the past. This should not be necessarily interpreted as a lack of progress—but as an indication of the complexity of the problem being addressed and the changing nature of the systems and networks needing the protection.

ADVANCES IN COMPUTERS, VOL. 58
ISSN: 0065-2458

287

1.   Introduction

At no time in our past history has there been more emphasis placed on the means and methods to secure systems and software than at the present time. Although much of this focus came to public attention following the tragic events of September 11, 2001, efforts to bring trust and security to software and systems have actually been underway for approximately the past 30 years. This chapter addresses this progress, beginning with initial efforts by the federal government and ending with thoughts on what the future holds. The chapter is written for those who are not specialists in this area, yet wish to understand the field at the generalist level. Background and definitional material is provided in Section 2 to facilitate concepts presented later and references are periodically given for those that desire to pursue any specific topic to greater depth. When web links are available and likely to remain present for the foreseeable future, they too are included for the reader's benefit.

The organization of this chapter is essentially chronological. A section discussing terminology and concepts is presented following the introduction to assist the reader with the context and content that follows. A section on historical perspectives follows which documents the many efforts in research and policy to bring trust, confidence, and correctness to our systems and software. The historical presentation contains comment and observations made by the author that often represents personal opinion and experience over the years. Sections then follow to discuss the state of current practice, security engineering capabilities, examples of what problems remain unsolved, and what the future may hold in this important area. Along the way, the reader may encounter recommendations and need for additional research effort. This chapter is not offered as a comprehensive treatment of the subject of computer security (aka, information assurance). Many good textbooks have been published on this subject, yet none of them would likely claim to be comprehensive. The problem of providing a secure solution for a specific software system or network is simply too difficult and too complex to be reduced to a single text or to a set of practices that will guarantee success. While there are commonly accepted best practices and some fundamental science involved, most would agree that securing systems and networks is today primarily a function of experienced, skilled, and knowledgeable systems administrators who constantly monitor and improve the protection mechanisms associated with that which is being protected. The reader will undoubtedly find that much of what is presented here appears to have a strong government emphasis to it. This is because most of the work done over the past thirty years has been government sponsored and promoted, but is still applicable to the commercial world and systems.

2. Concepts of Information Assurance

2.1 Overview

Information assurance or IA can mean something different to various individuals—depending on their position, interest, business, employer, and many other factors. To some, the focus is on a network; to others, the interest may be on a particular software system or may involve a complete systems engineering effort (which should include hardware, software, people, processes, and procedure). In truth, security in any automation environment (networks, software, systems of systems, etc.) must take a holistic approach and include a complete systems engineering view—to include people and process as well as hardware and software. An attack or threat of any kind (intentional or unintentional) has a high likelihood of occurring at the point of the least resistance (or the weakest link). A comprehensive defense means that each point of attack or risk must be identified, assessed for threat, and some sufficient defensive measure taken or planned. When we say holistic treatment or comprehensive approach, this normally means that the security engineer must consider hardware security, software security, policy, procedures, personnel employed, electronic emission security, and physical protection when constructing a protection strategy. Failure to properly address security in any one of these areas can and will introduce a point of vulnerability.

The process just described is in no way trivial and forms the essence of the information assurance discussion that follows and the research that has occurred over the past three decades. First, we need to make a distinction between the study of penetrating systems and that of defending systems. These two areas are sometimes referred to as offensive operations and defensive operations. On the offensive side, the penetration of systems can be a legal or illegal activity. Illegal activities may include authorized individuals inside the organization (we refer to this as an *insider* threat) who are misusing or abusing the computing assets in some manner that results in a violation of law or policy. This may be intentional or unintentional on the part of the employee. Examples of such actions could be installation of an unauthorized modem connection in a corporate network that then provides an unprotected entry point into otherwise protected assets (unintentional side effect), deletion of important and sensitive data by a disgruntled employee (intentional action), or use of corporate hardware and software to establish and run an adult web site (intentional action). In each case, damage to the organization occurs and policy (or perhaps law) is likely violated. Illegal activity can often occur from outside the organization (we refer to this as an *outsider* or *external* threat) by an unauthorized user. This again can be intentional or unintentional, although the preponderance of such activity is assumed intentional. Examples of such attacks might include overwhelming an organization's networks by sending a very large amount of spurious traffic to a single entry point and causing a system failure (or at least an availability issue), discovering a flaw in the operating system that allows the outsider to bypass protection and gain entry to a system (a hacker threat), downloading or receiving harmful (malicious) code or email that damages the system (unintentional outsider), or providing easy access to an unauthorized outsider which results in their ability to penetrate system defenses (e.g., providing one's password and user identification by failing to properly protect it).

While illegal activities might be more intuitive to the reader, legal (from the U.S. point of view) penetrations are also a subject of interest to readers. A common method of testing system defenses is known as "penetration testing" (also known as "red teaming")—a sanctioned activity to attempt (in a controlled fashion) to gain unauthorized access. This form of testing can be accomplished by insiders (employees of the organization involved in testing system security) or outsiders (third party testing). In either case, the penetration is done on behalf of the organization with the intention of discovering weak defenses so that they can be shored up. It has been argued that this form of testing is one of the more useful measures of a system's overall protection [9]. Additionally, there is another form of penetration that is not often considered on first thought—that of information warfare [4] (or information operations, network centric warfare, or other similar terms). Government sponsored technical staffs generally accomplish this form of penetration activity as part of its intelligence gathering activities or in preparation for military action (declared or undeclared) against another government. This may include mapping networks to discover topologies and weak points, covert insertion of malicious code, denial of service attacks, or traffic analysis. We will not further address this form of legal penetration testing but wish to include mention of it here for the sake of completeness.

On the defensive side of information assurance, the security engineer tries to create what is referred to as a defensive perimeter (also known as a security perimeter) around the object of protection (e.g., the system, a network, a single host, a physical facility). The objective is to create enough penetration difficulty for the attacker so that the level of effort to penetrate exceeds the value gained if the penetration is successful. This is the same concept one uses when securing a home against possible invaders—that is, to make the level of effort necessary to gain entry more difficult than the attacker is willing to exert. Just as no home is one hundred percent secure, no useful computer system can guarantee total security. Because we cannot guarantee total security and because there is always risk present, we tend to use the term *assurance* to mean strength of protection. High assurance means a very strong system in terms of the security protection it offers and low assurance means very little security protection. A better characterization might be to think of assurance as trust in a system's ability to provide protection. Trust can come from many sources—experience, examination of the code, testing, certification by experts, and others. Hence, this chapter is concerned with information assurance (a term that indicates a property having various scalable values) more so than computer security (an objective that is either present or not).

The degree of assurance that we arrive at for a system (through whatever means we employ) is not a static value. That is, a high assurance system yesterday may be reduced to a low assurance system tomorrow though many means. This might occur because a previously undiscovered vulnerability in a specific operating system is announced, an update to the software configuration is installed with flawed code, a lapse in security procedures occurs due to a change in key personnel, or a firewall[1] is accidentally misconfigured by a systems administrator. Many other examples could be provided here, but the point is that past performance in terms of trust says very little about future performance characteristics. It is incumbent on the systems and/or security engineer to continuously update the security perimeter and to check on its effectiveness. There is simply no guarantee of impenetrability and today much of our reliance is on the individual skill set of those that administer the system and its protection. The advantage always lies with the attacker of a system in that, with patience, the attacker must only find a single unguarded entry point into the system while the defender must block them all. Even when penetration is prevented, the majority of systems are certainly subject to being taken out of service though a denial of service attack, which may overwhelm its processing capacity or network resources to the point of failure.

---

[1] A firewall is a collection of components (hardware and/or software) that is placed between networks for the purpose of protection of the inner network. Network traffic from the outside is filtered and restricted by a set of rules that enforce a policy or a part of a policy.

2.2 Background Concepts

Initially, security for computing systems was thought to be primarily an issue of access control to data so that users could be assured that others having access to the computer system could not obtain access to data in the system that they did not have permission to see. In other words, early attempts to protect systems worked within a confidentiality paradigm. Section 3 will address more of the rationale for this early view. As the professional and technical communities learned more about the security problem and the needs of specific organizations, other definitions began to surface that were not confidentiality issues. In fact, before a security engineer can accomplish any work, it is important that a firm understanding of the organizational definition of security be achieved and agreed to. This is often referred to as the security "policy" for an organization. Once a firm understanding of the policy is obtained, the security engineer (working with the organization) may develop a "model" of proper system behavior which complies with the policy and which can serve as a system specification. Common security concerns today are generally one of or a combination of the following characteristics:

- *Secrecy* or *Confidentiality*: A guarantee that assets of a protected system are accessible only by authorized parties.

- *Integrity*: Data assets can only be modified by authorized parties and only in authorized ways. Related issues include the preciseness of the data, consistency of data, and accuracy of the data.

- *Availability*: Computing assets (e.g., data, processing power, network bandwidth) are accessible to authorized parties when needed. Note that the absence of this characteristic is known as a *denial of service*.

- *Accountability*: The ability to establish correspondence between an action on the system and the responsibility for the action. This characteristic also includes a more specific area called *non-repudiation*, which is the establishment of responsibility for a computing action that cannot be denied.

A primary object of concern when developing a protection strategy is the data maintained by the computing system. Data must be in one of three electronic states—processing (active manipulation), storage (passive or at rest), or in transmission. The security engineer's objective then becomes to preserve the security characteristics of interest to the organization (i.e., confidentiality, availability, integrity, accountability) across all possible states of processing—a very difficult problem and one which involves significant analysis, testing, the weaving together of several disparate products (also known as mechanisms) into a protection perimeter, and then monitoring its effectiveness over time.

Often information security is thought to be synonymous with encryption.[2] While encryption is indeed a strong tool to use in developing a protection scheme, it is not a complete solution. When one considers how to protect data in transmission, encryption is the obvious solution, but it does not adequately or completely address protection needs while data is being processed or stored. Strong encryption is useful to keep data confidential while transiting a network for example. It is also a means to guarantee integrity of the data in that unauthorized modification of encrypted packets is likely detectable when the data is deciphered at the receiving end. Because of these characteristics, encryption has been the tool of choice in not only protecting data while moving it over a network, but also in specific protocols that result in the ability to digitally sign an electronic document in such a manner that the signature cannot be repudiated—to exchange encryption keys securely and to carry out secure dialogue in a client server environment. Encryption is more of a commodity today to those that must employ it (with the exception being the intelligence community, who create their own). It comes preinstalled in web browsers, is available in many commercial off-the-shelf products, and is available as freeware from web sites. Encryption strength is always a subject of concern and the length of time needed for a dedicated adversary to break it changes over time as computing technology improves. Web browser security offers sufficient security today for web transactions, but would not be sufficient to protect national secrets. The complete study of encryption and its progress through the years is beyond the scope of this chapter. It is treated here as one of many mechanisms that the security engineer must consider using in providing a total solution.

When taking a necessary holistic approach to the security problem, there are many areas of concern that encryption will not solve. There are many examples of such areas and the following are provided as a representative sampling.

– *Physical controls.* A good security perimeter requires solid physical controls so that an attacker does not have access to the equipment, the network wiring, employee workspace, files, or other sensitive items. A lack of such controls can result in the theft of equipment which contains sensitive data, a *social engineering* attack where the attacker uses human error or a lack of attention to policy and procedure to discover sensitive information or to gain access, the installation of a network recording device (called a *sniffer*) to record sensitive packets, or the installation of malicious software (e.g., a trap door or Trojan horse which can be used later by the attacker to gain system access). Good physical controls are necessary to protect against the outsider threat.

---

[2]Cryptography is the use of secret codes to transform and hide data from those that are not authorized to view it. It is sometimes used to authenticate origin and content. It is distinguished from information hiding where no transformation takes place (e.g., stenography or invisible inks) [7].

– *Policy*. Written policy and procedures that are made known to all authorized users of the system and enforced are paramount to overall system security. Studies in the past have shown that a large number of reported security incidents are unintentional, insider actions—that is, mistakes by an otherwise well-intentioned employee. Written policy, which is known and understood by employees, addresses this vulnerability. Examples of such policy might include disallowing an employee to install a dial-up modem on their office computer because such a device may introduce an unprotected entry point into the corporate network; prohibiting employees from downloading Active X controls (a form of what is known as *mobile code*) from a web server (accomplished by a simple browser setting) because such action can introduce malicious code into the corporate system; or, establishing a policy requiring frequent changing of passwords that are at least 8 alphanumeric characters long as a preventative measure against password discovery (e.g., *cracking attacks*). Policy is an excellent non-technical risk mitigation strategy—but only if employees understand the policy and the reason for it.

– *Software controls*. Any useful computing system contains a vast quantity of software integrated into a suite of services and functionality for the user. Software can contain intentional or unintentional hidden functionality that might be exploited by an attacker. Acquiring software with high assurance mitigates risk associated with software that might be of lesser assurance. Using an operating system that has been certified as having high assurance by a government agency (e.g., the National Institute of Standards and Technology) is preferred over using one that has not. Acquiring application software from a responsible and reputable source is preferred over downloading such software from an unknown author who may have posted it free of charge on a web site. This area of concern also includes protection against malicious code attacks such as computer viruses, worms, or Trojan horses. Charles (Chuck) Pfleeger addresses this topic nicely in Chapter 5 of his book, "Security in Computing" [13].

– *Inference or aggregation*. In the modern world of Internet connectivity and web servers, organizations must exercise caution with respect to the amount of information that is placed in various publicly available areas that might be independently accessed and combined together by an attacker to gain confidential or sensitive insights that should not have been publicly disclosed. This is referred to as the problem of aggregation. An example might include a corporate web site that on a general news page carries an announcement that there are confidential discussions underway with a competing company that may lead to a merger. A link from the main page to the human resources page may contain new information on a plan to move to a new employee benefit program that is generally known to be a benefits provider for competitor X. A third link may appear on the corporate web page housing "other links of interest" to competitor X's web site. Each piece of information by itself is not sensitive—but combined it begins to leak sensitive information to the detriment of the organization. Inference is a close relative of aggregation and occurs when non-sensitive information is obtained from a computer system and mathematically manipulated to discover sensitive information. Inference is generally associated with database queries, but need not be strictly isolated to that area. An example might include obtaining the total of all executive salaries in a small organization (non-sensitive aggregate data) and subtracting from that the total of all male executive salaries in the same organization (non-sensitive aggregate data) to arrive at the salary for the only female executive in the organization (sensitive, specific data). Defenses against inference and aggregation attacks are difficult to achieve since, in the majority of cases, the attacker uses information obtained outside the organization, and combines it with information obtained freely and legally from the organization resulting in disclosures that should not have been allowed.

The examples above were provided to demonstrate the wide area of concern that a practicing security engineer must be concerned with and to show that a single solution set is not adequate for an organization. It is imperative that a suite of products, policy, procedure, and training be combined by a knowledgeable engineer and constantly monitored over time if risk of attack is to be reduced to an acceptable level. This is often more art than science today.

3.   A Historical Perspective

3.1   Introduction

Protection of information while in transit has far deeper roots than does computing security. The use of cryptography, our most useful tool in this regard, can be traced back more than 4000 years to ancient Egypt and in some reports, even earlier (for a good overview of historical notes, the reader is invited to review Ron Gove's historical perspectives in the Information Security Management Handbook [7]). The history of the origin of computing machines is somewhat more recent and can be traced back to the seventeenth century when gear driven computing machines were described and constructed. Credit for these advances is often given to notable early scientists such as Blaise Pascal of France, Gottfried Wilhelm Leibniz of Germany, and Charles Babbage of England. All of these machines were capable of following some algorithm (a precursor of computer programming). Even the historically famous automated weaving loom developed by Joseph Jacquard of France in the early

1800s was an example of a programmable computing device used to control an industrial process. Security in these devices was not an architectural consideration and some would agree that even if security were a recognized need, it was provided for by the obscurity of the technology and the high level of knowledge needed to understand the mechanics and mathematics associated with these devices. Similar thought processes occurred when electronics was applied to these mechanical structures and modern day computers began to evolve. During the early 1940s, the truly first computers (as we know them today) were built. These included early prototype work at Bell Laboratories, Harvard University (the Mark I computer), Iowa State University (the Atanasoff–Berry machine), the University of Pennsylvania (ENIAC), and a code breaking machine developed in England for the intelligence community, known as the COLOSSUS. Other machines followed over the years, gradually moving from highly specialized and dedicated machines to general purpose computers that were cost effective for use in administering business or government, as well as useful in scientific exploration. Interestingly, the time between the introduction of the first prototype specialized computers and their widespread general use was only approximately 20 years. During this evolution of general purpose computing, engineering emphasis was placed on ease of use, speed, operating systems, programming languages, utility software, storage advances, and memory to name a few. Security, as a serious requirement, was not a high priority, or even a major consideration, beyond the need for some basic auditing (for cost accounting purposes). Physical access controls were generally thought to be sufficient to address any other concerns in this area. During the decade 1960–1970, however, security and protection of information assets began to assert itself as a requirement in modern computing systems and one that could be difficult to resolve. The interest in security was being driven more by evolving technology at this time than by user demand. Computing machines were becoming more affordable and as a result were proliferating quickly into society at large. Additionally, advances such as multiprogramming, networking, disk storage, large and persistent memories, application layer programs, resource sharing, and databases were increasing the amount of shared space and data exposure. The serious study of computer security began toward the end of this decade (circa 1967) sponsored by the U.S. Department of Defense as a response to growing concern with resource sharing computers and the risk they posed to loss of National classified information. One of the earliest reports addressing this concern was a Defense Science Board report [23] titled "Security Controls for Computer Systems" that was chaired by Dr. Willis H. Ware, then of the RAND Corporation. This paper is often cited as seminal work and the first that truly outlined the security problem in computing. It set in motion a series of events and responses by the Department of Defense (DOD) and the Federal government that resulted in international impact and advances through research that continue today. The historical overview that follows in this section is intended to provide the reader with a broad sense of past efforts and where they have led us over time to the present day. In the large, the problem remains unsolved, but important progress in understanding the problem has been made.

The remainder of this section is an attempt to overview significant events beginning with the 1970 Defense Science Board (DSB) report and ending with perspectives on where we are today. Apologies are extended if in the opinion of the reader, an important historical event is omitted in the remainder of this chapter. Admittedly, the events discussed here are based on this author's opinion of their importance.

3.2   The Defense Science Board Report

This report [23] is generally considered the first major scientific work reviewing and documenting the computer security problem. It was commissioned in the summer of 1967 by the Department of Defense (the Assistant Secretary of Defense, Deputy Director for Administration, Evaluation, and Management) in response to growing concerns that computer systems were proliferating throughout the military which were then being used to process and store sensitive information. Both defense contractors and DOD technical staffs were pressing the issue of security, the need for appropriate policy, and safeguards. The task eventually fell to the Advanced Research Projects Agency or ARPA (the forerunner of today's Defense Advanced Research Projects Agency or DARPA) and a task force, operating under the authority of the Defense Science Board, was eventually formed with Dr. Willis Ware, of the Rand Corporation, as its chairperson. Two panels were organized to review the problem and to make recommendations—a technical panel and a policy panel. Membership on these panels was diverse and well chosen. Many members were later recognized for their strong contributions to addressing the problem of computer security and are known today for their seminal work in this area. A full list of the membership is contained in the report, which is publicly available on the web at http://seclab.cs.ucdavis.edu/projects/history (note: this report and other key early papers were collected and stored electronically for public review under a grant by the National Security Agency to the University of Maryland). The report was originally classified at the Confidential level by the DOD and later downgraded to unclassified and made publicly releasable.

The report clearly addressed the need for holistic security controls—a theme that still exists today. Technical measures, as well as administrative policy and procedures, must all work together to address the security problem. They also characterized two important environments within which secure computing systems must operate. These environments still generally exist today, albeit with some modification as a result of technical advances over the years. They were identified as *closed* and *open* environments, where a closed environment was one that consisted only of trusted (or in the DOD vernacular, "cleared") users, working at physically protected workstations, connected to a physically protected computer system by protected communication circuits (i.e., physical, cryptographic, and electronic protection). Such an environment offers opportunity for the construction of a high assurance system that can process very sensitive information. This kind of closed system can reasonably be established in the commercial world also—for example, in the domain of banking. The other environment, and the more problematic, is known as open and is characterized as one in which there is a mixture of trusted and untrusted (or cleared/uncleared) users. The untrusted users use the system at unprotected workstations, connected to a central computing system by communicating over unprotected communication lines. The trusted users work from protected workstations and communicate over protected communication lines. Such an environment is far more difficult to establish assurance for and at the time of the DSB report, the authors believed that technology did not exist to fully address this problem [note: There is good argument that this has not changed a lot in the ensuing 30 plus years]. Furthermore, in a memorandum to the Chairman of the Defense Science Board, Dr. Willis wrote, "Thus, the security problem of specific computer systems must, at this point in time, be solved on a case-by-case basis employing the best judgment of a team consisting of system programmers, technical hardware and communications specialists, and security experts." This same truth holds today in that security engineers employ best judgment in a specific environment against a specific set of threats [22]. The conclusions reached by the task force in 1970 are reported verbatim below, as taken from the memorandum written by Dr. Ware to the Chairman of the DSB, and are annotated with this author's comments and thoughts. The annotations are enclosed in brackets following each conclusion for ease of separation.

- Providing satisfactory security controls in a computer system is in itself a system design problem. A combination of hardware, software, communications, physical, personnel, and administrative-procedural safeguards is required for comprehensive security. In particular, software safeguards alone are not sufficient. [This conclusion holds today and refers to the need for a holistic approach by the security engineer. An attacker will penetrate the point of least resistance so a weakness in any of the areas identified in this conclusion will become a potential target. In general, most penetrations today are not technical.]

- Contemporary technology can provide a secure system acceptably resistant to external attack, accidental disclosures, internal subversion, and denial of use to legitimate users for a *closed environment* (cleared users working with classified information at physically protected consoles connected to the system by protected communication circuits). [The key to this conclusion is the "acceptably resistant" phrase. This means that we can provide a sufficiently secure solution in most cases if we can assume trusted users and protected systems and networks. The same is true today.]

- Contemporary technology cannot provide a security system in an *open environment*, which includes uncleared users working at physically unprotected consoles to the system by unprotected communications. [Recalling that an open environment means a mix of trusted and untrusted users coupled with protected and unprotected systems and networks, this conclusion is only partially true today. Research and advances in security engineering have allowed for a much greater degree of protection in open environments today than in 1970. While it is still unwise to place national secrets in such an environment, e-commerce and other business applications today operate in this environment quite comfortably with, in most cases, sufficient security.]

- It is unwise to incorporate classified or sensitive information in a system functioning in an open environment unless a significant risk of accidental disclosure can be accepted. [Again, most would agree that significant advances have been made with respect to this conclusion. While it is still unwise to mix highly sensitive information with public information in an open environment, some lower level sensitive information can be resident on the same system accessible by the public with adequate assurance of separation today.]

- Acceptable procedures and safeguards exist and can be implemented so that a system can function alternately in a closed environment and in an open environment. [This conclusion addresses a work around that the panel came up with, sometimes called periods processing. The procedure can still be used effectively today for a stand-alone system. It requires that the system be brought to a halt, all sensitive information is removed, and then the system is reinitialized for open processing.]

- Designers of secure systems are still on the steep part of the learning curve and much insight and operational experience with such systems is needed. [Most security engineers would agree that the learning curve is still steep and that operational experience and insights are still required.]

- Substantial improvement (e.g., cost, performance) in security-controlling systems can be expected if certain research areas can be successfully pursued. [This conclusion initiated significant government funding of trusted computing systems which continues today in various forms.]

Clearly, the authors of the DSB report recognized the lack of architectural guidelines for secure systems and the risk that the Federal government was taking in the use of resource sharing computers. The call for research in this area was not ignored and resulted in a research focus that continues today. Specifically, the DSB report called for research in the following areas:

- Facilitate progress toward handling the open environment. The development of encryption devices to function internally within the computer proper was seen as a strong need as was the development of special hardware configurations that could provide satisfactory security controls in an open environment.
- Improve the understanding of failure risks. This suggestion was designed to initiate a program of research leading to a better understanding of the processes and policy needed to certify and re-certify systems for sensitive processing. In today's world, the federal government does have such processes in place, but there remains much room for improvement and the need for qualified certifiers remains.
- Improve the efficiency of security controlling systems. This suggestion reflected the need to develop new architectures for resource sharing computers that had, as a fundamental design principle, a security requirement. The members of the DSB study believed that with appropriate research focus new computer architectures could implement security controls more efficiently and correctly than present day systems did. They also recommended a parallel program of research to predict failure probabilities and failure modes in systems. The suggested focus on creating security architectures was taken to heart by the Department of Defense and major investments were made in this area throughout the 1970–1990 timeframe. In fact, this work continues in various forms even today.
- Solve a latent and not fully understood leakage point. In the context of the DSB report, resource-sharing computers were viewed as information repositories that were porous in nature with a tendency to "leak" protected information in a large variety of ways such that compromise of the information could occur. The report specifically mentioned leakage occurring from improper "erasing" of magnetic media—but within the entire report, many other leakage points were identified. This call for research was insightful for its time—particularly in the area of magnetic remanence where researchers were discovering the persistent nature of magnetic memory and that with highly specialized techniques, information could be retrieved even after having been erased. Additionally, this suggestion was directly related to the whole area known as object reuse which in the years following the DSB report became a required architectural component in trusted systems (note: object reuse will be discussed later in this chapter, but involves the requirement to clear information from shared resources prior to allocating that resource for reuse by another subject).

The authors of the report also prophesied that although the Department of Defense had initiated the study on computer systems security controls, this subject would very soon transcend the DOD and become an area of interest to the entire federal government and industry. Although not specifically addressing this thought in detail, it proved entirely accurate as in the next few years confidentiality concerns in the DOD were joined by integrity and availability concerns from the private sector and from the federal government. As time passed, sensitive but unclassified, privacy data, non-repudiation, and other such issues demonstrated that security in computer systems extended far beyond what was initially thought to be only a confidentiality problem.

This report has long been considered a seminal work in computer security and one that still deserves study today. It bounds the problem nicely for students and outlines the fundamental areas that are of concern to those that are charged with securing systems. Much of the work that is reported on in this chapter is a result of the DSB report and its recommendations.

3.3   The Reference Monitor

One of the DSB recommendations was for architectural change in computing systems such that security could be enhanced. An important response to that call was suggested by James P. Anderson [1] in 1972, within a report prepared for the U.S. Air Force. In this report, Anderson outlined the need for strong access controls and recommended the use of hardware and software to implement a *reference validation mechanism* (later referred to as a *reference monitor* concept). Although there are fine differences between the terms reference validation mechanism and reference monitor, they are used interchangeably in this chapter. The idea was elegant in notion and design and later became an important feature of operating system security and was adopted by the DOD as a fundamental architectural concept for trusted systems and was included in national level guidance and standards (specifically the DOD 5200.28-STD, the DOD Trusted Computer System Evaluation Criteria or "Orange Book"). It persists today in other trusted systems documents to include ISO Standard 15408 (The Common Criteria).

In the Anderson report, the computer system was modeled as a set of *subjects* (active entities in the system, e.g., processes) and a set of *objects* (passive entities in the system, e.g., file storage). Anderson suggested the use of a reference validation mechanism that would intercept every request by a subject for access to an object and validate that access based on a set of rules. These rules could, in effect, implement a security policy for the system—both discretionary (user/owner determined) and mandatory (organizationally determined) policy. In fact, the reference validation mechanism could be used to enforce a mandatory policy over a user's desire to share information or provide access to another subject if the organizational policy would be violated as a result. Although a specific implementation of a reference monitor was not given in the report, three important properties that any implementation of it would have to have were provided. These are given below with brief explanation.

- The reference validation must be tamperproof. This requirement was one of protection against attack and modification. If the hardware, software, or firmware components were modified, then no guarantee of its proper action could be made for access control. In any trusted system that employs the reference monitor concept, protection must be convincingly demonstrated to evaluators of that system. This characteristic is sometimes referred to as *isolation*.

- The reference validation mechanism must always be invoked. This characteristic is sometimes referred to as a no bypass capability or *completeness*. There must be no path in the system such that a subject can access an object without invoking the reference monitor. In practical systems, this rule is violated by privileged users such as system administrators or security officers, but each such exception increases the risk of a security failure.

- The reference validation mechanism must be small enough to be subject to analysis and tests so that its completeness can be assured. There is more requirement in this simple sentence than may first be observed by the reader. What is implied here is that the reference monitor must be correctly implemented and that correctness determination is enhanced if the mechanism is small enough to be comprehensible. The word "assured" was used by Anderson, and in computer security study, that term (assurance) means "a degree of trust." Trusted systems, for example, offer more "assurance" to the user that their information assets will be protected than do systems that are not trusted. Software from a reputable and known source generally offers more assurance that it has no malicious components than does software from unknown sources. The desire for the reference validation mechanism to be small stems from a desire to inspect (but formal inspection as well as informal inspection techniques) the software code and to use mathematical rigor to prove it correct for high assurance systems. This is known as *verifiability*.

An Air Force officer by the name of Roger Schell was actively involved in the study of computer system security vulnerabilities in the early 1970s and is generally credited with first specifying the concept of a reference monitor in 1972, as a security kernel. The implementation of the reference monitor concept has become known as a *security kernel* since that time and over the past thirty years there have been many commercial attempts to implement one. Although existing reference monitors have primarily been implemented in software, the concept itself is not restricted to software implementations. During the late 1970s several security kernel implementations were accomplished—primarily as research projects. MITRE is generally given credit for implementing the first on a DEC PDP-11/45 in 1975. For a full treatment of the advances in security kernels and the history behind them, the reader is invited to review Chapter 10 of Gasser's excellent book titled *Building a Secure Computer System* [6].

A closely related concept is the *trusted computing base* or TCB defined in the DOD Trusted Computing Systems Evaluation Criteria (TCSEC) [5]. The TCB was defined as the totality of protection mechanisms within a computer system— including hardware, firmware, and software—the combination of which is responsible for enforcing a security policy. The TCB concept is broader than the security kernel and in a system using the security kernel it becomes that kernel plus various trusted processes. Not all systems that are certified to process sensitive information use the reference monitor approach. The TCB description was offered as a matter of convenience so that protection components of a computer system could be described as a set of elements. The TCB is sometimes referred to as a *security perimeter* and includes all parts of the operating system that enforces a security policy. While it may seem better to use a reference monitor approach, in reality it may not be possible with legacy systems. A reference monitor is an architectural decision that must be implemented during the initial construction of an operating system—not a retrofit added later. In cases where software systems not employing a reference monitor concept are used in sensitive environments, a description of the TCB may be sufficient to convince a certification authority that security policy enforcement is sufficient for the degree of assurance required by the system and its users.

3.4   More Architectural Principles

Corresponding with the increased research activity brought on by the 1970 DSB report and the emphasis being placed on the development of more trusted systems for use by the government, Jerome Saltzer and Michael Schroeder (in 1975) [16] published eight fundamental principles for secure system design. These have been cited many times since and still today form an important basis for those constructing trusted systems or networks. They are repeated below with a brief synopsis taken from Saltzer and Schroeder with additional comments included in brackets.

- *Economy of mechanism*. It is important to keep the security design as small and as simple as possible. Security errors do not tend to manifest themselves in normal use and special examination techniques are required to find and eliminate them. By keeping the design small, examination and discovery of security errors is made less difficult. [This is also a common software engineering best practice. The principal can be difficult to implement in a security context since security functionality touches so many other areas in an overall system.]

- *Fail-safe defaults*. Access permissions should be based on explicit permissions and not exclusion. Defaults should always be the more secure option. [In modern day firewall practice, a similar practice is encouraged in that behavior not explicitly allowed is denied. Many operating systems today are shipped with defaults set to relatively open permission and the installer has to close these permissions explicitly. The fail-safe default principle would tell us that such systems should be shipped with all permissions turned off and only those that are to be allowed in operation should be explicitly turned on. There is debate as to whether or not this is a truly practical approach.]

- *Complete mediation.* Every access to every object must be validated and mediation cannot be bypassed. [This is a reinforcement of the reference monitor concept presented earlier.]

- *Open design.* The design itself should not be the basis for secrecy nor should it be a secret at all. The more open a design is, the more likely it is that the community of reviewers will find flaws and repair them. [Salter and Schroeder might be considered early advocates of the open source movement. This argument is one that open source advocates espouse and claim that such software is more robust, efficient, and secure due to the inspection process that tends to occur with open source development. There has been other research that disputes this and claims made that there is 'security in obscurity.']

- *Separation of privilege.* This principle advocates not putting too much authority in a single mechanism and requires, for critical or sensitive applications, that two or more separate process cooperate to accomplish a function.

- *Least privilege.* It is important that all mechanisms run at the lowest privilege required to appropriately perform their intended function. If an application program invokes a system utility, that utility should run, if at all possible, at the application program level or privilege and not at "root" level.

- *Least-common mechanism.* The idea behind this principle is to design system mechanisms such that they tend to operate on behalf of a single user and perform a single function. If we have a mechanism that operates on behalf of several users at the same time, we increase the risk of information compromise or having the mechanism itself used as a means to upgrade user privilege.

- *Psychological acceptability.* The security features used in a system must meet with user acceptance or they will be ignored or bypassed. Human factors engineering is important.

The Saltzer and Schroeder principles are not complete and there are other good best practices found in the literature, but their principles are the most widely cited. Inherent in the message they tried to communicate in their paper is another principle that has been widely regarded as key—build security into a system from the very beginning. Security must be a fundamental design objective and not an afterthought.

One of the major difficulties faced today by practicing security engineers is to take an existing system or network that was not constructed with security as a design constraint and to then secure it. Adding security to a completed system is not effective in the majority of cases and can lead to what is known as a penetrate and patch philosophy—that is, various mechanisms are added to counter each penetration of the system.

3.5   A Government Infrastructure Is Built

During the late 1970s and early to mid 1980s, the Federal Government began to build an infrastructure and publish standards and guidance in the area of computer security and computer controls. This activity was partially in response to the DSB report discussed in 3.2 above (within the Department of Defense) and partially in response to US Congressional legislation—the Brooks Act of 1965. As members of the DSB had predicted, concerns with security issues were not unique to the DOD and would most certainly involve other government activities and industry. The Brooks Act specifically named the National Bureau of Standards or NBS (later renamed the National Institute of Standards and Technology or NIST) as the federal agency responsible for the creation and promulgation of federal computer standards, implementation, and research. This legislation officially marked the beginning of a long partnership between the National Security Agency (representing DOD) and the federal government in the area of computer security—a cooperative arrangement that continues today.

In response to the Brooks Act, NBS initiated several studies to define the security problem and to organize their own internal effort to begin standards production. In 1977, NBS began an important series of workshops [15] (by invitation only) to investigate the needs for audit and evaluation in computer systems. The goal of the workshops was to determine "What authoritative ways exist, or should exist, to decide whether a particular computer system is 'secure enough' for a particular intended environment or operation, and if a given system is not 'secure enough' what measures could or should be taken to make it so." Nearly sixty attendees participated from the federal government and supporting contractors and their work resulted in a series of NBS publications—but more importantly the workshop formalized for the federal government, conclusions very similar to those already reached by the DSB in their report a few years earlier, that the provision of security in a computer system involved much more than just technical solutions. Attention to policy, hardware and software mechanisms, and a way to measure the strength provided by the system (known as assurance) was needed. Secondly, the workshop concluded that no then present day operating system could be considered secure in terms of its ability to separate users of that system from data that they were not authorized to see. They noted that computer systems could of course, process highly sensitive data, but that specialized process and procedure had to be employed to protect the confidentiality of the data processed. Reliance on the operating system for such protection was not technologically possible. While this statement might not seem too insightful today, it represented a formal beginning to the quest for what today is known as *multilevel security*. A second NBS workshop was held the following year (1978) that resulted in a call for specific actions that needed to be taken. These included the need for a national computer security policy for information considered sensitive, yet not covered by existing policies (this later became known as "sensitive but unclassified" or SBU information); the need for the creation of a government process leading to formal evaluation and accreditation of computer systems; and a formal technical means to measure and evaluate the overall security of a system (assurance evaluation). Embedded in this report was also a call for the government to maintain a list of "government approved" products that could be used for sensitive environments—essentially a list of evaluated products whose assurance level was known and trusted. These recommendations were key events in the evolution of a government infrastructure that exists today to evaluate and recommend products. Also beginning in 1979, in response to the NBS workshops, was the DOD Computer Security Initiative consisting of a series of workshops and resulting in a new mission assignment to the National Security Agency (NSA) in 1980—that of promoting trusted information systems and products within the DOD (although their actual impact was far outside the DOD community). As an outcome of the NBS workshops and interest from the DOD, MITRE assumed the task of creating computer security evaluation criteria that could be used to measure assurance (trust) in a computer system. This project resulted in several documents and proposed criteria [11,12,19] that formed the foundation for later DOD and national standards in this area.

3.5.1 Birth of the National Computer Security Center (NCSC)

In January of 1981, the DOD formally established and chartered what was then known as the DOD Computer Security Center (later renamed the National Computer Security Center or NCSC, in 1985). In the evolution of trusted systems, this was perhaps one of the most important events. Established originally by DOD Directive 5215.1, the Center was assigned the following goals.

- Encourage the development of trusted computer systems.
- Evaluation of the protection capability (strength) of systems.
- Provide technical support and advice to those involved in computer security R&D and conduct and sponsor research efforts.

- Develop and publish technical criteria to be used in the evaluation of computer systems and products.
- Apply these technical criteria to the evaluation of commercial computer systems and products.
- Develop tools to assist in building trusted systems.
- Publish computer security guidance.
- Conduct computer security training.

One might notice at this point that both NIST and NSA were key players in the emerging government interest and standardization of computer security guidance and the efforts of one were consistent and supportive of the other. This strong relationship was forged over time and continues today. The initial MITRE efforts for NBS in the area of evaluation criteria became the foundation documents for the evaluation criteria published by the NSA as the DOD Trusted Computer System Evaluation Criteria in August 1983 and later re-released as DOD Standard 5200.28-STD in December 1985. This document became known as the *Orange Book* based on the color of its cover and, for the first time, established a method for evaluating and ranking trusted operating systems—satisfying at least part of the new mission assigned to NSA. An interesting component of this document was the promotion of a computer security model of behavior known as the Bell and LaPadula model. This model was the first to be implemented in useful operating systems with the government and remains today a widely accepted confidentiality model of behavior. Specifics of this model and others are adequately covered in Chapter 7 of [13] and will not be further discussed here. While there will be no attempt to present the details of this landmark document here, the interested reader is invited to review it in greater detail at http://www.radium.ncsc.mil/tpep/. The evaluation criteria itself consisted of seven hierarchical classes of assurance which were contained in four divisions (A, B, C, and D). Most divisions were further sub-divided into classes. Various security mechanisms were required at specific classes (e.g., mechanisms might include auditing of security relevant events or identification and authentication). At the higher levels of assurance, fewer mechanisms were required, but stronger assurance practices became necessary (e.g., security testing, covert channel analysis, and specification and verification procedures). A summary of the evaluation classes, and their meaning as taken from the Trusted Computer System Evaluation Criteria (TCSEC) Appendix C, is provided in Table I and is presented in order of increasing assurance.

The NCSC built an infrastructure around the TCSEC in order to respond to its mission assigned by DOD Directive 5215.1. The evaluation criterion responded to a specific mission requirement but was not complete in and of itself. The NCSC also established a strong research and development office, a criteria and standards office,

TABLE I
SUMMARY OF EVALUATION CRITERIA CLASSES

TCSEC class	General description
Class (D): Minimal protection	This class is reserved for those systems that have been evaluated but that fail to meet the requirements for a higher evaluation class.
Class (C1): Discretionary security protection	The Trusted Computing Base (TCB) of a class (C1) system nominally satisfies the discretionary security requirements by providing separation of users and data. It incorporates some form of credible controls capable of enforcing access limitations on an individual basis, i.e., ostensibly suitable for allowing users to be able to protect project or private information and to keep other users from accidentally reading or destroying their data. The class (C1) environment is expected to be one of cooperating users processing data at the same level(s) of sensitivity.
Class (C2): Controlled access protection	Systems in this class enforce a more finely grained discretionary access control than (C1) systems, making users individually accountable for their actions through login procedures, auditing of security-relevant events, and resource isolation.
Class (B1): Labeled security protection	Class (B1) systems require all the features required for class (C2). In addition, an informal statement of the security policy model, data labeling, and mandatory access control over named subjects and objects must be present. The capability must exist for accurately labeling exported information. Any flaws identified by testing must be removed.
Class (B2): Structured protection	In class (B2) systems, the TCB is based on a clearly defined and documented formal security policy model that requires the discretionary and mandatory access control enforcement found in class (B1) systems be extended to all subjects and objects in the ADP system. In addition, covert channels are addressed. The TCB must be carefully structured into protection-critical and non-protection-critical elements. The TCB interface is well defined and the TCB design and implementation enable it to be subjected to more thorough testing and more complete review. Authentication mechanisms are strengthened, trusted facility management is provided in the form of support for system administrator and operator functions, and stringent configuration management controls are imposed. The system is relatively resistant to penetration.
Class (B3): Security domains	The class (B3) TCB must satisfy the reference monitor requirements that it mediate all accesses of subjects to objects, be tamperproof, and be small enough to be subjected to analysis and tests. To this end, the TCB is structured to exclude code not essential to security policy enforcement, with significant system engineering during TCB design and implementation directed toward minimizing its complexity. A security administrator is supported, audit mechanisms are expanded to signal security-relevant events, and system recovery procedures are required. The system is highly resistant to penetration.

(continued on next page)

TABLE I — *Continued*

TCSEC class	General description
Class (A1): Verified design	Systems in class (A1) are functionally equivalent to those in class (B3) in that no additional architectural features or policy requirements are added. The distinguishing feature of systems in this class is the analysis derived from formal design specification and verification techniques and the resulting high degree of assurance that the TCB is correctly implemented. This assurance is developmental in nature, starting with a formal model of the security policy and a formal top-level specification (FTLS) of the design. In keeping with the extensive design and development analysis of the TCB required of systems in class (A1), more stringent configuration management is required and procedures are established for securely distributing the system to sites. A system security administrator is supported.

and an evaluation office to meet other missions assigned to it. The R&D effort invested time and resources in promoting advances in products and tools that could support the advance of trusted systems. Examples included strong support of multilevel secure database research, hardware based access controls, and secure operating system architectures.

The evaluation component of the NCSC was charged with evaluating commercial products against the criteria specified in the TCSEC standard and in maintaining an "evaluated products list" or EPL. A related endeavor was known as the rating and maintenance program or RAMP, which was a strong process involving certification for commercial vendors to modify their evaluated products (necessary because of normal software maintenance) and yet retain the original evaluation level. This office was populated with a very strong technical staff that worked closely with commercial technical staffs to evaluate products at the source code level as well as accompanying documentation. The evaluation process was, in concept, very straightforward and accomplished in three phases (a preliminary product evaluation, a formal product evaluation, and entry onto the evaluated products list). The preliminary product evaluation was characterized as "informal dialogue" to scope the level of effort and to make sure that all parties understood the evaluation process and its requirements. Target evaluation objectives and evaluation concerns were all addressed during this process. Once both the commercial enterprise and the NCSC evaluators decided to move forward with the actual evaluation, they entered a formal product evaluation phase during which appropriate non-disclosure agreements and memoranda of understanding were executed. During this phase, the product was subjected to intense scrutiny and a publicly available final report was created along with a rating. The product was then entered onto the EPL at the rating level assigned. As normal software maintenance occurred over time, the product was maintained at its evaluated level by the corporate technical staff through the RAMP program as described earlier in this section.

3.5.2 Experience with the Orange Book

The evaluation process quickly became a bottleneck to the overall objective of third party evaluation and ranking. Not only was the process exceptionally time consuming, but it also required an experienced evaluation staff possessing technical skills that were in high demand in industry as well as in the federal government. Many evaluators were offered much more lucrative positions in industry while replacement personnel became increasingly difficult to find. While backlogs grew, the federal government continued to press for purchase of evaluated products. Mandates such as "C2 by 1992" became unachievable because policy was ahead of reality in terms of ability to produce products and get them evaluated in time for necessary purchases. Prices for those products that were evaluated were often not competitive with non-evaluated similar software. Waivers to government policy promoting evaluated products were often granted so that vendors that had invested heavily in the TCSEC process felt that they had not been able to recoup their investment and that the government was not following though with its earlier commitment to buy the products produced to the TCSEC specifications. Overtime, the TCSEC and the NCSC became less relevant and other approaches began to surface. Challenges to the TCSEC approach came both nationally and internationally. In 1989, the U.S. Air Force began a program of product evaluation at their facility in San Antonio, Texas as a service to Air Force customers. This was partially a reaction to the bottleneck process at NSA as well as in response to a need for evaluation of products other than those submitted to NSA. At almost the same time, other countries began to publish evaluation criteria of their own which differed substantially in content and approach from the TCSEC. Other nations with evaluation interest and emerging criteria included Canada (Canadian Trusted Computer Product Evaluation Criteria or CTCPEC), Germany (IT—Security Criteria), the Netherlands, the United Kingdom, and France. The European efforts quickly joined together as what became know as a "harmonized criteria" in 1990, while the U.S. and Canada maintained their approach separately. The European harmonized approach became known as the Information Technology Security Evaluation Criteria (ITSEC) in 1991, and varied somewhat substantially from the North American approach. Whereas the TCSEC primarily addressed government systems and combined assurance and functionality into one rating, the ITSEC addressed commercial and government security and separated functionality from assurance. Both communities, North American and European, recognized that software manufacturers could not afford to build trusted products to different standards and began efforts to explore how they might couple the criteria in a way that the international and commercial communities could accept them. Initial efforts were directed at coming up with equivalence correspondence mappings so that a system or product rated by the European process could be viewed as some equivalent TCSEC class. These endeavors were never successful and were subject to much valid criticism. In 1992, discussions began to merge the two approaches into a "Common Criteria" that the international community—both government and industry—could accept. Work in earnest followed a year or two later with representation from Canada, France, Germany, Netherlands, United Kingdom, and the U.S. While many draft criteria were produced for comment, the first true version of the Common Criteria was published as version 1.0 in January 1996. Taking into account comments, reviews, and experience with this initial version, a revised version 2.0 was released in May 1998. A modification of this second version, version 2.1, was adopted by the International Standards Organization (ISO) as an international standard in 1999 (ISO Standard 15408).

3.5.3 The Common Criteria (CC)

Today, ISO Standard 15408 is the recognized computer security evaluation and rating criteria internationally and the TCSEC was formally retired in 2001 by the U.S. government. Following the development of the Common Criteria, the National Institute of Standards and Technology (NIST) and the National Security Agency, in cooperation with the U.S. State Department, worked with the CC Project to produce a mutual recognition arrangement for IT security evaluations. In October 1998, after two years of negotiations, government organizations from the United States, Canada, France, Germany, and the United Kingdom signed a historic recognition arrangement for Common Criteria-based IT security evaluations. The "Arrangement" (officially known as the Arrangement on the Mutual Recognition of Common Criteria Certificates in the field of IT Security) was a significant step forward for both government and industry in IT product security evaluations. The U.S. government and its partners in the Arrangement agreed to the following objectives with regard to common evaluations:

- Ensure that evaluations are performed to high and consistent standards and are seen to contribute significantly to confidence in the security of those products and profiles.
- Increase the availability of evaluated products for national use.
- Eliminate duplicate evaluations between the signatories.
- Improve the efficiency and cost-effectiveness of security evaluations and the certification/validation process.

In October 1999, Australia and New Zealand joined the Mutual Recognition Arrangement increasing the total number of participating nations to seven. Following a brief revision of the original Arrangement to allow for the participation of both certificate-consuming and certificate-producing nations, an expanded Recognition Arrangement was signed in May 2000, at the 1st International Common Criteria Conference by Government organizations from thirteen nations. These include: the United States, Canada, France, Germany, the United Kingdom, Australia, New Zealand, Italy, Spain, the Netherlands, Norway, Finland, and Greece. The State of Israel became the fourteenth nation to sign the Recognition Arrangement in November 2000. The Common Criteria continues to this day to gain in acceptance and several other nations are actively considering its adoption (e.g., Russia, China, and Japan).

The Common Criteria represents a departure from the TCSEC approach and is more closely related to the approach developed by the European community. A very brief overview will be presented here, but for a more detailed review of this document and its processes the interested reader is directed to http://csrc.nist.gov/cc/, http://www.commoncriteria.org/, and http://niap.nist.gov/. The CC is a lengthy document divided into three parts. Part 1 provides background information on the criteria itself, an overview of its processes, and serves as a general reference. Part 2 addresses functional requirements, assists users in formulating statements of requirements for secure systems, and assists developers in interpreting those requirements. Similarly, Part 3 addresses assurance requirements. Note that assurance and functionality have been separated in this document and are no longer coupled as they were in the TCSEC. The CC also introduced several new terms that were important to its processes. First is that of the Protection Profile (PP). A protection profile is an implementation independent requirements document that specifies a need. A consumer can use requirement statements from Parts 2 and 3 to describe the functionality and assurance needed in a product. Additionally, the PP contains a statement of the security problem to be solved by the IT product (which may include specific assumptions that may be made concerning the operating environment, the anticipated threats, and organizational security policies). The PP, although a requirements document, can be submitted for evaluation under the CC and receive a rating. Once rated, it can be placed on the list of evaluated products so that others can make use of it. There was no equivalent to this in the TCSEC process. An IT product that is to be evaluated is known as a Target of Evaluation (TOE). Actually, a TOE can be a complete product or a part of a product or system. It includes the product itself and all associated documentation. In order to have a TOE evaluated under the CC process, a Security Target (ST) must be created. For the most part, the ST follows the same specified format as the PP with the exception that the ST references a specific PP and contains a description (claims) of how the TOE meets the requirements of a PP or where it falls short of doing so. Whereas the PP is a generic requirement—the ST is specific to a particular TOE and makes specific claims as to its assurance, its functionality, and its compliance with the PP requirements. An evaluation, therefore, under the terms of the CC, would require the ST, the set of evidence about the TOE, and the TOE itself. The result of the evaluation would be confirmation that the ST is satisfied by the TOE. More simply stated, the PP is the end user requirement, the TOE is the product, the ST is the claim that the product meets the need, and the evaluation is the third party review that the claim is correct.

Under the terms of the CC process, a certified private laboratory accomplishes the evaluation of the actual product. Each signatory to the CC has a government oversight body that validates laboratories as being compliant with CC standards. Evaluations conducted at any laboratory certified by a signatory to the CC are acceptable (at the first four levels of evaluation only) to all nations that participate in the CC recognition agreement. Evaluations are paid for by the product manufacturer, as agreed to by the vendor and the laboratory. This is a major departure from the early U.S. TCSEC procedure that offered a single evaluation facility that was largely funded by the government.

The evaluation scheme consists of seven levels—evaluation assurance level (EAL) 1 through 7. Each level is only an assurance level and does not imply any specific mechanisms since the CC decoupled mechanisms and assurance. Their meaning is summarized below as taken from the Common Criteria introductory brochure [3].

- EAL 1: *Functionally tested*. Used where some confidence in correct operation is required, but the threats to security are not viewed as serious. The evaluation at this level provides evidence that the TOE functions in a manner consistent with its documentation, and that it provides useful protection against identified threats.

- EAL 2: *Structurally tested*. Evaluation at this level involves a review of design information and test results. This level may be appropriate where developers or users require a low to moderate level of independently assured security in the absence of ready availability of the complete development record (e.g., when securing legacy systems).

- EAL 3: *Methodically tested and checked*. This level is applicable where the requirement is for a moderate level of independently assured security, with a thorough investigation of the TOE and its development. An EAL 3 evaluation provides an analysis supported by testing based on "gray box" testing, selective independent confirmation of the developer test results, and evidence of a developer search for vulnerabilities.

- EAL 4: *Methodically designed, tested and reviewed*. This is the highest level at which it is likely to be economically feasible to retrofit an existing product line with security. It is applicable to those circumstances where developers or users require a moderate to high level of independently assured security and there is willingness to incur some additional security specific engineering costs.

- EAL 5: *Semiformally designed and tested.* This is applicable where the requirement is for a high level of independently assured security in a planned development, with a rigorous development approach, but without incurring unreasonable costs for specialized security engineering techniques. Assurance is supplemented by a formal model, a semiformal presentation of the functional specification and high level design, and a semiformal demonstration of correspondence. A search for vulnerabilities that includes resistance to penetration attacks and a covert channel analysis is also required.

- EAL 6: *Semiformally verified design and tested.* This EAL is applicable to the development of specialized TOEs for application in high risk situations where the value of the protected assets justifies the additional costs. The evaluation provides an analysis, which is supported by a modular and layered approach to design. The search for vulnerabilities must ensure resistance to penetration by attackers with high attack potential. The search for covert channels must be systematic. Development environment and configuration management controls are enhanced at this level.

- EAL 7: *Formally verified design and tested.* Applicable to the development of security TOEs for application in extremely high risk situations, and/or where the high value of the assets justifies the higher costs. For an evaluation at this level, the formal model is supplemented by a formal presentation of the functional specification and high level design showing correspondence. Evidence of developer "white box" testing and complete independent confirmation of developer test results are required. As a practical matter, a TOE at EAL 7 must minimize design complexity and have tightly focused security functionality amenable to extensive formal analysis.

There is a distinct break between EAL 1 through 4 versus EAL 5 through 7. EAL 4 and below can generally be achieved by retrofitting existing products and systems and can be done so economically. Evaluation certification of an IT product by any laboratory certified by a signatory of the CC at EAL 1 through 4 is acceptable in any other signatory nation. Products certified at EAL 5 through 7 must be certified by the nation that uses them in its government systems. At EAL 5 and above, specialized security engineering techniques are required and retrofit of existing products is generally not possible. A complete list of certified products can be found at http://www.commoncriteria.org/. The reader will note that most evaluated products lie in the EAL 1 through 4 range (see Table III).

One of the objectives of the CC effort was to maintain a backwards compatibility with the TCSEC (recall that it had been used by the U.S. for over ten years prior

TABLE II
EVALUATION COMPARISONS (APPROXIMATE)

Common criteria	TCSEC	ITSEC
–	D: Minimal protection	E0
EAL 1	–	–
EAL 2	C1: Discretionary access protection	E1
EAL 3	C2: Controlled access protection	E2
EAL 4	B1: Labeled security protection	E3
EAL 5	B2: Structured protection	E4
EAL 6	B3: Security domains	E5
EAL 7	A1: Verified design	E6

to the arrival of the CC) and the European ITSEC. This was made necessary due to the heavy investment that the software industry had made in producing evaluated products and in order for government agencies to remain compliant with specific regulatory guidance. The general equivalency between CC, TCSEC, and ITSEC evaluations is given in Table II as published by the CC working group. Although commercial vendors of trusted products sometimes cite this table, one needs to be aware that many valid arguments can be made that the mappings are not exact and that no direct comparisons can be made. It serves as a general guideline only.

It remains to be seen how effective the CC scheme will be over time. At the present, it seems to be gaining acceptance and strength. As of this writing, there are approximately fifty IT products on the evaluated list, which have been certified between 1997 and 2002 and several others undergoing evaluation. Table III depicts the number of products by year and evaluation level achieved. Clearly, early evaluations were concentrated on lower level assurance (EAL 1 and 2) while in more recent years higher levels of assurance have begun to appear on the list (EAL 3 to 5). While some of this trend is likely due to an initial effort by vendors to obtain the quickest and lowest cost evaluation, it also reflects a growing willingness to invest in the process and the desire to produce products that are more trustworthy than in the past. It is also interesting to note that evaluations at the very highest levels of EAL 6 and 7 are missing which may be a reflection on a lack of necessary software engineering tools to perform adequate formal analysis, verification, and proofs of correctness for large software based systems or perhaps it is an indication that vendors are not yet willing to risk the high cost of development of such systems until they are more confident of a return on investment. In order to achieve a multilevel security capability, IT products and systems will need EAL 6 and 7 levels of assurance. To promote the use of CC evaluated products within the U.S. government, the National Security Telecommunications and Information Systems Security Policy

TABLE III
COMMON CRITERIA PRODUCT RATING BY YEAR AND EAL

	EAL 1	EAL 2	EAL 3	EAL 4	EAL 5	EAL 6	EAL 7	Total
1997			1					1
1998	2	2	2	1				7
1999	4	3	1	1				9
2000	1	3	5	6				15
2001		2	2	4				8
2002		2	3	3	1			9
Total	7	12	14	15	1	0	0	49

(NSTISSP) number 11 was issued in January 2000 which requires that preference be given to acquisition of commercial off-the-shelf (COTS) information assurance (IA) products and IA-enabled IT products which have been evaluated in accordance with the Common Criteria, the National Information Assurance Partnership (NIAP), or NIST Federal Information Processing Standard (FIPS) programs. The policy further requires that, as of July 1, 2002, acquisition of such products will be *limited* to those that have been evaluated. It remains to be seen whether or not this policy will indeed have the desired effect to promote an increase in the number of evaluated products and their use—or whether the policy's waiver process will be used extensively to circumvent it. In today's environment, with a necessity to establish a strong defense in depth strategy, there simply is not enough diversity of products on the evaluated list from which one could construct a total defense so the waiver process will have to be used for valid reasons. Additionally, for the CC process to be a long-term success, it will need to gain acceptance in the industrial (non government) communities—an objective that has not been met today.

3.6   Other Notable Legislation

While some legislation and government guidance has been presented already, several key laws and directives were omitted. A reasonably comprehensive treatment of computer security mandates and legislation can be found in the Russell and Gangemi text titled Computer Security Basics [14], Appendix B.

The importance of the Brooks Act of 1965 has already been discussed. Although several additional mandates, directives, and laws pertaining to classified information processing and protection of signals were issued in years following the Brooks Act, it was not until 1984 that the next major computer security mandate was issued. That came in the form of National Security Decision Directive (NSDD) 145, which among other things, created a high level government computer security oversight committee which over time (and with the help of National Security Directive 42 in 1990) created a policy body known as the National Telecommunications and Information Systems Security Committee (NTISSC). This directive also required protection for sensitive, but unclassified information for the first time and assigned to the National Security Agency the tasks of encouraging, advising, and assisting the private sector in information protection. This appeared to be a major shift in national leadership responsibility for computer security from NIST to NSA—but not without controversy. The National Security Agency had long been regarded as a closed intelligence organization with almost no public presence. The assignment of a public mission to such an organization that involved assisting the public sector in the protection of information by an organization whose intelligence role included penetrating foreign government systems seemed, to some, a bit of a conflict. This role included providing encryption algorithms to the public sector to protect data in transit—while NSA retained the role of being responsible for breaking encryption algorithms for intelligence purposes. Not withstanding this appearance of a conflicting role, there was also a certain amount of mistrust prevalent in the public sector toward such an organization and its culture.

Responsibility for computer security at the federal level seemed to shift once more with the Public Law 100-235 (also known as the Computer Security Act of 1987), which became effective in the fall of 1988. This law assigned to NIST responsibility for computer security vulnerability assessments, standards, technical assistance, guidelines, and training and gave NSA a supporting role to NIST. The law did not apply to classified material and left responsibility for that with NSA. Additionally, the law required all federal agencies to create a specific computer security plan for their organization and to provide computer security training for their people. While these actions might have seemed fairly basic, they were needed in that few organizations had such plans and many that did had not exercised them or updated them for the actual environment they were working in.

In 1996 Congress passed what has become known as the Clinger–Cohen Act (also called the IT Management Reform Act) that assigned to the Office of Management and Budget the responsibility for acquisition and management of IT. While much of what the Act mandated was strictly procurement related, it did have interesting side effects related to security. These included giving authority to acquire IT resources to the head of each executive agency of the government and encouraging the procurement of commercial off-the-shelf (COTS) products as preferred over initiating special developments. Most importantly, the Act required the appointment of a Chief Information Officer (CIO) in federal agencies—an office that naturally assumes the responsibility for computer security in most cases. Later in 1996, President Clinton issued an Executive Order creating a CIO council that has today assumed computer security policy and mandates to be a part of their charter. The core responsibility for carrying out the requirements of the Clinger–Cohen Act and the follow on Executive Order 13011 (establishment of the CIO Council), lies with the Office of Management and Budget or OMB which has statutory responsibility for setting policy for the security of Federal automated information systems. It implements these responsibilities through OMB Circular A-130, Appendix III, "Security of Federal Automated Information Resources" (see http://www.whitehouse.gov/omb/circulars).

Nearly simultaneous with the actions in the preceding paragraph, President Clinton issued Executive Order 13010 in 1996, creating the President's Commission on Critical Infrastructure Protection (PCCIP). The order stated, "Certain national infrastructures are so vital that their incapacity or destruction would have a debilitating impact on the defense or economic security of the United States. These critical infrastructures include telecommunications, electrical power systems, gas and oil storage and transportation, banking and finance, transportation, water supply systems, emergency services (including medical, police, fire, and rescue), and continuity of government. Threats to these critical infrastructures fall into two categories: physical threats to tangible property ("physical threats"), and threats of electronic, radio frequency, or computer-based attacks on the information or communications components that control critical infrastructures ("cyber threats"). Because many of these critical infrastructures are owned and operated by the private sector, it is essential that the government and private sector work together to develop a strategy for protecting them and assuring their continued operation." The significance of this EO is that it was the first to recognize the vulnerability of the Nation's infrastructure systems and the dependence our national security places on their operation. In the words of the resulting report, "The cyber dimension promotes accelerating reliance on our infrastructures and offers access to them from all over the world, blurring traditional boundaries and jurisdictions. National defense is not just about government anymore, and economic security is not just about business. The critical infrastructures are central to our national defense and our economic power, and we must lay the foundations for their future security on a new form of cooperation between the private sector and the federal government. The federal government has an important role to play in defense against cyber threats—collecting information about tools that can do harm, conducting research into defensive technologies, and sharing defensive techniques and best practices. Government also must lead and energize its own protection efforts, and engage the private sector by offering expertise to facilitate protection of privately owned infrastructures." The report listed eight infrastructures "so vital that their incapacity or destruction would have a debilitating impact on our defense and economic security." These infrastructures and their importance were reported as:

- *Transportation*: moves goods and people within and beyond our borders, and makes it possible for the U.S. to play a leading role in the global economy.

- *Oil and gas production and storage*: fuels transportation services, manufacturing operations, and home utilities.

- *Water supply*: assures a steady flow of water for agriculture, industry, business, firefighting, and homes.

- *Emergency services*: responds to our urgent police, fire, and medical needs.

- *Government services*: consists of federal, state, and local agencies that provide essential services to the public.

- *Banking and finance*: manages trillions of dollars—from individual accounts to support of global enterprises.

- *Electrical power*: generation, transmission, and distribution systems that are essential to all other infrastructures and every aspect of the nation's economy.

- *Telecommunications:* includes the public telecommunications network, the Internet, computers used in homes, commerce, academia, and government, and all forms of communication that connect systems together.

The final report can be accessed at http://www.ciao.gov/resource/pccip/report_index. htm for those that are interested in further exploring the findings.

Based on the findings of the PCCIP, President Clinton signed Presidential Decision Directive (PDD) 63 on May 22, 1998. This event officially expanded the nation's policy interest to the cyber security world and, in effect, recognized a need to couple more tightly the nation's critical infrastructure industrial base with corresponding federal government offices and to establish a specific law enforcement focus on cyber protection and incident response. To this end, PDD-63 formally assigned lead government agencies to specific industrial sectors and for what was referred to as "special functions." Table IV depicts the agency/sector partnering.

As of the writing of this chapter, the lead agencies are as established by PDD-63, but the terrorist attacks of September 11, 2001 and the subsequent establishment of the Office of Homeland Security will likely change this assignment as responsibilities are realigned in the federal government. The President's decision required each lead agency to designate one individual of Assistant Secretary rank or higher to be the sector liaison official and to coordinate/cooperate with the private sector in addressing problems related to critical infrastructure protection. In addition to the sector liaisons, the PDD also established lead agencies for "special functions." Special functions were defined as those related to critical infrastructure protection that *must* be chiefly performed by the federal government (e.g., national defense, foreign affairs, intelligence, and law enforcement). The most important aspect of the special function lead is that they have responsibility for coordinating all the activities of the federal government in their assigned area. The lead agencies and their designated special functions are:

TABLE IV
PDD-63 LEAD AGENCY FOR SECTOR LIAISON

Lead Government agency	Critical Infrastructure sector
Commerce	Information and communications
Treasury	Banking and finance
Environmental Protection Agency	Water supply
Transportation	Aviation, Highways, Mass transit, Pipelines, Rail, Water-borne commerce
Justice/FBI	Emergency law enforcement services
Federal Emergency Management Agency	Emergency fire service, Continuity of government services
Health and Human Services	Public health services, including prevention, surveillance, laboratory services and personal health services
Energy	Electric power, Oil and gas production storage

- Department of Justice/FBI: Law enforcement and internal security,
- Central Intelligence Agency: Foreign intelligence,
- Department of State: Foreign affairs,
- Department of Defense: National defense.

The above is a high level overview of the structure established by the federal government. Other functions, such as the role of a National Coordinator for Security, Infrastructure Protection and Counter-Terrorism; the creation of a National Infrastructure Protection Center (NIPC); and the research and development role for the Office of Science and Technology Policy, are all discussed in the PDD. The full version of PDD-63 can be found at http://www.terrorism.com/homeland/PDD-63.pdf for the interested reader. While the objectives of the PDD were quite lofty, actual progress has been slow and real results are few. The greatest contribution, however, was its focus on the problem as a national policy issue and the formal structure it created.

As a reaction to the terrorist attacks of September 11, 2001, a new law known as the Patriot Act was hurriedly pushed though Congress and signed by the President on October 26, 2001. The bill is 342 pages long and makes changes, some large and some small, to over 15 different statutes. The government may now monitor web surfing activities of Americans, including terms entered into search engines, by merely convincing a judge that the monitoring could lead to information that is "relevant" to an ongoing criminal investigation. The person monitored does not have to be the target of the investigation. The judge must grant this application and the government is not obligated to report to the court or tell the monitored subject what has been done. The law also makes two changes to increase how much information the government may obtain about users from their Internet service providers (ISPs) or others who handle or store their online communications. It allows ISPs to voluntarily hand over all "non-content" information to law enforcement with no need for any court order or subpoena. Second, it expands the records that the government may seek with a simple subpoena (no court review required) to include records of session times and durations, temporarily assigned network (I.P.) addresses, and means and source of payments, including credit card or bank account numbers. Lastly, and most important, the Patriot Act makes a tie between terrorism and computer crime. This piece of legislation has the potential to become a defining point in combating computer crime, but will certainly be challenged in the courts over the next few years.

3.7   Worms, Viruses and other Malevolent Code

No historical treatment of computer security would be complete without some discussion of the impact that malicious code has had on the computing community. *Malicious code* is software that is created to intentionally violate policy or desired rules of behavior on your system—often with destructive intent. Code run on any computer system executes at some permission level—normally either the permission level of a particular user or at "system level." Access controls normally limit what actions user level permissions can take, while system level permission is generally unrestricted. The challenge of the author of malicious code is to have the code run at the highest permission level possible so that it activities are not restricted. Nonetheless, any malicious code run at a specific user's permission level can certainly damage, destroy, or compromise any information assets owned by that user and that alone is generally considered a significant threat.

Malicious code exists in many varieties and is classified in several ways. The intent of this section is not to define a taxonomy of malicious code or to present precise definitions, but rather to provide the reader with a sense of the types of malicious code, the basic way they operate, and to disclose some noteworthy incidents. We include the term *mobile code* in this discussion to refer to code that is downloaded from a server to a client machine and executes on the client. Mobile code is not necessarily bad and in the majority of cases it performs a useful and desired function, but the potential exists for such code to be malicious in the client's environment.

Malicious code either operates on its own (independent) or requires a host program (dependent). Some such code has the ability to reproduce (propagate) while others may not. The generally accepted types of malicious code are trap doors, Trojan horses, logic or time bombs, viruses, and worms. There are many more names, nuances, and descriptions of such code in the literature, but these are sufficient for this discussion. We begin with a brief description of each type of malicious code, followed by a discussion of some historical landmark incidents, and end with some thoughts on how one defends against such attacks today.

Malicious code is written intentionally to cause harm or at least mischief. It is different from legitimate software errors that may result in harm or system failure. While the end result is the same, the cause and defenses against it are different. Intent is the differentiator.

- *Trap door*—a secret, undocumented entry point into program software that can be used to grant access without going through the normal access authentication process. This might be, for example, software that recognizes a certain sequence of keystrokes or accepts a certain key word as input to turn control over to the attacker. This code does not reproduce itself nor can it "infect" other code. It is a specific entry point into executable code that is generally undocumented. Programmers often insert trap doors in code under development to assist in testing or as a shortcut in debugging. This practice is discouraged in most software development activities, yet it does occur. Occasionally, the programmer forgets to remove the trap door and it is discovered by others who exploit it for malicious purposes.

- *Trojan horse*—a computer program with an apparent or actual useful function that contains additional hidden functionality that surreptitiously exploits the legitimate authorizations of the invoking process to the detriment of security. These are often found in a useful utility program or game that when executed may also delete files or change file permissions or corrupt data. An example of this kind of attack might be a free computer game that when executed not only provides a game function for the user, but also accesses the user's files and writes them off to another location that the attacker can access later. A Trojan horse does not replicate or infect other programs.

- *Logic or time bombs*—a computer program that contains a malicious function and lies dormant in a computer system until triggered by a set of logical events (logic bomb) or a specific time/date combination (time bomb). Such bombs have been a nuisance for a very long time in computing. An example of a logic bomb might be code written into a financial system that destroys all financial records maintained by the system if a certain social security number is not present in the payroll file. This might be a tactic employed by a disgruntled programmer to guard against being fired. An example of a time bomb might be code that deletes files on Friday the thirteenth, April Fool's Day, or Halloween, for example. Logic or time bombs by themselves do not replicate or infect other files.

- *Viruses*—malicious software that is embedded within other code (normally another computer application program) or is hidden in a boot sector of a disk. It normally consists of three parts—a mission, a trigger, and a propagation (replication) component. A virus does not exist on its own and requires a host in order to execute and reproduce. When a legitimate (but infected) program executes, it will also execute the virus code unknowingly. The virus code will generally copy itself (infect) to another software program on the computer or imbed itself in memory and copy itself to every program that runs on that machine. After replicating itself, it may execute a specific function (mission) such as delete files, copy files, or modify data. In some cases, the virus has a trigger (logical or time condition) that it checks first before executing the mission. Similar to the logic or time bomb approach, this might be a trigger that looks for a specific program being ran before it executes or it may look for a specific time of day, month or year (e.g., Friday the thirteenth). Viruses are sometimes referred to as "self-replicating Trojan horses."

- *Worms*—malicious software that does not need a host to survive. Worm software is written to be independent code that replicates and travels through networks infecting machines. Like a virus, it can have a mission, trigger, and propagation component. It is designed, however, to attack networks and distributed systems.

- *Mobile Code*—came into existence as an efficiency technique associated with client server architectures and Internet usage. This is code that exists on a distant server and when a client connects, it is downloaded and executes on the client machine. There are many specific techniques used to accomplish this— some more risky to the user than others. Examples might include Java Applets, Active X, plug-ins, and JavaScript. While knowledgeable users have the ability to restrict or prohibit such code from running on their machine, in practice few actually do. The vast majority of mobile code implementations are beneficial and not malevolent but the technique itself does represent a vulnerability that can be exploited.

The use of malicious code has a rich and interesting history. It has been reported that even John von Neumann, often considered the father of the modern day computer, once published an article in 1949, titled "Theory and Organization of Complicated Automata" [18]—a report which dealt with what he referred to as self reproducing automata—an early description of what we now call a virus. Early scientists and computer technical staffs often used these techniques in games designed to prove their skill. A game originally called *Darwin* and later *Core Wars* was a contest between "assembler" programs in a machine or machine simulator, where the objective was to kill your opponent's program by overwriting it. The game was devised and played by Victor Vyssotsky, Robert Morris Sr., and Doug McIlroy in the early 1960s while working at Bell Labs. Most such exploits were harmless pastimes for technical wizards of the day. During the late 1960s and into the mid-1970s government penetration testing used the technique of a Trojan horse to exploit operating systems and achieve access. In the early 1980s, researchers at Xerox tried to create what we would refer to as a "worm" today that had no malicious intent and was designed as a maintenance program. Due to a flaw in the program logic, this Xerox worm [17] accidentally caused a denial of service issue. Essentially, there was very little, if any malicious activity, although the potential was there to exploit.

This changed dramatically in the early 1980s when a researcher by the name of Dr. Fred Cohen, then a professor of Computer Science and Electrical Engineering at Lehigh University, began a research effort focusing on computer viruses. The results of his work were published widely, but the initial publication came in a paper dated August 31, 1984 titled simply "Computer Viruses" and delivered at the 7th Department of Defense/National Bureau of Standards Computer Security Conference [2]. Within this paper, Dr. Cohen described the technique of creating a virus, general experiments with their propagation, concluded that virus detection by analysis is undecidable, and that countermeasures are extremely difficult to employ. Interest and experimentation in this technique quickly became widespread and continues into the present. Incidents have been reported involving computer viruses used for destructive purposes, industrial sabotage, as a terrorist tool, as an advertising ploy, and simply for the purpose of creating one. Over time as technology changes, the techniques of using a virus have evolved and have been adapted to macro languages (e.g., in Microsoft products like Excel or Word), some viruses have been created that change their appearance or signatures (called polymorphic viruses), and others have introduced code to help avoid detection and removal. While viruses have continued to plague the computing community, they have largely become more of a nuisance than the disaster they once were considered to be.

A major incident occurred in November of 1988 that is arguably the single most published computer security event, and the one incident that, more than any other, focused international attention on computer security and the fragility of operating systems and networks. While the incident is described in great detail in many publications since, the interested reader may wish to obtain a copy of the June 1989 issue of Communications of the ACM (volume 32, number 6) for a good synopsis of the attack. On November 2, 1988 a graduate student at Cornell University, Robert Tappan Morris, released a computer worm that he had created, into the Internet. Within hours the worm had penetrated thousands of computers and had caused many to fail due to a flaw in the worm that resulted in it consuming too many system resources and causing a denial of service (DOS) problem. The worm itself exploited several flaws in Unix operating systems that were, for the most part, well known in the technical community. It involved password cracking, exploitation of design flaws, and exploitation of design "features" to replicate and travel the Internet. Mr. Morris was identified within days of the incident and was eventually found guilty of violating section 1030 of U.S. Code Title 18 (the 1986 Computer Fraud and Abuse Act). He received a $10,000 fine and a suspended jail sentence with a community service obligation of 400 hours. This single incident not only focused community attention on computer security, but it also started a series of events to change the law, revisit the study of computing ethics, and the creation of Computer Emergency Response Teams (CERTs). The first of these CERTs was one created at Carnegie Mellon University's Software Engineering Institute (see http://www.cert.org). This CERT has assumed a national leadership role and is generally accepted as the "lead" CERT. Many other CERTs (over 200 worldwide) have been subsequently established to service a particular clientele. While many of the details of the worm attack are omitted here, it is important to realize that the same kind of attack can and does occur today. Many of the vulnerabilities exploited by the 1988 worm still exist.

Defense against malicious code and mobile code is today an important consideration. A total defense is not possible but mitigation strategies are possible and recommended—primarily against viruses, worms, and malevolent mobile code. Many good virus detection software products are available on the market today and it is important that users have one and keep it updated. Most virus scanners look at incoming email, web transactions, and software distribution media (disk or CD), and resident software for the presence of viruses or worms. Since these products work on the basis of recognizing known viruses and variants of them, it becomes important to update the virus scanner code frequently (once a week or so). New or redesigned viruses are discovered frequently and their recognition patterns need to be added to a user's virus detection system. This is normally accomplished over an Internet connection to the vendor's web site. Some worms can be discovered by virus scanning software, but not all. Having a firewall in place, which isolates a network, is helpful as a worm defense mechanism. Keeping operating systems up-to-date with the latest patch version is also an important defense. During the early 2000s a new software product began to appear known as operating system behavior based tools. These products are useful as a defense against virus or worm attacks that are new or have not yet been added to a virus scanner. The idea behind this approach is to establish user-defined rules of un-allowed behavior at the operating system kernel level so that if executing code attempts to perform some malicious function in violation of a rule, it is prevented. Finally, policy, procedure, and training employed by the organization helps to avoid activity that can introduce a virus and assists employees in identifying when a virus or a worm has been introduced. Web browsers today have security settings that help to act as a deterrent to malicious mobile code. By accessing browser security settings, a user can allow or disallow various forms of mobile code. Additionally, many reputable software producers "sign" their mobile code with a certificate that is displayed on the client machine so that the user can accept or reject the code based on knowing where it came from. Certified code is generally reasonably safe, while code from unknown sources may not be. Many organizations today with centrally managed networks are establishing policy toward mobile code and implementing that policy through system settings established and maintained by the systems administrator.

3.8   Summary and Concluding Comment

This section has presented a historical treatment of computer security with concentration on many events that the author considered important over the past thirty years. This is by no means a complete historical and topical treatment, but it does show progress over time and an increasing understanding of the problem. The motivations for computer security have been presented, design principles introduced, attempts to mandate security through law and policy were discussed, and significant events were related. In each case, the historical event was related to today's approach (as in movement from the orange book to the common criteria). It was the intent of this section to show advances over thirty years of work in the computer security/information assurance area, yet also demonstrate that much of the basic problem that one must grapple with in security has not really changed although technology itself has changed substantially. As Dr. Ware and the Defense Science Board so effectively pointed out in their landmark 1970 report, securing an information system is a difficult process that involves more than technical solution sets. It remains a combination of effective policies, procedures, strong (high assurance) software products, and defensive in depth architectures all coupled with trained and trusted employees.

We must also conclude with a note on network security. Saltzer and Schroeder [16] tell us that security must be designed in as an architectural objective. Gasser [6] reiterates that concern in his book. The current Internet, however, did not evolve with security as a requirement. It was, in fact, a project sponsored by the Advanced Projects Research Agency (a Department of Defense research organization) with much of the construction taking place in the academic sector. The protocol for network communication became known as the Transmission Control Protocol/Internet Protocol (TCP/IP)—again, without significant security measures being considered. This development activity was taking place in the mid-70s at about the time the DOD was coming to understand security as an issue in networks and resource sharing computers. This ARPANET (as it became known as) eventually split into two networks—each evolving a bit differently. One became the open, ubiquitous Internet and the other became a closed military Intranet (originally known as MILNET, but today called NIPRNET and SIPRNET). Because the networks were created with no underlying security architecture and were thought to be simply useful for global sharing of computational resources, countless vulnerabilities have been uncovered and exercised by attackers using the system. This led to a proliferation of add-on security products to address vulnerabilities. Such products now include various firewall appliances, virtual private networks, encryption, virus detection software, vulnerability scanners, and many others.

4. Today's Threat and Countermeasures

4.1 Overview and Awareness

While the actual problem of securing computing systems and networks remains largely unsolved, substantial progress has been made over the past thirty years. Even the realization that perfect security is unobtainable must be considered a form of progress in understanding and allows the community to factor this risk into policy and procedure in today's information infrastructure. Improvements can be seen in the number of security products available today, the strength of those products, the number of security engineers, training of employees, strong internal policies, stronger operating systems, better networking procedures, and more effective laws. Awareness alone is not sufficient to fully address this problem, but does help employees understand and adhere to policies and helps managers support the IT budgets necessary to safeguard systems. In present day security, a security engineer has a broad experience base on which to examine the effectiveness of products and has the advantage of an evaluation process that many products have been exposed to through either the old Trusted Computing System Evaluation Criteria program (aka, the Orange Book process) or the newer, more current ISO Standard 15408, or Common Criteria. In short, today's security engineer knows more about the problem, the threat, and what comprises sufficient defenses than was generally known twenty or thirty years ago. On the negative side, the problem of knowing how to compose together a set of products that offer sufficient protection for a system is still a matter of individual engineering expertise and, to a certain extent, an art more than a science. Measurement of a protection structure, in terms of "how much" security is achieved by a specific architecture, is not possible today. It is also often not possible to shape a realistic return on investment strategy when one is faced with convincing the financial watchdogs that a particular security product or capability should be purchased for an organization.

The ability to secure systems would appear to have not advanced much—but such an observation would be deceptive at best. First, the field of computing itself is roughly only 50 years old. The interest in securing such systems has only been the focus of any serious attention for the last 30 years. Security of desktop machines at home and office has been an issue for less than 20 years. While these are relatively short periods of time in the field of scientific advances, one must also consider that the field of computing has been advancing rapidly while the investigations into its security aspects continued. A more succinct way of stating this might be to say that the provision of computing security has been a moving target with technology moving ahead faster than the security solution set seems to move. On top of advancing technology has been the issue of unreliable software. Major vulnerabilities exist in software today that allow outsiders to acquire unauthorized access or elevate their privileges, cause denial of service attacks, or affect the integrity of stored and processed data. Rather than become more secure over time, software seems to have become less secure. While software engineering principles are reasonably well understood, they are simply not practiced well today in many organizations nor has the community that relies on reliable software been very insistent on reliable code. For the reader interested in pursuing this observation a bit further, an article [10] addressing this topic written by Charles Mann in *Technology Review* is worth reviewing. An interesting observation made by Mr. Mann is that "Microsoft released Windows XP on Oct 25, 2001. That same day, in what may be a record, the company posted *18 megabytes* of patches on its Web site: bug fixes, compatibility updates, and enhancements. Two patches fixed important security holes. Or rather, one of them did; the other patch didn't work." This, as well as many other such episodes, attests to the fact that several dynamics are at play here—they include the expanding complexity of software systems today (Windows XP has approximately 45-million lines of code) versus systems of several years ago; the lack of programmer quality focus (a focus which seems to be decreasing over the years); and the lack of appropriate software engineering tools to prove code correct (verification and validation tools). The overall quality of software is an important consideration in the overall security of a system. The evaluated products process sponsored by the National Institute of Standards and Technology (NIST) implementing the ISO Standard 15408 helps to improve confidence in the quality as well as the trustworthiness of software.

4.2   Products and Procedures

Early researchers believed that access control by the operating system was the key technical focus to providing trustworthy computing and that if access control could be guaranteed to conform to some established security policy, then enforcement by the operating system could insure that no unauthorized access of a user to data could occur. While this model may have been satisfactory in a standalone, mainframe world—it could not scale up to technology changes, which included networking, database systems, wireless technology, high performance computing clusters, electronic commerce, and other advances. While this statement is not meant to diminish the role of strong access control in any way, it is meant to show that there are issues beyond access control that need to be solved as well in order to truly establish

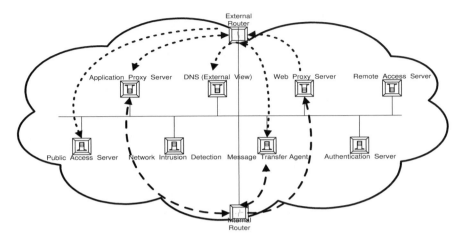

FIG. 1. Typical architecture for an information protection network.

a secure environment. Today, a defense in depth strategy is necessary in order to provide security in a networked environment. An example of such a strategy at a high level is shown in Fig. 1, where a typical architecture for an information protection network (IPN) is shown. When operating in a networking environment, a security engineer may be charged with insuring that the assets of the protected company network are secure from attacks from the outside world over Internet connectivity. To do so, the engineer will weave together an intermediate network of protection mechanisms and products that is fitted between the protected network and the open Internet. This is sometimes referred to as a Demilitarized Zone or DMZ. The IPN can process and analyze incoming and outgoing traffic in this "buffer zone" and add a significant degree of protection for the internal user. Using this IPN template in Fig. 1, a security engineer can make adjustments by adding or deleting products that lead to the engineered solution needed. For example, the engineer may decide that a web proxy server is actually not needed and delete that device based on a risk analysis or vulnerability assessment performed on the system being protected. Similarly, the engineer may decide that a network filter product is needed to filter outgoing and incoming emails looking for unauthorized communications. A wide variety of products can be accommodated in the IPN, but the final solution set is determined on a situation specific basis by a trained security engineer who uses personal knowledge and skill to design it and tweak it over time. Note that the IPN does include a strong access control component at the network level—an important fundamental consideration. The IPN also, however, accommodates other security concerns such as privacy of network addresses, proper policy enforcement, malicious code detection, remote

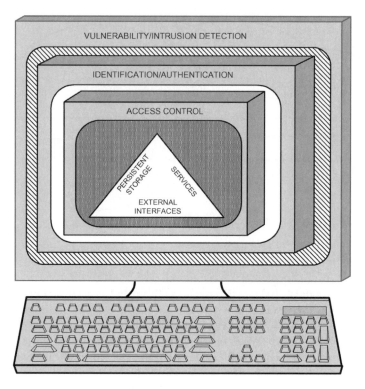

FIG. 2. Host level security concerns.

authentication, and other important functions. The security engineer will also be concerned with products that operate at the host level (which may be a desktop machine,
a large central server, a mainframe, a traveling laptop, or some combination of these).
Certainly the trustworthiness of the OS is important, but so are many other features
that may result in product selection for each machine. Figure 2 depicts a template
of concerns for a specific host that once again may be tweaked and modified by the
engineer to meet a particular risk or address a specific vulnerability. Access control
and identification and authentication (I&A) are generally included in the operating
system, but stronger I&A may be required. In such a case, the engineer may need
to choose from an array of products that might be useful to strengthen this function. That may include choosing a smart card product or perhaps a biometric device
(e.g., fingerprint scanner, voice identification, or retina scanner). Similarly, products
to combat intrusions, malicious code, or misuse of the computing resource may need
to be added (e.g., a personal firewall, a virus scanner, and a network filter). If a wire-

TABLE V
PREVENTION, DETECTION, AND RESPONSE/RECOVERY STRATEGY EXAMPLES

Prevention and deterrence	Detection	Response and recovery
• Firewalls	• Firewalls	• Backup procedures
• Public Key Infrastructure	• Malicious code scanners	• Forensic tools
• Smart Cards for I&A	• Intrusion detection systems	• Law enforcement
• Encryption devices (hardware/software)	• Content filters	• Policy
• OS behavior monitors	• Audit log analysis	• Procedure
• Employee training	• Employee training	
• Enforcement of security policy	• Forensics tools	
• Use of high assurance products	• Procedures	

less card is present and used, special encryption software may need to be installed so that a virtual private network (VPN) can be accommodated.

In general, the engineer must insure that protection coverage is applied in three broad areas—prevention and deterrence, detection, and response and recovery. Again, these responsibilities must be translated into procedures and products. These concerns and their countermeasures are synopsized in Table V. The specific method used to address each concern is again a decision left to the organization and its engineers. The solution chosen is often based on non-technical rationale to include budgetary concerns, return on investment models, risk assessments, personal experience with a product, salesperson emphatic assertions, and recommendations from others. Better approaches might include reviewing evaluated product lists and internal testing of products in the operational environment if possible.

This section would not be complete without a brief comment on response and recovery—an often overlooked, but essential, security service. Without doubt, an unauthorized outsider will eventually penetrate a system regardless of its protection architecture. Recovery from this penetration and its likely consequences is a necessary planning function. This involves such mundane tasks as insuring system backups are acquired on a regular basis and stored in a location that would be safe should the system infrastructure be attacked or damaged. Response is an important consideration too. If a system is damaged maliciously and business loss occurs—what will be the organization's response? Will legal remedies be pursued? Will employees that violate policy be terminated? Will law enforcement agents be called in? Such plans and decisions will need to be made ahead of time and invoked when the incident occurs. Thirty years ago, little response would be possible in that laws did not exist to prosecute against, forensics tools did not exist to gather evidence with, and law enforcement expertise in this highly technical area was virtually absent. Today this is not the case.

4.3   The Art of Security Engineering

As with other requirement elicitation difficulties that exist in traditional systems engineering, determining what the information security requirements of a customer are and how they can be best satisfied is left largely in the hands of the systems security engineer. In turn, this security engineer develops a security architecture that can address the needs of the customer and meet comprehensive system-level requirements. Customers and end users are, for the most part, incapable of articulating their security needs as anything more than high-level declarations. To develop a common understanding (or perhaps a common mental model) between the engineer and customer, some form of a business process reengineering (BPR) generally occurs. This BPR involves the engineer, the end customer, and perhaps other stakeholders who work together to understand the current business process. Over the life of the BPR review, the team reaches a comprehensive understanding of what the current business processes are and how they can be changed within business constraints to improve security to some level acceptable in the organization. Henning [8] makes the case that existing requirements engineering tools, such as Zachmann Business Process Models, can be augmented to allow common requirements engineering tools to collect raw input on information security data flows. Sufficiency in information security is achieved when *the solution's cost, in operational terms, does not exceed its value in terms of the protection it affords*—a principle previously described by the author [20,21]. Starting with information gained from working closely with the customer (current processes, constraints, security policies, desired outcomes, etc.), the security engineer will generally conduct a risk assessment/analysis, a vulnerability analysis, propose an engineered solution, implement the solution, test, document procedures, and train the organization in new procedures. This process, depicted in Fig. 3, is cyclic and needs to be periodically repeated, because the solution set tends to deteriorate over time as new vulnerabilities are discovered and promulgated and as new attack schemes are discovered and employed.

What appears to be the current pervasive view is an approach to securing systems that applies a defense in depth architecture to mitigate the risk to information assets down to a sufficient level as determined jointly by the engineer and the customer. A representative process for this approach is provided in Fig. 4. In this environment, the security engineer composes various security products to define sufficient protection. In some cases this judgment proves accurate and in other cases it does not. In suggesting the architecture, the engineer generally has several templates of tried and proven solutions that are then adjusted to provide the best fit to the specific customer's solution need.

Building a system to meet a security requirement is often difficult, because the problem being addressed is not static, but rather dynamic. Requirements such as providing an easy to use interface, online help facilities, or real time scheduling are

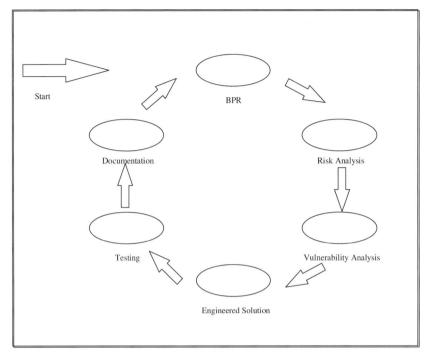

FIG. 3. Security engineering process view.

static requirements. For static requirements, the technical solution can be determined when the system is built and delivered and that solution is generally viable for the life of the system. A security requirement is dynamic for several reasons. First, the security solution is dependent on several factors:

- the threat against the system,
- the likelihood of the threat being exercised,
- the state of technology available for system protection,
- the state of technology for system attack, and
- the perceived value of the enterprise's information assets.

Second, a security solution, in most cases, needs to be developed to defend against the most likely threats. The security solution itself is also a dynamic factor. The threat against an enterprise can change depending upon specific, identifiable events. If the security solution proposed by an engineer is viewed as static, then the engineer must endeavor to establish a protection solution that addresses the greatest threat

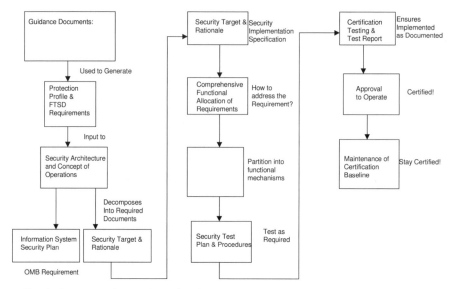

FIG. 4. A representative security engineering process applying a defense in depth solution to mitigate the risk profile to an acceptable level [22].

that can occur. If the solution is viewed as dynamic, then a range of protections can be proposed that address specific threat conditions and events leading to those conditions.

Third, there are no agreed upon or accepted information assurance measures or metrics that one can apply today to determine "how" secure a system is. We have no "composibility" metrics that help us understand the algebra of integrating several products together into a solution and how strong that solution is to a set of known attacks. We rather tend to use our base of empirical experience to suggest security solution sets that we have confidence in from experience or reputation and then we monitor the solution's success during test attacks (aka, red team penetration testing) or actual performance. We also note that the security threat changes over time based on a number of factors specific to each customer we work with and that change needs to be accommodated in the eventual solution that is engineered.

Earlier in this section, the point was made that new technology often comes along and that old security solutions do not apply or new security solutions need to be considered. In reality, this may not be a completely fair statement. What is really meant is the essential principals of security, those that were presented in Section 3, need to be reapplied in a new domain or problem set. Recent examples of this can be seen in the emergence of wireless computing and high performance computing. In the future, quantum computing will again introduce new security challenges for the security engineer.

5. Conclusions

We have attempted in this chapter to outline advances over a period of some thirty years in the area of information assurance (or computer security). We have moved through a discussion of what the problem is, historical efforts to address it, design principles and commonly accepted engineering practices. We have also presented challenges that the modern day security engineer faces in bringing an adequate defense in depth strategy to bear in a specific environment. It seems appropriate to end this chapter with some challenges to conventional wisdom and historic practices as well as some heuristics applied by the author and others over time.

The world is changing and so is our ability to secure its automation. We have many products in the market place today, but we are also finding that the products do not keep pace with the problems needing solutions. Old models of security engineering do not always work well with today's problem sets. Much of security engineering is still based on the experience of the engineer, risk management, and even luck. Software that we rely on and expect to work correctly often does not. The creation of correct software adhering to the best development practices seems to not be occurring and in fact, some suggest that the situation is worsening over time. One might suggest that, even with over thirty years of research and progress, we should be closer to being able to protect our systems, but in reality, it is easier today to mount a significant attack against systems than it was in years gone by. This is primarily due to automated attack scripts, the abundance of attack information available to malicious users, higher speed machines, higher speed networks, advances in parallel and distributed computation, and global interconnection.

Training and experience for employees and technical staff still goes a long way toward addressing much of the problem. Awareness programs and user training are important. Most important however, is the training of our systems administration staff—an area of increasing importance and one that is often sorely neglected. The technical talent shortage continues to grow and finding capable staff with experience is becoming much more difficult. Security engineering service providers that have managed to acquire a critical mass of these individuals are lower risk companies to the clients that they provide services to. Past history is important. Beginning in 2000, the U.S. Government initiated strong university scholarship programs designed to encourage faculty and students to study this area and to enter federal service after graduation as a partial means to address the skill set shortage. Meanwhile, both commercial and government entities must be educated on the value of their information, exposures in their networks, threats, risks and thus their need to consider security as a vital requirement within their larger networked computing systems.

Information assurance or security engineering is sometimes referred to as a "black art" or "arcane science." A good security engineer should know and understand a good security design or implementation by intuition vice quantifiable measures. In some regards, security engineering is more closely related to the legal profession: it relies upon a common body of knowledge and "case law" precedents for given architectures. Security engineers are reluctant to use the first known implementation of a particular architecture—the penalty for being first is additional scrutiny and analysis, causing cost and schedule impacts. Given that commonly accepted information assurance metrics are not agreed upon today, much of what we do, the tools we choose, and the perimeters we employ are based on empirical measures and past experience. Listed below are some observations and heuristics that are founded on experience in practicing security engineering.

- *There are different security assurance needs for different application domains*. Government intelligence agencies are far more likely (for good reason) to demand evaluated products, formal verification of code, trusted development environments, and high-end encryption. They are more prone to use evaluated products and support international efforts to build more trusted products. Government agencies, not in the intelligence business, are far more likely to settle for less assurance to handle their abundance of sensitive but unclassified data. Intelligence agency system security must start with the initial design of the system and build security into the overall system itself. Others in Government applications may not need this rigor. Most, in fact, can quite easily accept "add on" products to build an acceptable trust perimeter around a vulnerable system. In this domain, evaluated products are important to the customer, but not an overriding priority. Commercial encryption of browser quality is often acceptable here. Meanwhile, the commercial customer will almost exclusively rely on composition of commercial off the shelf products for their security. Evaluation of the product by third party laboratories is not a key factor today. Within this customer base, experience with products or protection architectures is the key to acceptance.

- *In many applications—past performance and emphatic praise DOES count*. This is particularly true with commercial clients who want to use products that have an excellent reputation and service providers whose livelihood depends upon reliable, predictable systems. If a product has performed well for other clients, is reasonably straightforward in its installation, has a good support structure from the vendor, and has proven itself over time—the customer and security engineer are both likely to favor it. This decision is often made without the benefit of formal product evaluation, trusted development environments, or code verification. There is nothing wrong with this approach in most applications today. Experience does count and is important.

- *History in the business keeps one from repeating past mistakes—even if it isn't the lowest cost proposal.* There are many "start-up" companies that are beginning to seek business in the information assurance business area. Government agencies are sometimes bound by the proposal process and low bid selection. Selection of a security engineering capability based on price can (and has) led to disaster. Experience, past performance, company commitment to the IA business area, and permanent staff can be contractor pluses. Others may involve more risk. A software engineer, systems engineer, and security engineer do not have the same skill sets.

- *There are frightening new programming paradigms taking hold in the dot com world (e.g., extreme programming—http://www.extremeprogramming. org) that will likely have a negative impact on trusted development or even controlled development.* Security starts with the coders and the code that is written. This is true whether the code is for an operating system, compiler, application layer, or any other executable. Testing, quality assurance, documentation, standards, life cycle development and other standard software engineering practices are important to the assurance that we look for during execution. Trends that produce code without such quality measures are also trading off assurance for time to market. Such practices represent a threat to the security of systems. Time to market pressures can lower software safety/trust/reliability. The consumer then becomes the testing ground for the program. Many have suggested that coding practices have become worse over time and not better. Programming practices that emphasize speed over peer reviews, documentation, testing, and formalism in development tend to result in less secure and perhaps less safe code.

- *Integration and system composibility is a great challenge and is not being addressed to any great extent.* What we mean by this is that the ability to add on products to a system and know what results is still a black art. In part, this stems from the complexity of systems and their emergent properties. It is entirely possible to install several products that individually each provide some security features/protections, yet the combination of products results in system failure. So systems must be viewed as a whole, and not just considered piecemeal. It is also possible that individual products have data that if combined with other data would signal an attack or penetration—but there exists no framework from which products can communicate with each other. In the network management area, such products do exist. We need them in the security area too. We also need these strength measures for product compositions to support business case analysis in industry when dollar costs must be weighed against risk mitigated. The entire area of metrics and measures in information assurance is an interesting one and largely unsolved. The interested reader is invited to review the proceedings of the Workshop on Information-Security-System Rating and Ranking (ISSRR) [9] available on line at http://www.acsac.org/measurement/.

Thirty years is a long time in the technical world and progress should be expected over such a time frame. In the area of information assurance, this has been the case. The problem areas defined by the Defense Science Board and discussed early in this chapter still exist. Our understanding of this problem set and the skills to address it have vastly improved. Attacks against systems have become easier over this same thirty years as the speed of computation increases, networking becomes more pervasive, and attack methods become better known and readily accessible to those that would use them against systems.

The information assurance area of research still requires greater attention and far more research to address future needs. Coupled with this is a need for software engineering to adopt more quality development practices and produce code with fewer latent errors and vulnerable components that later become exploitable. As computing becomes more ubiquitous and a part of every person's daily routine, it will also become a target for those that wish to damage an individual's system or data holdings or simply commit acts of electronic vandalism.

Acknowledgements

The author wishes to gratefully acknowledge the assistance and support of several individuals that have been helpful in providing material and advise for this work. First, Dr. Jack Murphy, EDS US Government Solutions Chief Technology Officer located in Herndon, Virginia, who provided the template graphics used in Figs. 1 and 2. Dr. Murphy has always been willing to help and lend advice and EDS has always allowed him to so in support of outside activities. Similarly, my good friends Ms. Ronda Henning and Dr. Kevin Fox of Harris Corporation in Melbourne Florida have contributed to this work in many ways by offering their comments and by working with the author on several related efforts. Ms. Henning and Dr. Fox are both practicing security engineers with many years of experience in the field. Many of the lessons learned that were presented in the concluding remarks came from their experience. I am grateful to my students at Mississippi State University who took the time to read this Chapter, comment on it and discover errors. I also wish to thank the editor of "Advances in Computers," Dr. Marvin V. Zelkowitz for inviting me to author this chapter and for the collaboration we have had together for two years while developing a Center for Empirically Based Software Engineering—a collaborative effort between the University of Southern California, the University of Maryland, Mississippi State University, and the University of Nebraska-Lincoln. This effort was partially supported by the National Science Foundation Grant number CCR-0085749.

References

[1] Anderson J.P., in: *Computer Security Technology Planning Study, ESD-TR-73-51*, Vol. I, ESD/AFSC, Hanscom AFB, Bedford, MA, October 1972.

[2] Cohen F., "Computer viruses—theory and experiments", in: *7th DOD/NBS Computer Security Conference, September 24–26*, 1984, pp. 240–263.

[3] Common criteria, An introduction, Available from http://csrc.nist.gov/cc/info/cc_brochure.pdf.

[4] Denning D., *Information Warfare and Security*, ACM Press, New York, 1999.

[5] Department of Defense Standard, *Trusted Computer System Evaluation Criteria, DOD 5200.28-STD*, 1985.

[6] Gasser M., *Building a Secure Computer System*, Van Nostrand Reinhold, New York, 1988.

[7] Gove R., "Fundamentals of cryptography and encryption", in: Tipton H., Krause M. (Eds.), *Information Security Management Handbook*, 4th edn., CRC Press, Boca Raton, FL, 2000, pp. 339–366, Chapter 19.

[8] Henning R., "Use of the Zachmann model for security requirements engineering", in: *20th National Information System Security Conference, Baltimore, MD*, 1997.

[9] ISSRR 2001, "Proceedings Workshop on Information-Security-System Rating and Ranking (ISSRR) held in Williamsburg, VA, May 21–23, 2001", http://www.acsac.org/measurement/.

[10] Mann C., "Why software is so bad", *Technology Review* **105** (6) (2002) 33–38.

[11] Nibaldi G., *Proposed Technical Criteria for Trusted Computer Systems, M79-225, AD-A 108-832*, MITRE, Bedford, MA, 1979.

[12] Nibaldi G., *Specification of a Trusted Computing Base (TCB), M79-228, AD-A108-831*, MITRE, Bedford, MA, 1979.

[13] Pfleeger C., *Security in Computing*, Prentice-Hall, NJ, 1997.

[14] Russell D., Gangemi G., *Computer Security Basics*, O'Reilly, Sebastopol, CA, 1991.

[15] Ruthberg Z., McKenzie R. (Eds.), *Audit and Evaluation of Computer Security, NBS Special Publication 500-19*, 1977.

[16] Saltzer J., Schroeder M., "The protection of information in computer systems", *Proceedings of the IEEE* **63** (9) (1975) 1278–1308.

[17] Shoch J., Hupp J., "The worm programs—Early experience with a distributed computation", *Communications of the ACM* **25** (1982) 172–180.

[18] Taub A.H., in: *John von Neumann: Collected Works. Volume V: Design of Computers, Theory of Automata and Numerical Analysis*, Pergamon Press, Oxford, 1961.

[19] Trotter E., Tasker P., *Industry Trusted Computer Systems Evaluation Process, MTR-3931*, MITRE, Bedford, MA, 1980.

[20] Vaughn R., "Sufficiency in information security", in: *Proceedings of the 21st National Information Systems Security Conference, Crystal City, VA*, 1998.

[21] Vaughn R., Henning R., "A pragmatic applications oriented approach to information assurance", in: *12th Annual Canadian Information Technology Security Symposium, Ottawa, Canada*, 2000.

[22] Vaughn R., Henning R., Fox K., "An empirical study of industrial security-engineering practices", *Journal of Systems and Software* **61** (3) (2002) 225–232.

[23] Ware W., *Security controls for computer systems, Report of the Defense Science Board Task Force on Computer Security*, The RAND Corporation, Santa Monica, CA, 1970.

Author Index

Numbers in *italics* indicate the pages on which complete references are given.

Subject Index

A

Abstract syntax trees (ASTs), 72
Abstractions, 145, 225, 226
Acceptability, psychological, 304
Access auxiliary function, 105–6
Accountability, 292
Active Design Reviews, 208, 214
ADL, 177
Adobe Acrobat Reader, 155
Aggregation, 294–5
Algebraic specification languages, 59
Alleles, 169
Analysis of variance, 22–3, 24
ARPANET, 326
Artificial Intelligence, 127
Aspect-oriented programming (AOP), 56–7
Assembly code, 66
Assignments, 138, 139
  implied, 139
ASSIST, 230–1
Assurance evaluation, 306
Atomic propositions, 122, 126, 127
Attack scripts, automated, 335
Availability, 249, 253, 292, 301

B

Back loop, 127
Backtracking, 138, 139
  non-chronological, 139
Base longevity interval, 274
BDDs, 119–21
  compared with BMC, 121, 141–4
  FORECAST model checker, 143, 144
  RULEBASE model checker, 142, 143
BEA, 246
Behavioral models, 168–70

Bell and LaPadula model, 307
Bell Laboratories, 272, 273
Benchmarking, 17, 40–3
  data collection, 40–1
  data comparability, 41–2
  data sources, 43
  project comparability, 42
Binary Decision Diagrams, *see* BDDs
Block structuring, 55
BMC, 120–1, 126–9
  compared with BDDs, 121, 141–4
  completeness techniques, 134–8
  conclusions, 144–6
  propositional SAT solvers, 138–41
  reduction to SAT, 129–34
  THUNDER, 143, 144
BNF grammars, 72, 75, 76
Boolean Constraint Propagation (BCP), 138, 139
Bounded Model Checking, *see* BMC
Bounded semantics, 128, 129, 132
Brooks Act (1965), 305
Buffer overflows, 254–7
Bugs, 53, 244–5
Business process reengineering (BPR), 332
Byte code evaluator (BCE), 104–5

C

C code documents, 216
C language, 256–7, 268
Canonical forms, 87–8, 102, 108
  offset indexing (Canonical Form 3), 87, 99–101, 107
  relevant constant pool construction (Canonical Form 2), 87, 98–9, 107
  removal of indirection (Canonical Form 1), 87, 88–98, 107, 108

349

Contents of Volumes in This Series

ISBN 0-12-012158-1

9 780120 121588